MW00559969

ELSEWHERE TEXTS

EDITED BY

GAYATRI CHAKRAVORTY SPIVAK AND HOSAM ABOUL-ELA

The series takes as its charge radical new directions in the engagement with the literary culture of the non-European. The point of departure here is the scandalous notion that the literary figure of the Global South is as human as the European, complex, subject to the dynamism of history, fluid, unrepresentable, and impossible either to essentialize or reduce to any glib *counter* essentialism.

As such, ELSEWHERE TEXTS emphasizes those aspects of this subject's dynamism that have been radically de-emphasized in the stock metropolitan representations. So, the series centers the intellectual dimension of literary culture elsewhere. The regions that Orientalists represented as *non-idea-producing areas* are revealed to be the opposite. Furthermore, modernity of ideas is engaged by the series' metatheoretical under-standing of the process of translation, the mechanism through which the unfixed nature of intellectual work may be most fully acknowledged. Finally, ELSEWHERE TEXTS understands theory as commitment, emphasizing that genre of theoretical discourse which through its engagement—its heightened sense of the social power of ideas and rhetorics—calls into question the supposed abstract transcendence of the god terms 'theory', 'text', 'idea'. This engaged dimension of the elsewhere text insists on the historicism of theory at the same time as it forges a new intellectual globality embodied here in intellectual work translated for the critical traditions of Asia, Africa, the Caribbean and Latin America in all their diversity.

RENÉ ZAVALETA MERCADO

Towards a History of the National-Popular in Bolivia,
1879–1980

TRANSLATED BY ANNE FREELAND

LONDON NEW YORK CALCUTTA

Seagull Books, 2018

Originally published as *Lo nacional-popular en Bolivia*, 1986
© Alma Reyles, 2014
Series Introduction © Gayatri Chakravorty Spivak, 2018
Introduction © Sinclair Thomson, 2018
English translation and Afterword © Anne Freeland, 2018

ISBN   978 0 8574 2 358 0

British Library Cataloguing-in-Publication Data
A catalogue record for this book is available from the British Library

Typeset by Seagull Books, Calcutta, India
Printed and bound by Maple Press, York, Pennsylvania, USA

CONTENTS

General Introduction

GAYATRI CHAKRAVORTY SPIVAK

'Theory' is an English transcription of the Greek *theorein*. Corresponding words exist in the major European languages. Our series, 'Elsewhere Texts', works within these limits. 'Theory' has been creolized into innumerable languages. Yet the phenomenon of 'seeing or making visible correctly'—the meaning in Greek that will still suffice—does not necessarily relate to that word—'theory'—in those languages. That describes the task of the editors of a translated series on theory in the world. How does 'theory' look elsewhere from the Euro–US? Since our texts are modern, there is often an at-least-implicit awareness that 'proper' theory looks different as the 'same' theory elsewhere.

Heidegger thinks that truth is destined to be thought by the man of 'Western Europe'.[1] Our series does not offer a legitimizing counter-essentialism. Take a look at the map and see how tiny Europe is, not even really a continent, but, as Derrida would say, a cap, a headland.[2] Such a tiny place, yet who can deny Derrida's description, which is a historical and empirical observation? Look at the tables of contents

---

1 Martin Heidegger, *What Is Called Thinking?* (J. Glenn Gray trans. and introd.) (New York: Harper and Row, 1968).

2 Jacques Derrida, *The Other Heading: Reflections on Today's Europe* (Pascale-Anne Brault and Michael B. Naas trans) (Bloomington: Indiana University Press, 1992).

of the most popular critical anthologies and you will see corrobora-
tion of the essentialist conviction that goes with the historical claim.
The counter-essentialism is reflected in the choice of critics from 'the
rest of the world', and today's espousal of 'the global South'. Just being
non-white is the counter-essence.

The influential *Norton Anthology of Theory and Criticism*, for
example, lets in only Maimonides before the modern university system kicks in.[3] But even if they had let in Khaled Ziadeh, Marta Lamas
and Marilena Chaui, the material would be determined by the epistemological procedures of that system.[4] Norton lets in W. E. B. Du
Bois, the first African-American to get a doctorate from Harvard,
the man who felt that 'of the greatest importance was the opportunity
which my *Wanderjahre* [wandering years] in Europe gave of looking
at the world as a man and not simply from a narrow racial and
provincial outlook'.[5] Du Bois emphatically claimed that the African-
American was the best example of the subject of the Declaration of
Independence (the Founding Fathers were standing in). It is therefore significant that here he claims to inhabit the persona of Wilhelm
Meister, Goethe's hero, with trajectory not fully reversed. Meister
came to the United States to act out the European Enlightenment
in this new land—a trip described in Goethe's *Wilhelm Meisters
Wanderjahre* [Wilhelm Meister's Travels]—a hope which Du Bois
nuanced, perhaps as soon as his scholarship to the Friedrich Wilhelm
University from the Slater Fund for the Education of Freedmen was

---

3 Vincent B. Leitch (ed.), *The Norton Anthology of Theory and Criticism* (New
York: W. W. Norton, 2010).

4 These authors were published by Palgrave in a series similar to this one,
under the same editorial collaboration.

5 Cited in Henry Louis Gates Jr., 'The Black Letters on the Sign: W. E. B. Du
Bois and the Canon' in *The Oxford W. E. B. Du Bois, Volume 8: Black Folk
Then and Now: An Essay in the History and Sociology of the Negro Race* (New
York: Oxford University Press, 2007), p. *xvi*.

cancelled, the year after President Rutherford B. Hayes' death [1893], by a Standing Committee on Education chaired by a former lieutenant colonel in the Confederate Army, the army that had fought to retain slavery and the slave trade in the US Civil War. (Hayes himself might have destroyed the possibility of Reconstruction by the 1877 Compromise with the Democrats. Du Bois as a young man was critical of his racism but probably not aware of political details, as he was later.)

In the *Norton Anthology*, we get Zora Neale Hurston (Columbia), Langston Hughes (Harlem Renaissance via Columbia), Frantz Fanon (University of Lyon), Chinua Achebe (University College, Ibadan), Stuart Hall (Oxford), Ngugi wa Thiong'o (Leeds), Taban Lo Liyong (Iowa), Henry Owuwor Anyuumba (Iowa), Spivak (Cornell), Houston Baker (UCLA), Gloria Anzaldua (UCSC), Homi Bhabha (Oxford), Barbara Christian (Columbia), Barbara Smith (Mount Holyoke), Henry Louis Gates Jr. (Cambridge), bell hooks (UCSC). The point I am making is not that these writers have not challenged Eurocentrism. It is that they are sabotaging from within, and this is a historical fact that must be turned around so that there is a chance for widening the circle. Fanon stands out, not because he is not a university man but because he is the only one who clearly operated outside the Euro–US, though he was what Du Bois would call a Black European, literally fighting Europe, also from within, located in a geographical exterior.

(In the next most influential anthology, the rest-of-the-world entries are almost identical, but for Audre Lorde [Columbia], Geraldine Heng [Cornell], Ania Loomba [Sussex], Chidi Okonkwo [University of Auckland], Jamaica Kincaid [Franconia and New School].[6] Again, Fanon is the only working 'outsider'. I am sure the general pattern is repeated everywhere. I have myself been so tokenized through

6 Julie Rivkin and Michael Ryan (eds), *Literary Theory: An Anthology* (Malden, MA: Wiley Blackwell, 2004).

my long work-life as representing 'Third World criticism' that I am particularly alive to the problem.[7])

Our position is against a rest-of-the-world counter-essentialism, which honours the history-versus-tradition binary opposition. We recognize that a hegemonic Euro–US series can only access work abroad that is continuous with Euro–US radicalism.[8] To open ourselves to what lies beyond is another kind of effort. Within the limits of our cause, we focus, then, on another phenomenon.

The history of the last few centuries has produced patterns of bilateral resistance. The formation is typically my nation-state, my region, my cultural formation over against 'the West'. These days there are global efforts at conferences, events, organizations that typically takes the form of the Euro–US at the centre, and a whole collection of 'other cultures', who connect through the imperial languages, protected by a combination of sanctioned ignorance and superficial solidarities, ignoring the internal problems when they are at these global functions.[9] The model is the fact and discipline of

---

7 An example that has stayed with me over the years remains Diane Bell's excellent *Daughters of the Dreaming* (Minneapolis: University of Minnesota Press, 1993), which, in response to requests for inclusion of Third World material, put in Trin-ti Min-Ha and me, longtime faculty persons in prestigious United States universities!

8 This continuity and the discontinuous are beautifully staged in the film *Bamako* (2006) by Abderrahmane Sissako. Jean-François Lyotard gave a clear articulation of the problem of discontinuity in *The Differend: Phrases in Dispute* (Georges Van Den Abbeele trans.) (Minneapolis: University of Minnesota Press, 1988).

9 My most recent experience is to encounter a Maori activist bookseller and an Indian feminist at such a convention, who had never heard of Frederick Douglass, where only in response to my questions did the South African participant admit to political problems with translation between indigenous languages, and the mainland Chinese participant to the barrier between Mandarin and Cantonese. Examples can be multiplied.

preservation. By the Nara document of 1994, Japan insisted that preservation should be not only of built space but also of intangible cultural heritage. What started was the model that I have described. It is now a tremendous capital-intensive fact of our world.

In and through our series, we want to combat this tendency. We want not only to present texts from different national origins to the US readership but also to point out how each is singular in the philosophical sense, namely, universalizable, though never universal. We are not working for area-studies niche-marketing, though the work is always of specialist quality. In the interest of creating a diversified collectivity outside of the English readership, a long-term feature might be a conference bringing the authors together.

The story begins for me in a conversation with the Subaltern Studies Collective in 1986—asking them if I could arrange the publication of a selection—because they were not available in the United States. A long-term preoccupation, then. To this was added Hosam Aboul-Ela's 2007 consolidation of a thought that was growing inside me: from the rest of the world, literary editors wanted fiction, poetry, drama—raw material. Theory came generally from 'us'. Seagull Books, the only publishing house based in South Asia with direct world distribution, and unlike most Western conglomerates uninterested in translations of theory not recognizable by the Eurocentric 'cosmopolitan' model, seems now the appropriate publisher.

In the intervening three decades, a small difference has imposed itself, the one I have been emphasizing so far, the justification for 'elsewhere'. Earlier I had felt that my brief within the profession was to share and show that the work overseas was really 'theoretical' by Western sizing. (I use the word 'size' here in the sense of pointure in Derrida.)[10] Hence 'strategic use of essentialism'. Now I also feel the

---

10 I have discussed this in 'Inscription: Of Truth to Size' in *Outside in the Teaching Machine* (New York: Routledge, 2009), pp. 201–16.

reader must learn that 'theory' need not look the same everywhere, that for the independent mind, too much training in producing the European model in stylistic detail might hamper. In my teacher-training work in rural India, it is the illiterate man who understands things best because his considerable intelligence has not been hobbled by bad education or gender oppression. The lesson here is not that everyone should be illiterate but that strong minds should not be ruined by bad education or imperatives to imitate.

The caution would apply to *Neighborhood and Boulevard* by Khaled Ziadeh (belonging to our earlier series, see note 4)—not bad education, obviously, but the imperative to imitate 'French Theory'.[11] Ziadeh, in spite of his time at Sorbonne, was not tempted. He theorizes by space and repetition; Hosam Aboul-Ela's introduction to that book walks us through it. There are plenty of people writing in Arabic who produce work competitive with the best in European-style 'theory'. Reading Ziadeh, as Aboul-Ela points out, we have to learn to recognize 'theory' in another guise. My own work profits from his account of the de-Ottomanization of the city by the French into an 'Islamic' space; because I think de-Ottomanization, still active in our time, has a history as old as the Fall of Constantinople, and, reterritorialized, backwards into Byzantium. Today's Khilafat movement can be read as an example of how imperial historical violence can produce a counter-violence of no return.

Our series has only just begun. I have described our goal with appropriate modesty: to translate theoretical material operating outside

---

11 I use this phrase with the French nationalist irony reflected in François Cusset, *French Theory: Foucault, Derrida, Deleuze et Cie et les mutations de la vie intellectuelle aux États-Unis* (Paris: Éditions la Découverte, 2003), available in English translation as: *French Theory: How Foucault, Derrida, Deleuze, & Co. Transformed the Intellectual Life of the United States* (Jeff Fort trans., with Josephine Berganza and Marlon Jones) (Minneapolis: University of Minnesota Press, 2008).

the Euro–US, not readily available to metropolitan readership but continuous with the episteme, even as 'hybridity' keeps the local elsewhere. Yet there are also singular enclaves in many places where teaching and thinking apparently take place in less continuous epistemic formation. To acquire texts from these enclaves would require the kind of preparation, partly traditionalist, partly anthropologistic, that I do not possess. Perhaps, if our initial forays succeed, we will be able to fling our net wider: particularly important in the context of sub-Saharan Africa, where strong theoretical writing in the imperial languages (also languages of Africa, of course) flourishes and holds influence. For theoretical writing in the indigenous languages, not necessarily imitating the European model, contained within internal conflict, avoiding the anthropologist in the name of tradition will be on our agenda. *Towards A History of the National-Popular in Bolivia* by René Zavaleta Mercado is our inaugural text.

To begin with, my understanding of an activist 'Task of the Editor' was as I have outlined above: to combat the bi-lateralism—my place and your Euro–US—that legitimizes Eurocentrism by reversal. Today this is complicated by the confrontation between nationalism and globalism. Can an elsewhere text supplement both?

Our series starts, then, with René Zavaleta Mercado, sometimes called the 'Bolivian Gramsci', perhaps because he introduced questions of culture into a generally Marxist position. In fact, his life, of a young bourgeois ideologue from the country going through many transformations by way of varieties of journalism and a periodic apologist's involvement in the state has a trajectory somewhat different from Gramsci's. The two held one conviction in common, resonating with our conjuncture as well, that education into social justice is both one-on-one and collective, thus countering the tired mechanical Marxist accusation of 'individualism'. This is not only a recognizable 'Latin American' theoretical imprint today but also shared widely elsewhere, as witness Darko Suvin's variation in his

New Year's message for 2017: 'Whoever doesn't fight collectively will lose singly'.[12]

Down the line, a translation of Luis Tapia's groundbreaking book *History and Politics in the Work of René Zavaleta* is under editorial scrutiny. Translation work is well under way on the collected literary writings of Paik Nak-Chung, the brilliant Korean public intellectual. He is important for our world because he grasps the 'literary' in all its worldliness, and philosophizes the possibilities for a way out of gated nation-states. Translation has begun on *Mononer Modhu*, a philosophical text by Arindam Chakrabarti which, in the best comparativist tradition, deconstructs European philosophizing into ways of thinking that it otherwise ignores. Also underway is *Gender, Context and the Politics of Writing* by Dong Limin from China, a powerful critic of many accepted social gender paradigms. We are waiting for a reader's report on a book of essays in Sesotho—one of the languages of South Africa—by S. M. Mofokeng, *Pelong yak ka* (literally, 'In My Heart'), published in 1962. Our thanks to Njabulo Ndebele for this suggestion.

Our translators share with us the problems of translation for each unique text, at least hinting to the reader that, although the activity of translating is altogether pleasurable, to accept translations passively as a substitute for the 'original' closes doors. We will not give up the foolish hope that a careful translation, sharing problems, will lead to language-learning.

---

12 See Darko Suvin, 'Tko se ne bori zajedno, izgubi pojedinačno . . .' [Whoever Doesn't Fight Collectively Will Lose Singly . . .], interview with Saša Hrnjez, July–August 2015. Available at: https://goo.gl/X7Kkto (last accessed on 7 January 2018).

Read our series as a first step, then. Come to the projected conferences if they happen, where all of the authors and translators will gather to ask: What is it to theorize elsewhere, in our world?

Self-Knowledge and Self-Determination
at the Limits of Capitalism

SINCLAIR THOMSON

> Sooner or later, each society learns that to know itself is almost to prevail.

René Zavaleta Mercado

On 23 December 1984, at the age of 47, Bolivia's greatest political theorist René Zavaleta Mercado died of brain cancer in Mexico City. His wife had rushed him from La Paz back to Mexico in order to try to save his life but the late-hour emergency efforts turned out to be in vain. At the time, Zavaleta was still in the early stages of drafting his most original and ambitious work, *Towards a History of the National-Popular in Bolivia, 1879–1980*. It remains difficult not to associate his death with the simultaneous crisis and collapse of the Democratic and Popular Unity (UDP) government which upheld elements of Zavaleta's own democratic, socialist and anti-imperialist politics. That catastrophe set the stage for the orthodox structural adjustment and implementation of the neoliberal model the following year. Broadly viewed, Zavaleta's own life and thought were inseparable from the unfolding and unravelling processes of revolution and counter-revolution that he interrogated and illuminated with such depth in his writings.

More than 30 years after the agonizing denouement in 1984, with the crisis of the revolutionary left and the truncation of his own radical intellectual project, Zavaleta's final work is here offered for the first time in English for an international audience. What are the reasons for bringing out his book today?

I

If we follow Zavaleta's own method here, we can address our question from both specific historical-political and general conceptual angles. Zavaleta died at a time when an important historical cycle of left-popular political struggle had recently peaked and a socialist alternative whose potential had been briefly glimpsed was now rapidly dissolving. From the 1950s to the time of his death, Zavaleta had himself moved from a revolutionary nationalist affiliation towards a more orthodox Leninism and ultimately to an increasingly creative and heterodox Marxist position. From the late 1970s to the early 1980s, democratic trade-union struggle, with proletarian centrality and key collaboration from the peasantry, had successfully brought to an end 20 years of right-wing military dictatorship. The role of the national trade-union confederation (Central Obrera Boliviana [Bolivian Workers Central] or COB) in the UDP government had initially posed the promise that the power of workers could chart a new course for economic and political organization in the country. Yet the administration finally imploded amid state economic mismanagement and private-sector financial speculation, staggering hyper-inflation and government inability to channel the mass mobilizations flooding the streets and plazas of the capital. The full-blown chaos set the stage for a counter-revolutionary turn in 1985, immediately after Zavaleta's death, which would lead to a consolidated neoliberal regime, one of the first in the world to operate under civilian rather than military political control.

A generation later, there nevertheless emerged a new conjuncture reminiscent of Zavaleta's own times. The neoliberal cycle in Bolivia began to fall apart in the years after 2000 as a series of popular insurgencies swept away the old regime and created an opening for new leftist, indigenous and nationalist projects. The process in

Bolivia accompanied simultaneous challenges to the Washington Consensus around South America and a regional shift towards a social-democratic centre-left option that became known as the Pink Tide. In this regional context of opposition to neoliberalism, Bolivia stood out as the insurrectionary frontline and its mobilizations were distinguished by the centrality of indigenous social movements. By 2006, they would catapult into power Evo Morales of the Movimiento al Socialismo [Movement to Socialism or MAS] party who would consolidate alliances particularly with Venezuela, Ecuador and Cuba to challenge longstanding US hegemony in the region.

There was also an accompanying intellectual ferment that caught the attention of some international observers on the left. In 2009, Emir Sader of Brazil commented that the 'post-neoliberal' political developments in Latin America had not generated a corresponding body of theoretical and political analysis on the left.[1] The prominent exception to the rule, he asserted, was the Comuna group in Bolivia, whose nucleus consisted of Luis Tapia, Alvaro García Linera, Raquel Gutiérrez and Raúl Prada. Tapia and Prada were independent intellectuals on the Bolivian left and García Linera had met Gutiérrez, a Mexican militant, while studying abroad in Mexico City. The couple returned to Bolivia to organize a guerrilla movement with an Indianist profile, which led to their detention. The collective coalesced in the late 1990s after Gutiérrez and García Linera were released from prison. Its production combined Marxist theory with concrete and conjunctural inquiry into power relations in Bolivia, while Gutiérrez included radical feminist reflection among her contributions to the group.

Sader appreciated how Comuna had elaborated an interpretation of the political and economic cycles and the formation of political subjects in contemporary Bolivian history in a way that illuminated the potential for an alternative to neoliberalism in the new millennium.

---

1 Emir Sader, *The New Mole: Paths of the Latin American Left* (New York: Verso, 2011), pp. 75–9.

Sader deserves credit for perceiving the creativity and insight of the left analysis in Bolivia in the 2000s. Yet he did not ask what gave rise to this current of critical Marxist thought. The answer has to do with the rich tradition of radical nationalist, *indigenista* and left political writing in Bolivia going back to the time of Bolivia's national revolution in the mid twentieth century. Despite the collapse of Marxism as a political and intellectual option in much of the West and despite the deep defeats of popular forces in Bolivia in the late twentieth century, an organically rooted intellectual tradition persisted in the political subsoil. The foremost figure in that radical tradition was none other than René Zavaleta Mercado, and the Comuna group was in many ways a new generational offshoot from that long tradition of political reflection.[2] If that generation of critical left thought has recently acquired some visibility internationally, especially with the election of García Linera to the vice-presidency of the MAS government in 2006, it is now time for the deeper tradition out of which it emerged to come to light. It seems opportune to revisit the rich legacy left by Zavaleta at a time when Bolivia has become, more than ever in its history, an international reference point for activists in social movements and intellectuals on the left.

II

If Zavaleta continued to offer appreciable reserves and resources for critical political thinkers in the revolutionary conjuncture of the early twenty-first century in Bolivia, it was ultimately because of the overall coherence and depth of his theoretical project. The rationale for translating Zavaleta for an international readership today ultimately rests on the value of this project.

---

2 The Zavaletian prologue to one of Comuna's first collective books, *El retorno de la Bolivia plebeya* (La Paz: Muela del Diablo, 2000) offers perfect evidence. It noted: 'The possibility of reconstructing a worker and popular horizon is not in simple resistance, in the prolongation of the agony, but in radically thinking through the crisis, learning from it, to understand the weaknesses and blockages of the past and to understand the world.'

*Main
Thesis*

The fundamental problem that Zavaleta came to grapple with in his late work was how to conceive of historical development in societies that were not fully governed by capitalist social relations. He saw that the conceptual apparatus of social science and social theory developed for capitalist societies could not be automatically applied to social formations that were not themselves fully regulated in capitalist terms. As he wrote in his essay 'The Masses in November': 'The pretension of a universal grammar that can be applied to diverse formations is usually no more than dogmatization.'[3] He believed that Marxism provided the most profound and coherent apparatus for social explanation, yet it had been developed to understand the capitalist formations of the industrialized West. The categories and frames for understanding modern England, France or Germany could hardly be applied to make sense of a country such as Bolivia that was largely rural and agrarian, lacking the more developed class dynamics of industrial society, the political frames of liberal citizenship, the aesthetic fields of bourgeois culture, the private realm of individuated subjectivity. If the analysis of such societies could not be productively apprehended simply in terms of an intrinsic deficit (or a yearning for what might be) compared with a Western ideal-type, where did that leave social theory if it were to be produced outside the capitalist West?

Zavaleta's response to this dilemma was to begin from a metropolitan Marxist framework—which he referred to in typically condensed allusive fashion as 'the theory of value'—while acknowledging the inherent limits of doing so. The epistemological challenge for the theorist on the periphery, in his view, was to produce a distinct conceptual framework and a set of concepts suited to the distinct social conditions that were the object of analysis. This procedure

---

3 René Zavaleta Mercado, 'Las masas en noviembre' in *Obra completa*, VOL. 2 (La Paz: Plural, 2013), p. 107. The important two-volume publication of Zavaleta's complete works was splendidly edited and introduced by Mauricio Souza Crespo.

could only be carried out through a serious inquiry into the specific historical and political processes that had given rise to the society in question. Such an engagement provided an alternative to the sterile option of applying an abstract framework devised for another reality or to the empty option of holding reality to a standard it could only meet in some imagined and ever-postponed future. Instead, the task was to work off a more universal frame while producing intermediate concepts elaborated through concrete analysis of particular historical and political realities. What makes Zavaleta's approach so rich, deep and dynamic is that he acknowledged the partiality of the theorist's intellectual position and saw that conceptual production itself inevitably depended on the very historical and political conditions that the theorist sought to understand. There was, however, no alternative method for a society at the margins of advanced capitalism to come to know itself and thereby to determine itself.

III

Zavaleta was in fact only embarking on this ambitious project when it was cut off. If he certainly had not drawn any sort of theoretical closure and we do not know how he might have gone on to revise and refine his work, he did succeed in outlining some general postulates and generating a cluster of concepts that indicate the overall direction and potential of his approach.

Some of these notions are of more global applicability. For example, the first of the hypotheses announced in the prologue to his book immediately indicates his distance from vulgar or economic-determinist interpretations of modern state formation as a reflection of surplus accumulation. Bolivia did not produce a modern state in the nineteenth or early twentieth century not because the country was poor but because it was incapable of internalizing its surplus and, more fundamentally, because it had neither the social 'receptivity' nor the state 'willingness' (*disponibilidad*) to do so. A second example comes from the third set of hypotheses in the prologue where he indicates that the famous problem of political instability in Bolivia derives from the question of legitimation, which can only be understood in terms of the history of the mass' own perspective on things. We can already see in such points a Marxism that is not economistic and that takes seriously the past experience and optic of the subaltern.

But a yet-more-crucial set of his notions about the relationship between state and civil society are also of global relevance. Zavaleta speaks of this correspondence in terms of a 'social equation' or 'social optimum', which will be higher where the patterns and codes of state power conform to the institutions and ideology present in civil society. Bolivia, by this standard, had a historically low degree of such correspondence in comparison with the bourgeois societies of Western Europe. Another term used by Zavaleta in this period (though not in this book) to refer to this fundamental relationship is the 'primordial form' and he sought to historicize it by referring to the 'constitutive moment' in which that relationship took on its basic structural composition.[4] The idea is not that a given constitutive moment—such as the Spanish conquest in the colonial period or the Federal War of 1899 in the liberal-oligarchic period or the national revolution of 1952—locks society and state into a fixed condition, but that it sets deep parameters for subsequent historical development until another moment of profound crisis and transformation resets those parameters. These concerns run throughout Western sociology, and not only Western Marxism, and hence Zavaleta begins his prologue citing Max Weber to declare that his project examines the connection between social democratization and state form.

In other respects, however, Zavaleta is interested to move from such universal conceptual problems towards those that concern social formations like the Bolivian one in which capitalism has had but a partial purchase historically. Hence in the third set of hypotheses in

---

4 René Zavaleta Mercado, 'Forma primordial y determinacion dependiente' in *Obra completa*, VOL. 2.

the prologue, he speaks of the degree of homogeneity required for representative democracy to be effective, a condition not found in Bolivia where, he writes, 'It is more important to know the result of an election in the three main cities, in the mining centres and in two or three peasant districts than in the country as a whole.'[5] By this token, institutions such as the political party or the trade union cannot be assumed to exercise the same roles in Bolivia that they would in Europe where they originated. In other late work, he would take up the question of 'dependent determination', referring to the degree of foreign influence or imposition in societies in which the state–society relationship is less cohesive and more conflictual and hence in which sovereignty is less solid.[6]

But the essential question in Zavaleta's final work is the heterogeneity of the economic and social formation in such regions peripheral to the metropolitan capitalist core, a phenomenon which he idiosyncratically termed *abigarramiento*, meaning 'motleyness'. For Zavaleta, the unitary nature of the political state is consistent with the more homogenized condition of civil society in industrial capitalist formations but inconsistent with the composite and disarticulated condition of formations in which capitalist relations do not prevail thoroughly and effectively. (It is this inconsistency that gives the state its merely 'apparent' aspect in a place like Bolivia.) This is not a superficial assertion about the presence of cultural diversity and mixture. A common but erroneous notion in Bolivian discussions is that *abigarramiento* is a peculiar way of talking about the country's 'multiethnic and pluricultural' reality, to use the terms enshrined in the 1994 constitutional reform.

Rather, the category captures a deeper and more complex historical phenomenon and draws from a sophisticated debate about modes of production within Latin American Marxism in the 1970s. In that period, theorists and historians concurred that the colonial

---

5 See p. 16 in the present volume.

6 Zavaleta Mercado, 'Forma primordial'.

history of Latin America made it impossible to apply any exclusive notion of a feudal or a capitalist mode of production to the region, or to describe any simple transition from one to the other, according to a Western European model. Ernesto Laclau's formulation concerning the articulation of coexisting but distinct modes of production within a single economic and social formation, in which one mode or another could subsume or exercise a prevailing influence over the others, thus generated substantial interest. Yet an alternative interpretation emerged as well—namely, the historical possibility that no one mode of production might prevail over the others and that a given social formation might be characterized by the *lack of any effective articulation*.[7] Zavaleta's category of the *abigarrado* refers precisely to such an unresolved fragmentation in Bolivia, and suggests this possibility for other colonial or postcolonial societies outside of advanced capitalism and the metropolitan centre.

In the Bolivian case, we can conceive of a gamut of types of production. Communitarian forms emerged with the pre-conquest development of agriculture in the Andes. Nomadic hunting and gathering in the Amazonian and Chaco lowlands likewise preceded European settlement and continued thereafter. Seigneurial forms arose with the implantation of the colonial hacienda system (and overlapped with the longer-term phenomenon of tributary extraction). Production based on servile and enslaved labour was also present in Andean and colonial forms. Capitalist forms of production took early root and spread from the colonial mining centres, especially Potosí. Over centuries after the conquest, commercial capital partially linked some of the disparate spheres of production. Ultimately in Zavaleta's view, capitalism never managed to achieve an effective reorganization and total absorption ('real subsumption') of other existing modes of production.

---

7 For a review of the historiographic positions in this debate, see Steve J. Stern, 'Feudalism, Capitalism, and the World-System in the Perspective of Latin America and the Caribbean', *The American Historical Review* 93(4) (October 1988): 829–72.

Zavaleta's conception was not narrowly economic but, rather, contemplated how the social and technical relations involved with any given mode of production entailed cultural, moral, legal, ideological and other civilizational features. He saw the heterogeneity of the productive modes as existing within two major civilizational matrices, the agrarian and eventually the industrial. He notably associated these civilizations with the coexistence of distinct temporalities or temporal densities within society.

Finally, Zavaleta elaborated certain concepts with specific reference to the Bolivian case, in an attempt to move beyond a merely negative conception of the society as lacking the characteristics of the European ideal type and to construct a more compelling understanding of the Bolivian historical process. An example of this is his notion of the seigneurial paradox, mentioned in the second hypothesis of the prologue. Seigneurial power for Zavaleta was found not only in the rural landlord sector but also in the quasi-sovereign territorial and political dominion exercised by the great mine-owning magnates into the twentieth century. He held that, contrary to what a conventional historical model might expect, seigneurial power in Bolivia was surprisingly resilient, capable of reconstituting itself even out of major transformations such as the national revolution of 1952. This capacity could be explained by the fact that its underlying productive relations were not necessarily modified by juridical and political shifts in the course of modern history. But by the same token, agrarian civilization in the Andes had also been transformed only partially and superficially through colonial and republican history, thus explaining its ongoing conflict with elite and state projects such as liberalism.

IV

Considering Zavaleta's late work in the light of critical intellectual developments at the global level, it is also notable that it was simultaneous with, in some ways complementary to, and yet also different from the move made by the Gramscian historians in the original South Asian subaltern studies project. The Indian historians certainly were prompted to engage with methodological and epistemological problems, just as Zavaleta, unlike most of the other Latin American Gramscians in the 1960s and 1970s,[8] was compelled to move towards history. For one and the other, the aim was not simply to apply metropolitan theory uncritically to a local case but also to deploy it as a tool to explain historical reality in the complex and fragmented specific conditions of the colonial and postcolonial world. Yet the national-popular was not a Gramscian category appropriated in a significant way by the South Asian historiography, and the subaltern category did not particularly preoccupy Zavaleta. When the subaltern studies school did reach Latin America, after its sometimes touted and sometimes disparaged reception in the metropolitan academy, it was not through the more globalized academic circuits of Buenos Aires or Mexico City. In a seeming paradox, the Latin American reception passed through Bolivia, long seen from outside as an intellectual backwater. Part of the reason had to do with the rise of Bolivia's autonomous indigenous political and cultural movements which could fit the bill for properly 'subaltern' subjects. If anything, the national-popular theme, with its connotations of cultural homogeneity and its potential implication of an alternative state project, could sound at odds with a subalternist vision of indigenous autonomy intrinsically counterposed to state power. Yet in their 1997 translation and edition of a set of key subaltern studies texts, Silvia Rivera Cusicanqui and Rossana Barragán would cite Zavaleta as a

---

8 Anne Freeland, 'Gramsci in Latin America: Reconstitutions of the State' (PhD dissertation, Department of Latin American and Iberian Cultures, Columbia University, New York, 2017).

prime example of the rich critical tradition of theoretical and historical analysis of colonialism produced within Latin America, if often overlooked by writers based in the US and Europe. The richness of that tradition in Bolivia—itself reflected in the work of the two women who edited the volume—is surely another reason why it would become the site for translation of the South Asian project for a Latin American audience.[9]

For radical historiography in a global scope, Zavaleta's book stands out as a rare effort to follow through in grounded historicizing fashion on Antonio Gramsci's intriguing if bare sketch of the national-popular concept. But we must acknowledge that if Gramsci's category was tentative, Zavaleta's historical project was likewise only incipient. The very title of the work is significant in this sense. The Mexican edition of Zavaleta's text, published in 1986 by Siglo XXI, was titled simply *Lo nacional-popular en Bolivia*, conveying an abstracted sociological object. The Bolivian re-edition in Zavaleta's complete works retains this title.[10] In this English translation, Anne Freeland has opted instead for the title that Zavaleta himself left. *Towards a History of the National-Popular in Bolivia, 1879–1980* acknowledges the open-ended but also the centrally historical nature of his project.

For Zavaleta, the national-popular was not an essence or object that existed outside history but, rather, a phenomenon that could be identified within its contingent, complex and shifting causal processes. He sought to identify the emergence and occasional coalescence of distinct popular sectors as a political force that could challenge the domination of an elite group which did not exercise

---

9 Silvia Rivera Cusicanqui and Rossana Barragán (eds), *Debates post coloniales: Una introducción a los estudios de la subalternidad* (La Paz: SEPHIS/ Aruwyiri, 1997).

10 René Zavaleta Mercado, *Lo nacional-popular en Bolivia* in *Obra completa*, VOL. 2 (La Paz: Plural, 2013). Plural had also republished the work in an independent edition in 2008.

power in the interests of the masses. He conceived of this coalescence as an intersubjective process that constituted, in Gramscian terms, a historical bloc that could alter the terms of coercion and consent prevailing within the society. What bears emphasis is that, in this account, there was no foreordained subject to follow the prescribed steps of any revolutionary teleology. If Zavaleta saw Bolivia's mining proletariat as exercising a central role in the fraught political struggles of the mid twentieth century, its very centrality supposed the existence of other popular subjects with which it was in political interaction and intercommunication. His attention to the anticolonial insurgencies led by Tupac Amaru and Tupaj Katari in the late eighteenth century, the community mobilizations under Pablo Zárate Willka in the late nineteenth century and the neo-katarista mobilizations during the general strike of 1979 reveal that he came to take very seriously the indigenous peasantry as a political subject in its own right and one that could have a decisive role in the formation of a national-popular project in Bolivia. In other words, he acknowledged the complexity of the class and ethnic dynamics that could play into any national-popular movement. By exploring the history of the subaltern actors and their alliances which had taken shape since the eighteenth century, he sought to frame an understanding of the revolutionary and post-revolutionary period of his own time. The lucidity with which he did so would help his successors do the same in our own.

Here again, we must come back to the critical issue of Zavaleta's own self-reflexive epistemological approach in a sociological context of 'dubious quantifiability', as he put it. For the national-popular was not only an object of historical analysis. It was no less a cognitive strategy which he elaborated, given the limits of a general theory of value in the Latin American setting, out of the specific historical and political conditions that marked the late phase of his own life. The 1979 general strike, which brought together mineworkers, indigenous peasants and other urban popular sectors to confront the reactionary military regime of General Alberto Natusch Busch, made a powerful impression on Zavaleta. It allowed him to see beyond his earlier concentration on the working class as a vanguard political actor and to understand proletarian centrality as part of a wider irradiation of democratic forces and a fuller process of the self-determination of the masses. This expansion of his own vision allowed Zavaleta to rethink Bolivian history more generally and to experiment with the national-popular as a crux for interpreting the fundamental relationships between society and the state.

This raises the question of the potential scope of national-popular politics and intersubjectivity. Zavaleta's own conception expanded from a narrow focus on class to one that included ethnic subjectivity, as a result of the unfolding of political struggle in his own time. In the early twenty-first century, the social mobilizations in Bolivia included a range of forces aside from indigenous and proletarian ones, such as territorial organizations of neighbourhood associations, generational groups of students and street kids, and middle-class professionals, which could also be thought of as part of a national-popular bloc in Zavaleta's terms.

One of the noticeably absent elements in Zavaleta's analysis is gender. This is perhaps unsurprising given its relative neglect within formal theory and practice on the left. On the other hand, it is intriguing that gender themes did not push themselves more fully into Zavaleta's field of awareness given his view of the vanguard role of miners and the particular protagonism of women mineworkers in key moments of national-popular struggle in Bolivia. According to the legendary account of the Catavi massacre, it was María Barzola who, Bolivian tricolour in hand, led the striking miners into the line of fire of the government troops in 1942. After the 1952 national revolution, the Movimiento Nacionalista Revolucionario [Revolutionary Nationalist Movement or MNR] named the members of its militant female auxiliary force 'Barzolas'. The trade-union federation of Bolivian mineworkers had a longstanding 'housewives' organization which played the leading role in bringing down the right-wing military regime of General Hugo Banzer Suárez with its hunger strike in 1977–78. It is true that middle-class feminism had limited political force in Bolivia and that class and anti-imperialist discourse was pre-eminent in the 'housewives' organization. However, if we follow Zavaleta's own reasoning about the production of local political knowledge as a result of local political conditions, it cannot be said that women themselves have been absent from national and popular struggle.

In the international context, socialist feminism, feminist social history and postcolonial feminist theory all provide bases upon which to rethink critically the history and politics of the national-popular project from a gender standpoint. In the Bolivian context, to take the case at hand, there are also local political and intellectual bases. For example, Domitila Barrios de Chungara was one of the women mineworkers who led the hunger strike that ultimately restored democracy in the country, and her classic 1978 book *Let Me Speak!* is often taken as an original instance of the Latin American literary genre of *testimonio*, in which a narrator from an oppressed group relates her or his life as a witness of popular suffering and struggle. Barrios de Chungara's account reflects the fact that gender power relations in the household and the community were a signif-icant concern of working-class women and were connected to their wider political consciousness and engagements.[11] To take another example: Silvia Rivera Cusicanqui began her radical sociological career in the late 1970s and early 1980s writing about indigenous Aymara history and political struggle in the era of the neo-katarista mobilizations. In fact, her intellectual work and activism contributed to Zavaleta's own move to take seriously the role of indigenous move-ments in Bolivian history. Over time, Rivera herself began to take

---

11 Domitila Barrios de Chungara and Moema Vizzier, *Let Me Speak! Testi-mony of Domitila, a Woman of the Bolivian Mines* (New York: Monthly Review Press, 1978).

more seriously the phenomena of patriarchal power in the country and their connection to the structures of internal colonialism that persisted after national independence.[12] Truly decolonized and democratized social relations in the nation would entail, to draw from only one aspect of Rivera's work, a challenge to the political culture of male authority found widely across class and ethnic lines. Likewise, Rossana Barragán's historical work on the principle of *patria potestad* reveals how gender exclusions, alongside ethnic ones, were built into liberal legislation regarding citizenship in the nineteenth century.[13] After prison and after her phase of social-movement activism and participation in the Comuna group, Raquel Gutiérrez returned to Mexico where her Bolivian experience has continued to influence her thinking about masculinist logics in politics and the role of women in creating the material and affective conditions for communal action.[14] Considering such a range of historical and contemporary examples, future reflection on a truly emancipatory project in the country—whether identified as national-popular or not—can be tested by its confrontation of patriarchal hierarchy and its openness to the constitutive social roles and political initiatives of women.

---

12 For a sample of her work, see Silvia Rivera Cusicanqui, *Anticolonialism as a Planetary Struggle*, forthcoming in the Elsewhere Texts series from Seagull Books.

13 Rossana Barragán, *Indios, mujeres y ciudadanos. Legislación y ejercicio de la ciudadanía en Bolivia* (*siglo XIX*) (La Paz: Fundación Diálogo/Embajada del Reino de Dinamarca en Bolivia, 1999).

14 See, for example, Raquel Gutiérrez Aguilar, *Desandar el laberinto. Introspección en la feminidad contemporánea* (La Paz: Comuna, 1999); and her 'Políticas en feminino: Transformaciones y subversiones no centradas en el estado' in *Horizontes comunitario-populares. Producción de lo común más allá de las políticas estado-céntricas* (Madrid: Traficantes de Sueños, 2017).

V

Zavaleta's book can be seen as part of a long current within Marxism in which grounded historical-political analysis has served as the basis for elaboration of key conceptual categories. Marx's *18th Brumaire* and Gramsci's 'Notes on Italian History' are two preeminent examples. The connections between Zavaleta and Gramsci's historical writing go beyond the general inspiration that the latter provided or Zavaleta's specific redeployment of some of his language and inquiries. There is the fact that Gramsci was himself writing from the southern periphery of European capitalism in the early twentieth century. There is also the similar truncation and open-endedness of their projects. The very incompleteness of Gramsci's work left it open to multiple readings and appropriations, like those made by Zavaleta himself. By the same token, if Zavaleta's life was cut off before his project had come to fruition, it allowed for a subsequent generation to pick up the themes and pursue the implications under new historical circumstances.

France in 1848 or Italy during the Risorgimento might be somewhat familiar to an international readership, perhaps in part thanks to Marx and Gramsci themselves. For an audience unversed in Bolivian, Peruvian and Chilean history, one of the challenges of reading Zavaleta's final work is its level of historical specificity. Such readers are advised to consult Anne Freeland's afterword to this book which provides a concise overview of the historical processes examined by Zavaleta.

We might draw an additional comparison here between Zavaleta's methodological approach to Bolivian history and Gramsci's approach to subaltern history. Like social historians in the present, Gramsci was aware of the difficulty of writing the history of subaltern social groups (and hence of Italian history as a whole). Given their relative lack of consolidation within the state and the corresponding limits to the accessibility of their experience for the researcher, any attempt to write subaltern history would inevitably be fragmentary and episodic. Zavaleta similarly saw that, given the degree of disarticulation or *abigarramiento* in Bolivia, the writing of its history would be necessarily sketchy, disjointed, discontinuous. His methodological solution was to focus on crises as moments of revelation of society (and hence the state): 'Moments of crisis operate not as a form of violence against the routine order, but as a pathetic manifestation of the points within society that would otherwise remain submerged and gelatinous.'[15] Gramsci drew the conclusion that subaltern history could only be written monographically, pulling together a mass of material not always easily accessible.[16] Zavaleta himself embarked on an equivalent monographic project, fully cognizant of the limits of his sources and his own historical knowledge. The result is not the smooth, homogenized product that passes for standard academic or successful commercial history, nor was it intended to be.

If Gramsci's writing was indirect and coded to guard it from the prison censors, the gnomic language, cryptic style and dense composition in Zavaleta flowed from other sources. Luis Tapia describes his vigorous, creative form as a Baroque-modernist expression corresponding to the very heterogeneity of the society that Zavaleta sought to apprehend and from which his own knowledge derived. Reflecting the society itself, argues Tapia, Zavaleta's writing is marked by manifold proliferating nuclei that lack an ultimately unified overarching frame and that spill over their own margins. Zavaleta's comment on crisis methodology might be extended to apply as well to literary approaches, and be taken as implicitly self-referential: 'Critical knowledge, as a result of the agglutinated form of heterogeneous presentation within that pathos, is proper to unquantifiable societies

---

15 See p. 17 in the present volume. Pathos in Zavaleta concerns the affective dimension in collective identity formation.

16 Antonio Gramsci, *Selections from the Prison Notebooks of Antonio Gramsci* (Quintin Hoare and Geoffrey Nowell Smith eds and trans) (New York: International Publishers, 1971), pp. 52–5.

such as Bolivia.'[17] By such a reading, Zavaleta's own literary bid could be seen as an effort, from a subjective and affective stance of revolutionary commitment, to approximate a composite synthesis of the disconnected elements of Bolivian history. His style is closer to essay than tract, resistant to schematic systematization, experimental more than conclusive, given to concentrated aphorism and assertion rather than evenly proportioned exposition. His peculiar language seems deliberately designed to contravene academic, technical or bureaucratic norms. The difficulties of Zavaleta's writing are notorious for his readers and might seem to pose an insuperable obstacle for translation, yet Freeland has met the challenges admirably in her elegant and scrupulous English translation. Her afterword also provides a glossary of a set of Zavaleta's key categories.

Finally, it must be said that this superficial sketch of Zavaleta's intellectual project cannot do justice to its complexity and depth. For an enhanced appreciation, the essential reference is the deep study of Luis Tapia, the masterful interpreter of Zavaleta and his foremost successor in Bolivian political theory.[18] Zavaleta is known primarily in Bolivian and Bolivianist circles, where his thinking has circulated and been absorbed in the social sciences, history and cultural studies as well as in public discourse. Yet, even his prominent position as director of the Latin American School of Social Sciences (FLACSO) in Mexico City did not lead to the international theoretical notoriety that might be expected for someone of his intellectual calibre and originality. Zavaleta has remained an intriguing figure but often an unread or underestimated author even in the Latin American context. It is to be hoped that this translation of *Towards a History of the*

---

17 See p. 17n2 in the present volume.

18 Luis Tapia, *La producción del conocimiento local. Historia y política en René Zavaleta Mercado* (La Paz: Muela del Diablo, 2002). An English translation of this work is forthcoming in the Elsewhere Texts series from Seagull Books as *The Production of Local Knowledge: History and Politics in the Work of René Zavaleta Mercado*.

National-Popular in Bolivia may spur reflection on the problems of
state–society relations and hegemonic and counter-hegemonic projects in different social formations around the world in which the
effects of capitalist development, however striking in some spheres,
however pervasive in others, remain only partial and uneven. His
final work-in-progress may also signal an avenue for producing critical theory from the global South and capitalist peripheries that is
historically informed and politically engaged as well as conscious of
and building from its own limits.

Prologue

I. Introduction

The problem that this study seeks to investigate is that of the formation of the national-popular in Bolivia, that is, the connection between what Max Weber called social democratization[1] and state form. By this we mean the different patterns of socialization as they existed and their indices of power, as well as the so-called mass projects. In other words, the relation between programme and reality. Our study of this problem will refer to the period between 1952 and

---

[The text of *Lo nacional-popular en Bolivia* was unfinished when René Zavaleta Mercado died. There was to be at least one more chapter, and he wrote footnotes only for the prologue and the first chapter, inserting asterisks in the text where there would have been footnotes in the second and third chapters. The first Spanish edition (Mexico City: Siglo XX, 1986) included the asterisks as in the manuscript without further citations. The second and most recent Spanish edition (La Paz: Plural, 2013), thoroughly revised to correct transcription errors in the first, omits the asterisks and includes footnotes with references for works cited in the second and third chapters, compiled by Mauricio Souza. I am deeply indebted to Souza as I have reproduced almost all of these, with minor modifications. References from Souza's edition have been omitted in a few cases where a particular text is cited as the source of a concept that is generally well known and present in multiple works of a particular author or discourse, and in most cases of texts in Spanish translation, I have changed the reference to either the original or an existing English translation. A few explanatory footnotes are mine, marked by brackets.—Trans.]

1 See Max Weber, *Economy and Society: An Outline of Interpretive Sociology* (Guenther Roth and Clauss Wittich eds; Ephraim Fischoff, Hans Gerth and A. M. Henderson trans) (Berkley: University of California Press, 1978). Weber uses this term in the sense of the concrete process of equality, that is, of the production of juridically free men, as opposed to democracy as political system.

1980, although its causal explanation will bring us back to the War of the Pacific (1879–84).[2] It should be understood as a general argument about the Bolivian social formation, empirically supported by data from the period. From a methodological perspective, we will proceed by isolating certain events, circumscribed in time, or regional situations, circumscribed in space. This is a response to a scarcity of information and it undoubtedly entails a symbolic selection. In defence of this method it must be said that no social science is possible otherwise in a country like Bolivia.

II. Background

The phase known as that of the National Revolution, which unfolds around the moment of rupture of 1952,[3] is at the centre of our analysis because it constitutes an organic development: latent elements are suddenly compelled to perform a radical act of manifestation or appearing, and it is here that it becomes evident, for example, that the category of marginality, perhaps valid as a quantitative criterion within a moment of gnomic subordination, is nonetheless not at all valid in a moment of critical revelation.[4]

---

2 In 1952, a popular insurrection instituted the current Bolivian state model. The War of the Pacific, with Chile on one side and Peru and Bolivia on the other, involved a displacement of the logic of protectionism with regard to the towns of the interior in favour of the mercantile logic of the peripheral ports. It is the starting point of the oligarchic state in Bolivia.

3 The 'National Revolution' in Bolivia refers to the period of democratic transformations that began in April 1952. The term is attributed to Carlos Montenegro, the foremost theorist of revolutionary nationalism, and it indicates in a way the privilege that tends to be afforded to national objectives over democratic ones. 'Not to be like those who feel themselves to be a class rather than nation,' he writes.

4 For the role of crisis in social knowledge, see René Zavaleta Mercado, 'Movimiento obrero y ciencia social: La revolución democrática de 1952 en Bolivia y las tendencias sociológicas emergentes', *Historia y Sociedad: Revista Latinoamericana de Pensamiento Marxista* (Mexico) 2(3) (1974): 3–35. Also in *Obra completa de René Zavaleta Mercado* (La Paz: Plural, 2011–15) VOL. 1,

Since this moment is characterized by a hierarchical fluidity or void, there is in effect a mode of identification that each of the social classes adopts in relation to the new general articulation, in relation to one another,[5] and also to the state, which does not merely receive the consequences of this interaction but also contrives to test its own nascent autonomy amid a set of events that can only be construed as a typical constitutive moment.[6]

In a way, the subsequent history of Bolivia is but the unravelling of the elements of the crisis of 1952. Thereafter, the class subjects only reproduce the conditions of their performance at that crucial moment. This of course leads us to consider the singular role of catastrophic or constitutive moments in relation to the reformulation of ideological models and also of what we might call the 'temperament' of a society. The inquiry itself should tell us if this is a way of compensating for imbalances or disjunctions between silent structural events and the constitution of power, that is: In what way does a society that is to a great extent invertebrate like that of Bolivia coordinate the moments of its determination, given that here this could not be done by means of representative democracy?[7]

---

pp. 691–726. See also Zavaleta Mercado, 'Clase y conocimiento' *Historia y Sociedad: Revista Latinoamericana de Pensamiento Marxista* (Mexico) 2(7) (1975): 3–8; *Obra completa*, VOL. 2, pp. 383–9.

5 It is obvious, for example, that the peasants are formally organized in the image of the workers, yet this does not create a relation of immersion in the working class but in the state *from* which the working class had operated. Other movements within the hegemonic exchange that is active beginning in 1952 include the particular mode of association between the military and the peasantry, and between the students and the workers.

6 A 'constitutive moment' can be understood as the originary point of a society in the most remote sense, for example, the irrigation of the Nile in Egypt, or the conquest of the elements in the Andes. In the sense in which we are using it, it refers to the manner of acquisition of the ideological tone and the forms of domination adopted by the state, that is, the moment of its construction.

7 See René Zavaleta Mercado, 'Cuatro conceptos de la democracia', *Bases: Expresiones del pensamiento marxista boliviano* 1 (1981): 101–24; *Dialéctica*

The period itself, understood as a revolutionary period, is thoroughly illustrative of the contents of each of the social classes and their 'national' scope. The reorganization of the relations between the new political classes (the working class and the peasantry) and the mediations that were established almost as if to reconnoiter the situation[8] necessitated the founding of a new state system that we will call the state of 1952. It inaugurates the second phase of the Bolivian state in the twentieth century.[9]

The first had been established with the Federal War (1899). An alliance between the oligarchic subclass and the indigenous peasantry imposed then, by military means, a new dominant social bloc, a new geopolitical axis, certainly new principles of legitimation and, to a great extent, even a new repressive apparatus, all this within the context of Bolivia's new mode of insertion into the world market with the tin mines.[10]

The structural composition of the state of 1952 is based on the expansion of the demographic base of political consensus (which had collapsed as a result of liberal defection in 1899) through the inclusion of the workers in the political sphere in the 1940s and of the peasantry in the 1950s, on a new spatial conception of the country (although spatiality is a constant in the reasoning of the Bolivian state),[11] a new

7(12) (September 1982): 11–30; *Obra completa*, VOL. 2, pp. 513–29; 'De Banzer a Guevara Arze: la fuerza de la masa', *Cuadernos de Marcha* (Mexico) 2(3) (September–October 1979): 29–41; *Obra completa*, VOL. 2, pp. 471–93.

8 See Zavaleta, 'Movimiento obrero y ciencia social.' The conduct of the peasant leaders in relation to the guerrilla of 1967 is especially eloquent. See René Zavaleta Mercado, 'El Che en el Churo', *Semanario Marcha* (Mexico), 10 October 1969, pp. 16–18; subsequently published in *Temas Sociales* 7 (1971): 10–22; *Obra completa*, VOL. 2, pp. 621–32.

9 See note 41.

10 See Ramiro Condarco Morales, *Zárate, el temible Willka: Historia de la rebelión indígena de 1899* (La Paz: Talleres Gráficos Bolivianos, 1965).

11 See Carlos Badía Malagrida, *El factor geográfico en la política sudamericana* (Madrid: Reus, 1946); Jaime Mendoza, *El macizo boliviano* (La Paz: Imp. Arnó hnos., 1935), etc.

ideology (the 'ideologeme' of revolutionary nationalism),[12] and a new repressive apparatus. More important than all of this, however, is the emergence of structures of mediation and mediators in a modern sense.[13] A comparative analysis of the constitution, the forms and the decline of the two Bolivian states (of these two phases) serves as a valuable frame for the study of Latin American social formations. In other words, this study is intended as an intervention in the recent debates on the problem of the state on the basis of the analysis of a concrete case.[14]

If it is obvious that the revolutionary event is not the result of direct economic determination but of class accumulation, we can nonetheless infer connections between elements belonging to the official country and those of its inner nature. None of the moments proper to the state mode of 1952, some of which constitute absolute shifts with regard to the entire history of the country (such as the definitive incorporation of the peasantry),[15] would have been possible

12 See Luis H. Antezana Juárez, 'Sistema y proceso ideológicos en Bolivia, 1935–1979' in René Zavaleta Mercado (ed.), *Bolivia hoy* (Mexico City: Siglo XXI, 1983), pp. 60–84; Ernesto Laclau, *Política e ideología en la teoría marxista: capitalismo, fascismo, populismo* (Madrid: Siglo XXI, 1978).

Juan Lechín, for example, was the classic mediator throughout the period. But so, in a way, was Alfredo Ovando in relation to the army. The advent of what has been called 'mediation through privilege' (see Zavaleta, 'De Banzer a Guevara Arze'; Walter Guevara Arze, 'Los militares en Bolivia' [unpublished manuscript, 1980]), on the other hand, is characteristic of the moment of decline of the state of 1952.

14 See Ernesto Ayala Mercado, *¿Qué es la Revolución Boliviana?* (La Paz: Talleres Burillo, 1956); Guillermo Lora, *La revolución boliviana: Análisis crítico* (La Paz: Difusión, 1964). For the general problem, see Biaggio de Giovanni, 'Crisis orgánica y Estado en Gramsci' in Giacomo Marramao et al., *Teoría marxista de la política* (Mexico City: Cuadernos de Pasado y Presente, 1981); Giuseppe Vacca, 'Forma-stato y forma-valore' in Louis Althusser et al., *Discutere lo Stato: Posizioni a confronto su una tesi di Louis Althusser* (Bari: De Donato, 1978).

15 See Silvia Rivera Cusicanqui, 'Apuntes para la historia de las luchas campesinas en Bolivia (1900–1978)' in Pablo González Casanova (ed.),

without certain precursory events like the Chaco War.[16] War is always a force of renewal in societies and not for nothing has it been said that it is the way in which nations progress. We must nonetheless consider the function of a more or less universal mobilization in a country that lacked truly national events.[17] The role of modern warfare as a sociological event of great pathetic intensity in the transformation of social classes is clearly evident (for example, the emergence of a state pathos within the military), but, above all, in the preparation for depeasantization and certainly as an arena of ideological nationalization. The relation between military mobilization and the peasant movement now seems easily demonstrable.[18]

In fact, the social catastrophe of 1952 itself suggests heterodox positions with regard to the most representative sociological literature in Latin America, at least that of recent years. It is claimed, for example, that we are dealing with a social formation whose character is determined by its marginality and dependency.[19] In principle, we are compelled here to abandon a purely statistical analysis. The ample participation of the peasantry in the implementation of the process

Historia política de los campesinos latinoamericanos, VOL. 3 (Mexico City: Siglo XXI, 1985).

16 See David H. Zook, *The Conduct of the Chaco War* (New York: Bookman Associated, 1961); Roberto Querejazu Calvo, *Masamaclay: historia política, diplomática y militar de la Guerra del Chaco* (La Paz: Los Amigos del Libro, 1975); Aquiles Vergara Vicuña, *Historia de la Guerra del Chaco* (La Paz: Litografía e Imprenta Unidas, 1940–44).

17 The same can be said of the mobilizations that took place during the period of the rise of the masses after 1952: here the mobilization itself has a validity independent of its proportions; that is, what is irreversible is the act of the masses and not its scale.

18 See Jorge Dandler, *El sindicalismo campesino en Bolivia: Los cambios estructurales en Ucureña* (Mexico City: Instituto Indigenista Interamericano, 1969).

19 See Aníbal Quijano, *Dependencia, urbanización y cambio social en Latinoamérica* (Lima: Mosca Azul Editores, 1977). Also, Ministerio de Planificación y Coordinación, *Estrategia socioeconómica de desarrollo nacional, 1971–1991* (La Paz: Ministerio de Planificación y Coordinación 1970).

of agrarian reform (in certain regions in particular) proves that the quantitative criterion of marginality is too reductive.[20] As for the structure of dependency, it is clear that if we were to adhere strictly to this principle, we would have to understand history as a closed circle in which the dependent could produce nothing but dependency: there would be no national histories. It is obvious that there are non-dependent forms of articulation, that the metropole itself faces great obstructions with regard to its capacity for knowledge of dependent societies. The nucleus of 1952 reveals a significant degree of political self-determination in a very backward context,[21] although this self-propulsion gave way almost immediately to the coercion of external conditions.[22]

In any case, it seems that in the interpretations of these events that have been advanced until now, there has been a certain Manichaeism, that is, they have almost always lacked what is called a 'total perspective'. The various factors tend to be subordinated either to the existence of a political caucus (the MNR) or to the undoubtedly impressive actions of the working class, not to mention explanations that emphasize the role of charismatic leadership.[23] It

20 This is evident in the events of Sacaba, Tolata and Epinaza in 1974 and the great peasant movement in support of the workers' strike of November 1979.

21 We know, for example, that US diplomats were sure in March 1952 that Movimiento Nacionalista Revolucionario (Revolutionary Nationalist Movement, MNR) would never rise to power, when an insurrection would erupt just days later. With Sergio Almaraz, I was able to see correspondence on this matter in the archive at the Calvo office in La Paz.

22 See Jackson Eder, in his memoirs, cited in Laurence Whitehead, *The United States and Bolivia: A Case of Neo-colonialism* (Oxford: Haslemere, 1969) and Victor Andrade, *My Missions for Revolutionary Bolivia, 1944–1962* (Pittsburgh, PA: University of Pittsburgh Press, 1976).

23 See Herbert S. Klein, *Orígenes de la revolución nacional boliviana: La crisis de la generación del Chaco* (La Paz: Juventud, 1968); Liborio Justo, *Bolivia: La revolución derrotada* (Buenos Aires: Juárez Editor, 1971); Luis Peñaloza, *Historia del Movimiento Nacionalista Revolucionario: 1941–1952* (La Paz: Dirección Nacional de Informaciones, 1963).

is more profitable, in our view, to discern instead the contradictory development of the different factors, as if the subjects of this history intended one thing and the course of events led ineluctably elsewhere. Jacobinism here turned out to be an ineffective school of thought. The idea of the peasantry as a class that receives and the proletariat as the class that gives, for example, merely follows a dogmatic line. In reality, there is every reason to believe that the peasantry had its own class accumulation and also, as it were, its own class history within the history of classes. It is significant that it serves successively as a hegemonic mass at the moment of the constitution of power,[24] as a conservative body throughout the so-called military –peasant pact, when it was considered a 'peaceful class', and, finally, as the site of the disaggregation of the class bloc of 1952, that is, of the dissolution of the state.[25]

The Bolivian working class, in its history as a constitutive class and as a separatist class, has consistently put into question the degree to which we can say that there is in Bolivia, and, in all likelihood, anywhere else, a necessary correspondence between the indices of economic and cultural development and the level of political development of the workers. The Bolivian experience seems to show, as do other cases, that this correlation is at best indirect, so that for a class like this, its own organic accumulation or hegemonic history, something that is necessarily related to the degree of efficiency achieved by the state presence, is of greater importance.[26]

---

24 It was surely the success of the peasant mobilization that ensured the survival of the MNR's power in the critical years of 1952–56.

25 The substitution of the 'military–peasant pact' by an alliance between the peasantry and the COB towards 1978 and the support of the UDP in the three elections that Siles Zuazo won between 1978 and 1980.

26 See Juan Rojas and June C. Nash, *He agotado mi vida en la mina: Una historia de vida* (Buenos Aires: Nueva Visión, 1976); Domitila Barrios de Chungara and Moema Viezzer (eds), *'Si me permiten hablar': Testimonio de Domitila, una mujer de las minas de Bolivia* (Mexico City: Siglo XXI, 1977), available in English as: *Let Me Speak! Testimony of Domitila, a Woman of the*

But this apparent margin of autonomous political development proved valid only in a less perspicuous way for other sectors. Scant economic development was not a real obstacle for the development of the working class, but it probably was an obstacle for the formation of a local bourgeoisie. In other words, while the peasants demonstrated an almost general capacity for mobilization (for non-marginality) and the workers for what was practically an impromptu hegemony, to a remarkable extent on the Latin American scale, at the same time the 'seigneurial paradox' emerges. What do we mean by this? The old Bolivian class or caste proves incapable of gathering within itself any of the subjective or material conditions of its transformation into a modern bourgeoisie, perhaps because it is a bourgeoisie that lacks bourgeois ideals, or because all of its cultural structures are of a precapitalist order. The paradox consists in that at the same time it possesses an extraordinary capacity for self-ratification qua dominant class throughout the different phases of the state, through immense social changes, and even several modes of production. Thus, just as the National Revolution is something like a bourgeois revolution carried out against the bourgeoisie, its development is the placing of its elements in the service of a repositioning of the oligarchic-seigneurial class. This seigneurial orientation, then, proves to be a constant throughout the history of Bolivia.[27]

Bolivian Mines (New York: Monthly Review Press, 1978); Carlos Soria Galvarro, *Con la revolución en las venas: Los mineros de Siglo XX en la resistencia antifascista* (La Paz: Editorial Roalva, 1980).

27 See Gonzalo Romero, *Reflexiones para una interpretación de la historia de Bolivia* (Buenos Aires: Imprenta López, 1960); Jorge Siles Salinas, 'Reflexiones sobre la ejemplaridad' in *Lecciones de una revolución: Bolivia, 1952–1959* (Santiago: Editorial Universidad Católica, 1959), pp. 27–36; Marcelo Quiroga Santa Cruz, *La victoria de abril sobre la nación* (La Paz: Burillo, 1964); Jorge Siles Salinas, *La aventura y el orden: reflexiones sobre la revolución boliviana* (Santiago: Bustos y Letelier, 1956).

III. Some Hypotheses on the Subject

In short, our intention is to apply concepts from state theory and from a theory of social classes to a study of a concrete, historical nature centred on the preliminary hypotheses or postulations outlined below:

1. *The Relation between Surplus and Constitutive Moment*
The role of social 'receptivity' as the basis of the formation of modern states is more or less generally accepted. This receptivity or general opening refers, with regard to civil society, to moments of emptying, that is, to the conjunctures in which great masses are prepared to assume new collective beliefs.[28] From the perspective of the state, however, this 'receptivity' is clearly related to the problem of economic surplus, that is, a haphazard malleability of the masses is not enough, but, rather, a degree of capacity for emission or infusion is necessary on the part of the state, of power as a programmatic act. There is a parallel development: the deeper the 'receptivity' of society as ideological flux and the greater the surplus, the better the conditions for the construction of a modern state, that is, one in which ideological inflection predominates over the repressive fact and democratic mediations replace or mask traditional forms of domination.[29]

In Bolivia, there have been at least two constitutive moments in the period that interests us here: 1899 and 1952. The extent and depth of each of these is a matter of debate. That of 1899 had national consequences, but it was not a truly 'national' event and ultimately it translated for the most part into shifts of power within the dominant social bloc. Even the participation of the Aymara occasioned,

---

28 This notion of 'emptying' is really a metaphor, but it is clear that ideology is a thing of great tenacity and that only in very exceptional moments are people open to such a substitution.

29 See Louis Althusser, 'Ideology and Ideological State Apparatuses' in '*Lenin and Philosophy' and Other Essays* (New York: New Left Books, 1971), pp. 127–88; Claus Offe, 'The Abolition of Market Control and the Problem of Legitimacy', *Kapitalistate* 1–2 (1973–74): 109–16.

above all, the establishment of what has been called 'social Darwinism' as the internal ideology of the oligarchic state.[30] This is of course not the same thing as a democratic revolution in which great masses are active and take up arms, those in which military action is more or less global, such as the Mexican Revolution, or insurrections like that of Bolivia in 1952 that are concretized in a concentrated nucleus which later distributes its revolutionary effects, only after these have been mediated by ideological subsumption, etc.[31] In any case, even if we accept such objections, we would have to speak in terms of a lack of extension or depth of these constitutive moments, but not of their nonexistence. It is clear that the course of Bolivian history prepared the way for this type of innovation.

Here the explanation of the weak constitution of the nation-state on the basis of a supposed lack of economic surplus is an unfortunate commonplace.[32] Bolivia would never have had the articulatory economic capacity required to produce more advanced institutions. This would not explain, on the other hand, why countries like Cuba in the 1920s and Argentina during the half century that spans from 1880 to 1930 failed nonetheless, as did Bolivia, in the construction of modern political superstructures.

In the nineteenth century, Bolivia disappears from the world market for all practical purposes.[33] A state apparatus is then organized

30 See Marie-Danielle Demélas, *Nationalisme sans nation? La Bolivie aux XIXe–XXe siècles* (Paris: Éditions du C.N.R.S., 1980); Bautista Saavedra, 'Proceso Mohoza: Defensa del abogado pronunciada en la audiencia del 12 de octubre de 1901' in *El ayllu: Estudios sociológicos* (La Paz: Juventud, 1971), pp. 133–56.

31 See René Zavaleta Mercado, *El poder dual en América Latina: Estudios de los casos de Bolivia y Chile* (Mexico City: Siglo XXI, 1974).

32 See Wálter Guevara Arze, *Plan inmediato de política económica del gobierno de la Revolución Nacional* (La Paz: Letras, 1955) and all of Paz Estenssoro's speeches on 1952.

33 See Luis Peñaloza, *Historia económica de Bolivia* (La Paz: El Progreso, 1953).

with an economy founded almost exclusively upon what is called indigenous tribute.[34] This institution is perhaps the most worthy of study in relation to the Bolivian social formation: it refers in principle to a 'tributary' sector but not to a 'constituent' sector. With various modifications, this would continue to be the case until well into the twentieth century; but the character or spirit of the material base of the state, its 'structural conception', would not change until 1952 and even then it would retain substantial residual tendencies.

The appropriation of the surplus has always been an alien concept for the Bolivian ruling class, and this was the case during the two silver booms as well as the tin boom.[35] In other words, we must review the conditions as a result of which Bolivia was unable to absorb its surplus, but the claim that no surplus existed is clearly untenable.

2. Conservative Aspects of the Seigneurial Paradox and the Agrarian Question

If we bear in mind the dramatic universality of the events of 1952 and of several other contiguous events,[36] the seigneurial reconstruction of the ruling class in the subsequent period is all the more surprising. This is what we have called the problem of the seigneurial

34 See Nicolás Sánchez-Albornoz, 'Tributo abolido, tributo repuesto: Invariantes socioeconómicas en la Bolivia republicana' in Tulio Halperín Donghi (comp.), *El ocaso del orden colonial en Hispanoamérica* (Buenos Aires: Sudamericana, 1978), pp. 159–200; Rivera Cusicanqui, 'Apuntes para la historia de las luchas campesinas en Bolivia'.

35 See Antonio Mitre, *Los patriarcas de la plata: Estructura socioeconómica de la minería boliviana en el siglo XIX* (Lima: IEP, 1981); Juan Albarracín Millán, *El poder minero en la administración* liberal, VOL. 1 (La Paz: Urquizo, 1972); Sergio Almaraz, *El poder y la caída: El estaño en la historia de Bolivia* (La Paz: Los Amigos del Libro, 1967); Jan Kñakal, *Vinculaciones de las empresas transnacionales con la industria del estaño en Bolivia* (Santiago: CEPAL, 1981).

36 See note 25.

paradox in the history of Bolivia.[37] It is a feature of the traditionalism that Bolivian society exhibits in contrast to others of great dynamism and initiative, and it is likely (though this remains to be proven) that it has to do with the semicrystallized state of the agrarian question. Although this is a far more complex problem and anything we might say about it here would entail a measure of audacity, there are certain apothegms within the discourse of social analysis in Bolivia that should be pointed out. We could say in general that there has been, from a schematic perspective, a difference between the juridical moment of taxation or tribute and the structural moment of production, that is, that the juridical forms of the agrarian question have been conflated with the practical models of agricultural appropriation of the land, which is, in our view, where the crux of matter lies.

This is perhaps already evident in the persistence of the agrarian form of the 'community,' given that the defence and reproduction of this form in practice constitutes the mode of insertion of the peasantry in the democratic movement.[38] But despite the apparent forms of the haciendas and even smallholdings, at least as far as the classical Andean habitat is concerned, it is clear that it is merely a matter of juridical modalities in which the model of production is maintained; in other words, there is ultimately a single agricultural form that has persisted over time. The Spaniard, the *hacendado*, the civil servant, would serve as state mediators or tax collectors but never as administrators in the sphere of production; that is to say, there would be a juridical subsumption but never a real subsumption.[39]

---

37 See note 27.

38 Erwin Grieshaber, 'Survival of Indian Communities in Nineteenth-Century Bolivia' (PhD dissertation, University of North Carolina, Chapel Hill, 1977); Rivera Cusicanqui, 'Apuntes para la historia de las luchas campesinas en Bolivia.'

39 See E. Boyd Wennergren and Morris D. Whitaker, *The Status of Bolivian Agriculture* (New York: Praeger, 1975).

This hypothesis, although certainly belied by patent instances of privatization of communal lands, of inter-peasant economic accumulation and of differentiation (and unification), nonetheless exerts a certain influence that compels us to test it. In any case, the resistance of the Andean agrarian civilization would demonstrate the impenetrability of this universe to the interpellation of a nondemocratic state and the incompatibility of the seigneurial elite with democratic legitimation. That this is still true in the present conjuncture is evident, for example, in the striking resonance between Tamayo's ideas in 1910 and the millenarian project of the contemporary Katarists.[40]

3. *Problems of Theoretical Formalization*

This period of Bolivian history presents interesting problems for its theoretical formalization. This is the case, for example, with regard to those questions related to the stability or instability of the power system, the role of representative democracy and authoritarianism and, finally, the originary formation of the organs of power.

Bolivia has known two periods of civilian representative-democratic stability (1899–1934 and 1952–1964) and two phases of military rule (1934–1946 and 1964).[41] In general, Bolivia is known as a country of political instability. We must, however, account for why in the first period of civilian stability there was sufficient legitimacy despite minimal electoral participation, why in the second a

---

40 See Franz Tamayo, *Creación de la pedagogía nacional* (La Paz: Biblioteca del Sesquicentenario de Bolivia, 1975[1910]); Gamaliel Churata, *El pez de oro: Retablos del Laykhakuy* (La Paz: Canata, 1957); Fausto Reinaga, *La revolución india* (La Paz: Partido Indio de Bolivia, 1969).

41 The liberal period, strictly speaking, only lasts until 1920, but the subsequent republican governments were ultimately a continuation of this period. From 1952 to 1964, the MNR governed through a peaceful succession of elected civilian administrations. The first period of military government begins with Toro (1934) and ends with Ballivián (1952). But this is too formal a classification.

much more extensive sphere of legitimation was required, and why after this second period not even the complete universalization of suffrage was a sufficient legitimating element. This has to do with the perception of the masses, which is to say, in this study a double perspective is sought: first, how things occurred in the complexity of their contents; second, the way in which they were recognized and internalized by the masses. Why, for example, in the eyes of the collectivity, Busch or Villarroel represented democratic periods and not Herzog or Barrientos is a question that has to do with the history of the perspective of the masses.[42]

Consequently, with regard to representative democracy, the following problems, among others, will be addressed: the problem of the territorial axis, that is, Bolivia's failure to establish such an axis, even when it expressly attempted to do so with the Federal Revolution. There is no Piedmont or Buenos Aires in Bolivia.[43] But the social topography itself is irregular. It is more important to know the result of an election in the three main cities, in the mining centres and in two or three peasant districts than in the country as a whole.[44] This suggests that representative democracy, in order to be effective, requires a degree of homogeneity that Bolivia does not have. Therefore, the site of the 'nucleus of good sense' of legitimacy must be negotiated because, on the other hand, it is clear that representative democracy at a certain point becomes a popular demand.

The same can be said of the paradigm of the political party or the union. Bolivian society has been capable of building a party system since 1880 and has generated at least one party on the scale of

---

42 See René Zavaleta Mercado, 'Bolivia: Algunos problemas acerca de la democracia, el movimiento popular y la crisis revolucionaria' in René Zavaleta Mercado (ed.), *América Latina 80: Democracia y movimiento popular* (Lima: DESCO, 1981), pp. 39–61.

43 Although the Federal Revolution was a frustrated attempt to give the department of La Paz the role of Piedmont.

44 To capture La Paz, Cochabamba and Santa Cruz, plus the mining districts and peasant towns like Cliza and Achacachi, is to capture all of Bolivia.

the strongest in the region. Our task, however, is not to investigate what is called a party, which is basically a social bloc, but what it means in relation its original model, which is the European party. The same goes for the decisive history of the unions. If the union is the organization proper to the free circulation of labour power, we must ask what its function was prior to the full freedom of the market (the union preceded the internal market) or, rather, how 'alienation' or depeasantization was the mode of its constitution.

CHAPTER ONE

The Struggle for the Surplus

'In short, one has to make an outline of the whole history of Italy—in synthesis, but accurate.'[1]

Crisis can be understood in general as an anomalous instant in the life of a society, as a moment when things appear not as they are experienced in the quotidian but as they truly are. Yet, if the quantification of society is possible only through capitalism disseminated as a general form, and although certainly there is not a single way of knowing each thing, crisis acquires a special connotation in relation to those societies like the Bolivian that are incalculable and incognizable. Each mode of being necessarily engenders a form of knowledge, and therefore we maintain that it would be wrong to speak of a general method of knowing common to all societies.[2] In this society specifically, moments of crisis operate not as a form of violence against the routine order, but as a pathetic manifestation of the points within society that would otherwise remain submerged and gelatinous. Quantification itself, as we shall see throughout this history, plays a more limited part in more heterogeneous societies; on the other hand, it is at the moment of crisis or its equivalent (a moment

1 Gramsci, *Selections from the Prison Notebooks*, p. 131.

2 A 'general method' is at least as remote a possibility as is a general theory of the state. Each society must identify the method that can refer or apply to it. There are cognizable and incognizable societies, societies that are cognizable in one way and societies cognizable in another; in short, quantifiable societies and societies in which the mode of articulation between different forms is qualitative. Critical knowledge, as a result of the agglutinated form of heterogeneous presentation within that pathos, is proper to unquantifiable societies such as Bolivia. See René Zavaleta Mercado, *Las masas en noviembre* (La Paz: Juventud, 1983).

of intensity) that, in its results or synthesis, for this constitutes the only phase of concentration or centralization, a formation that otherwise would appear only as an archipelago can be seen. If this is true, it is not true in all cases, because not every crisis is generally eloquent and here the degree of revelation is also proportional to the degree of generality of the crisis, nor is quantification as such something that can be dispensed with altogether. The important thing is that, sooner or later, each society learns that to know itself is almost to prevail. The will to self-knowledge is not an insignificant phase of existence. War, in turn, is an intense moment, but not every war is a crisis and neither one nor the other encompasses in all cases the whole of the social object. The history of these hundred years in Bolivia will therefore necessarily be the history of a series of crises or pathetic social agglutinations.

Now, if we were to distinguish between how the War of the Pacific was experienced and how the Federal Revolution was experienced[3] (by which we mean to refer not to the externality of these events but to their collective internalization), we would have to say that the former should be considered, strictly speaking (at least in its initial moment), a matter of the state, that is, something won or lost by the ruling class, since at that time this class was not differentiated from the state[4] as an entity accountable to itself. In its different degrees of integration, a war can involve society and affect the state

---

3 In the War of the Pacific, Chile fought against Peru and Bolivia between 1879 and 1884; the so-called Federal Revolution was a civil war between the departments of the south, under the leadership of Chuquisaca, and those of the north, basically La Paz. See Condarco Morales, *Zárate, el temible Willka*.

4 Although it had been at times, for example, with Santa Cruz. A true distinction between the government as apparatus and the ruling class does not formally exist until the Revolution of 1952. Still, here we must take into account the tendency of the state to *return* to society—as a result of its power, it returns to society far stronger—and, conversely, the continuous impulse of every aspect of society, but more forcefully of certain particular groups, towards the state. The more or less prolonged stability of the state and of society is the privilege of but few societies.

only in a limited way, or it can be between a faction of society and the state, or, finally, it can remain solely at the level of the state. We maintain, then, that in the immediate ideological form it took when it occurred, the War of the Pacific was an affair of the state and of the state class, and not of society, at least not in any immediate way. In what follows we shall see why. The Federal Revolution, on the other hand, revealed the vital core of the paradigmatic conflicts of civil society.[5]

This nomenclature (civil society, state) is not always convincing. Especially in a country like that which Bolivia undoubtedly was at the time, in which the relative separation of the state, its autonomy, had not yet been achieved in any way. What we call the state at that time was rather the fraction of the ruling caste (because it was hereditary) within civil society itself that took over the government (here this expression, *to take something over* [*hacerce de algo*], must be emphasized) in an arbitrary way, with a characteristic transience. That is, this caste dominated continuously in civil society and intermittently in government, alternating between its parties or factions.[6] What in fact distinguishes Hilarión Daza from [Narciso] Campero, or [Mariano] Melgarejo from the second Ballivián (who was his child's godfather)?[7] At best a difference in degree of legitimacy within the ruling caste, which, after all, was important because one needs a

---

5 See the following chapter.

6 We should note, for example, the triviality of the skirmishes between Santa Cruz's and Ballivian's factions, although the penetration of *crucismo* in *belcismo* is indeed significant. In any case, the naturalness with which the conservative ruling class of Chuquisaca adapted to the ascendancy of the liberal ruling class of La Paz indicates that the connections between the two were considerable.

7 Manuel Rigoberto Paredes, *Melgarejo y su tiempo* (La Paz: Isla, 1962). Adolfo Ballivián, indeed, had spoken to Melgarejo of 'the sincerity and tenderness of my affection for your person' in a letter dated 29 January 1863, in which he also maintained that his decision would be carried out 'even if cherished and sacred ties did not bind me to you'. Melgarejism was no doubt at least one side of the oligarchic tradition and it was tied to the other, as this letter shows.

certain rational *hereditary right* even within a system of caste privilege. The unity or division of the ruling class is always a decisive factor in the assessment of the state. In any case, that this caste should
admit almost indiscriminately its traditional heroes, such as [Jose]
Ballivián, or the enigmatic sort of a brutal charisma like Melgarejo,
is ultimately of little importance since either case constitutes only the
internal movements within a single class. Ballivián or [Tomas] Frías
represented at best a spurious proposition of the principle of the
rational constitution of power that [Mariano] Baptista or [Aniceto]
Arce would later practise inconsistently.[8] The so-called Federal
War, on the other hand, is a far more profound event. It is the sum
of Melgarejo and [José María] Linares, of Daza and Ballivián that lost
the earlier war, that of the Pacific, whose significance Bolivia was
only belatedly able to discern.

And why, we might ask, did Bolivia take so long to take account
(to render account to itself) of what had happened? A people that
fails to recognize its own defeat is a people that is far from itself. The
indifference or perplexity with which this country dismissed an event
so decisive not only for its immediate being but also for all of its fore-
seeable future is indeed striking. The territorial loss represented an
indisputable defeat, the gravest and most decisive for the fate of
Bolivia. If we consider its most immediate implication, it can be said
that this rupture imposed a pseudo-autarchic future upon a country
ill-suited to autarchic development. The very heterogeneity of this
land reminds us perpetually that there is no homogeneity but that
imposed by history, that is, by men, through conscious and cumula-
tive acts. Only a certain penetrating contact with the world could
allow for some kind of surplus that might supply the no doubt costly
requirements of an articulation of the diversity that could only
convert the logos of the traditional space into a coherent national
market through a systematic programme. Here life is anything but

---

8 Joaquín de Lemoine, *Biografía del general Eliodoro Camacho* (Buenos Aires:
Peuser, 1885), cited in Alcides Arguedas, *Historia general de Bolivia* in *Obras
completas*, VOL. 2 (Mexico City: Aguilar, 1960).

spontaneous action. Consequently, with scarcely a kind of abject consciousness, Bolivia lost the possibility of developing a fluid and self-determined relation to even a minimal extent (that is, in its non-dependent territorial access) to a world market that, moreover, had just then begun to set the foundations of what would become a global economic system. Certainly the fetishization of this loss or failure often functions as an ideological scapegoat to explain the inferiority of the Bolivian nation, a common Jeremian refrain, as if to say, 'Thus began our misfortune.' What we might call the model of success, that is, the seductive effect of the fortunes of the core countries, operated in the production of this exutory. England, therefore, from that so-insular perspective, seemed to be the alliance of commerce and the sea, which was moreover what a capitalist form whose only modality of existence had always been commercial capital was prepared to believe.[9] The truth is that of these peoples of which Bolivia is made up has always been an inland culture: it is not a culture that closed itself off, but one that has constituted itself inwardly, which might have something to do with a certain inclination towards historical perseverance.[10] Under no circumstances could Bolivia have become a seafaring people and the conclusive nature of its dispossession shook the formation in two ways. First, because in the era of the world market, no country can acquire any degree of autonomy (and without autonomy, that is, without a degree of self-determination that does not impede its existence in the world, no nation can effectively be a nation) except through exchange with it, that is, real autonomy consists in a relation of belonging and at the same time of non-contingence vis-à-vis the world. In other words, the least that can be said is that this circumstance impeded Bolivia's untethered emergence at a decisive moment in the history of the world, a moment of such importance that it could be said that not to have participated in it is also not to know the world as it exists here and now. Bolivia became a tributary

---

9 Carlos Sempat Assadourian et al., *Modos de producción en América Latina* (Buenos Aires: Siglo XXI, 1973).

10 Tamayo, *Creación de la pedagogía nacional.*

both to the metropolises of the world and to this now ineluctable geographic mediation. It would be fair to say that from then on, whatever surplus was produced[11] had to contend not only with the incapacity for absorption common to all the countries of Latin America, but also with the logic of the two borders. Bolivia's wealth, still, besides its relatively modest scale, is internal. It is clear that sovereign control of the port, or at least access to it, would not have made it less so. Isolation merely exacerbated that which must of necessity be the nature of any Bolivian project, that is, its non-referral to any axis but its own. It is, then, a country that, although it must take into account its mode of insertion into the world market, must focus to a far greater extent than other countries on the self-referential aspects of its development. Indeed, there is no more absurd method of knowing a social formation like that of Bolivia than through indices with pretensions of general validity.

As we shall see, the *spirits of the state* in Bolivia could only see the geography of the country from a *gamonal*[12] perspective. The traditional state form was that of *gamonalism*.[13] The territory, of course, is an essential element of ideology, the nodal material support for the way in which a people sees itself, and this is why the notion of the nomadic or errant has such a pejorative connotation. The important thing about the War of the Pacific, infinitely graver than the fact

---

11 Guevara Arze, *Radiografía de la negociación con Chile* (La Paz: Universo, 1978); Daniel Sánchez Bustamante, *Bolivia: Su estructura y sus derechos en el Pacífico* (La Paz: Banco Central-Academia Boliviana de la Historia, 1979); José Fellman Velarde, *Réquiem para una rebeldía* (La Paz: Los Amigos del Libro, 1967); Edgar Oblitas, *Historia secreta de la Guerra del Pacífico* (Buenos Aires: Peña Lillo, 1978).

12 An Andean Spanish term for a landowner and local political boss. The word is derived from the name of a weed; it therefore has a connotation of illegitimacy that distinguishes the concept from that of feudalism.

13 Carlos Montenegro, *Nacionalismo y coloniaje* (Buenos Aires: Pleamar, 1967), p. 190: 'The predominance of the colonial spirit in that stage of the life of Bolivia is revealed in these unmistakable signs: the abandonment of the national territory to the invaders, and a zealous constitutionalism.'

of disconnection from the Río de la Plata or the dispossession of the banks in the Amazon,[14] is the loss of Atacama, or at least of the main part of the Atacaman territory that was Antofagasta, which entailed a rupture of the spatial logic through which that historical unit had been constituted. Andean agriculture, which is surely the most important civilizational event that has occurred here and in all of Latin America, and then Potosí, or Charcas,[15] are organized around and derive their identity from this territorial matrix. Santa Cruz is called *de la Sierra* because it refers not to the Río de la Plata or to the Amazon, but, precisely, to the Sierra.[16] It could not be something alien to it and perhaps, in certain circumstances, it could be at the heart of the Sierra. Atacama was an archetypically *appropriated* territory, incorporated into the ecological logic of the Andeans, and it is therefore not just any coast suitable for modern commerce that could have occasioned such a collective feeling of disintegration. The struggle for existence in the great Andes entails such extreme precariousness that such existence is not possible without the support of those surrounding regions, which do not define it but which give it a certain existential security.[17]

Certainly, these are far from insignificant incentives. Why, then, did this society, which had always fought so hard, fight so little then?

We are inclined to consider how an event is lived to be something of ever-greater importance; this, in the social sphere, is perhaps more decisive than its exteriorization (or at least a substantial element of its objectivity). In any case, it would be impossible to experience such an event, which either has not been totalized or has

---

14 J. Valerie Fifer, *Bolivia: Land, Location and Politics since 1825* (Cambridge: Cambridge University Press, 1972).

15 Josep M. Barnadas, *Charcas: Orígenes históricos de una sociedad colonial (1535–1565)* (La Paz: CIPCA, 1973).

16 Hernando Sanabria Fernández, *Breve historia de Santa Cruz* (La Paz: Juventud, 1973).

17 John V. Murra, *Formaciones económicas y políticas del mundo andino* (Lima: IEP, 1975); Ramiro Condarco Morales, *El escenario andino y el hombre: Ecología y antropogeografía de los Andes Centrales* (La Paz: Librería Renovación, 1971).

lost the forms of its totalization, as a coherent totality. The very idea of totalization or general intersubjectification[18] refers to something that is never acquired once and for all, and thus the nation can exist more within a collective project or prognosis than within an exhaustive homogeneity; moreover, even what has been generalized sooner or later tends towards its transformation into a conservative symbol of the particular. Intersubjectification must, therefore, be constantly reproduced. Men such as Prudencio Bustillo who were the vanguard or spirit of the consciousness of the state (not of social consciousness, because that would be an overstatement; we say this because *in practice* the Bolivian state itself would have been Bustillo)[19] had warned of this ineluctable situation. It was not, after all, so complicated, and ultimately, Bustillo is but the common sense of a truly parochial lack of common sense. Portales himself would have had no more than a rhetorical existence had he not produced the War of the Pacific. An insensitivity to the seriousness of the conflict is evident in Daza (although it is also evident in the rest of the men of state, including Baptista and, of course, Arce, who resolved to join in his enemies' victory, founding a whole school).[20] What is worth noting in all this,

---

18 See p. 47.

19 Ignacio Prudencio Bustillo, *La misión Bustillo: Más antecedentes de la Guerra del Pacífico* (Sucre: Imprenta Bolívar, 1919). At any rate, it is an isolated case. It can easily be said that there would be no bourgeois national consciousness of such depth until Montenegro. At some point Bustillo's polemic against Alberdi published under a pseudonym should discussed.

20 Aniceto Arce was an associate of Melchor Concha y Toro, of whom Ramírez Necochea says: 'An influential liberal politician. Member of Parliament for more or less 30 years. [. . .] He opposed the Balmaceda government and, when civil war broke out, he declared himself on the side of Congress. He made a name for himself as a businessman; he had powerful banking and mining interests; he extended his activities to Bolivia and was closely associated with British capital' (Hernán Ramírez Necochea, *Balmaceda y la contrarrevolución de 1891* [Santiago: Ed. Universitaria, 1969], p. 84. Arce said: 'The only hope for Bolivia's salvation is Chile's need to enlist it to ensure its own

however, is that the ideologeme of space is very different in society understood as the masses (which can also be conceived in terms of confrontation) and in the oligarchic stratum which is *there and then* the *whole* state (although the state is not the whole oligarchic stratum).

The problem should be posed, in our view, in the following manner: the originary event of this society makes space predominate over time. Adaptation to the harsh environment marks its elemental historical time.

Those *mitmaq* were just a belated and distorted manifestation of an ancient Andean pattern that I have called 'the vertical control of a maximum of ecological tiers.'[21]

The unity of space, therefore, is but an extension of this historical time, which is not that of capitalism (which does indeed break with agricultural time), but a local form of seasonal agricultural time.[22] Here political unity is derived from the necessities of subsistence and subsistence itself can only be conceived as collective time. The first consequence of this is that intersubjectivity is a precocious and violent event.[23]

---

conquests' (Santiago Vaca Guzmán, *El doctor Arce y su rol en la política boliviana; exámen de sus opiniones concernientes a la celebracion de la paz entre Bolivia y Chile* [Buenos Aires: Coni, 1881], p. 37).

21 Murra, *Formaciones económicas y políticas*, p. 60.

22 'In the formation of the Andean state and in the structure of the revenue system, one of the first and most important steps was the census of towns, *chacras* or *papakancha*, livestock and herders, and annual production levels' (ibid., p. 31).

23 'Most of the potatoes harvested are true alpine crops, frost-resistant but also highly dependent on human intervention' (John V. Murra, *La organización económica del Estado inca* [Mexico City: Siglo XXI, 1978], p. 33; available in English as: *The Economic Organization of the Inca State* [New Haven, CT: JAI Press, 1980]).

Early in the history of the Altiplano a political authority emerged that continuously demanded a growing fraction of the productive energy if its inhabitants, herds and lands.[24]

From this we derive the unity of space conceived as territorial reciprocity or politico-geographic pact (the geographic, understood as geology occupied by history, is not possible without the state) in the traditional Andean sense: one space cannot be conceived except in relation to another.[25] And this is what has been called the 'archipelago' or 'vertical control of a maximum of ecological tiers'. Agriculture in the highlands is not sufficient in itself without the complement of the agriculture of the lowlands, although certainly the latter would not have the capacity to fulfil this role if not for *telos* or solidity of the state proper to highland agriculture. The proof of this is that the subsistence agriculture of the fertile lowlands in this period generated only primitive state forms.[26]

The precondition of the state, therefore, is not surplus value but the conscious mode of its acquisition. At the same time, if we turn now to consider the problem at the level of the internalization of the event at the time of the War of the Pacific, we must say that this was then a buried and innate attribute, proper and at the same time unknown to the ancestral actor of the event, which is the Andean collectivity. Since the decisive thing here is the ideologico-cultural impotence of the gamonal-Hispanic elite, it was inevitable that their conceptions of life and of the land would be inimical.

The traditional Andean idea of space will always be different from the oligarchic-seigneurial, regional and non-national idea. The

---

24 Murra, *Formaciones económicas y políticas*, pp. 213–14.

25 On the 'enormous productivity in such harsh geographic conditions, Choy suggested that the proximity of such diverse climatic zones could be an explanation' (Murra, *La organización económica*, p. 15).

26 Such capacity for quantification has not been seen since. 'An efficient census system is, among other things, an indication of the strength of the state' (ibid., p. 168).

originary idea of space, because that space was the matrix of the primordial organization of life, is opposed to a patrimonial conception. It is well known, however, that space plays a determinative role in the relation to the state, that is, we have here two competing conceptions that are both spatialist. On the seigneurial side, which is that of the state, we have the hereditary notion of power in its double sense: on the one hand, as the idea of private power (the *rosca*)[27] and, on the other, as an extension of the seigneurial or feudal relation to the land, an absolute dominion over the land as an entitlement tied to a lineage, as a general principle of power. That regional or particularist conflict is so intense within the Hispanic contingent and, on the other hand, that the coexistence of Aymaras and Quechuas is so natural, although in theory the whites are said to ultimately belong more or less to a single ethnic group while, strictly speaking, a Quechua should be as foreign to an Aymara as a Spaniard, bears witness to the existence of these two conceptions or principles.[28] It is

---

27 This local epithet speaks to the Bolivian ruling class' sense of being an absolute minority. It is said to have been first used by Bautista Saavedra.

28 All this is quite complicated. It is not clear that Aymara was the language of La Paz, for example, and there is some evidence that it might have been Puquina (Alfredo Torero, *El quechua y la historia social andina* [Lima: Studium, 1975], p. 57). Moreover, 'nobody has found valid reason to maintain that Quechua existed in Bolivia prior to the arrival of the Incas,' although there is no doubt that Quechua ultimately became the lingua franca of the colony (Gary Parker, 'Falacias y verdades acerca del quechua' in Alberto Escobar (ed.), *El reto del multilingüismo en el Perú* [Lima: IEP, 1973], p. 117). In other words, the borders between Quechua and Aymara were never absolute. This means that there is an identity, even if it is produced between two languages, which is like a paradigm of intersubjectivity. Meanwhile, the Hispanic sector, which is assumed to be of greater homogeneous and monolingual provenance, is very far from such an identification. The fragmentation of reality proper to the gamonal mentality has cost the Hispanic group dearly. Indeed, it remains to be seen whether the chief obstacle to nationalization in Bolivia is not in fact the degree of cultural and symbolic dispersion of its ruling class and not, as has been said almost by reflex, the presence of the indigenous.

not that the oligarchs like Arce or Pacheco had no sense of belonging to the space, but that the feelings they had were connected to a seigneurial notion of space. This is the deep origin of what is called regionalism in Bolivia, that is, the incapacity for an experience of space as a national reality or even as something not directly linked to a personal relation to the land, as something conceived trans-personally or collectively.[29]

A country, or a society (or human nucleus), wages war with what it is, but also with what it is not. If a war is a radical event, if it is universal, it creates social receptivity. If it is not, it can shatter the society that it was supposed to defend. The true optimum for this purpose is produced when, as is said to have occurred with the ancient Scandinavians, the society goes to war en masse, that is, when no particle of the social body is unaffected by the war. For this to occur, first of all, the social corpus as such must feel itself to be unified to a certain extent (the principle of connection) and, on the other hand, and this is related to the first point, it must regard the object of the war as something central, vital and unrenounceable, something that must not be lost except when all is lost. Where the nation does not exist, men cannot be asked to take part in a national war or to possess a national sensibility in relation to the territory. That of the Bolivian ruling class is a particularist idea of the nation. These men experienced the dispossession of the coast as something inessential, as if, conserving the main part of the country, it was merely an incidental loss (this is why they accepted money for a territory that should never have been for sale), because such was their mentality: this land had no seigneurial connection whatsoever nor did it have a seigneurial use; to lose it, then, was like losing nothing at all, a mere inconvenience.[30]

---

29 'The oligarchic notion of territorial integrity was merely a notion of property' (Montenegro, *Nacionalismo y coloniaje*, p. 207).

30 Aniceto Arce attributed the war to 'our madness' (Arguedas, *Historia general de Bolivia*, p. 1341).

We must of course explain why the other Bolivia, that which should indeed have seen these things as the gravest injury, took so long to assess the situation. The perplexity with which the social body experienced so considerable a loss can be explained by the fact that the prior spatial logic, which was in reality a combination of traditional Andean agriculture and the despotic state as its natural culmination (because without an authoritarian organization agriculture was impossible),[31] had withdrawn to what we will call the crystallized or ossified aspect of the country's history (for it also has dynamic aspects). Modes of production would come and go without interrupting the repetition of the productive patterns of Andean agriculture, and would merely be translated into juridical forms of circulation superimposed upon local practices of the transformation of nature.[32] The old state had retracted into the moment of production itself and, therefore, the apex of the state in relation to this would never be more than a weakly supported facade. Strictly speaking, the local mode of production would not change over the course of several juridical forms, from Asiatic despotism to commercial capital, from gamonalism to simple mercantile production, which only concealed or masked it. A country is always what its agriculture is. Agriculture even today remains the characteristic mode of relation between man and nature, and even when it is said that industry predominates over agriculture, industry in fact functions in the service of this essential human activity. In a comparison of the kinds of agriculture practised in Bolivia, its true nature comes to light. Nomadic agriculture that necessarily creates certain errant and sporadic representations is one thing, and the pillage of the land, the only kind

---

31 See note 23.

32 This should be qualified. Toledo, for example, effectively transformed the community in all the Andes. Still, it is true that the productive act in itself (what we might call the logic of the highlands and the microclimates plus the collective pattern of productive organization) survives, permeating its superstructural expression. The latifundium, for example, is but a superficial form of plunder of the surplus; never has something so brutal been so impotent.

of capitalist agriculture that has been practised here, is another; yet another, lastly, is the form of exploitation in which ecological conservation is one of the central objectives.[33] In the plot of *Raza de bronce*[34] or in the geographic logic of Santa Cruz, in the Economic Plan of the National Revolution[35] or in Mendoza's *Macizo boliviano*,[36] we find only more or less sketchy reminiscences of the principle of ecological tiers. At the level of its superstructural expression, this might be a repressed or buried concept, but it cannot be eradicated from the collective mind. It is, therefore, an *inherent thinking*. The breaking off of Atacama was a violation of this integral body.[37]

The dispersion or nonexistence of a collective sense of space, on the other hand, leads to a kind of fragmented hypersensitivity towards certain spaces. It appears that the question of the Pacific seemed more significant for La Paz and Oruro in the beginning and only later for Tarija or Potosí.[38] In any case, if the ruling class is the official synthesis of the country (as every ruling class is), its disarticulation is clearly evident in the immediate defection of almost all of this class, in all of its expressions. This wretched country found itself forced to defend a city that had been christened Antofagasta

---

33 'From Cobo we learn that the use of fertilizers was one of the things the Europeans learnt in Peru' (Murra, *La organización económica*, p. 61). We might also mention the effects of irrigation on the coast, etc., for the state.

34 Alcides Arguedas, *Raza de bronce* (Buenos Aires: Losada, 1972).

35 Guevara Arze, *Plan inmediato*.

36 Mendoza, *El macizo boliviano*.

37 'The Pacaxas [. . .] had possessions on the Pacific coast, apparently interspersed with those of the Lupaga' (Murra, *Formaciones económicas y políticas*, p. 753). 'The Aymara-speaking kingdoms extended their control not only towards the Pacific, but also to the edge of the rainforest and beyond' (ibid., p. 77).

38 The 'Colorados' join the fight in El Alto de la Alianza with the rallying cry 'Long live the youth of La Paz!' See Alcides Arguedas, *Historia general de Bolivia*, p. 1338.

after an estate owned by Melgarejo's brother,[39] and its select troop was the regiment created and favoured by that drunken brute.[40] Barbarous caudillos like Melgarejo, because he foresaw cause of the dispossession,[41] or like Daza, because he was oblivious to the magnitude of the event, but also the lineage of the lettered caudillos, those of relative constitutional legitimacy (Arce, Baptista) and their great successors (Montes, Pando), men revered to this day—in all of them was the sole emphatic decision not to fight for that which was deemed pure periphery. It would surely have seemed to them more terrible to lose the Virgin of Copacabana. The same men who, like Daza, proved overzealous when it came to military privileges regarded it as no dishonour at all for the army not to have fought or even to to have considered fighting at any point in time.

Closed off in the agricultural sphere and practising a moral economy of resistance,[42] conservation and persistence, the vast popular corpus, although it only belatedly came to an awareness of the problem, would do so with an intensity that can only be explained by the interpellative force of space over ideological interference in this society.

*

---

39 'Melgarejo changed the name of La Chimba to Antofagasta, which was the name of an estate that a brother of his owned in the puna of Atacama' (Roberto Querejazu Calvo, *Guano, salitre, sangre: historia de la Guerra del Pacífico* [La Paz: Los Amigos del Libro, 1979], p. 136).

40 Arguedas, *Historia general de Bolivia*, p. 934.

41 Querajazu, *Guano, salitre, sangre*. Melarejo was of such a character, such was the paucity of his sense of sovereignty, that he asked Chile 'to send a garrison of fifty Chilean soldiers with their respective officers to reside in Cobija' in view of his 'confidence in the discipline, morality, and determination of the Chilean troops' (Gonzalo Bulnes, *Resumen de la Guerra del Pacífico* [Santiago: Ediciones del Pacífico, 1976], p. 16).

42 E. P. Thompson, 'The Moral Economy of the English Crowd in the Eighteenth Century', *Past and Present* 50 (1971): 76–136.

We might say that at the heart of the War of the Pacific was a conflict over the surplus because, as we shall see, Chile wanted to be Peru,[43] which, with Potosí, had been a symbol of the wealth of the world, surplus as magic; Bolivia thought that it was not Peru because Chile had snatched the philosopher's stone from it and Peru wanted only to go back to being itself, at least that of the guano surplus, but to do it better this time. Everyone here was seduced by the idea of a panacea. Meanwhile the Federal Revolution, which is the next moment of this history, would pose the question of the axis of the state, understood as a pivot of the spatial articulation of the country (one of the aspects of the optimum), which already brings us to the core of the national question as one of the central problems of the Bolivia of that time, that is, as a relation of the territory to the terri-tory and of men with men, space understood as a relation to space but also as a struggle among men and between men and the spaces they inhabit.

We must return to the question of Bolivia's non-combativeness. It is true that the first thing that strikes us in the War of the Pacific is the lack of a collective will (this is not an exaggeration) to fight for a portion of the territory that was vital to the core of the country, that is, the refusal (because the people were unarmed and as a con-sequence of the field of vision of the elite) to see it as something abso-lutely crucial. Here we must distinguish between territory that has been socially incorporated or appropriated and that which has not,

---

43 Peru and Bolivia together, according to Portales, 'would always be more than Chile'. In this remarkable letter, he says that 'we cannot view the existence of the two confederated peoples without great consternation and alarm and, in the long run, as a result of their common origin, language, habits, religion, ideas and customs, they will naturally form a single nucleus'. The explanation for this was their 'greater white population', 'the combined wealth of Peru and Bolivia barely exploited until now', 'the greater number of learned white men well connected to the Spanish families in Lima' (Diego Portales, quoted in Jorge Basadre, *Historia de la república del Perú, 1822–1933* [Lima: Editorial Universitaria, 1968–1970], VOL. 2, p. 149).

because this indicates the extent to which it has penetrated the ulti-mate ethos of a nation. There are inherent or essential territories, that is, those without which a people cannot be what it is, and marginal or supplemental territories, which are those that accom-pany or complement the vital core. Since Atacama was a limit or frontier made fit for human life by the Andeans and no one else,[44] and considering, moreover, that neither Spaniards nor Araucanians had ever settled there, the Andeans considered it in their collective soul to be part of their central home, which, incidentally, goes against Tamayo's exceedingly narrow *latifundista* ideas on the subject.[45] In other words, it belonged to the intellectual horizon of the Aymara, to their spatial discourse. In a radical rupture with this general con-ception of the space, the seigneurial class experienced its disposses-sion with a kind of ease or indifference scarcely moderated by the flagrant humiliation with which the rather inexperienced Chilean emissaries, newly risen to glory, were inclined to treat them.[46]

In any case, had there not been a general failure to understand that the territory in question was one socially incorporated into the innate logic of the nation, the nation would not have been able to lose it without first facing the loss of the whole of the nation itself. A man or a nation of sound mind does not lose something vital without losing or at least risking his very life. Here, however, the territory was lost because those who knew that they were losing it thought of it as dispensable.

Just as today it is perpetually said on the subject of imperialism that since we cannot beat it we must live under it, it was said then that Chile's material superiority was so insuperable that retreating to

44 See note 37.

45 See Mariano Baptista Gumucio, *Yo fui el orgullo. Vida y pensamiento de Franz Tamayo* (La Paz: Los Amigos del Libro, 1978).

46 Abraham Köning, Chilean minister in Bolivia, wrote in 1900: 'Our rights are born of victory, the supreme law of nations' (Jorge Escobari Cusicanqui, *Historia diplomática de Bolivia: Política internacional* [La Paz: Casa Municipal de la Cultura Franz Tamayo, 1975], p. 79).

the mountains was the only reasonable option. This was false, of course, even from a military standpoint. Even under radically inferior conditions, the dispossessed nation fights with a certain paradoxical advantage because it moves within itself, on the condition that what is at stake belongs to it, something that, as we have seen, was only true for a buried part of the nation.[47] The very fact that the invader moved with greater ease in that environment shows that, in terms of immediate, effective belonging, Bolivia, because it was Arce's Bolivia and not Willka's,[48] was even farther from that Bolivian territory than was the Chilean state.[49] That was the real conquest. The war was just its inevitable consummation.

Arce himself was determined that the vanquished partner was the victor,[50] and indeed his role in this history is that of the advocate of a repetition, with the silver of Colquechaca,[51] of Chile's felicitous coastal nitrate venture. It is surprising, to say the least, that this man is even today considered a paragon of Bolivian patriotism. No less can be said of Baptista, who proposed an alliance between Bolivia and Argentina, or of Montes, who sought unification with Chile (no longer just as a partner but to form a single country, in which Bolivia

---

47 If we adhere to Francisco Antonio Encina's account, in Antofagasta, out of a total population of 8,507 residents, there were 6,554 Chileans in 1878. This speaks to the fact that, whatever the importance of the Andean sphere in its constitutive moment, the *capitalist formation* of the Chilean nation had claimed the same *locus*.

48 'Willka' was the patronymic adopted by various *kolla* leaders over the course of their struggles in the last two-thirds of the nineteenth century (Condarco Morales, *Zárate, el temible Willka*).

49 There were 40 Bolivian gendarmes in the territory that would supply the greatest economic surplus of the subsequent period in the Americas.

50 See note 20.

51 It is significant that Chilean capital had such great expansive capacity when it came to the raw materials of the coast and not, or at least not to the same extent, with those of the Altiplano. Thus, Patiño's expulsion of Artigue from La Salvadora contributed to his future prestige.

surely would not fare especially well).[52] These distinguished figures,[53] all of them adhering to the sacred doctrine of regional patriotism, betray the poverty of geographic consciousness of the nation that pervaded this class. As we shall see, the state revenue of the liberal era did not come from tin and the other minerals, which could have supplied it in abundance, but from payments from Chile and Brazil in exchange for territory, namely, Cobija and Acre.[54] It is impossible to express the incalculable damage done to the soul of a country, that is, to the ideology with which it sees itself, when it loses land without defending it, receives money for it (it makes no difference how much), wishes to disappear in the face of the enemy. The ailing caste saw the land as it saw everything else and as it would see the world thereafter, as something of little importance, so long as it did not serve the logic of its lineage in an almost familial way.

The territory is the foundation of a people; only blood itself is as important.[55] Still, there are nations or peoples that have pre-existed their space and territorial unity can increase or decrease, or even disappear to a certain extent and for a certain period of time, because the desideratum of their constitution as a people or nation is not in that element. Here, however, *it is the space that creates the people*, as the element in which the nation must come to be. The territory, then,

---

52 Montes at one point in fact came to propose the fusion of Bolivia and Chile into a single country, a notion decried by Franz Tamayo.

53 In the local lore, indeed, the names Arce, Baptista and Montes are never absent from the pantheon of national heroes, which can only be explained as a whitewashing of the facts within the history of a single continuous caste that persists to this day.

54 In exchange for its coast, Bolivia took 2,500,000 pounds sterling. Brazil paid no more than 1,000,000 for all of Acre.

55 'The territory [. . .] is the first and most sacred of national possessions, because it contains within it all of the others' (Rafael Bustillo, in a letter to President Morales dated 12 March 1872 [Querejazu Calvo, *Guano, salitre, sangre*, p. 91]).

conceived in terms of its quality or substantiality, is of crucial importance here.

Of course the *territory* of a country as the term is generally
understood is merely a cartographic fact. When it is said that Brazil
has an area of 8 million square kilometres, what this really means is
that this is Brazil's territorial project or objective. In the 5 million
empty square kilometres of the Amazon, meanwhile, Brazil does not
yet exist nor does anything; it is an unassimilated territory. We can,
therefore, distinguish between the cartographic area and the state's
legitimacy in a territory because for the latter what counts is that the
authority of the state can be enforced, albeit by means of pure, immediate military force, that is, even if the state does not occupy the territory but impedes its occupation by anyone else. This constitutes a
primitive form of territorial legitimacy because it is founded only on
a threat, a practical circumstance: neither you nor I have any right
to anything here, but I can punish anyone who challenges my claim.
This kind of legitimation, however, has little to do with the notion
of *socially incorporated space*.[56] Here it is not just a matter of the invo-
cation of a juridical apparatus or objective, or even of the military
capability of imposing its claim. It is a matter of the real efficacy or
internalization of the essentially external phenomenon that is a territory. It is a performance transformed into a constant flow of determination that affirms: I am myself and my space; this space will not
be recognizable without me; I am not myself outside this space. There
is a particular kind of relation between a certain space and a certain
man, and even a certain form of relationality between them, that is,
a particular, palpable cultural event has occurred.

In other cases, the pathetic encounter with the external is a problem of state power; this occurs with peoples whose origin is the state,
which also becomes their end. On the other hand, articulation or

---

56 The interpellation or hailing to identification or interpenetration can come
from war or from any profound event. Here, undoubtedly, the nucleus of the
call to intersubjectivity was determined by the space.

unification can be produced outside of the territory or conceiving the territory as something external to it, and also outside of the state, that is, both territory and state can be its product and not its origin. Here, on the contrary, we have a particular mode of relation between space or collective matter, identity and power. Geography, as sign, as challenge, as calling, has determined everything.[57]

Let us turn then to the problem of the scene of nationalization. Modern men exist at once as individuals and as certain forms of totalization or collectivization. Ours is an era of the predominance of the ideological. We can discuss it in genetic, instrumental or determinative terms, but the fact is that the mode of participation in the world today is determined by the primacy of intersubjectivity. It is not just a matter of interaction among men, but a particular type of intersubjectivity that is proper to juridically free men. *Juridically* means having the choice; one is not free simply because one is juridically free, but one has the right or claim to freedom. Wise men know the importance of a consecrated or inalienable right as a call to praxis. It has the same function as myth or immutable belief, *mutatis mutandis*. The territory is the locus where intersubjectivity has been produced; it is the non-spatial determination of space and it is here that the material world begins to have a history. It is upon this path that we would have to embark were we engaged in a purely academic discourse on the rather serious problem of precapitalist nations. The territory contains the potentiality of nature. The transformation of nature is consciously witnessed only in processes whose organizational principle is one of territorial annexation (so-called Asiatic despotism) and in the capitalist

---

57 This is persistently intuited in Bolivian thought, although of course without much rigour. 'The greatness of a race is directly proportional to the difficulties overcome in its struggle with the environment' (Tamayo, *Creación de la pedagogía nacional*, CHAP. 9), and also: 'The *kolla* have conquered the land through permanent submission to it.' What is undeniable is that behind the collective form is a particular logic of the natural world conceived as habitat [*escenario*] (cited in Guillermo Francovich, *La filosofía en Bolivia* [La Paz: Juventud, 1966], p. 91).

mode of production, for very different reasons.[58] The role of the witness is decisive here, although in the first case it is collective, and in the second case it is so only in a differed way. In examining the construction of a discourse, would it be of little account to ask *where* the discourse occurs? Hegemony, if it is produced, is produced somewhere. It is, therefore, linked to a symbol-space, to a kind of geological totem. The god of Andean culture is the space determined by the Andean mountain chain, which, of course, cannot have the same function as the Pyrenees or the Apennines for the Spaniards or the Italians.[59] In any case, to derive ideological and state forms from a space, like the Andeans, is not the same thing as to conquer a territory not bound to the people's own identity, something which, in order to succeed, must be the consequence of a previously existing identity.[60] In this case, the people constructs its space; in the other, the space forms the people.[61]

But what was really at issue here between Peru, Bolivia and Chile? The thesis that on one side was perfect treachery and on the other total innocence is ultimately untenable. It is a fact, for example, that just as Portales formulated a policy against Santa Cruz, the latter assumed the categorical superiority of Peru and Bolivia. We should say, rather, that it was a confrontation between a vain self-satisfaction, that of Peru to a greater extent but also that of Bolivia, since they were ingenuous countries,[62] and a certain sense of adventure, a certain inferiority complex and a precociousness of the

---

58 In Asiatic despotism, because the state tends to be originally determined by a spatial foundation. In capitalism, because to a great extent there is a conquest of space by time, that is, the qualitative abolition of space is the necessary condition of the concentration of time.

59 The function of a border; the Andeans live *in* the Andes.

60 The most characteristic case is the construction of its space by the nation in the United States—the nation preceded its environment.

61 Although surely no one can uproot and resettle himself without simultaneously transforming himself.

62 Countries in which what Vico called the 'vanity of nations' replaces the production of the most elemental certainties.

state on the part of Chile. In effect, the antagonism was between conflicting constitutive moments or irreconcilable vital principles. Yet in the form in which this antagonism appears or is phenomenalized, it revolved around the question of the surplus or an irrationalist view of economic development,[63] a view that, irrationalist or not, was deeply rooted in the tangible experience of these peoples. We must, therefore, discuss the relation between economic surplus and state receptivity. From the outset, each nation saw the greatness of the others or what appeared to be their greatness as something inimical to it. This certainly has to do with the forms of originary accumulation proper to each. The colossal and boastful a spectacle of the guano boom in Peru, which added wealth to the excess of titles and the anticipation of so neat a surplus as that of the nitrate fields, however, turned that latent tension into something urgent. What gives a certain politico-economic content to Chile's project is, moreover, the marked decline of its prospects in the global wheat market.[64]

We have here, then, the geopolitical consequences of what is perhaps the most fundamental and intrinsic myth of Latin America. The surplus is, of course, a global symbol and not just one of capitalism. The philosopher's stone or manna constitute such fantasies

---

63 See note 67.

64 'Chile had its first economic crisis between 1858 and 1861 as a result of the closure of the Californian and Australian markets. Having overcome this hurdle, it experienced another period of distress beginning in 1873 and ending in 1877 or 1878. This intense crisis was brought upon the country by a decrease in the price of agricultural products' (Julio César Jobet, *Ensayo crítico del desarrollo económico-social de Chile* [Mexico City: Centro de Estudios del Movimiento Obrero Salvador Allende, 1982], p. 54). It does not follow that the 'grave situation', the 'intense crisis', was the efficient cause of the war. What matters here is that within a national project, sustained over the course of successive governments, a critical method could be transformed into an economic and military policy. A. Edwards, however, maintains that 'if not for the War of the Pacific, the Pinto government might well have ended in a revolution' (in ibid., p. 64).

of abundance. In any case, a culture of second sons[65] combined with the avarice inherent to mercantilism to produce the ideologeme of El Dorado or Gran Paititi,[66] which is like the ultimate spirit of the Conquest. 'Gold,' Columbus would say, 'is a marvel.' Without the surplus supplied by America, there could have been no world market and indeed no political reorganization of the globe such as followed the price revolution. From this we can draw two conclusions: on the one hand, that the surplus, in effect, could generate a state of receptivity, of plasticity and of inclination towards the new; on the other, it could be a source of aggression and disorder. Of course, the surplus in itself means nothing except in relation to the previous society to which it refers and therefore it is said that the gold of America impoverished Spain. It is nonetheless true that the toolkit of the modern state has something to do with the notion of surplus. If by mediation we understand the transformation of the fury of the oppressed into part of the programme of the oppressor, which is after all a hegemonic relation, it is obvious that mediation is all the more possible the greater the surplus because to represent the state to society and society to the state is something that involves money, concessions or privileges. Still, the concept of surplus is, in the first place, a relative concept because it must refer to a surplus relative to a given moral-historical norm,[67] and, secondly, the relation of surplus itself to the

---

65 Ruggiero Romano and Alberto Tenenti, *Los fundamentos del mundo moderno: Edad Media tardía, Renacimiento, Reforma* (Mexico City: Siglo XXI, 1979), p. 185.

66 Hernando Sanabria Fernández, *En busca de El Dorado: La colonización del oriente boliviano por los cruceños* (La Paz: Juventud, 1973); Svetlana Alekseevna Sozina, *En el horizonte está El Dorado* (La Habana: Casa de las Américas, 1982).

67 The basic idea here is of course Marx's. The necessary labour of each epoch gives it a moral level. The moral dimension of compensation, consumption, the horizon of life, is defined by the level of purchasing power. The surplus, therefore, should also be measured in relation to this; however, it is possible, strictly speaking, to generate a surplus by means of a stripping of that moral-historical measure.

question of receptivity is one of species to genus.[68] In the established dogma of surplus as the only possible form of receptivity lies the legacy of the mercantilist core of the Spanish foundation of America, as perpetual tributary to commercial capital. If receptivity is the originary moment of the state, insofar as it signifies an openness or general malleability before a proposition, this leads to a double consequence: conservative in one sense, because the idea that wealth creates power is a vertical, reactionary and elitist notion, while the receptivity generated by popular action, as a mass will to transformation, is a revolutionary event. We have, then, two conceptions of the problem: the democratic form of production of receptivity and the vertical form. While it is true that surplus generates receptivity, this, in the sense of men prepared for a substitution of loyalties, beliefs and principles, occurs even more powerfully when it entails a concrete rupture with their routine. The conflict between the force of habit and the replacement of loyalties underlies all this. In this sense, America is a conservative continent because it believes more readily in transformation through surplus than through intellectual reform. This is indisputably at the core of our inheritance. It might seem absurd to speak of conservative ossifications in a continent with a young population and that is itself practically a symbol of youth— it has been called 'the triumph of health'[69]—but this is indeed the case. It is not necessary to be successful in order to be conservative. Even the indigent of America are undoubtedly quite conservative.[70]

Receptivity reveals a moment of internal groundlessness, of nonconditionality. This is a serious matter if we consider that the general foundation of modern societies is determined by the way in which

68 In the sense that a surplus enables the development of receptivity or malleability, but not all receptivity is born of a surplus.

69 Romano and Tenenti, *Los fundamentos del mundo moderno*.

70 Occidentalism, for example, is in practice a popular school of thought in Latin America; its insertion in this context cannot but have a profoundly reactionary sense.

they achieve their totalization. That is, totalization plus the qualitative form in which totalization is realized.

> [T]he same division of labour that turns them into independent private producers also makes the social process of production and the relations of the individual producers to each other within that process independent of the producers themselves; they also find out that the independence of the individuals from each other has as its counterpart and supplement a system of all-round material dependence.[71]

We have, in the first place, generalized circulation, that is, everyone produces for another and no one for himself. This in itself speaks to a specific form of totalization, no doubt superior to previous forms. The crux of the issue resides, however, not in the simple fact of generalization but in the interaction that comes with it, which is an interaction among free men, that is, if circulatory totalization itself contains a moment of receptivity or emptiness, because man has been untethered from the conditions of his previous discourse, he immediately gives himself over to the formation of a new ideology, the ideological substitute, which is a particularly powerful intersubjectivity for it is grounded in the will of juridically free men. This interpenetration clearly must be greater than that produced among men who do not construct such an interaction but are passively homogenized because they have a common master.[72] If the existence of juridically free man is a *sine qua non* of capitalism and such are the collective-ideological consequences of originary accumulation, this nonetheless should not be oversimplified. Ultimately, we can

---

71 Karl Marx, *Capital: A Critique of Political Economy*, VOL. 1 (Ben Fowkes trans.) (New York: Penguin, 1992), p. 202–03. Here we see the development of a new entity (the *social process*) which is the result of the specific form of independence in capitalism that is founded upon a *mutual* or general-market dependence.

72 In a way, here men make one another in their own image, but no one emerges unscathed from such an interpenetration.

speak of the *farmer* and *junker* modes of intersubjectivity and surely even if the entire ritual of what is called the capitalist mode of production is fulfilled, we would still have to discuss the historical conditions in which it occurred, that is, its specific content.[73]

Our claim, then, is that the three countries involved in the conflict obstinately shared the same myth of the surplus.[74] We have also claimed that not all surplus generates receptivity, although it is indeed a favourable element in its production. What interests us, then, is receptivity and not the surplus; receptivity, moreover, only as it relates to the question of the constitutive moment.

This is a concept that will have to be used repeatedly over the course of this exposition. [Alexis de] Tocqueville defined it almost ingenuously: 'Every people bears the mark of its origin'. 'The circumstances that surround its birth and aid its development also influence the subsequent course of its existence.'[75] The concept is more complex than this, but this definition will do for now. If it is true that men cannot experience anything without making it into a representation, or experience a representation without translating it into a discourse, this means that the 'conception of the world' is an instinct. Ideology is essential and it is durable. No one is willing to sacrifice his conception of the world except when he is compelled to do so by

---

73 The social process can be constructed either as the self-constitution of civil society or through the subsumption of the state in society (*junker*). In any case, if intersubjectivity exists in the abstract, we must still determine which route has been taken to arrive at it because here what is important is the category plus the determination of its origin or accumulation.

74 Paul Alexander Baran takes up Bettelheim's definition, which says that 'the economic surplus [. . .] is constituted by a portion of the net social product appropriated by the non-working classes' (*Excedente económico e irracionalidad capitalista* [Mexico City: Cuadernos de Pasado y Presente, 1980], p. 75). Here we use the concept in the sense of the difference between the product of labour and the non-confiscated portion of the goods produced.

75 Alexis de Tocqueville, *Democracy in America* (Arthur Goldhammer trans.) (New York: Library of America, 2004[1835]). p. 31.

a momentous and imposing force. Of course, there may be peoples with more diffuse constitutive moments than others, more syncretic and weaker. Still, there are certain profound events, certain unfailing processes, even certain instances of collective psychology that found the mode of being of a society for a long period of time. An interpellative event at a moment of general receptivity, at a constitutive moment, is destined to survive as a kind of unconscious or substrate of that society.[76] This is the tragic role of the past in history; in a way, one can only ever do what has already been foreseen. Great epidemics and famines, wars and, in our time, revolutions, are the classic moments of general receptivity: men are prepared to substitute the universe of their beliefs. This role was fulfilled by the constitution of space—by agriculture—in the Andean world, by the Arauco War in Chile, and by the conquest with its attendant demographic catastrophe and the chimera of gold in all the Latin American countries.[77] It can therefore be said that the delusion of surplus led to a confrontation of social formations governed by very different constitutive moments. The constitutive moment refers to the ultimate source of each society, to its deep genealogy, as Hegel said, to its orginary essentiality.

To continue along this line of reasoning, according to the general understanding of the problem (that of the surplus), it has been determined that development can take place only where a constant and substantial economic surplus exists. The history of Latin America itself, however, has provided concrete examples of what we might call the infecundity of the surplus (or at least its relative infecundity).

---

76 For the concept of interpellation, see Louis Althusser's work.

77 Nicolás Sánchez-Albornoz, *La población de América Latina: Desde los tiempos precolombinos al año 2000* (Madrid: Alianza, 1973); Sherburne Friend Cook and Woodrow Wilson Borah, *Ensayos sobre historia de la población: México y el Caribe* (Mexico City: Siglo XXI, 1977); available in English as: *Essays in Population History: Mexico and the Caribbean* (Berkeley: University of California Press, 1971); Darcy Ribeiro, *Configuraciones histórico-culturales americanas* (Montevideo: Centro de Estudios Latinoamericanos, 1972).

THE STRUGGLE FOR THE SURPLUS ● 45

Even Potosí emphatically proved that it is not the surplus that matters but who appropriates it and for what. Great surpluses like that of Argentina in the last third of the nineteenth century and the first of the twentieth, that of Chile's nitrates and copper, even that of Venezuela's oil and Cuba's heyday, attest to the absolutely supplementary role of this factor.[78] The history of the period immediately prior to the war shows how a great surplus, that of the guano boom, had not sufficed for the construction of a nation. On the other hand, Mexico in the period between 1910 and 1920 and then in the 30s produced a very high level of state receptivity without the benefit of a large surplus. Here receptivity was the result of the activity of the society. Even Chile ultimately had demonstrated that state receptivity is one thing and the surplus is another. Indeed, when Chile took hold of an immense surplus, its social optimum was impoverished and it clearly once enjoyed a considerable level of state accumulation on the basis of a rather modest surplus.[79]

---

78 Roberto Cortés Conde, 'El "boom" argentino: ¿una oportunidad desperdiciada?' in Tulio Halperín Donghi et al., *Los fragmentos del poder: de la oligarquía a la poliarquía argentina* (Buenos Aires: J. Álvarez, 1969), p. 217–41; Oscar Zanetti, 'El comercio exterior de la República Neocolonial' in Juan Pérez de la Riva et al., *La República Neocolonial: Anuario de estudios cubanos*, VOL. 1 (Havana: Ed. de Ciencias Sociales, 1975), pp. 45–126; Héctor Malavé Mata, *Formación histórica del antidesarrollo de Venezuela* (Havana: Casa de las Américas, 1974), p. 203.

79 In fact, given that the railways did not yet compete with maritime transport, California was closer to Chile than to the eastern United States, which proves how relative the concept of space is. This was surely a decisive factor in Chile's weak boom of the middle of the nineteenth century. Based for the most part on wheat and grains, trade with Chile in California rose from US$250,195 in 1848 to US$1,835,466 in 1849 and US$2,445,868 in 1850 (Jobet, *Ensayo crítico del desarrollo económico-social de Chile*, p. 35). In other words, the rapid growth of the Chilean economy during the decades prior to the war ensured that the crisis that followed it was experienced as something intolerable. 'From 1848 to 1860 trade figures tripled', 'the urban population increased by 50 per cent' (ibid., p. 42). Chile was the world's top producer of copper even before the

From all this it should be clear that the concept of the surplus is not to be privileged a priori. In a tentative analogy, it could be said therefore that the surplus refers to absolute profit and to formal subsumption, while receptivity is connected to real subsumption or the internal or essential reorganization of the productive act. The significance of the surplus here, however, derives from the fact that it is a requirement of large-scale reproduction which, in turn, contains the whole logic of the new experience of time. Since it is as if men today live many days in the space that used to occupy a single day, since they have taken hold of time and concentrated it, they must construct far more elaborate mechanisms so that this precarious agglutination does not explode. A separate excursus would certainly be in order regarding the relation between surplus and receptivity, and of both to the structure of the state, the expansion of the state, and the theory of mediations.[80] The form in which the surplus exists and the form of its absorption, then, determine the very succession of modes of production. On the other hand, capitalism itself is the history of the construction of its state or, in other words, the history of the capitalist state is that of the production, distribution and application of the surplus. To be precise, it is clear that the surplus does not have an autonomous function because the optimum is composed, in reality, of the relation between surplus and receptivity. Where there is no receptivity, the surplus has no function. The greater the degree of receptivity, the more we must take into account the datum of the surplus. Receptivity, as we have seen, can ultimately exist even with a meagre surplus, although with a greater degree of material social erosion.[81]

---

conquest of the great Bolivian deposits (Chuquicamata). In 1869, Chile already produced 61 per cent of the world's copper (ibid. p. 55).

80 Giacomo Marramao.

81 Peru was a typical example of a surplus that could not be made into accumulation, while Chile paradoxically degraded its margin of receptivity with the conquest of an immense surplus. The Meiji represent a case of great receptivity and a precarious surplus, at least at first.

THE STRUGGLE FOR THE SURPLUS ● 47

This is the basis on which we can define the formal character of the state, that is, its degree of development on the basis of the division of surplus value.[82] The model of circulation of surplus value determines the type of capitalist state. Although we cannot embark here upon a technical analysis of the problem, it is one thing if, for example, surplus value is largely absorbed in an essentially non-productive moment, which is that of luxury consumption, and another if the consumption of surplus value is fundamentally directed towards the erection of the general capitalist and, on the whole, we could say that appropriation primarily by the general moment of the state or the total capitalist and by the productive moment itself tends to coincide with a more rapid rotation of capital, which has its own significance. It is within these parameters that we must understand that it is not by chance that representative-democratic structures were established in areas where there was a greater retention of the global surplus because this also applies to the global logic of surplus value.

This has to do with the function of the optimum. We will consider the national problem in greater detail below. For now, it would be fair to say provisionally that the nation expresses the degree of cohesion, interpenetration and intensity of civil society while the state is political power in action (politics understood in its practical relation to power and not as pronouncement or deliberation), whose force in society can be either dependent upon democratic process or arbitrary, of systemic stalemate or omnipotent. In any case, the contemporary notion of the state cannot convincingly be reduced to the classical model of the political state because there is a politics of society and a politics of the state and, furthermore, there is no doubt

---

82 In theory, indeed, the circulatory model of surplus value should determine the extent to which the total capitalist exists, which has to do with the totalization of the bourgeois class. Without totalization or identity neither the expansion of the state nor organized capitalism is possible. In any case, the state can be tax-based, as the Spanish state was, and have little pretension of totalization; the retention of surplus value in its most general moment or that of the state does not in itself indicate a primacy of accumulation.

that the state must act as a person in civil society to assert its autonomy or separation.[83] The modern state must then adapt to expanded reproduction or perpetual mobility and, on the other hand, also to the totalization of society, that is, general circulation (or the generalized social market). In the binary or transfigurative movement that things in this structure tend to have, it could be said that, perhaps as a result of the accumulation of time, a much more decisive measure of organic solidarity or subjective interpenetration emerges here as well as far more structural forms of contradiction, contestation and counterhegemony. Solidarity, therefore, as well as dissent or resistance, are inscribed with the mark of their provenance from men who command the use of their own will. The work of interaction modifies subjects in relation to one another; they are reformed by one another. This necessarily produces, at least in its prototype, a particular mode of totalization that constitutes the unequivocal specificity of the phenomena of the nation and the state in capitalism.

The very sense of time, the idea of the provisionality of the world, that is, the expansion of circulation and generalized interaction, because the old particularity has been destroyed and one cannot take refuge within what no longer exists but only in the particularity proper to the collective (no one acts for himself and the self ultimately resides in the first person plural),[84] would have translated into the simple suppression of capitalism if here the originary construction of ideology in its new form, that is, the superstition of the indestructibility of the state, had not taken place. The establishment of consent, whether by means of an impression of power of the state or through the seduction of a new culture, is only the extension of the real subsumption of labour under capital. There is an element

---

83 In truth, the more organic the insertion or inclusion of the state in society, the more consistent its autonomy founded on distance. This should not be confused with the state that has not differentiated itself from the units of society, that which has no choice but to act as a faction that governs arbitrarily.

84 Zavaleta, 'Clase y conocimiento', p. 3.

of gratification that comes with the institution of the forms of mediation without which totalization itself or the generalization of capitalism would do itself in. To invite men to be free and to interact among themselves without mediation would be an act of self-destruction. Hence the far more actively conservative function that we expect of the capitalist state.[85] It must, in other words, move within a world of uncertainty—a world uncertain but cognizable. Mediations, in turn, like enclaves or bunkers of the state within society and of society in the state, belong to the common expenses (and the degree to which they are taken on as such reveals the extent to which a bourgeois mentality has been assumed) of the circulation of surplus value and this, at least at its initial moment, is the function of the surplus. Rentier profits can guarantee a few years of prosperity, but then the *raison d'état* is accidental.[86] No investment is ever so successful, on the other hand, as an investment in total capital.[87]

The surplus, therefore, is in principle a transmitter of ideology but it could not operate as such if at its base there did not exist a certain receptive appetite or desire, which is proper to material events that are or are deemed to be supreme. Societies cannot live without gods and there are certain events or dogmas that give each society its deities. On the other hand, given that the surplus is remitted primarily

---

85 Clauss Offe.

86 Peruvians like Pardo used the guano surplus to abolish indigenous tribute, which was like an attempt to win Peru its independence from the Indians. Around 1830, indigenous and *casta* tribute in practice made up half of all tax revenues (Ernesto Yepes del Castillo, *Perú 1820–1920: Un siglo de desarrollo capitalista* [Lima: IEP, 1972], p. 43). The surplus conquered in the Pacific, on the other hand, enabled the 'Chilean experts' [*duchos de Chile*] (the expression is Matte's) to 'win their independence' from the state (Jobet, *Ensayo crítico del desarrollo económico-social de Chile*, pp. 67–8).

87 The history of the relation between the Bolivian state and the tin barons, who in practice never contributed anything, is an example of absolute non-contribution to total capital and its consequences. They were ruined by their own greed.

to the ruling class and only in a secondary way to the oppressed, it cannot be thought of as something that acquires effective validity except where it can produce a culture and knowledge linked to a system of mediations, a system that is always local. Institutions generally belong to the sphere of a *national* (and not a global) view of history. In all cases, as we have seen, the powerful idea of the surplus blurs into the vague but fundamental idea of receptivity. There is a relation of species to genus and of appearance to essence between them.

The surplus is not spontaneously transformed into the substance of the state. If this were the case, advanced states would exist wherever a surplus existed. Potosí possessed a surplus that it was incapable of appropriating and the same could be said of Spain, in an intermediary position in the chain.[88] The surplus is conditioned by what for Marx is an element of value: a *moral-historical* dimension.[89] We must now consider the importance of the fact that the quantitative limit of the economy is a non-economic factor in a differed way. In essence, this is a certain quality of the social, a kind of relation between the overdetermined or the moment of the state, and the self-determined or democratic. It is therefore something dynamic, something that must be formulated, that must evolve by trial and error. A sudden material discovery (which is what every Latin American, because he is an 'eldoradianist', ultimately longs for) surely generates a surplus and one that is not always used in a sensible way. However, a surplus can also be generated through the redistribution of the

---

88 Pierre Vilar, *A History of Gold and Money, 1450–1920* (Judith White trans.) (New York: Verso, 1991).

89 Both Marx and Gramsci use the term 'moral', in the sense of 'moral-historical' or 'intellectual and moral reform'. This does not refer merely to the theft of man's labour power in the first case, or the internal form of valorization of conduct in the second. It seems to us that in both cases it involves the principle of action according to ends, the transformation of which ought to be in daily life and the hegemonic internalization of the present foundations of the social.

existing product, which is the path of reform; this is feasible too but at a higher cost. Reforms excite or move people in a way that is even more dangerous than revolutionary measures. Finally, especially at decisive political moments, new canons of the moral-historical measure itself can be generated, that is, there can be a moral act that founds a new surplus. Even the appropriation of that measure, in what can be called the negative formation of ideology, the apology for self-plunder, can be conceived as a foundational event.[90]

Let us turn now to consider the behaviour of the three countries engaged in the struggle for the surplus, which is the motivating core of the conflict, although it is surely attended by powerful dispositions accumulated in the social or collective unconscious[91] of each. The idea of possessing Peru or destroying what could not be possessed of it (to possess the fortune it never had) was no doubt a bitter collective compulsion in Chile[92] which, moreover, proved to be an organic people or a nation although this could not be explained by the general market. This concept is often used as a cipher, as if it could explain everything. But in itself it ultimately leads nowhere if it is not integrated into a certain deliberation on the problem of the *social optimum*, as a necessary theoretical matrix, and if we do not take into account the fundamental inability of the three countries

---

90 On the authoritarian construction of hegemony, see the work of Erich Fromm; Hubert Bacia, 'La predisposición autoritaria' (The Authoritarian Personality) in Wolfgang Abendroth et al., *Capital monopolista y sociedad autoritaria: La involución autoritaria en la R.F.A.* (Barcelona, Fontanella, 1973), p. 209; Oskar Negt, 'Hacia una sociedad autoritaria' in Abendroth et al., *Capital monopolista y sociedad autoritaria*, p. 237.

91 Ernst Bloch.

92 The collective attitude towards Bolivia was no better: 'There was soon a general, unrestrained hatred of Bolivia among the Chilean people' (Francisco Antonio Encina, *Resumen de la historia de Chile* [Santiago: Zig-Zag, 1954], VOL. 3, p. 1411).

(and of several others):[93] their patent incapability of building structures of self-determination. This means only that we must set aside casuistic exegeses of the event such as that which would attribute its outcome to Chile's long diplomatic and military preparation. We could indeed say that Chile was prepared for victory and, on the other hand, it is as if Peru and Bolivia had prepared themselves for defeat but, since it is not our intention to uncover genetic or social Darwinist explanatory formulas here (because no one really desires his own ruin, at least not in an organized way), the fact is that if Chile prepared itself for victory, it is because it was able to do so. That is, if it could initiate a coherent diplomatic action 30 or 40 years before its inevitable conclusion, for example, it is because it had political peace. If it had political peace, however, it was because its social equation or optimum (more on which later) was superior to those of its rivals, who, on the contrary, were unable to formulate a state policy. We have come, then, to the problem of the construction of the policy or ideological transmission of the state. In other words, its preparation or policy is but the mode of appearing of a certain efficient relation between the power structure and man as a group, between the form that power has assumed and the real distribution of those men in those circumstances. The obstinacy with which all risked their

93 The war in fact marks the end of the self-determinative tendencies that ostensibly existed in the previous Chilean state. 'Harvey, working with North, played a prominent part in the operations carried out during the war' (Ramírez Necochea, *Balmaceda y la contrarrevolución de 1891*, p. 45). There could be no other outcome. 'In 1889, the British dominated the vital centres of industry' (ibid., p. 28), Curtis, an American cited by Ramírez Necochea, said, 'Valparaíso, with its trade entirely controlled by the British, its market transactions conducted in pounds sterling, its English newspaper and extensive use of the language, was no more than a British colony' (ibid., p. 39). The great protagonists of diplomatic intrigue such as Carlos Walker Martínez, a good friend of Baptista, and Concha y Toro, an associate of Arce, were concrete agents of the British. In the end, there was no doubt that Chile had made a lot of money but that it was less a of country than it had been before.

lives for the surplus and their common failure when it came to the transformation of the surplus into self-determination, along with certain other significant factors such as the seigneurial worldview, indicate that these are countries that have something in common, which perhaps has to do with a certain quality of their colonization that we might call 'Peruvian'.[94] Of course all this should be qualified, but certain identities can become entangled in a tragic history like the one that transpired here. War is an atrocious mode of relation between societies but it is a mode of relation nonetheless.

In one case after another, the idolization of the surplus is always the same. With the level of development that the Incas had reached and with the demographic volume that they had attained practically overnight, the conquest itself entailed the acquisition of an unprecedented surplus. The conventional indices, moreover, fail to adequately explain a certain elasticity or capacity for sudden regeneration that the Peruvian economy continually displayed over the course of its history.[95] For example, independence did not devastate the territory as it did in Upper Peru, Venezuela or Mexico. And yet Peru had to sustain a good part if not all of the cost of the other side,

---

94 'No Spaniard came to Chile with such modest intentions. All of them were lords or aspired to be. The West Indies were the perfect environment for a mentality that belonged to a feudal society in decay and in an arena too confined to satisfy the ambitions of the many hopeful lords that were the Spanish hidalgos. On the other hand, those who previously could not even come close to claiming such a rank could do so the moment they set foot on American soil. All of them viewed the Indian as a true serf destined to ennoble their new masters' (Álvaro Jara, *Guerra y sociedad en Chile: La transformación de la guerra de Arauco y la esclavitud de los indios* [Santiago, Ed: Universitaria, 1971], p. 40).

95 To the point that, of this country destroyed in 1870, it could be said that, between 1917 and 1921, 'in contrast to what was then occurring with other Latin American countries, Peru had no problems balancing its budget' (Julio Cotler, *Clases, Estado y nación en el Perú*, [Lima: IEP, 1978], p. 143). Exports rose from 91.6 million sols in 1913 to 269 million sols in 1919. Cotton exports grew twentyfold between 1900 and 1919, sugar grew sixfold and copper eightfold.

that of the royalist defence, as well as Bolívar's campaigns.[96] The recovery of this cost bears no comparison to the aftermath of the war in Bolivia, which had to wait 50 years to return to the world. The revival of the Peruvian economy following the systematic dismantling imposed by the war is a truly surprising event.[97] Not to mention the guano boom which constitutes in absolute terms one of the greatest surpluses known to Latin America and perhaps the world. Here what stands out surely is the capacity for continual reconstruction of new forms of economic surplus and, at the same time, a persistent impotence when it come to its internalization or retention (and, of course, to its transformation). In the entire century that followed, indeed, Peru would generate new surpluses out of a devastated economy but it would repeat over the course of various political models the same inability to forge an effective nation-state.

Since Chile was a precocious state that could afford to commit the same blunders in relation to its society as Peru, its connection to the problem is even more eloquent. Two moments can be discerned in its development. In the first it resembles that of Costa Rica or nineteenth-century Colombia in some aspects (in the modest scale of the surplus), or even twentieth-century Mexico (in the primacy of receptivity over the surplus, strictly speaking). It is true, for example, that at the *decisive moments*, the British placed their bets on Chile and not Peru, and this is what gave rise to the myth of an Anglo-Chilean victory. In reality, the relation of dependence to England was quite similar with Peru and Chile, with the paradoxical difference that Peru was a more promising market.[98] Chile, however, was able to pursue an

---

96 Yepes del Castillo, *Perú 1820–1920*, pp. 33, 45, 46.

97 See note 95.

98 'Between the mid-1850s and the mid-1860s, the value of Peruvian guano imported into Britain was greater than that of any other single national product imported from Latin America' (W. M. Matthew, 'The Imperialism of Free Trade: Peru, 1820–70', *Economic History Review* 21[3] [December 1968]: 563). For 25 years, Britain maintained closer relations with Peru than with any other

autonomous policy within the structure of dependency, that is, in the rupture of that moment, a certain principle of self-determination was produced. In other words, with a modest surplus, although within a deep framework of receptivity, Chile was able to sketch out a *state policy* that cannot be explained merely as active subordination to British interests. If we leave it at this, the plunder and slaughter of the war would appear to be no more than one of so many atrocious events through which countries advance, a characteristic phase of originary accumulation in which the action of the state is decisive— first, for the extra-economic acquisition of monetary wealth and, second, for its transformation into capital. Chile, in fact, conquered the spoils of the age, comparable only to Texas and the other territories lost by Mexico.[99] The combination of an optimal social equation in which the state predominated over society, which is the most advantageous in these circumstances (because an excess of society disorganizes the process of accumulation) and an immense surplus seemed to indicate that in this case there should have been a stable organization of a logic of self-determination. No such thing occurred and the Chileans themselves spoke of the 'Peruvian malady' [*mal peruano*].[100] Victory accentuated the most reactionary elements of the national ideological discourse, reinforced the inferiority of the masses in relation to the state and, in short, a century later, the

---

Latin American country. Still, it is also true that Chile was the fifth largest supplier of wheat to England and that in the months leading up to the war Chile came to be a more important trading partner of the British than any other country in the region with the exception of Brazil. (Hernán Ramírez Necochea, *Historia del imperialismo en Chile* [Santiago: Austral, 1970]).

99 Chile's trade increased from 65,452,467 pesos in 1879 to 136,280,478 pesos in 1890 (ibid.). Export taxes on nitrates and guano increased suddenly from 15.4 million pesos to 35.4 million pesos in 1881 (Jobet, *Ensayo crítico del desarrollo económico-social de Chile*, p. 73).

100 Chile, according to González Prada, 'was infected with the Peruvian malady'.

Chilean situation roughly resembled that of Peru during the same period.[101]

As for Bolivia, the oligarchy was unable to perceive except in a vague way the magnitude of the wealth in question, which means that it was totally unable to retain the same economic surplus to whose absence it would later attribute all of Bolivia's misfortunes and backwardness, that is, it first handed over what it would later fetishize; that great surplus lost, the oligarchy could at least have held its sovereign passage to viable ports as something inalienable, that is, it could at least have preserved its effective access to the world market given that it could not conserve its inheritance. What was done is truly inexplicable. Those who were unwilling before, during and after to put up a real fight, those who had no awareness of the scale of natural resources at stake, those who lost them, which was like losing the most extraordinary opportunity to generate a surplus after Potosí, those same men consecrated in the juridical sphere a loss of access in the form it took at that time and still takes now to the world market, that is, the sea lanes. Why did they do it? For money, that is, once again, they handed over everything in exchange for two days' bread. As we shall see in the following chapter, the Bolivian ruling class learnt nothing from this disaster and it is indeed worth reflecting on the fact that the Gran Chaco itself, where certainly far fewer interests were at stake, precipitated a social movement of greater scope and consistency.[102]

If we look at things in this way, since neither the victors nor the vanquished were capable of transforming the conditions of their existence, conditions of marginality and subordination, we might speak

---

101 The current indices of each country, if favourable to Chile, are no more so than those before 1879.

102 In this case, there was certainly a collective instinctual resolve that new territories should not be lost. It is nonetheless striking that Bolivia made much greater sacrifices for the Gran Chaco, which was practically empty, than for the coast, which was a great source of wealth.

of the gratuitousness or futility of an event that was nonetheless an orgiastic squandering of life, passion and wealth. Yet it cannot be denied that there was an absolute victor and here we should note that one never vanquishes without consequences—that one does not vanquish with impunity. It is true that even without guano or nitrates, it took Peru only two decades to reach a situation at least similar to its previous one; and, more importantly, the deep sense of humiliation gave way to a moral uneasiness which characterizes the milieu out of which figures such as [Manuel] González Prada and [José Carlos] Mariátegui and perhaps even [Víctor Raúl] Haya [de la Torre] emerge. An atmosphere of collective discontent and anxiety was necessary for moral and intellectual personalities like Gramsci or Mariátegui, thinkers of reconstruction, to appear. It is also true that the patent ethico-intellectual bankruptcy of the oligarchy was a necessary condition in Bolivia for the buried substrate of the nation to be expressed through the Fearsome Willka,[103] that is, perhaps this tragedy, the confusion in which the nation lived, could only have been followed by another upheaval. In truth, the national question in Bolivia—Tamayo's book clearly shows this[104]—is not articulated explicitly at the political and intellectual levels until then. Defeat teaches many things but it is a good school only insofar as there is a full recovery. This, of course, has not yet happened.

Victory, in turn, as Chile's absolute victory and, to a lesser extent, Paraguay's illusory victory in the Gran Chaco demonstrate, can have consequences for the construction of self-consciousness which is, after all, the precondition for all tasks. In the case of Chile, the conquest of the Pacific surely led to an exacerbated validation of the hegemony of the oligarchic core of the state. Even the masses took to living the insidious but radical authoritarianism of its national discourse, of its political system, and of its state not as the inevitable

---

103 Condarco Morales, *Zárate, el temible Willka*.
104 Tamayo, *Creación de la pedagogía nacional*.

collective inheritance of a difficult consolidation but as a virtue in itself. The collective deification of authority would cost Chile dearly.

*

We must now turn to the problem of the equation or result in a society. Historical bloc, socioeconomic formation, state axis are all concepts that refer to the same thing—to the felicitous or frustrated, high or low relation between the state as the sum of all aspects of power and civil society as the set of material conditions in which power is produced. Returning to the problem under discussion, it should be said that when a war takes place, it is waged not just with what one is at that moment but with all of the history that one carries. There is, therefore—and this is critical—an ideological engagement in the war. One really cannot free oneself from the past except when it is destroyed, or at least when it can be understood in its material ultimacy and made to serve the present instead of being its master. Since war, like a general crisis, involves an ultimate tension or intensity of a society's resources, there is a confrontation of everything that each society can muster at that moment. The shrewd capacity to concentrate everything that one is in an instant is what proves one's superiority, and the most obvious thing about Peru and Bolivia in the War of the Pacific is that they could not bring together what they had. The very concept of national mobilization was alien to those countries, but it was an easy, natural and accustomed notion for Chile, for reasons that we shall see later. Loyalty to the state became a kind of reflex or instinct for the Chilean people following the Arauco War, and therefore the capacity for mobilization became an internalized habit. Bolivia's half-hearted participation in the war, with a few thousand men, represents almost the antithesis of this attitude. In the case of Peru, it is clear that it could not base its prospects of success on the greater prestige of its society. The War of the Pacific, then, was a confrontation between three historical accumulations or, rather (although this requires some qualification), the apex or end of each— which is the state. It must be noted that there are wars that are more properly a matter of the state and more popular wars, by which we mean to designate the different degrees of penetration in the collective ideological formation. Of course the Manichean, statist nation is as fallacious as the societarian or autonomist or populist idea of the dissection of politics. The state can indeed have a more national-popular or, as it were, more societarian determination, against less democratic sectors of society (and, in fact, the state has on more than one occasion been ahead of society) and, certainly, since here the principle of centralization is felt more strongly, it can embody the national against antinational sectors of society. Civil society, in turn, can have a significant degree of continuity with the state. That is, a society may have been nationalized or unified prior to the full existence of its state (the unification of society by society, which is the opposite of the fetishism of unity), although in most cases a society's unification comes from a conscious act of the state, generally as a hostile reflex against previously unified nations. In this case, the popular element was weak. We might mention the discontent of the Chilean workers in revolt, which was ardent;[105] it is also true that, since Chile was operating from the position of an optimum that it would never again attain to the same extent, the state would prove its capacity to summon society, which is to say, there would be a significant popular engagement below the interpellation of the state—this is the function of the optimum; and finally, the peasant resistance (Cáceres)[106] in Peru. In any case, the central quality or feature of the war is its interstate character. In Peru and Bolivia, it was *purely* an affair of the state; in Chile, the state had the capacity to mobilize the people psychologically and administratively. The administrative aspect is not secondary because it must not be forgotten that Chile always had a numerical advantage in each of its actions. This, of course, says nothing of Peruvian or Bolivian heroism but reveals a patent logistical incompetence.

---

105 Gonzalo Bulnes, *Resumen de la Guerra del Pacífico*.

106 Nelson Manrique, *Las guerrillas indígenas en la guerra con Chile* (Lima: Centro de Investigación y Capacitación, 1981).

Marx wrote that wars are not waged between countries but between gross products. Today we can affirm that this betrays a certain —necessary—economistic bias. Gross product is really only a valid criterion of comparison between countries with a similar level of capitalist development and even then certain qualifications would have to be made. It is, first of all, a purely statistical datum and refers only, somewhat crudely, to the quantitative aspect of a society. A society with a greater gross product might not have it concentrated or might not be able to concentrate it when it wants to do so, while one with an inferior gross product might have the ability to mobilize it effectively, swiftly and at the opportune moment. Thus in this conflict (and this approximates the logic of dependency theory) the more powerful, the country possessing the greatest gross product, should necessarily have won. Even with a greater gross product in absolute terms, the social optimum can be inferior (this is the case with Argentina at present, for example).[107] In reality, then, since Peru lost the war when it was richer than ever,[108] the conflict is between different types of social equations or the degree to which each of them is the bearer of an optimum. We must explain what it is that we mean by what we have reiteratively called the social equation or optimum, which is nothing but the relational quality of a society. We will base our discussion on a passage from Antonio Gramsci:

---

107 In Argentina, the Falklands tragedy exemplifies the high price of a low optimum in the relation between society and the state.

108 Peru exported more guano in 1876 than at almost any other year, apart from exceptional years such 1869 and 1870, and even then it exported almost twice as much in nitrates and triple the figure from 1870, just six years earlier. Even sugar exports increased almost twentyfold and amounted to almost half the income from guano. Sugar production rose from 4,500 tons in 1871 to 60,763 tons in 1878 (Luis Raúl Esteves, *Apuntes para la historia económica del Perú* [Lima: Imprenta Calle de Huallaga, 1882], p. 16). While revenues remained constant between 1865 and 1868, spending increased from 13.36 million pesos to 20.5 million pesos (Yepes del Castillo, *Perú 1820–1920*, p. 84). It was not as a result of economic inferiority that Peru lost this war.

This does not mean that the tactics of assault and incursion and the war of maneuver should now be considered to be utterly erased from the study of military science; that would be a serious error. But in wars among the most industrially and socially advanced states, these methods of war most be seen to have a reduced tactical function rather than a strategic function; their place in military history is analogous to that of siege warfare in the previous period.

The same reduction must take place in the art and science of politics, at least in those cases pertaining to the most advanced states, where 'civil society' has become a very complex structure that is very resistant to the catastrophic 'irruptions' of the immediate economic factor (crises, depressions, etc.): the superstructures of civil society resemble the trench system of modern warfare. Sometimes, it would appear that a ferocious artillery attack against enemy trenches had levelled everything, whereas in fact it had caused only superficial damages to the defenses of the adversary, so that when the assailants advanced they encountered a defensive front that was still effective. The same thing occurs in politics during great economic crises. A crisis does not enable the attacking troops to organize themselves at lightning speed in time and in space; much less does it infuse them with a fighting spirit. On the other side of the coin, the defenders are not demoralized; nor do they nor do they abandon their defensive positions, even in the midst of rubble; nor do they lose faith in their own strength of their own future. This is not to say that everything remains intact . . . .

And finally:

In the East the State was everything, civil society was primordial and gelatinous; in the West, there was a proper relation between State and civil society, and when the state tottered, a sturdy structure of civil society was immediately revealed.

The State was just a forward trench; behind it stood a succession of sturdy fortresses and emplacements.[109]

Here Gramsci offers a brilliant analysis of the 'immortal',
crystallizing, ossifying nature of ideological superstructures, of their
persistent tendency to ratify and sustain themselves. This is really
not only valid for the superstructures of capitalism, where it is more
visible as a result of expanded reproduction, but for all systems:
superstructures—law, ideology, the state itself—are made in relation
to or oriented towards the source of their determination, not to transform but to preserve it. In this sense, law and the state are always
conservative. Of course, just as in capitalism, the state must adapt to
a perpetually moving base, it must also act through methods of
reading or methods of social knowledge such as political democracy
in this sense. The *trench system* is thus nothing but the set of mediations, structures and supports through which civil society exists
before the state and the political state before civil society, that is, the
intermediate phase without which the conscious will of politics or
power (the state) and society (the space of production of the conditions of a political will or of its reception) cannot know one another.
It is also clear, moreover, that when we speak of the *external surface*
of the state, we refer to its old form of violent coercion or repressive
apparatus while the *effective line of defence* is the space of the perpetuity or tenacity of its ideological constitution, the hegemonic core.[110]

In this master metaphor of the modern state, there is, however,
more than one arguable point. We would have to distinguish, for
example, between states of long duration and situations of state fluidity, such as those proper to the apparent state. It is absolutely true
that the 'assailants' do not organize themselves immediately because
they are themselves immersed and absorbed within bourgeois

109 Antonio Gramsci, *Prison Notebooks* (Joseph A. Buttigieg and Antonio
Callari eds and trans) (New York: Columbia University Press, 2007), VOL. 3,
pp. 162–3, 169.

110 See Michel Foucault.

hegemony and its discourse; they exist in a relation of internality, of belonging, or of inseparability to the hegemonic discourse. Their life, simply put, cannot be conceived outside of the hegemonic radius. The *truth principle*[111] fails here because both its assailants and its defenders deeply believe in the truth of the state.

This is most rigorously applicable to the advanced capitalist state. Its defenders who *believe deeply and are not demoralized* are what Hegel called the *general class*, or the bureaucracy in a basic sense, as the bearer of the secret of the state or ideology for itself. [Augusto] Pinochet, of course, at the moment of the coup, felt himself to be the bearer of that self-certainty of the state. The assailants, therefore, are dominated not only by force as violence (which also exists) but, above all, by the memory of force, which is ideology, *generalized discipline*. The state here is the *superego*[112] of civil society; it contains the collective memory of what is called the real subsumption of labour under capital or formal subsumption, that is, the sacrifice of the autonomy of the *state of separation* to the despotic power of productive capital.[113]

We consider the premise that capitalist societies are more complex than precapitalist societies to be patently false. It is true that capitalism multiplies social time but it is no less true that it homogenizes, standardizes society. Ultimately, national classes, the nation itself, vast, relatively uniform social units, are proper to capitalism and, in this sense, any backward society is more heterogeneous and complex than a capitalist society.

Therefore, although Gramsci fails to consider this fact (he omits it; he does not deny it), the general validity of this apothegm on the state must be based upon a kind of simultaneous and homogeneous determination of the superstructure by the economic base or civil society. In reality, the moment of determinative efficacy of civil society

111 See Foucault.

112 That is, the internalized authority of the voice of the father.

113 Zavaleta, 'Cuatro conceptos de la democracia'.

is heterogeneous, that is, it is above all an erratic result in complex or motley societies, in illegible societies. Even in capitalist societies simplified by industrialization, the determinative moment is at least sequential or mobile, and here, if the impediment of incalculability is absent (and the proof of this is representative democracy), the state must still adjust to the aleatory determination proper to expanded reproduction.

What seems most questionable is the premise that civil society in the East was 'primitive and gelatinous' in comparison with the *robust* character of civil society in the West. It has been said that here Gramsci uses the term East in a metaphorical sense, although in any case it is a metaphor with a proper name. It is a culturalist exaggeration to suppose that capitalism exists in Europe because it is Western. In this case, there could be no mode of capitalism but that of the West. Gramsci's statement can be interpreted to mean that the political state is powerful where it results from a *farmer* path,[114] or from the free choice of juridically free men. This distinction is important. If it is true that freedom is the necessary condition of capitalism, a man can be free as one who has received his freedom from the state, as one who has conquered his own freedom *before* the state, or as one whose freedom *has determined* the mode of existence of the state. In all three cases, the precondition—the formation of free men—is wholly fulfilled. Nonetheless, the spirit with which this common condition is experienced is different in each case.

In any event, the strength or robustness of the state is gauged only in relation to the civil society to which it refers, and vice versa.

---

114 Lenin: 'The peasant [. . .] becomes the sole subject of agriculture and is gradually transformed into the capitalist farmer' ('The Agrarian Question in Russia Towards the Close of the Nineteenth Century') [Translated from the Spanish. This reference is untraceable.—Trans.]. This has to do with the mode of constitution of the free individual. In other words, a 'pact' between free individual smallholders is one thing, and it is quite another if the peasants are subjugated, by debt or in any other way, even if they have been granted juridical 'freedom'.

What matters here is the degree of intensity or correspondence. The mere ascendency of the state over society does not constitute an optimum but the paralysis or circular life that Marx called Asiatic despotism. Conversely, the mere unorganized supremacy of society over the state constitutes only an aleatory relation and can disorganize or negate all politics, good or bad. Thus the supremacy of society (at least) or the absorption of the state by society that is assumed to be a progressive feature of socialism constitutes a specific kind of supremacy of the latter over the former and does not refer to *all* supremacy.

We can set aside the somewhat culturalist sense that resides in the letter of this paragraph. It goes without saying that the optimum in its paradigmatic form emerged in the United States, strictly speaking not a Western state, unless the term refers to the originary stock in a racial sense, and then it would be unclear why the same culture would function badly in Latin American hands, of 'Western' descent in this sense, and well in the hands of Anglo-Saxons, equally Western, unless *mestizaje* had the effect of weakening the political consequences of Western blood. It is obvious, moreover, that it would be mistaken to think of Norway or Portugal as more instructive in the history of capitalism in the world than Japan. Bearing in mind our whole previous digression, we must also take into account European and North American privilege in the appropriation of the global surplus, which in itself does not explain the capitalist state, although it certainly made it viable.

We know, however, what Gramsci meant at the core of his reasoning. There is no doubt an often forgotten sequence from the abolition of the old collectivity or at least its reorientation towards the consecration of the juridically free individual, in its two phases, as man unbound from the soil and as citizen, and the constitution of the capitalist model of intersubjectivity, which differs from somatic homogeneity in that here what homogeneity there is is the fruit of the transferable interaction *from* the general market. The very separation of the state from society is possible only on the basis of the concept of the total capitalist, which, in turn, refers to a specific pattern in the circulation of surplus value. Therefore, if this is the necessary prodrome of the relative autonomy of the state, it is true that the relation of symmetry or reinforcement in the equation, which is what we are here calling the optimum, is impossible, or it is possible only to a lesser extent so long as these particular forms of interaction and this degree of independence of the state, which is a product of the more general and less and private appropriation of surplus value as well as of democratic knowledge of society, are not present. This, in our view, is what we may learn from this absolutely decisive analogy offered in the thought of Antonio Gramsci.

*

What we are calling the optimum is of course a metaphor and in reality it can only be approximated. In any case, even if it exists, it does not exist once and for all but is something that is gained and lost. There is in every equation an inherent tendency towards a loss of equivalence between the two terms. A typical example might be the dramatic difference between the Russian formations of the two world wars.[115] In the case under discussion, there is no doubt that, of the three countries that took part in the conflict, Chile possessed a greater social equation than its adversaries. The difference in the national product, if it gave some slight advantage to Chile, was not significant. Or at least not militarily significant. It is a fact that Bolivia and Peru had far greater populations. Even if we concede the military advantage resulting form the superiority of its preparation and equipment, the Chilean victory, if we adhere to these indices, should have been, in theory, far more difficult and less crushing than it was. In military terms, it is said that a victory of such proportions should be the result either of an overwhelming superiority or of some absolutely decisive stroke of luck. Neither of these things occurred and

---

115 Or also, of course, the radical difference between Baptista's soldiers and the volunteers in South Africa or Ethiopia.

our analysis of this history leads us to seek more structural and constant causes.

'Chile,' [Oswald] Spengler once wrote, 'is a robust state.' Let us leave aside for now the general question of the state in Chile and reduce the exposition to its elements or essence. Whether Chile was or was not then already a robust state remains to be seen; in reality, it is demonstrable, rather, that the Chilean state was capable then and there of constructing a state policy, which in turn was able to engage the entire society, to lead it towards the objective of war. It is perhaps worth pausing to consider this question, that of the construction of a state policy. With states as with individuals, decisions that are in fact imposed by circumstance or external conditions are often attributed to the will of their executors; in some cases, the subjective support for the decision might even believe itself to be resolving something that in reality has been determined by events.[116]

This is particularly true for the world of the periphery, the proletarian nations.[117] As we have seen, the problem of receptivity is always decisive. In normal circumstances, they are countries that lack receptivity, that is, self-determination. This emerges under certain conditions, such as in moments of conflict between core countries, or through the social receptivity that results from a general crisis or the seizure of an unforeseen surplus.[118] What we call the 'economic policy' of these countries is often no more than the sum of measures demanded by the hegemonic core. This is of course relative. Every society, even the weakest and most isolated, always possesses some

116 This is the problem of what we must call illusory self-determination, widely present in apparent states.

117 Pierre Moussa, *Les nations Prolétaires* (Paris: Presses Universitaires de France, 1959).

118 The most spectacular surpluses of this century in Latin America are that of Argentina, as of 1890; that of Venezuela, after 1940; and that of Mexico, after 1975. The highest revenues in Peru's history are attained in the decade of 1870–80 (Heraclio Bonilla, *Guano y burguesía en el Perú* [Lima: IEP, 1974], p. 139).

margin of self-determination, but such a society is utterly incapable of exercising it unless it knows the conditions or particularities of its dependency. In other words, each national history creates a specific model of autonomy, but it also engenders a particular mode of dependency. One of the most striking features of Chile at that time is the aptitude of its ruling class for an accurate analysis of the kind of dependency that governed its relations with the core countries[119] and, on the other hand, a knowledge of the degree of social receptivity to determination by the state. Self-determination in any case cannot mean the disappearance of external constraints; it means, rather, the elaboration of one's own objective or will within a set of external constraints, that is to say, these can be eluded insofar as they are known. Knowledge of the world and a realistic view of oneself are the absolute prerequisites of self-determination. In this sense, moments of self-determination in Bolivia, for example, have always been rare.[120] Ultimately, telic consciousness, or, in more common terms, sovereignty in determining its own ends, is the object of state.

119 Despite the fact that the state had ownership of Peru's guano since 1840 and its nitrates since 1878, despite the fact that all loans had been controlled by the state, this did not proffer a privileged position in relation to Chile. 'Harvey, working in partnership with North, occupied a special place in the operations carried out during the war' (according to Ramírez Necochea's account [*Balmaceda y la contrarrevolución de 1891*, p. 45]). To some extent at least, British capital would favour Chile's acquisition of the deposits and then decide what to do with Chile itself. Indeed: 'John Thomas North had contributed a sum of 100,000 pounds sterling [to the anti-Balmacedists]' (ibid., p. 192). A British trading company, one of whose centres was the Gibbs house, maintained that a Chilean victory could be beneficial in the long term because this republic was the most efficient and energetic of the South American Pacific. (Basadre, *Historia de la república del Perú, 1822–1933*, VOL. 8, p. 30). So it is not that the British decided the war in Chile's favour but that they immediately understood Chile would inevitably win.

120 The moment of greatest receptivity was certainly 1952, when the MNR rose to power despite the disapproval of the United States. The lowest, perhaps, with the immediate loss of that receptivity, was reached in 1956 when Jackson Eder commandeered the political life of the state.

It is clear that not every state is capable of formulating policies and, of course, few can sustain them and carry them through. The diktat in itself reveals an attitude of confidence in the conformity of the social body or in the state's ascendency over it. This is why in countries like ours, it is crucial to thoroughly examine the question of what has been called the *apparent state*. In too summary a fashion, it can be defined as equivalent to Lenin's notion of the semicolony.[121] As a state, a colony does not exist because its territory, its population and what could be its political power are in foreign hands. A semi-colony, on the other hand, possesses an illusory sovereignty over all three. For Lenin, it refers to countries with political independence that are economically dependent. Obviously, the political and the economic cannot be separated like this. Where a certain degree of economic sovereignty does not exist, there can be no political sovereignty, etc. In any case, there is no doubt that the Latin American countries, which are the founders of political independence in the periphery, share this characteristic: they have had constitutions but no constitutional moment; the state form as a whole (although the form itself here is part of the history of its content) resembles that of advanced states; in short, they appear to be Western (in the Euro-centric sense of the term) in all respects but somehow they are not. What misfires here is a structural concept of sovereignty that is ulti-mately incompatible with the condition of non-centrality in the world, at least in history such as it has occurred until now. This must be taken with due caution. Still, we are speaking of states in which what predominates, if not total dependency, which sometimes exists for long periods of time, is at least an incomplete self-determination (keeping in mind that absolute self-determination is a theological idea); they have only a vague sense of self-certainty, that is, identity. We can therefore also call them uncertain states.[122]

---

121 V. I. Lenin, *Imperialism, the Highest Stage of Capitalism* (1917), in *Selected Works*, VOL. 1 (Moscow: Progress Publishers, 1963), pp. 667–776.

122 Non-self-determination is a problem of identity. In other words, one who does not have the desire for self-determination in this age lacks visibility and

Chile had a surprising capacity for the construction of a political programme. Our task here is to ascertain the nature, origin and end of that programme. The fascinating figure of Diego Portales illustrates this process.[123]

It is a case in which the temperament of a man became the character of a nation or, as it were, the personality of a nation was revealed in the character of a man. There is no doubt that the mimetic or seductive relation between societies and states is of great importance. If we consider the seduction of El Dorado,[124] it is true that Chile defined itself as a project in the image of Peru or, rather, Potosí,[125]

---

therefore recognition by those who should be one's fellows. This kind of renunciation of sovereignty is perhaps the most aberrant feature of the politically and economically dominant classes in Latin America.

123 Let us leave aside the idea that Chile could be explained by the predominance of 'Castilian-Basque' ancestry, espoused by Francisco Antonio Encina. In any case, it is true that Portales very clearly expressed something that had been silently developing within that society. The characteristic combination of legality and authoritarianism, the formation of impersonal power and the constitution of a certain degree of independence of the state in relation to the 'special apparatus' of repression are surely part of Portales' legacy. But so are the very conditions of impossibility of the utopia or national ethos that he founded. He defined Chile's sovereignty in relation to Peru and Bolivia, not in relation to the world; conceived of success solely in terms of surplus; and, finally, believed that Chile's purpose was to 'affirm the conquests of European civilization' (*Resumen de la historia de Chile*, VOL. 2, p. 834).

124 Sanabria Fernández, *En busca de El Dorado*; Sozina, *En el horizonte está El Dorado*; Romano and Tenenti, *Los fundamentos del mundo moderno*, p. 178.

125 In a famous letter to Blanco Encalada, then head of the Chilean naval and military forces against the Confederation, Portales wrote these telling words: 'We cannot view but with apprehension and the greatest alarm the existence of two confederated peoples who, ultimately, given their common provenance, language, habits, religion, ideas, and customs, will naturally form a single nucleus'; it was a matter of impeding what Chile had done early on, because 'those two states united [. . .] would always be greater than Chile' and this 'as a result of its greater white population' and 'its greater number of learned

which was the secret of Lima and then, long after, of Charcas. The truth is that every nascent state is born in relation to another state or paradigm or tendency. It must be something desirable, but not remote. Such is the function of alterity for the state. One cannot found oneself in relation to oneself. The *other* for Chile was always Peru. Chile, a state constituted against the Indians, in spite of the Indians, and excluding the Indians; Peru, a state built on the backs of the Indians and therefore with a concupiscent tolerance for them; Chile, a state fashioned out of a frugal surplus; Peru, the paragon of a surplus without a state. Peru (which in this ideologeme includes Potosí), the locus of vast natural resources, and Chile, endowed with limited natural resources, at least for the period. All of this is, ultimately, illusory because time proved that the most important source of natural wealth in Bolivia then was that which it lost.

Portales said that power in Chile is sustained by 'the weight of night'.[126] Herein lies the essence of the authoritarianism of the Chilean state. If the people is awake, democracy is not possible. Democracy is founded on the force of night, that is, the slumber of the people. Here we have an early theorist of the social market state. Authoritarianism, however, is only of consequence if it is converted into power; without this, it is no more than a feeling. A state, in effect, can only formulate policy within the sphere of its ideological or at least its actual reach, as the actualization of something that exists as a potentiality or virtuality in the administrative and repressive apparatus, because the state is itself plus the radius of its legitimacy or authority. If it is true that to be is to choose oneself, as André Gide once wrote, the production of policy has to do with the logic of ends

---

white men in Lima with ties to the Spanish families' (quoted in Basadre, *Historia de la república del Perú 1822–1933*, VOL. 2, p. 149).

126 The full passage is richer: 'The social order in Chile is maintained through the weight of the night and because we have no keen, astute, and discerning men; the general tendency of the masses towards repose is the guarantee of public peace' (letter from Portales to Joaquím Tocornal, 17 May 1832).

without which the state would respond only to the instinct of self-preservation of the strongest. History would be a stupid, continuous line in which the powerful always prevail. The capacity to imagine or a kind of telos is what distinguishes man from spider because he weaves towards a preconceived object.[127] Hence we must infer the conscious substantiality of the state, that is, if the state has no self-consciousness or self-certainty, it is not a state but a factual consequence of the confrontations, hostilities and pacts between anomic groups in civil society.[128] If utopian action can respond to a future determination (not effective in the present), certainly the optimum requires a selection of possible objects and apposite means, that is, the call to action must be something underlying or latent in the social equation. Therefore, if the true production of politics is like the self-determination of the subject, it is in fact also the expansion of the social subject. This does not depend only on free will in the sense that to be is to choose oneself, but to do so successfully. Why, then, was Chile, that Chile, able to produce a *state policy* while Peru and Bolivia achieved only its simulacra? Bolivia struggled just to remain where it was. Surely it attempted a to produce a policy, but its 10 cents per quintal of nitrate not only provoked the war but also led to its condition of geographic inferiority.[129] Peru, in turn, tried belatedly

---

127 'A spider conducts operations which resemble those of a weaver, and a bee would put many a human architect to shame by the construction of its honeycomb cells. But what distinguishes the worst architect from the best of bees is that the architect builds the cell in his mind before he constructs it in wax. At the end of every labour process, a result emerges that had already been conceived by the worker at the beginning, hence already existed ideally' (Marx, *Capital*, VOL. 1, p. 284).

128 G. W. F. Hegel, *Philosophy of Right* (T. M. Knox trans.) (London: Oxford University Press, 1979[1952]), §270: 'The state [. . .] knows what it wills and knows it in its universality, i.e. as something thought. Hence it works and acts by reference to consciously adopted ends, known principles, and laws which are not merely implicit but are actually present to consciousness.'

129 'The Antofagasta Nitrate Company founded with Chilean and British capital was granted special privileges by the Bolivian government to exploit the

to nationalize its nitrate fields.[130] Chile, meanwhile, instituted a policy that consisted in overcoming its relative inferiority and the conquest of a surplus that was like the spoils of the age. As far as Chile could see given the limits of its field of vision, these ends were achieved. Whether it was all an illusion—whether success in the end was indistinguishable from failure—is another question.[131] We must insist,

---

nitrates discovered near the port of La Chimba (Antofagasta). In 1873, the company built the first railroad in Bolivian territory to facilitate the transport of nitrates from the deposits of Salar del Carmen to the Antofagasta port. Just a few years later, in 1879, the nitrate tax levied by the Bolivian government (10 cents per quintal) provoked the ire of the Nitrate Company and unleashed the War of the Pacific. A few months later, the Bolivian coast was occupied by Chilean forces. With the war over, the Chilean government, attentive to the interests of foreign and domestic capital, ordered a classified study of mining and agricultural conditions in the provinces of Lípez and Sud Chichas in the interior of Bolivia with the decree of 22 May 1882. In 1884, the government of the Bolivian oligarchy signed a truce with Chile in the fourth article of which it was established that the products of each country could be freely imported to the other. With this measure, Chile won a new victory, this time economic, since it was clear that Bolivia could export nothing but its minerals. Thus the conquest of Bolivian markets was methodically prepared. The Antofagasta Nitrate Company took the next step, initiating the construction of the railroad towards the postwar border in occupied territory, *without consulting the Bolivian government*. The regime of the mining oligarchy took preparatory steps, raising duties on products imported from Peru by 30 per cent. This measure, intended to benefit Chile, was a hard blow for trade in the northern districts and further degraded relations with their allies from the war of 1870' (Mitre, *Los patriarcas de la plata*, p. 165).

130 In 1875 (Ramírez Necochea, *Historia del imperialismo en Chile*). The nitrate fields had already belonged to the state since 1840 (Heraclio Bonilla, *Guano y burguesía en el Perú*, p. 165). Even the loans were all overseen by the Peruvian state. In theory, therefore, a large surplus such as had seldom been seen was at the disposal of the state.

131 Each of the three countries went through an economic crisis in its own way. Bolivia really suffered only the exacerbation of a destitution that was perhaps indistinguishable from a virtual economic nonexistence before the world. Peru had created its own crisis. Chile, meanwhile, attempted a *fuite en*

however, that such an achievement cannot be explained solely on the basis of the indisputable preparedness or ascendency acquired since the capture of the Huáscar or even by a kind of privileged position in relation to British interests. It is something founded on the level or potentiality of the social optimum, surely more efficient than those of its rivals. It was Chile's history, at that moment, that had readied itself to defeat Peru and Bolivia. We must consider the essence of the event and not its phenomenon.

Chile's constitutive moment, as a state and as a nation, is determined by the Arauco War just as the Nile is Egypt's ultimate cause and constitutive moment and the combination of the price revolution, the black plague and depeasantization is England's. Of course it would be absurd to attribute the determination of the emergence of a society or of a state to a precise moment or even a central cause. It is true, and has been proven in practice, that a process of gradual and even conscious accumulation can supplement the nonexistence of such a moment or irruption, which is decisive either for its precise location in time, which gives it its visibility in the future, or for its momentousness, as with the Nile or Andean agriculture. It is, moreover, a typical ex-post notion, in that we can know with some certainty what the originary moment of a society is but not how future

---

avant (and succeeded): 'The economic crisis that had reached its peak with the declaration of the inconvertibility of banknotes in 1878 came to an unexpected end with the War of the Pacific. And we say that it came to an unexpected end because with the war the country came into possession of vast resources' (Daniel Martner, cited in Jobet, *Ensayo crítico del desarrollo económico-social de Chile*, p. 65). This is indisputable, for Chile conquered the world's only natural nitrate deposits. The direct prelude was, first, the Peruvian stagnation of 1873 and the subsequent expropriation of the nitrate fields in 1878. 'These events [the Peruvian crisis and expropriation] are those which established for the Chilean capitalist class the need to conquer the nitrate fields as a solution to the economic and financial crisis that was ruining the country' (ibid., p. 64). According to Alberto Edwards, 'without the War of the Pacific, the Pinto government might well have ended in a revolution' (cited in ibid.).

societies, through a weaving that remains inscrutable, will be constituted. It is true that to have a constitutive moment that is conspicuous and in a sense decisive (because it defines the character of the society for a long time to come), visible to and shared by the entire people, is initially beneficial. But the history of a country is often the result of more than one constitutive moment, although one constitutive moment can be more profound, more radical and ancestral than others. This, which proves at first to be an advantage, can in fact be an obstacle to the attainment of the most suitable form for the fulfilment of what we might call the tasks of the age; a deep-rooted identity can obstruct the formation of a new identity.

The concept of the constitutive moment refers to the formation of a society's essential discourse. Our previous discussion of the concept of receptivity is instructive for its understanding. A constitutive moment must be something potent enough to interpellate an entire people or at least certain strategically important groups within it because it must bring about a replacement of beliefs, a universal substitution of loyalties, in short, a new horizon of visibility. If we attribute so integral a symbolic function to this moment, it is because it is from here that the social 'cement' that is the ideology of a society is derived or founded.[132] It is one of the most persistent social facts,

---

132 González Prada said that 'Chile was infected with the Peruvian malady.' This seems to be corroborated by the following facts: 'the nitrate region was transformed into a British factory. Through it and through the supremacy that the British had achieved in the economic life of the country prior to the War of the Pacific, Chile's total subordination to British imperialism was secured' (Ramírez Necochea, *Historia del imperialismo en Chile*, p. 103). 'Around 1890, the British dominated the main towns of the north, especially those of Tarapacá, exercising an unchecked influence in that province' (ibid., p. 102). Note that it is a date very close to the end of the war.

The national subordination of this same state that had been capable of setting its own objectives was obvious, that is, the Chilean optimum had deteriorated. 'Valparaíso [. . .] with its trade entirely controlled by the British, its market transactions conducted in pounds sterling, its English newspaper and

to the point that we might say that the constitutive ideology often cuts across several modes of production and historical periods. Yet the omnipresence of this moment cannot mean the absolute hegemony of the past or origin. Over the course of this study we will see the role assigned not only to the principle of selection in history, which is the foundation of anthropocentrism, but also to complementary constitutive moments, to the flux of historical reform within an originary movement.[133]

Chile, then, was blessed with a sharply delineated constitutive moment, and one that included the whole of society and supplied the

---

extensive use of this language, was no more than a British colony' (Ramírez Necochea, *Balmaceda y la contrarrevolución de 1891*, p. 39).

Harvey himself declared to the *Financial Times* that 'a conversation of a few minutes between the Chilean minister and a man with the capability of Colonel North would be sufficient for the purpose' (ibid., p. 55)

Whether such subordination was a general fact or not is still open to question, but it did not exist to this extent prior to the Chilean victory. What is indisputable is the contagion of the 'Peruvian virus' in the form of political corruption: Gonzalo Bulnes, for example, 'took advantage of his position as governor of Trapacá to carry out major nitrate deals in the province that had been entrusted to his governance' (*Resumen de la Guerra del Pacífico*, p. 27). An account in *El Tarapacá* (28 August 1886) makes clear that this had not been common practice before: 'This is the first time that a civil servant has given up his post to devote himself to business affairs that had previously been within the domain of the state.'

Afterwards, this conflation of the positions of partner of the British or of the capitalists and civil servants would become increasingly frequent. This reveals a growing erosion of the relative autonomy of the Chilean state that would reach its peak when Jorge Alessandri, one of the Chilean millionaires, became president, which already implies a complete abandonment of the conventions of the Chilean oligarchy in the tradition of Portales. At the same time, it is telling that a population that had increased between 1843 and 1865 at a rate of 2.35 per cent would slow its growth rate to 1 per cent between 1865 and 1907—a not a result of demographic modernization but of poverty.

133 See Ernst Bloch, *Sujeto-Objeto: El pensamiento de Hegel* (Mexico City: FCE, 1949).

early elements of its precocious acquisition of an efficient social equation. That moment was the Arauco War or, rather, the encounter between the colonization of Peru (seigneurial at its core; Pizarro said: 'Here one goes to Peru to get rich,' that is, to be a *señor*)[134] and the circumstances surrounding the Arauco War. 'In Chile of the sixteenth and seventeenth centuries, it would be difficult not to perceive the pervasive militarism that seemed to dominate all of society.'[135]

This was true from the beginning. Already in the fifteenth century, the priest Diego de Rosales had described Chile as the Flanders of the Indies. As Álvaro Jara aptly says—and we will follow his account throughout this exposition—it was effectively a clash between a colonization at once seigneurial and private and the pre-state organizational and military forms of the Araucanians. We might say, rather, that it is a question of the failure of the Spaniards in that encounter.

If the number of hidalgos was in itself very high within the Spanish population of the time, the demeanour of the 'second sons,'[136] along with their subordinate status and their vast numbers, set the seal on things. 'All were lords or aspired to be' and 'those who had not even remotely been gentlemen, upon setting foot on American soil claimed that rank.'[137]

From then on, the set of mediations of the three societies, although in different ways, would be founded on the seigneurial principle, which will be discussed later. If the conquest of Chile is heir to the conquest of Peru, the conquistadores with their already Peruvianized minds encountered an indomitable social structure there.[138]

---

134 Raúl Porras Barrenechea, *Pizarro* (Lima: Ed. Pizarro, 1978).

135 Jara, *Guerra y sociedad en Chile*, p. 13.

136 Romano and Tenenti, *Los fundamentos del mundo moderno*, pp. 185–6.

137 Jara, *Guerra y sociedad en Chile*, p. 40.

138 Jara refers to 'the absence of a chief or king to lead them [the Araucanians]: if in one sector there was peace, others would remain outside the accords, since there was no single authority to rule them all; or, rather, if several groups made peace, this could not last for the same reason' (ibid., p. 48). This is also

The war in effect *became endless and interminable*.[139] The development of the state in Mexico or in Peru, which was clearly despotic, favoured a logic of conquest because here, once its peak was captured, the entire pyramid set to obeying as it had before.[140] Since Araucanians had no general organization but only military alliances, this led to a kind of indefinite multiplication of the centres of society and consequently to the futility of peace because what was agreed upon by some was not valid for others. In terms of defence, therefore, here society would acquire a contingent consistency as a result of its instability or, as it were, the military form of a mobile, scattered state.

The first consequence of this is that war itself is modernized. A long war always entails a certain modernization of warfare. Not just because of the adoption of cavalry by the Araucanians, who are said to have assembled 3,000 horses and 5,000 foot soldiers in one battle (in Purén), but also through their collective military ingenuity with tactics like that of the 'hedgehog' (clusters of spikes as a trap for the cavalry). The Spaniards, in any case, did not yet use infantry, at least not in its later sense, when cavalry had become useless.

---

relatively valid for the Chiriguanos. Still, without facing the same danger of extermination as the first Spanish colonies in Chile, for the inhabitants of eastern Charcas, the consequences in terms of *provocation of the state* were less serious as a result of the support of Charcas and Lima, which was immediate, and because of the greater spatial dispersion or lower numerical concentration of indigenous aggression.

139 Ibid., p. 21.

140 This is almost an established principle: the greater the state consciousness, the less individualist consciousness there is in military resistance (because this does not apply to the economic). 'Where Indian resistance was scarce or insufficient, the indigenous community survives—arduously—to this day' (Romano and Tenenti, *Los fundamentos del mundo moderno*, p. 183). On the other hand: 'Its efficiency [that of the conquest] was greater in those territories in which the indigenous masses, as a result of their greater social development, had been subjected to a social and productive regime that compelled them to render a surplus to the ruling caste' (Jara, *Guerra y sociedad en Chile*, p. 19)—which, of course, was not the case with Chile or with any frontier region.

Jara notes, on the other hand, the private character of the conquest inherent to what was called the *hueste indiana*, a private enterprise with a necessary seigneurial tendency at its core. In those
conditions it was clearly impossible for 'the conquerors-turned-
encomenderos[141] to successfully shoulder so heavy a burden over so
many years.'[142]

But it was not just an offensive failure; what was at stake was the
very survival of the new community, now undeniably besieged. The
rebellion that began in 1598 destroyed the seven existing cities and
the whole of the south was recovered by the Indians. We must ask
what role such a brutal, imminent, and global threat plays, for the
Araucanian objective was clear: the Spaniards, 'subjects and slaves,
obeying the Indians as their lords, and the Indians, ruling like masters and proprietors.'[143] The answer to this is the emergence of the
state whose point of origin is the army: 'Then, and only when the
abyss was opening, a state army paid for entirely with public funds
as had long been the norm in Europe was created.'[144]

In what did this *opening of the abyss* consist? In a willingness to
accept whatever was necessary for the survival of that which was

---

141 [Spanish soldiers or officials to whom a specified number of indigenous
inhabitants of an area (an *encomienda*) was 'entrusted'. The *encomendero* was
formally charged with the protection of the population and exacted tribute.]

142 Jara, *Guerra y sociedad en Chile*, p. 72. The problem lies always in the
transformation of (private) pacts into a (public) *frontier army*. The ideological
institution of the category of the public is essential in understanding the modern state, because civil society is the private sphere that, although it contains
state substance in potentia, has not *yet* assumed a public or state form. 'The
conquest was conditioned by its private nature, one that has largely persisted'
(ibid.). This means that it was not Spain that carried out the conquest but
gangs of second sons commanded by outsiders.

143 Sg. Alonso de Ovalle (Jara, *Guerra y sociedad en Chile*, p. 45).

144 Ibid., p. 116. The indigenous rebellion (that of 1598) 'ended in the
destruction of the seven cities, and the entire south was recovered by the
Indians' (ibid., p. 45).

threatened, that is, of that society that even if in the most embryonic way nonetheless possessed the elements of its initial recognition. On the other hand, the claim that war forced the substitution of the private nature of the *hueste indiana* by the national and state army carries important implications. The seigneurial privileging of the private sphere gives way here to the requirements of a national form of repression, because in absolutism the state precedes the nation.

We find in these passages, cursory as they are, traces of the Chilean optimum. We can say then that a general war organized the components of Chile's constitutive crisis. The *frontier army* becomes the foundation of the future Chilean state, a fact that is significant in itself.[145] The nucleus of a society's constitutive determination defines things and distinguishes them from one another. An originary intersubjective act constituted by agriculture or the logic of the councils, for example, is not the same thing as one constituted by a military imperative to rule and obey because the price of not doing so is annihilation. Men do not change their habits without good reason and those men (those of the *hueste indiana*) who had come to be their own masters in the seigneurial utopia of the time would not have accepted the implacable and precocious logic of the *regular army* if not for an urgency that prevailed over any kind of belief. This is the

---

145 Which means that the constitutive act is war, and, therefore, in the core ideological discourse, it would refer in the future to the logic of war. Hence, it makes a difference whether the constitutive act is a charismatic or messianic moment, if it is an act of submission or negative war, or an act of victory, active war, or war directed outwards. Moreover, the mode of the 'frontier army', which is a consequence of the frontier mentality, in turn organizes its own economy: 'A far-from-trivial market for the consumption of the products of the creole economy, since the last quarter of the sixteenth century and especially as of 1600, was constituted by the frontier army' (ibid., p. 37). In other words, the state is born of its repressive apparatus or army; the army exists outwardly and not inwardly; and, finally, the economy is produced by the state.

'deep crisis'[146] of the sixteenth century on which Chile is founded. The very fact that the Mapuche even today speak of 'the Chileans' is proof that the process of national integration in Chile excluded them. This blocks the most divisive aspects of the *hueste Indiana* ('within the seigneurial style of creole society, no one prided himself on being a soldier, and everyone wanted to be a captain').[147]

It was, however, a transformation and not a substitution or eradication. This is the characteristic fusion of the Chilean formation. If the principle of compliance, of obedience, is a deeply ingrained feeling, general and unshakable, this only transposes the individual habit of seigneurial rivalry to the collective plane (at least in principle) of the state, but it does not mean that the spirit of the seigneurial was extinguished and in essence the beginning of the separation of the oligarchy in Chile has always been its foundation in the image of its enemy, which was like its father—namely, Peru.[148] Because along with this kind of vertical solidarity that is the military rule of obedience, and as its base, there is an essential but xenophobic internal sympathy, which also ensues from the decisive moment. Herein lies the logic and legitimacy of Chilean racism (which is entirely ideological, that is, without further foundation than belief itself).[149] There is no doubt that the radical threat posed by the Araucanians put Chile's germinal existence into question; we do not tend to think well of those who have wanted to kill us. It is the reasoning of all frontiers with pre-statist Indians. If there is a progressive gradation consisting of a condition of inorganicity with a capacity for aggression or threat, organicity with a capacity for memory but without a state, and

---

146 Ibid., p. 94.

147 'The private and seigneurial style was imposed in the Indies' (ibid., p. 26).

148 'Valdivia was a prominent *encomendero* in Peru' (ibid., p. 19).

149 A large majority of the Chilean population has the blood type O, which indicates indigenous presence, that is, it is a mestizo population.

organicity capable of memory, of the reconstruction of an ideological heritage and of a state policy, the Araucanians did more for a nascent Chile than for themselves, and we might even say that they were incapable of producing their own memory.[150] This surely distinguishes them in an important way from Katarism, which is also militarist, as a movement within Tupaj Amarism. What has been called Chilean democracy is founded on this: on an ancestral feeling of equality among Spaniards. A disciplined equality was a military necessity. It did not mean that they believed in universal equality. The persistence of egalitarian features within an fundamental order, of a certain general cohesion along with an unquestionably seigneurial ascendancy of the state, then, constitutes the characteristic composition or synthesis of this formation.

It is interesting to compare the results of the military and social siege laid by the Indians in the three societies. In Chile, as we have just seen, the violence of the Araucanian programme precipitates the early establishment of the state. The state, in turn, is configured not as a bureaucratic entity as was the case with colonial Peru but by the army conceived as state substance, that is, not as corporate, private or spontaneous violence but as a general coercive latency. As for Peru, or at least that Peru of 1879, the triumph of a counterrevolutionary ideology (viceroyalist, Hispanicist and anti-indigenous) and a false and bureaucratic unification constitute the basic determining factors. As we shall see, it would have been difficult for Peru as a society to escape either of these conditions. There is no doubt, if we turn once more to the Chilean model, that war must provoke either dispersion, if its object is something disperse, or vigorous and passionate forms of pathetic unity, with an intensity in proportion to the extension, universality and duration of the event. The challenge of the war produces a response of solidarity or nationalization. For this reason it can be said that Chile is born unified by the Arauco War; the Other is something so powerful that it demands the production

---

150 For problems of historical memory, see the works of E. P. Thompson.

of a self-identity. This is not merely a logic of *carpe diem*. Not to adapt here was to perish.[151]

Our discussion of Peru must take other criteria into account. In the first place, because Peru represents a paradigmatic case of multiple constitutive or originary moments (with the systematization of space through agriculture and the moral-historical foundation of the conquest)—Peru is a more pre-Hispanic country than most in Latin America yet a more typically colonial country.[152] Here, there was not so much an enemy to be defeated as a whole world to administer; the problem of power, from the beginning, lay in the radical impossibility of controlling the very thing it possessed because it was not a case of the conquest of one people by another but of the occupation of the apex of a social pyramid.[153] Even in our discussion of the national question, we must, in all rigour, speak of a second Peru, because the Inca and their predecessors were successful, at least to a considerable extent, in the construction of something that can only be called a precapitalist mode of national formation. That Peru, like China, Egypt and so many other cases, testifies to the foolishness of the idea that only capitalist formations can be considered national.[154]

---

151 *Challenge and response*, used in this sense of the induction of a constitutive act, are Arnold Toynbee's terms. However, Tamayo employs the same concept in 1910: 'Is a rich and fertile environment better for man, for a race? Perhaps not, because the ease of such an existence would hardly stimulate and develop man's (or a race's) activity and strength. A hard and barren environment would then be preferable, because then man would be forced to exert himself, and his greater effort would impel his historical progress' (*Creación de la pedagogía nacional*, CHAP. 53).

152 Murra, *Formaciones económicas y políticas*; Emilio Choy Ma, *Antropología e historia* (Anthropology and History) (Lima: UNMSM, 1979).

153 See note 140.

154 This is Stalin's concept: 'A nation is not merely a historical category but a historical category belonging to a definite epoch, the epoch of rising capitalism' (Joseph Stalin, *Marxism and the National Question: Selected Writings and Speeches* [New York: International Publishers, 1942].)

We are speaking, then, of the second nationalization of Peru. But we must consider the cultural effects of bureaucratic organization. For the Spaniards, administering Mexico or Peru meant administering something immense—all of America. If the Chilean national ideology is that which is born of the abyss of Arauco, Peru's, at least in its traditionally dominant stratum, is that of viceregalism.[155] On the other hand, if it is true that war is a unifying event, so is the institution of a bureaucratic order, in another way and to a different degree. Bureaucracy generates a kind of unification from above that while certainly inconsistent can generate new customs, affinities and articulations. Received habit can be translated into material forms in a society; the subjective exercise of power is capable of producing objective consequences that then cease to be entirely dependent upon it.[156] Here we must take into account that there are different forms or degrees of unification. Peru, as the name of this bureaucratic or aristocratic form of unity, does not constitute a deep nation,[157] as it would if it referred to the historical consequences of Andean agriculture, that is, to its modification oriented towards the present. There is an important difference between the unity that comes from a fundamental experience of war and that which comes from a

155 'Peru today is a coastal formation' (José Carlos Mariátegui, *Siete ensayos de interpretación de la realidad peruana* [Lima: Amauta, 1975(1928)], p. 205; available in English as: *Seven Interpretative Essays on Peruvian Reality* [Marjory Urquidi trans.] [Austin: University of Texas Press, 1971]).

156 The transformation of the spirit of the state into social potentiality is an unduly neglected aspect of most analyses of the so-called Hegelian–Marxist theories of the state (see David Gold, Clarence Y. H. Lo and Erik Olin Wright, 'Recientes desarrollos en la teoría marxista del Estado capitalista' in Heinz Rudolf Sonntag and Héctor Vallecilos [eds], *El Estado en el capitalismo contemporáneo* [Mexico City: Siglo XXI, 1977], pp. 23–61).

157 It is indeed still to be seen whether the Peruvian axis of nationalization will be Lima and its ideology, which is viceregalism, or a contingent democratic interpellation with an necessarily indigenous connotation. 'Peru,' Mariátegui wrote, 'must choose either the gamonal or the Indian' (*Siete ensayos*, p. 194).

vertical bureaucratic act, which, moreover, is extrinsic in this case. This form of interpellation obviously cannot compete in terms of penetration and density with the unification proper to the general capitalist market that unquestionably produces superior forms of intersubjectivity. Peru thus encountered a set of adverse conditions. Given that Andean agriculture could not exist except in an organized manner, with all the consequences that this entails, it had to set up a power structure that could not but enter into a contract with regard to the surplus generated prior to it. Further, given that the pyramid of the state (that of the Incas) was compact, to occupy its apex meant at once to adhere to its methods, even if practised in a degenerate way.[158] This could not lead to a military logic but only to an administrative or bureaucratic logic—and this is what happened. *Perricholismo*[159] was really the creole version of the bureaucratic-seigneurial system, which produced a thinking in terms of capital and not of territory, of tribute and not of cohesion, of status and not of identity. Peru had more noblemen than any other Latin American country but this was in no way to its benefit.[160]

We can therefore maintain that Peru was a nation and that it ceased to be one in a kind of social recomposition that is surely not unique in history. The system of ecological tiers[161] or the spatial organization was translated into a juridico-political system that has had considerable success in the conscious task of homogenization, at least to the extent that this was possible in a context of non-market exchange. We can also reasonably contend that the collapse of this

---

158 The *mita*, for example, was used in mining—a non-capitalist form was carried over to a commercial form of exploitation. *Yanaconaje* was the recuperation of a pre-existing form, etc.

159 This is what the creole was called in its courtier version. From *perra* [whore (literally, bitch)] and *chola* [half-breed; educated or assimilated Indian woman]: the Peruvian lover of a viceroy, Amat, was called Perricholi.

160 Basadre, cited in Yepes del Castillo, *Perú 1820–1920*, p. 38.

161 Murra, *Formaciones económicas y políticas*.

system, added to the demographic catastrophe and the colonial reorganization of this world, necessarily instilled a general state of shock
or vacancy. Bureaucratic unification was but an attempt to escape
this situation of general provisionality by the juridico-formal route.[162]
The most radical and organic attempt to restore the old Andean logic
of space and to reconstruct that society within the new parameters,
now under a democratic principle of interpellation, was the campaign led by Tupaj Amaru. His failure represents the failure of the
democratic constitution of the Peruvian nation.

The first thing that strikes us when we consider Amaru's rebellion, or even the series of Indian rebellions known by this name, is
the brevity of its duration, which in no way diminishes its enormous
social intensity. We could say that everything began in Chayanta in
July 1780 and ended, little more than a year later, with the siege of
La Paz in October 1781.[163] The rebellion of Condorcanqui itself was
even briefer: it broke out in Cuzco on 4 November 1780 and ended
on 5 April the following year, when Amaru was defeated.[164] Now, is
the Hispanophilia displayed, if not by Peruvian society, at least by its
core at the time of the War of Independence, and then certainly by a
vital part of its subsequent ideological contents, not disconcerting
for a country with such a rich historical and cultural presence of the

---

162 Oscar Cornblit, 'Levantamientos de masas en Perú y Bolivia durante el
siglo dieciocho' in Tulio Halperín Donghi (ed.), *El ocaso del orden colonial en
Hispanoamérica* (Buenos Aires: Sudamericana, 1978), pp. 57–117.

163 In reality it was a series of rebellions. The first in the series took place in
Chayanta with Tomás Catari in July of 1780 (not to be confused with Tupac
Katari [Julián Apaza], although it is revealing that one caudillo takes the name
of the other, as occurred with the Willkas, as though to signify the perpetuity
of leadership and the circumstantiality of its support). The Chayanta rebellion
ended in the siege of La Plata (Chuquisaca) in February of 1781. La Paz was
besieged for less than eight months, between March and October of 1781.

164 Condorcanqui was executed in Cuzco on 18 May 1781; the siege of La
Paz would last for another five months after his death.

Indians? Peru, surely, is not merely a semantic excess.[165] Amaru, then, must be designated as the new underdeterminative point of rupture. It is a moment of transformation of the ideological discourse of the society. We could say that after Tupaj Amaru, nothing in Peru remains as it was before.[166]

We must ask why so brief an event had such vast repercussions. Today no one remembers dozens of viceroys and jurists but Amaru and Katari are present, especially in the unconscious of these societies. The depth of the programme proposed by the political genius of Condorcanqui [Amaru] resides in a way in its eclecticism, because it was a programme for *all of society*. This was determined by his own personal context. It is debatable whether Amaru was a descendent of the Inca but there is no doubt that he belonged to a certain hierarchy in the Incan aristocracy, which indicates that his relation to colonial society was one of belonging and not of exclusion.[167]

---

165 This expression, more felicitous as such than as a concept, belongs to the historian Pablo Macera.

166 There is a subtle shift even within the seigneurial articulation itself. Its axis becomes strictly Hispanic. Previously, 'if an Indian was of noble caste [. . .] then his nobility was as valid as a Spaniard's and he neither paid tribute nor was required to fulfil the duties of the mita, and was eligible to occupy administrative and military positions' (Jan Szeminski, 'La insurrección de Tupac Amaru II: ¿Guerra de independencia o revolución?', *Estudios Latinoamericanos* 2 [1974]: 9–40). After Amaru, an 'organized annihilation of the traditions of the Inca state and a *forced hispanicization* were carried out, and the creoles understood that without the support of the Spaniards they were in no condition to maintain their situation. [. . .] Above all, they had to transform their culture and renounce all family, cultural, and other ties with indigenous society' (ibid.). Finally, there was even an attempt to eliminate the Quechua language in what was like an inversion of Apaza's programme which had prohibited the use of Spanish. This is [José Antonio de] Areche's ideological legacy.

167 John H. Rowe speaks of 'the tradition of using the indigenous nobility for the execution of administrative orders' ('El movimiento nacional inca del siglo XVIII' in Alberto Flores Galindo (ed.), *Sociedad colonial y sublevaciones*

'Making one body of Indians and creole Spaniards, doing away with the Europeans, who were to be killed making no distinction of persons, class or age, because the government had to be wholly sloughed off.'[168] It is now clear beyond all doubt that Amaru was referring to the entire people and not only to the Indians: 'Documents from the time of the campaign reveal that José Gabriel Amaru expected the support of powerful groups in Cuzco.'[169] This, then, was an Incan interpellation of the whole society, a call for unification within certain models of legitimacy and not outside of them. In a way, this is akin to Bolívar's programme and that of the great majority of those who fought after independence, but inverted, because here the interpellative nucleus was constituted by the indigenous.

With Amaru, on the other hand, there is a political articulation of the Andean spatial system, now embodied in the consequences of the Potosí market. As the owner of a transport company that served that market, this space was Amaru's only possible frame of reference. In reality the uprising was centred on the Potosí region; it could be said that where this region ended, the influence of [José Antonio de] Areche, that is, of Lima, began. This also explains the fact that the abolition of the *mit'a* and the right of Indians to occupy government posts, indeed the emancipation of black slaves, figure among the first points of his programme.[170]

---

populares: Tupac Amaru II, 1780 [Lima: Retablo de Papel, 1976], pp. 11–66; here, p. 15). It is true, moreover, that Condorcanqui filed a legal claim that took four years for his direct descent from the Inca lineage to be recognized. He would not have sought such recognition within the Spanish juridical system had he already had the intention of abolishing it.

168 Dámaso Katari, one of the leaders of the Chayanta rebellion (Boleslao Lewin, *La rebelión de Tupac Amaru* [Buenos Aires: Hachette, 1943], p. 282).

169 'But at the same time the movement became too powerful for the middle and upper classes, which up until then had been their potential allies' (Cornblit, 'Levantamientos de masas en Perú y Bolivia', pp. 112–13).

170 The points of the programme were: (1) the appointment of Indians to administrative positions; (2) the right to travel to Spain without prior

In our view, the subsequent course of events must be explained by programmatic contradictions within the general movement. We can indeed distinguish two wings or tendencies within it. The first is what we might call the peasant or universal branch for the whole of the colonial society (an *Incan* programme for all of Peru), which is that represented by Condorcanqui himself but also by the Rodríguez brothers and even the first Katari, Tomás.[171] The other is the millenarian, militarist and ethnocentric wing, which is directly and rather violently epitomized in the figure of Julián Apaza. And we of course cannot ignore the existence of a sector integrated into colonial society and deeply invested in the status quo, the indigenous reaction constituted by Pumacahua and the 12 ayllus of Cusco.[172] There is, then, a conflict between a general democratic programme, although with an indigenous connotation as its interpellative nucleus, and a radical messianic proposition that swiftly mobilizes armed support.

The military action, as is well known, was concentrated in Apaza's area. Its culmination was the blockade, the constant general siege, of La Paz and Sorata. In La Paz alone, which was then a modest town, 6,000 people died.[173] A number of remarks of a more properly military nature could be made on the subject, for example, on the

permission from the local authorities; (3) access to ecclesiastic ranks; (4) more education for the Indians; (5) the abolition of the Potosí *mita*; (6) the abolition of the *reparto de efectos* [forced distribution of goods] (Rowe, 'El movimiento nacional inca del siglo XVIII', p. 35). Of these points, at least the first four are oriented towards the integration of the Indians within the system, that is, its democratization and not its abolition. As for the last two, the abolition of the *mita* implied a defence of the community because the *mita* had produced the *forasteros*. The sixth point refers to the resistance to forced commercialization.

171 The leaders of the rebellion in Oruro were Spaniards (the Rodríguez brothers), and Tomás Katari had named a Spaniard governor of Tupiza.

172 Indigenous aristocrats such as Pumacahua and Coquehuanca fought against Amaru (Cornblit, 'Levantamientos de masas en Perú y Bolivia').

173 According to Segurola's diary written during the siege (ibid.).

transformation of social quantity into military quality, but the important thing is its repercussions. As an act of re-foundation, there is no
doubt that the rebellion would not have had the same meaning if the
movement had not been split between Apaza's ultimatism and
Amaru's doctrine. In contrast to what happened in Peru, in Charcas
the movement had a global scope that can be ascribed to the fact that
it is within the sphere of Potosí, that is, it was the extension, in the
form of insurgency or war, of the immense depeasantization process
of Potosí. It is also here that a certain temperament, which is that of
the *masses in action*, is founded. The ferocity of Apaza's proclamation
contained its own impracticability, but impossible movements often
found enduring schools. If the idea of mass accumulation is so crucial in Bolivian history it is because it is inspired in this kind of ini-
tiation. After all, the logic of the siege of La Paz resembles that of
Willka in the Federal War.[174] Apaza *educated* the masses in a kind of
democracy of the multitude, a self-determination and irreverence
that would be repeated later in the Fifteen Years' War,[175] with
[Manuel Isidoro] Belzu,[176] and at all their critical moments. The agi-
tated character of the masses would besiege the state, which could
not in its routine existence be anything but this, a state under siege.
This is the importance of this moment in the formation of Bolivian
civil society.

To found a discourse of contestation or an ideology of insubordination, whatever its merits, is not the same thing as to propose a
programme of social reform. Katari ordered the tongues of those
who spoke Spanish in his presence cut out and he is said to have
banned bread because it was not Andean, but Amaru's actions were
far more terrifying because they constituted a concrete project for
the abolition of the seigneurial system in the form in which it existed.

---

174 See Chapter 2 in this volume.

175 José Santos Vargas, *Diario de un comandante de la independencia americana (1814–1825)* (Mexico City: Siglo XXI, 1982).

176 Rigoberto Paredes, *Melgarejo y su tiempo*.

What is significant in this interpellation is its subject.[177] Amaru's was not the only egalitarian project in the history of Peru but an egalitarian project in which the call had as its core the Indian, the only project that called for a nationalization founded on a deep-rooted idea of Peru and not merely on a process of homogenization. Such an egalitarian process, that is, the general constitution of a market of free men, however, must also take into account the form in which it is instituted. To be the recipient of freedom as a concession is not the same thing as to conquer one's own freedom. The interpellative core of the process of nationalization in turn leaves its mark. Here Amaru proposed that equalization be produced under the interpellation of the indigenous, but as a convocation *urbi et orbe*, that is, for all men. Hence the radical character of the Hispanocentric reaction, which was like a reformulation of the Peruvian identity.

A number of conclusions can be drawn from this: that what is decisive militarily is not always effective at the level of the state (Katari); that the differed consequences of the failure of a military project in the constitution of a state can nonetheless be organized or absorbed in the form of habits of equality and self-determination; and finally, that a universalist project, as a result of its very feasibility as a national programme, produces an antithesis at least as powerful as the project itself—but in inverted form. This is what happened in Peru during the War of Independence 30 or 40 years after Amaru. *Peru became a bastion of loyalty to Spain.*[178] These were the decades of forced de-Quechuizaiton, of the foundation of ideological Hispanophilia, and surely that San Martín encountered 'the curious spectacle of the formation of a government for an independent Peru,

---

177 In the Althusserian sense: 'All ideology hails or interpellates concrete individuals as concrete subjects' and "transforms' individuals into subjects (it transforms them all) by that very precise operation which I have called interpellation or hailing' (Althusser, 'Ideology and Ideological State Apparatuses', p. 173).

178 Szeminski, 'La insurrección de Tupac Amaru II'.

made up of the same elements that had governed under Spanish rule'[179] should come as no surprise. Neither events like those of Torre Tagle's presidency nor the extensive enlistment of Peruvians in the royalist armies can be seen as fortuitous or imposed by violence alone.[180] Peru's relation to the Spanish question was quite different from Venezuela's or Mexico's, or even El Plata's. The war, therefore, at least in this context, became largely a confrontation between Charcas and Lima, crystalizing the bifurcation that had become inevitable after the failure of Amaru.[181] Lima would have been vice-regal but not viceroyalist as it in fact came to be, nor would Hispanophilia have become a kind of official religion, nor could one ever have spoken of the 'Indian stain' [mancha india] had Amaru succeeded in carrying through to the end his rare capacity to convoke a national-popular bloc.

This is what we might call the floating form of ideology. The old *junker* path was possible in Germany because Münzer's path had failed. There is a moment of organic uncertainty in which the practice of historical selection defines things for a long time to come and it was clear that here society had to reconstruct itself in Areche's

179 Rowe, 'El movimiento nacional inca del siglo XVIII', p. 53.

180 Bolívar himself, who had said that 'these Peruvians are the most miserable men for war' (21 December 1825) and that he would not mince words on Lima—'Criminal Babylon', 'they see us as the usurpers of Peru', 'a country cursed with a moral plague'—would nonetheless admit of the Indian soldiers of the Spanish forces: 'The excellence of the Spanish army in Peru in marching without losing strength. The loyalist soldiers walk fifteen or twenty leagues a day, and they carry their food in a little coca pouch and in another of barley or cooked or toasted maize' (10 February 1824).

181 The myths about the border have always been very crude. Mitre, for example, believed that Argentina extended up to where a certain kind of man resided. This was not so. The separatist movements in Salta or the Confederation are not born of presumed racial identities nor, of course, of Santa Cruz's head. The sphere of the market that had been centred on Potosí made things seem to be in their natural place.

image and that it wanted to eradicate everything that recalled Tupaj Amaru. It is the history of every ruling class that has been threatened but not destroyed. Where there is a more or less serious crisis (and that of Amaru was extremely serious), the privileged classes have a greater awareness of what can be lost.[182] In other words, the provocation or explicit resolve to change things is felt here in an almost material way and produces a reactionary class consciousness. One who has gained something is less conscious of what one has than is one who has been on the verge of losing everything. Therefore, if Katari was fiercer, more extreme and more terrible than Amaru, the latter embodied a project for all, a utopia that was not merely utopian. The elite saw in it a society that could exist, a kind of national independence that it did not accept even with Bolívar, who represented an enlightened seigneurial project, although of course with a broader total perspective. This is, roughly, the Peru that would come to face Chile in 1879.

Of course it would be a Peru even more corrupted by the bacchanal of the guano boom (Bolivar had said: 'Peru [. . . is marked by two elements that are inimical to any just and liberal regime:] gold and slaves'),[183] which would only exacerbate the scorn of the viceroyalists, and less unified, because with independence the state had lost the centripetal tendencies of the bureaucratic structure that it had under Spanish rule.

---

182 A culture of fear of the Indians emerged after Amaru but this fear had existed previously: 'It had been revealed [to a priest] under the seal of confession that the plan was to attack the Palace and take out the guards at midnight, take the armoury and kill Your Majesty's ministers and principal persons and rise with the city, as the capital of the kingdom; the Indian conspirators demanded the restoration of an ancient empire' (Report to the viceroy Manso de Velasco, cited in Rowe, 'El movimiento nacional inca del siglo XVIII', p. 50).

183 But this was not, as we have seen, the only thing he said about Peru. [Simon Bolívar, *El Libertador: Writings of Simon Bolivar* (Frederick H. Fornoff trans.) (Oxford: Oxford University Press, 2003), p. 27. In Zavaleta's manuscript, Bolivar's famous phrase is condensed to 'Peru, gold and slaves.']

Centralism, or a bureaucratic identity, was for Peru what Potosí was for Charcas in that in each case there was a false unification or unfinished tendency towards an apparent articulation: in the organization of Potosí, the first internal market of what is now Bolivia and the surrounding region, because it disappeared along with its perishable wealth or a market linked not to the social substance that results from continuous exchange but to a contingent material fact; in the Lima system, because the force of the state cannot go beyond the limits of its enforceability and here the bureaucratic form was based not on an intrinsic authority but on external backing from Spain. The mercury crisis had the same divisive effect for Bolivia as independence for Peru.[184] In Bolivia, because the internal market was dependent on an ephemeral product and, on the other hand, because it had to restrict itself to the sphere of depeasantization or of what we are designating as such for the purposes of this study.[185] That is to say, it was dependent on largely fortuitous factors with no capacity for cohesion once the axis or primary cause was destroyed. In Peru, this led to what some have called the *gamonal* form of the state.[186] In other words, for somewhat different reasons, both countries not only were frustrated in their attempts to constitute themselves as nations

184 Tulio Halperín Donghi, *Revolución y guerra: Formación de una élite dirigente en la Argentina criolla* (Mexico City: Siglo XXI, 1972), p. 79.

185 Although it was extensive. We will return to this in the following chapters, especially in reference to the formation of the working class. In our view, the strong *mitima* roots of the pre-Columbian population, the *forasteros* of Amaru's time, the *ccajchas* and *obrajes* played a major part in the construction of the tenets of the proletariat.

186 'Gamonalism, within the central and unitary republic, is the ally and agent of the capital in the regions and provinces' (Mariátegui, *Siete ensayos*, p. 202). Indeed, it would be absurd to reduce the role of gamonalism to one of fragmentation. It was a backward kind of mediation and the gamonal, in a way, was a mediator and functionary of the state. In reality, gamonalism as such was an extra-economic form of extraction of a surplus. Alberto Flores Galindo suggests that we might speak, as Fontana did, of 'an aggregate of isolated rural cells'.

in the modern sense but also regressed with respect to their previous condition. 'The new independent state was incapable of imposing its hegemony at the level of the entire territory called Peru.'[187]

Gamonal mediation, like any other mediation, has no intrinsic value. It is the same as the corporation or the union, which can successively become apparatuses of the state, organs of mediation or counterhegemonic structures.[188] *Mutatis mutandis*, the traditional figure of the *gamonal* might have been a divisive element in Peru— in fact, it had not only fostered anarchy but was also the backward form of centrality of an extremely weak social equation. Once Lima's centrality—based on the colonial pact—was broken, the Peruvian provinces acquired conditions of increased contact with the emerging world market compared to the scattered Bolivian provinces, which had no such contact at all. In a process that bears some resemblance to that of Central America, each region could communicate autonomously with the world and only inefficiently with its own presumed centre.[189] Given the ancestral weakness of the state in Charcas,[190] if the same condition of autonomous geographic access had existed, perhaps the country itself would have fallen apart. In a way, the habits of bureaucratic centralization, to which must be added the further effect of the surplus, saved the unity of Peru through hereditary rule. But the *gamonal* component had to be added to the bureaucratic and seigneurial lustre of the general ideology, while in Bolivia the long stalemate between caudillism and the masses in action permitted only a feeble reconstruction of the

---

187 Alberto Flores Galindo, *Arequipa y el sur andino: Ensayo de historia regional* (*siglos XVII–XX*) (Lima: Horizonte, 1977), p. 46.

188 Against Althusser, for whom all mediation is also a state apparatus.

189 Ernesto Yepes del Castillo, 'Burguesía y gamonalismo en el Perú', *Análisis. Cuadernos de Investigación* (Lima) 7 (1979): 31–66.

190 Gabriel René Moreno, *La Audiencia de Charcas* (The Audience of Charcas) (La Paz: Ministerio de Educación y Cultura, 1970).

seigneurial, which had nearly lost its will to live.[191] In any case, the shift from a centralized power structure to a country of *gamonales* revealed the emergence of the centrifugal form that the state contract had assumed in Peru—a bankrupt form, utterly impotent before the challenges it faced. If this did not happen in Bolivia it is because the *gamonales* were themselves weak in their own impoverished and autarkic regions, reduced to mere subsistence, with no capacity for connection to the world. The society itself, moreover, had gotten used to living in its traditional stalemate. It is the Peruvian *gamonal* form that explains the disunity expressed in the country's three governments at the time of the war (because, in contrast to Chile, which had adopted forms of rational legitimation in the constitution of power with Portales, here there were no such forms at all), its non-transformation into a national war except when the fighting had reached the very heart of the country, even the flight of its president in at the height of the conflict.[192] By this we mean only to say that if Peru and Bolivia had had something even remotely comparable to Chile's social optimum, that is, a fluid relation between the state and society, they would have prevailed on Peruvian territory, even if Chile had a certain superiority in terms of its gross product.[193] To cite a

---

191 Adolfo Ballivián, in his style and person, is an example of a kind of decadence that overtook the traditional aristocracy in Bolivia. José María Linares is really no less representative of this.

192 Basadre, *Historia de la república del Perú*, VOL. 8; Heraclio Bonilla, *Un siglo a la deriva: Ensayos sobre el Perú, Bolivia y la guerra* (Lima: Instituto de Estudios Peruanos, 1980).

193 Economic arguments about military matters are one thing; military arguments about the economy, another. The Chilean 'military investment' was superior in tactical and strategic terms. This was well thought out by the political leadership. Still, the merit of this campaign lay in its low cost relative to the scale of its success. To achieve this, in conditions of any degree of normality or equilibrium, an overwhelming economic superiority would be required. It was the existence or semi-existence at the level of the state of the Peruvian and Bolivian societies that made the war into a kind of target practice.

recent example, it is obvious that the Vietnamese in the context of their war had an optimum superior to that of the United States in that space and in that situation.

Interpretations that attribute the defeat to a servility posited as the predominant mode of existence of the Peruvian-Bolivian population, which has a veiled social-Darwinist connotation,[194] are of little use. Ultimately, the Chileans were no more 'free-born Englishmen'[195] and in the last instance the *Weltanschauung* of its ruling class was as seigneurial and oligarchic as that of its enemies. In reality, a servant and even a slave can be a great soldier—but to be a great soldier, one must believe in servitude or in slavery, that is, there must be a relation of consent. Genghis Khan's men reached the heart of the West and not because his men were free, at least not strictly speaking.

Such is the Peru that was defeated by Chile in 1879. In the following chapter, we will speak more specifically of the Bolivian formation. In any case, it is with Amaru and not with Santa Cruz that the idea of Gran Perú[196] is dissolved. The rebellion or mobilization in effect spans the entire trade circuit that had been built between Lima, Potosí and Buenos Aires,[197] that is, the Potosí–Amarist wellspring was the last chance for the consolidation of the traditional space of the region. Santa Cruz himself later represented no more than an inter-seigneurial proposition, although conserving a certain sense of the traditional territory. The loss of Atacama and the Peruvian provinces was only an extension of that first dislocation.

What matters in the conflict, in its conclusion, is that Chile was able to set tasks equal to its ends while Peru and Bolivia were not. This is what we have been calling the level of the social optimum.

---

194 See Chapter 3 in this volume.

195 See Thompson, 'The Moral Economy'.

196 Oscar Cornblit, 'Levantamientos de masas en Perú y Bolivia'.

197 Flores Galindo, *Arequipa y el sur andino*, p. 17.

CHAPTER TWO

The World of the Fearsome Willka

In the absolute confusion or unease produced by the multiplication of objects in the world, men are alone in the midst of things which are increasing endlessly. Is this not now the solitude of the age, the general fallacy of its identity and, in short, what we might call the second loss of the self?

The era is multitudinous and it is as if it were fleeing from us, as if it always signified something other than itself, lost in the enormous number of its invisible events. Nonetheless, despite continually overwhelming us, it has a weak flank amid this sort of infinite siege and this consists in that it can be known. There is no doubt something astonishing in the fact that the very moment of the explosion of the world's quantity is at once that in which it can be known for the first time. This should lead us already to the distinction between cognizable and incognizable eras, and even between internally cognizable eras and eras that can only be known from the outside or after they have passed. The advent of abstract labour, which serves as the *raison d'être* of our temporality or horizon, ultimately could not but cause certain instances of social quantification and, in this general sense, quantification necessarily contains the assumption of iterability, that is, Bacon's method.

Yet if the quantification of the social remains a promise not wholly fulfilled, on the other hand, abstract labour, or the social substance or substrate, does not. This is something palpable, easily verifiable. The wish to bring Bacon to bear on the problems of society constitutes a desire for certainty that is proper to men who live in uncertainty. This has no doubt led to a closed preserve which is the positivist closure of the social sciences. We must operate with some certainties or at least attempt to construct them. In this respect it is strange that the certainties available to us are but certain aspects of that which is particular in the world, of what we grasp in its pulverization (because multiplication is also a form of atomization), that is, a knowledge by reduction, and, on the other hand, the second certainty arises which is the almost spontaneous, automatic, inevitable certainty of totality. Totalization is not something that has occurred in any prior age.

It seems to us that there are three crucial moments in Marx's thought, which are undoubtedly linked. In the first place, reductive certainty, understood as the originary or essential mode of relation of men to matter, is undoubtedly a process 'in which production is the real point of departure and hence also the predominant moment'.[1] In fact, if the primary event is the encounter between individuals and nature, then what is called a mode of production is already 'a [determinate] mode of expressing their life, a determinate *mode of life*', so that 'what they are, therefore, coincides with their production; both with *what* they produce and with *how* they produce'.[2] This, then, is a kind of fundamental identity, and if the most ancient form of transformation of nature is agriculture, this is why we say that a society is what its agriculture is. And it is here, in the mode of production understood in its strict sense, that is, the elemental relation to the productivity of the land, where we can see the extent to which Bolivian society, for example, still belongs to its constitutive moment. This means, in short, that there was never anything at the level of social distribution or of the superstructure that would affect this kind of inertia of the base.

The methodological strategy of sacrifice, the reduction of the phenomenon to the construction of a thought-concrete, therefore

1 Karl Marx, *Grundrisse: Foundations of the Critique of Political Economy* (Martin Nicolaus trans.) (London: Penguin, 1993), p. 94.

2 Karl Marx and Frederich Engels, *The German Ideology*, PART 1 (New York: International Publishers, 1970), p. 42.

had to occur; self-knowledge could not be produced without a moment of dissolution or separation, that is, of sacrifice. What is radical in Marx, however, does not consist in his deliberation as to the transformation of the world; rather, after the incorporation of a different perspective on the question of historical time, the knowledge that the world would transform itself became inevitable, and is Copernican in that it is a discovery of something that exists.

The substantive idea is undoubtedly the rupture with traditional temporality, that is, the seasonal idea of time, which includes prehistoric hunter-gatherers—man without conscious memory—as well as historical or agricultural man. In reality, in a qualitative sense, it is a question of the abolition of agriculture. Therefore, in what is like the prodrome of expanded reproduction, it is as if man suddenly began to live several lives within the physical-temporal space where he had always lived a single life. It is, in short, a concentration of time. This consists in a set of basic life events, from the extension of the human lifespan to real subsumption, from the subjugation of disease, as a negation of life, to the alteration of the female reproductive cycle, not to mention the spatial effects of concentration, that is, the industrial, urban and national ethos, to the new time of politics, that is, the emergence of the total form of social change, which is the contemporary phenomenon of revolution. This is a sequence whose moments are mutually contained. If real subsumption, for example, as such, *must* be a mass phenomenon, is it not true that it must therefore contain an anthropocentric element? Consequently, the notion of the self or of the modern individual, of the self-determination of the human, of the force of the masses as the application of ancestral experience to productive as well as historical effectivity, of the conscious exercise of human agency, which is therefore a logic of the multitude, all of this necessarily generates forms of intersubjectivity or totalization (here the second proposition has constructed the third) that, if they are strengthened by their self-knowledge, are consummated in a terminus that is conventionally called socialism, which in this case can indeed be considered scientific.

The concentration of time itself works towards collective knowledge as a mass force in the sense that there is a qualitatively different effect that makes accumulated or condensed time behave with a kind of infused certainty in a way that would not have been possible if the same time were conceived over a longer period. This tells us, therefore, that the distinction between cognizable and incognizable or unrepresentable eras is far from an arbitrary one. The acquisition of the concept of abstract labour as a measure of society is therefore an event in itself, and an event that is collectively produced. Let us leave aside the question of whether here a calculability of the social is in fact inaugurated, although there is no doubt that the introduction of accounting within domestic production must be its germ. In any case, what matters here is the emergence of what has been called the social substance or social matter, or at least its concrete revelation. Certainly, as the notes on Wagner indicate, in any age concrete labour could in theory be aggregated to obtain a kind of value, that is, a kind of socially necessary labour. But that, even if we grant that it is possible, could only have something like a statistical existence without any social effect. Here, however, the result, social matter or value, is something that acts upon its causes; without the method of sacrifice it simply would not have been possible to obtain the 'mode of life' with which we take part in the transformation of nature in the form it assumes in our times; this now leads us to ascertain the existence of a new actor, which is a concrete totality or intersubjectivity.

In other words: value as 'something that exists in all forms of society' is therefore composed of imaginary labour in that we must consider incommensurable forms of labour and different kinds of men, with no concrete traces of interaction, that is, labour irreducible to a common term. Here, however, abstract labour in its present form must constitute, at least in principle, a form of labour that somehow contains a whole other form of labour in the sphere of the measurable. It is, then, an interaction on the basis of an equivalent measure that is determined by the postulation of free man as the element or unit of the social.

The construction of the thought-concrete that is totality or at least social totality is only the continuation of this no doubt formidable point of departure that is the *state of separation*[3] or what we might call the interchangeable solitude of capitalist man. This solitude is indeed necessary, and implies a loss of the old identity or self submerged in the small community, so that the new intersubjectivity, which contains the form of totalization proper to this productive age, can be constructed. The production of this social substance is what enables the reduction of social activity, following certain ruptures that can be considered epistemological, to its substantive moment, which is value; but this could not exist as an effectively social and living substance without its unconscious, the inevitable result of so fundamental a totalization, which is the production of discourse or of an organic ideology. Totalization cannot be thought without the constitution of hegemony. The powerful logic of this paradigm is what we might call Marx's relevance for our time.

Totality, however, if it is not an idea that can designate an unstructured sum, cannot in principle mean more than this—that some partialities have had to do with the composition of others and that there is no independence or isolation within this sociohistorical formation. This can still serve as a correct description of what happens with the great events of the age (the nation, the class, the state) without yet describing the distribution of the elements within this totality; this is what [Karel] Kosik called an 'empty totality': 'False totalization [and synthesis] show up in the method of the abstract principle, which leaves aside the wealth of reality, i.e. its contradictory character and its multiple meanings.'[4]

The danger of so comprehensive a construction as that of the principle of totalization is that it tends to find its own validation

---

3 Karl Marx, *Capital: A Critique of Political Economy,* VOL. 2 (David Fernbach trans.) (London: Penguin, 1992).

4 Karel Kosik, *Dialectics of the Concrete: A Study on Problems of Man and World* (Karel Kovanda with James Schmidt trans) (Boston: D. Riedel, 1976), p. 28.

within itself, like in Hegel's metaphor of spheres within spheres. The problem really lies in deciding when we must refer to foundational forms or ultimacy as the nature of the age and when the internal histories or histories of a singular articulation, the ad hoc or simply incommensurable aggregation of a social association or correlation, without one thing becoming useless in relation to the other.

Formal subsumption, for example, contains the most central point of originary accumulation, which is subordination, in that it resolves the anxiety of alienation in a certain sense. This is why the determination of the constitutive moment or interpellation is so radical, so vital, so singular, and not only with regard to the study of the state. It is so decisive an event that it can be said that men live only to formulate an interpellative call or to answer it, or to live that which has been received previously.

Powerful as they are, these categories, however, perhaps like all categories, are slaves to their impossibilities or lacunae. We can speak of a productive regime or of productive labour or of real subsumption or even of a socioeconomic formation but each of these theoretical objects will have occurred in one way or another. Although they contain a thought-concrete of general validity, they inevitably have a history. A man, for example, is never wholly 'alienated' or 'separated'. The formulation *state of separation* or receptivity here is but a principle or, if you will, a *petitio principii*. Ultimately, the same state of separation is produced within a tribe of barbarians whose space has been seized by invaders as through a *farmer*-type accumulation, which is the revolutionary one according to Marx. Likewise, an inherited fortune in the hands of a usurer is, as inherited money, the same material substance as the inherited money of the capitalist before he turns it into productive capital: the difference is in the mind of each, of the miser and of the industrialist. It is one thing for a free man to be produced because he has been expelled by his master for whatever reason and another for him to conquer his freedom through his own will, against that of the master, although in both cases we obtain the same 'free man'. Finally, if by real subsumption we understand only de facto subordination and the internalization or somatization of discipline, we must concede that this can occur through an authoritarian process (because history proves that it is possible to transform one's dispossession into one's own idea of one-self) or through a purely hegemonic process (although it is also true that nothing has ever really occurred through a purely hegemonic process).

If we accept the premise that the closest thing to practice itself is the organized memory of practice, that is, if we agree that knowledge is the archive of past practices, then the idea of the simultaneity of totality must replace that of society as discrete spheres or a structure of structures and empirical, describable objects must at least incorporate theoretical or sacrificed objects. This is why the idea of a general, alocalist theory of the state proves so metaphysical; on the contrary, we could say that a local aggregation, emerging from its own causal chain or simply by chance, determines the form in which these universal-reiterable conditions that affect the history of power are fulfilled. These are the necessary supplements to a system of thought that would otherwise have been closed off in the hermetic universe of its great central ideas; without them, the concept of totality would not be translatable into the concrete. There is no doubt a healthy distance between the idea that 'the history of humanity is the history of class struggle' or the tactical logic of class against class and the *blocco storico* or the concepts of composite average and *irradiation*, but it is no greater than the distance between Marx's concepts of mode of production as *ideal average* and his analyses of socio-economic formations in motion, such as that of the *Eighteenth Brumaire*.

Thus, the appropriation of the world follows the path of a kind of social analysis of history, to the extent, of course, that history does not constitute its own solipsism. We can therefore speak only of a history of the major elements of the era and not of a history of all things. If we consider, again, the question of different paths, how can we explain the fact that the American South did not follow a *junker* path, while the Prussians did? Ultimately, the former was as thoroughly precapitalist as the latter, or as the Meiji, and in all three cases these societies found themselves faced with a fully developed capitalist world. A definition of formal subsumption, then, even if it includes the substitution of traditional temporality and the emptying-interpellation continuum itself, is of little use to us because we would have to determine in the first place who is doing the interpellating and in the name of what world or history it interpellates or why its call is answered, for where an interpellative process succeeds it is reasonable to suppose that others have failed.

Things are of course very different if the productive mentality comes from a kind of man like that which the English process produced, where real subsumption—if we think of Stephenson or Arkwright or so many others—was not just a task of the Enlightenment but also an act or affair of the people. Here, therefore, anthropocentrism is not just a doctrine of do-gooders but also a kind of general impulse or predisposition, while if the interpellation takes place under a parasitic form, for example, that of French usurious capital or the various levels of seigneurialism of the different bourgeois Spanish varieties, the process itself must orchestrate its own reproduction. It is also true that the English have had to pay for the precocious apparent perfection of their capitalist history.

These ideas will be useful as we attempt to describe the character of the Bolivian socioeconomic formation of the last four decades of the nineteenth century. In the previous chapter, we examined the explosive encounter between three social formations and to some extent their historical origins, especially those of Peru and Chile. It is not enough, for example, to say that Bolivia was not capitalist then. We would at least have to inquire into the substantive aspects in which it was in fact precapitalist and those in which it was not, and, if possible, where these different aspects come from. In any case, from even a preliminary study, it was clear that universal categories are of little use in understanding our subject. We came to a kind of aporia because whatever their logico-formal importance (to use a somewhat inadequate terminology) or even in the case of an effective incorporation or thought-concrete, these categories tend towards their own abolition by way of their qualification or contingency. It is a fact that appropriation must always occur in a particular context, even in the case of proven principles. If, as history has so often shown, a heteroclitic interpellation becomes a kind of non-capitalist mode of occurrence of capitalism, we should surely discuss the possible import of unconsciously bourgeois or democratic tasks within movements of a non-capitalist configuration. It is here, where the temptation to renounce a general analysis of particular phenomena is so strong, that we discover the flexible richness of certain intermediate notions or paradigms of inquiry such as the socioeconomic formation or historical bloc.

*

A socioeconomic formation is generally defined as the articulation of various modes of production. With good reason, this term itself—*articulation*—has been disputed because it is certainly not simply an accord between different elements but also the qualification of some by others, in such a way that none of them maintains its prior form. The concept is undoubtedly more complex. Paul Claudel wrote—granted, in a spirit of jest—that France is a thought, that is, something difficult to define but present in synthetic form in almost every man. It is like a complex self-evident fact that is more powerful in its obviousness than the definitions that have been ascribed to it.

Let us turn, with this in mind, to a description of Bolivian society in the nineteenth century:

> The Bolivian panorama in the middle of the nineteenth century is that of an essentially rural and agricultural society (Dalence 1851, pp. 197–230). Of the total of 1,373,896

inhabitants counted in a census during that period without counting the tribes of the Eastern plains, only a third lived in towns and cities. The city of La Paz, the largest and most prosperous commercial centre at the time, had a population of only 42,000. [...] Some 20,000 people were employed in artisanal production, including carpenters, stoneworkers, glaziers, potters, and others (Fellman Velarde 1970: II.113). The tradesmen dedicated to the satisfaction of the limited demand of those centres resented the import economy. Through their instinct of self-preservation, this group, which consisted mostly of mestizos, would support the protectionist measures of the old regime. The artisans, because of their long guild history and urban location and despite their limited numbers, represented an easily mobilizable strategic force in political revolts. [...] The country's ruling class was made up of creole landowners numbering approximately 23,000, including their families. This class, with some 5000 haciendas, owned 50 per cent of the best arable lands and exercised seigneurial control over 160,000 farm labourers (Dalence 1851: 234–7). This tiny group of *hacendados*—1 per cent of the total population—lived in the cities whence they directed the political and economic life of the nation. What is known as 'Bolivian history' of the nineteenth century refers largely to the activities of this class. On the opposite extreme were approximately half a million *comunario* Indians—close to 35 per cent of the population—who lived in more or less isolated *pueblos* occupying roughly 20 per cent of the arable land. Between these two poles were relatively numerous intermediate groups of indigenous and mestizo tenant farmers (360,000, including their families) and smallholders (160,000, including their families).[5]

5 Mitre, *Los patriarcas de la plata*, pp. 56–7. References in the passage are to: José María Dalence, *Bosquejo estadístico de Bolivia* (Chuquisaca: Ymprenta

An analysis of this excellent summary by Antonio Mitre shows
that the basic conflict was between a tradesmen-*comunario* axis and
the landowners. If mining, which is the quintessentially precapitalist
activity in that it precedes capitalism because it tends towards it, is
absent here, it is because of the 'chronic deficit of the trade balance
[that is, a virtual disappearance from the world market] and the
growing demonetization of the economy'—that is, the regression of
the embryonic domestic market that had been constituted around
Potosí. It is also clear that the class struggle emerges between the
countryside and the city or, rather, between the countryside allied
with a minority faction within the city and the city linked to a power
system rooted in the *pueblos* (which here means something very different from in Mexico, as is the case with the hacienda).

It is easy, however, to say of France that it is a thought. Here there
is an assumption of something that has been thought in common or
a thinking of France that has become that of all Frenchmen. Most
likely, it is a combination of the encyclopedists, Robespierre and
Napoleon. In any case, whether it is an ideological fact or not, nobody
doubts that this social body spans history from the Gauls to the post-
revolutionary Frenchmen, through slavery, feudalism and capitalism;
here the formation is defined by an identity that cuts across its development, its articulation. On this very point, for example, Bolivian
views of Bolivia differ from one another: from [Ernesto] Sanabria's,
which is in reality [Gabriel René] Moreno's—'Bolivianness in the
sense of a society with its own characteristics, self-aware and capable
of attaining the formal position of a nation-state, whose origins are
more recent and begin with the organization of the colonial Spanish
province known as New Toledo or Upper Peru or, more properly,
Charcas'[6]—to that of the Bolivian massif[7] or Tamayo's ideas, or those

---

de Sucre, 1851); José Fellman Velarde, *Historia de Bolivia, tomo II: La Bolivianidad semifeudal* (La Paz: Los Amigos del Libro, 1970).

6 Hernando Sanabria Fernández, 'Preámbulo' in Moreno, *La Audiencia de
Charcas*, p. 9.

7 Mendoza, *El macizo boliviano*.

that can be culled from the works of Murra, Choy and Condarco. This theory of the sterility of the non-Spanish inheritance is connected in its more or less Darwinist sense to Arguedas' theses, which, in essence, are nothing but those of José Antonio de Areche. In any case, if Bolivia is a thought, it is no doubt as a result of a certain prolonged coexistence of contradictory conceptions of its own formation.

The problem here lies in determining to what point it is legitimate to conduct a genetico-structural analysis of an existing formation; in other words, if it is true that the domestication of the potato, for example, in the way that Marx speaks of those formations whose base is constituted by communal property now dissolved, has something to do with Bolivia's present. It must be said here not only that the communal forms have not been dissolved by the (hypothetical) nucleus of irradiation, but also that, even to the extent that this has occurred, which is slight, they could not be dissolved without the nucleus that irradiates or suppresses preserving a certain residue or partial determination by the very thing that it irradiates or suppresses. Of course we cannot dismiss the problem posed by Sanabria, which is the question of the plausibility of the juridical origins of the formation, with the stroke of a pen. We could say that the organization of the highest spheres of the juridico-political system in fact comes from the Audiencia of Charcas, but this means only that it was the superstructure of the Potosí market; the Potosí market in turn was a particular form of mercantilization that surely had to adapt to the principles of the primordial formation, which is that which the Spaniards encountered at the time of conquest. If the point of departure is defined in so voluntarist a way, that is, if it refers to the current Bolivian nation-state, it could just as well be said that its project is unfinished as that it began with independence as the juridico-official moment of its existence. It's obvious that for the purposes of a social history like that which we propose to write, 'Bolivia' itself is but a moment in a much longer progression.

It is Sereni who, unsurprisingly as an important theorist of the national question, refers to the 'socioeconomic formation' as a synthetic-totalizing formulation: 'Generally used to designate not so much the process of formation of society in general as that of a particular society or succession of societies, or, as it were, the final result of this process,'[8] and, on the other hand, as a combination of different levels of analyses: 'This category expresses the unity [and we would add, totality] of the different spheres—economic, social, political, and cultural—of the life of a society; and it expresses it, moreover, in the continuity and at the same time in the discontinuity of its historical development.'[9]

What this notion says, therefore, is that not only can the social world be understood as a totality, and a totality that can be known, but also that the social substance that emanates from it (from totalization) can and in reality must be translated into the events, great or small, but significant, that make up its internal history. In other words, through a prescience à la Claudel, Mexico is Mexico, from the despotic-tributary system to the colonial system, to that of the Republic, that of Porfirism and that of the bourgeois revolution.

Moreover, there is no doubt that in Mexico there are at least two modes of production and its character is determined, therefore, by the pattern of articulation and irradiation. Industrialization, for example, can take place without a process of intellectual reform and in this case the conditions of the fundamental productive force that is the worker will be similar to those of servitude or slavery: a speaking tool. The same elements or modes of production, therefore, can be co-inserted in one way or another, in one proportion or another and with different degrees of irradiation. As a result of the depth of the bourgeois revolution understood as intellectual reform, French smallholding, for example, in no way implied a

---

8 Emilio Sereni, *La categoría 'formación económica y social'* (Mexico City: Roca, 1973), p. 59.

9 Ibid., p. 69.

spiritual resistance to capitalism. Meanwhile, smallholding in Bolivia or Peru was regarded as a true act of rebellion against the state because it prevented its appropriation of the surplus.

Ultimately, even countries that are identical in terms of their mode of production, in the collective form of transformation or appro-priation of nature (for example, Argentina, England and France), will have wholly different logics in their symbolic or politico-liturgical attributes, that is, in their superstructural effects and, above all, in the constitution of the state. It goes without saying, of course, that very different superstructures can nonetheless fulfil the same function enabling and guaranteeing reproduction, and this is why while the 'isolation of social relations from the relations of production' explains the new unity of the history of the world, an analysis of the superstructural level and of the socioeconomic formation itself refers to its qualitative diversity. In other words, if a law of correspondence between base and superstructure exists, history itself is a struggle between that law and the broken or oblique form of its fulfilment; if the superstructure has a kind of temperament or idiosyncrasy in its mode of relation to the base, all this is but part of the history of the complex form of belonging that connects the mode of production, as an isolation of the primary act, to its phenomenon or apparition, which is the superstructure, and the emergence of a particular totality, which is the socioeconomic formation.

*

Just as it is said that the Italians grafted commercial capital onto Spain[10] (although it could also be said that they grafted the impossibilities of Italian commercial capital onto Spain), there is no doubt that primitive forms of capitalism existed in Potosí from the beginning. 'The economic system is controlled by those who control the means of circulation';[11] from the beginning there is a predominance

---

10 Pierre Chaunu, *La España de Carlos V* (Barcelona: Península, 1976).

11 Juan Carlos Garvaglia, Introduction to Carlos Sempat Assadourian et al., *Modos de producción en América Latina*, p. 8.

of commercial capital over productive capital which, moreover, is capitalist only in an imperfect way (incomplete formal subsumption, only a primitive form of real subsumption).

The necessary forms of alienation would inevitably be produced; the production of free workers and even the forced introduction of wages would ensue. This is a typical *imperative form* of construction of free men.

> The *cuatequil* or the system of forced wage labor that was to develop on a much larger scale in Peru under the name of *mita* [. . .] a system of compulsory wage labour [. . .] in the end became the chief *source* of labour in the colony.[12]

And:

> In Potosí 708 men entered the mines every day. They worked for one week and had two weeks off [. . .]. They were *mingas* for the most part, that is, free Indians who were voluntarily employed, and *mitayos*, forced to work for a fixed salary.[13]

But our task here, in the context of this history, is to define the Bolivian socioeconomic formation first during the War of the Pacific, which was like its day of judgement, but even more importantly, at the moment of the general national crisis that was the Federal Revolution. We can pose a number of questions, although they may seem somewhat academic:

Why is it that Potosí, which supplied the conditions of possibility for circulation and even the price revolution and the depreciation of fixed rents, without which European capitalism would not have been

---

12 Silvio Zavala, *New Viewpoints on the Spanish Colonization of America* (Philadelphia: University of Pennsylvania Press, 1943), pp. 93–7. Cited in A. G. Frank, *Mexican Agriculture, 1521–1630: Transformation of the Mode of Production* (Cambridge: Cambridge University Press, 1981), p. 128.

13 Pedro Santos Martínez, *Las industrias durante el Virreinato (1776–1810)* (Buenos Aires: Eudeba, 1969), p. 117.

possible (Potosí, in a Toynbeean sense, is therefore a Western phenomenon), did not become capitalist itself?

Why did Spanish domination of agriculture not produce a 'Spanish' transformation of agriculture?

Why, in the silver mines themselves, if there was an owner of the means of production and a buyer of labour power, did neither the buyer nor the seller become capitalist, strictly speaking?

The facts tell us that even if we suppose that a formally capitalist sector existed, there was never a formally capitalist environment. In other words, what capitalist elements there were in Bolivia were always determined by that which was not capitalist. In reality, the capitalists themselves were invested not in bourgeois values but in the symbols of the seigneurial world.

The bulk of capital was reinvested in land. The silver miners, gradually displaced from mining and commerce, used their money to acquire rural properties and build extravagant palaces in keeping with the seigneurial way of life that they enjoyed. Pacheco bought numerous estates in the city of Sucre [. . .] Arce, at the end of the nineteenth century, found himself in possession of a number of haciendas—La Barca, La Lava, Santa Rosa, La Oroya—and several houses in Sucre and Potosí. [. . .] In the outskirts of the city of Sucre were the famous Palacio de la Glorieta de los Argandoña and the sumptuous La Florida property, built by Arce, 'where French cooks presided over gigantic ovens, European grooms watched over the stables, [. . .] black overseers, corpulent and lustrous, [. . .] travelled the roads on horseback seeing to the needs of that bustling hive of activity.'[14]

They were, then, a bourgeoisie with a pre-bourgeois mentality, which can perhaps be explained by Kula's observation that 'the delimitation of two sectors [. . .] does not lead to a classification of the

---

14 Mitre, *Los patriarcas de la plata*, p. 110.

different enterprises in two categories, but often occurs within each';[15] the ruling class had a split soul in which capitalist and pre-capitalist elements coexisted.

This has been explained on the basis of the premise that 'an interest in the land as a marketable asset for the acquisition of small-scale capital runs parallel to the interest in maintaining a stable income', which would prevent us from 'falling into purely superstructural explanations that attribute the agricultural backwardness of the country solely to the feudal 'mentality' of its ruling class'.[16]

There was, then, a certain rationality proper to to the seigneurial stratum or substrata. We can counter this in this way: if the most primitive horizon of visibility of the bourgeoisie is assumed, the world is conceived from the perspective of profit, and profit, therefore, can just as well come from usury or from the capitalist use of slavery, which indeed conforms to a certain style of rationality.

This recalls [Eugene] Genovese's argument about the American South:

In the South extensive and complicated relations with the world market permitted the growth of a small commercial bourgeoisie. The resultant fortunes flowed into slaveholding, which offered prestige and economic and social security in a planter-dominated society. [Independent merchants found their businesses dependent on the patronage of the

---

15 Witold Kula, *Teoría económica del sistema feudal* (Mexico City: Siglo XXI, 1979), cited in Juan Carlos Garavaglia, 'Un modo de producción subsidiario: la organización económica de las comunidades guaranizadas durante los siglos XVII–XVIII en la formación regional altoperuana-rioplatense' in Carlos Sempat Assadourian, Ciro Flamarión S. Cardoso, Horacio Ciafardini, Juan Carlos Garavaglia and Ernesto Laclau, *Modos de producción en América Latina* (Buenos Aires: Siglo XXI, 1973), pp. 161–92.

16 Silvia Rivera Cusicanqui, 'La expansión del latifundio en el Altiplano boliviano: Elementos para la caracterización de una oligarquía regional', *Allpanchis: Revista de Pastoral Andina* 13 (1979): 189–218; here, p. 196.

slaveholders.] The merchants either became planters themselves or assumed a servile attitude towards the planters.[17]

Seigneurial reason, however, was not bourgeois reason and, in
any case, it was not rationalistic; it is a rationality internal to the irrationalist premise of the existence of a caste. The notion of a feudal
'mentality', therefore, although it is perhaps too convenient an explanation, nonetheless has real objective validity. Even what was
obtained through capitalist activity was squandered in a seigneurial
fashion. The reason for this was none other than the nonexistence,
even as a remote project, of intellectual reform. It is easy, moreover,
to see the extent to which political power, ideology and juridical and
daily life were nothing like their capitalist models. After all, the Indians were forced to pay the indigenous tribute simply because they
the were Indians, that is, because of their racial status. This was a
national tax on the Indians. One could not ask for a more structural
example of legal inequality.

There is no need, at least for now, to focus on the remote origins
of capitalism in Bolivia. This is a task that requires further empirical
research which should take into account the various forms of disarticulation or alienation that the population experienced even before
the Spaniards as well as the consequences of that kind of bootlegging
racket that was the colonization of the east, and the fleeting nature
of the subsequent surplus, with no process of accumulation. We can,
however, discern the forms of the current stage of capitalism, which
emerges, let us say, in the sixth decade of the nineteenth century (and
indeed this has been done). The origin of this bourgeoisie, that of
the silver mines, is no doubt the latifundia; or, more precisely, it is
the small hacienda, that is, 'a sector of the oligarchy that was much
less differentiated [than the large landowners], which involved a vari-
ety of activities among which the most stable was the hacienda'.[18]

---

17 Eugene Genovese, *The Political Economy of Slavery: Studies in the Economy
and Society of the Slave South* (New York: Pantheon Books, 1965), p. 20.

18 Rivera Cusicanqui, 'La expansión del latifundio en el Altiplano boliviano',
p. 213.

Of this there is doubt: the only stable business in Bolivia was the Indians. We should add that this caste's only innate and unrenounceable belief has always been the conviction of its superiority over the Indians, a non-negotiable belief, with or without liberalism, with or without Marxism.

The precapitalist trap, moreover, was only comparable to the social siege laid by the Indians. Consequently, the surplus from the small hacienda and from trade, especially that of luxury goods, was the basic source of the 'capital' of men like Aramayo or Arce. In any case, as Genovese said, 'the road to power lay through the plantation'.[19]

Even in the mines, the workers were paid as far as possible in kind, that is, in products that often came from their employers' lands. And this was not the only precapitalist or protocapitalist aspect. The *ccajchas*, for example, functioned in a way that resembles what has been called the *putting-out system*. They were own-account (petty-bourgeois) workers commercially subordinated to capital but with no *productive* relation to it, in the sense that they did not work under its command. The 'voluntary *mita*' or *doblada* are certainly not capitalist forms of exploitation or recruitment. It is reasonable to maintain that, from the very moment the Spaniards set foot on these lands, the most consistent precapitalist element is the theft of labour power. All the phases of capitalism to this day have been based on this logic of appropriation and this translates, naturally, into demographic indices.

In any case, 'inclinations' or great existential choices prove most eloquent when it comes to the miners' vision of the world, granted only as the upper echelon of the dominant bloc. Theirs were not bourgeois sentiments. They are related, on the one hand, to the almost obsessive association with foreign capital (Chilean or British or French), and, on the other, to investment in land. The two great phases of originary accumulation in Bolivia (the silver and tin surpluses), then, involve at once the insertion of Bolivian capitalism in

19 Genovese, *The Political Economy of Slavery*, p. 29.

imperialist capital and the reactionary reconstitution of land tenure, both aspects of great importance, as we shall see. Xenophilia here is a school of thought and not just a method of economic management. This makes sense because the oligarchy is not only dominant but also foreign for a long time and in a way it maintains a sense of being in a country to which it nonetheless does not belong. The oligarchic caste failed definitively in the task of becoming rooted in the land, although it is also true that it has lost all connection to a lineage. Evoking vague symbols, its stunned spirit is trapped in a kind of reminiscence of its foundation on this soil and knows only that it must submerge itself at all times in a power that comes from outside (because its power has always been backed from the outside) and, above all, and this is its true religion, that it must maintain its supremacy over the Indians. It is an abhorrence without end.

As for the prestige of landownership, its relation to social status, it is not difficult to discern its origin. It is the function of the *ancestral home*. Here, however, it assumes a particular form because the land operates as a social fetish. There is a radical disregard for productive practice. The function of the lord is vertical. He is a state functionary who collects the surplus and, in turn, impedes the peasants' access to the market. The market and the world must exist through the lord. This, however, is what gives the system a kind of rationality:

> Most of the elements of irrationality were irrational only from a capitalist standpoint. The high propensity to consume luxury goods, for example, has always been functional (socially if not economically rational) in aristocratic societies, for it has provided the ruling class with the facade necessary to control the middle and lower classes.[20]

*

Hence the somewhat tiresome tone assumed in the recurring debates over free trade and protectionism, considered true historical parties

---

20 Ibid., p. 18.

at least over the course of the nineteenth century—protectionists, *crucistas* and *belcistas*; free traders, *ballivianistas*, *linaristas*, the 'reds' and the conservatives. The doctrine of free trade and its historical party triumphed decisively, with everything that this party contained, which was not, of course, only free trade. Here a programme and even a human group as such, a part of the oligarchy as a whole, comes out victorious and is given the chance to put its conception of the world into practice. One might reasonably ask if this history would have been very different if their enemies had prevailed, but this is a purely academic question and it's pointless to speculate about the counterfactual.

The debate in itself is insubstantial. However, its terms are suggestive: 'Under [protectionism] it was a question of concretely supplanting a technical insufficiency and weakness with the afore-mentioned measures, of prolonging the agony of colonial industrial production, based on feudal servitude and *gamonalismo*.'[21]

Of course, if protectionism is not attended by intellectual reform or a substantive embourgeoisement of beliefs and habits, it is nothing but the protection of backwardness. Marx said this most emphati-cally. But the context must be taken into account. The truth is that no latecomer has ever industrialized without protectionist policies. In the *reductio ad absurdum* of these positions, one would have to hand countries over to imperialism in order to accelerate the global development of the forces of production. But what good would it do to develop a country's forces of production if it is no longer a nation? There is a tendency to take the side of free trade or protectionism as if these were final objectives, of value in themselves. What is impor-tant, rather, is the subject of free trade or protectionism and the moment in which one policy or the other is applied. The British or the Americans alternate between the two in their economic history, the only constant being their national interest or self-referentiality,

---

21 Guillermo Lora, *Historia del movimiento obrero boliviano*, VOL. 1 (La Paz: Los Amigos del Libro, 1967), p. 80.

which is, as we have seen, one of the aspects of bourgeois transformation that did not come to fruition here. It is Machiavelli who made the world revolve around the *raison d'état*, which is to say, the reason of the nation-state and of sovereignty. 'The "conquest of the desert" between 1840 and 1870 fused Chilean and European interests in such a way that their conceptual separation proves problematic.'[22]

A 'conceptual separation' of Arce and the Chileans was equally impossible. The proof of this lies in that he did not hesitate to impose protectionist measures, but in favour of Chilean trade, after Bolivia's defeat. A nation, in short, favours peace when peace is to its benefit and war when war will strengthen it. It will therefore choose free trade or protectionism depending on its ends and for this it first has to desire itself, to determine itself.

Marx, of course, defended protectionism in other circumstances. In any case, a reading of Marx through literal and scattered citations is impossible because there are certainly more than a few cases in which his diatribes are intermixed with his arguments. And we must also take into account the constraints of his time. We could say that the myth of indefinite progress enveloped everything then, including, of course, at least at certain moments, Marx himself. It was the idea that the development of the forces of production, through their quantitative expansion, would entail necessary qualitative changes, that progress would correct history's vices. The privileging of production in socialist experiments and the deferral of the political tasks of socialism is to some extent part of this legacy. In any case, Marx's prognosis that British investment in India would result not only in the development of the forces of production but also in the bourgeois revolution itself was an economistic and linear idea; British capitalism in India in fact deepened the precapitalist and ossified caste system; when India came to face its bourgeois revolution, it had to do so against the caste system and against the British.

---

22 Mitre, *Los patriarcas de la plata*, p. 93.

We are therefore more interested in studying the men, the classes, the contents and politics behind protectionism and free trade—in other words, not what free trade or protectionism are in the abstract but what they have been historically in Bolivia. We would also have to consider the transformations within each party because Santa Cruz, the founder of protectionism, liberalized his party when he needed British support for the Confederation, and Palmerston respected him but not as the leader of a protectionist party. Linares, meanwhile, adopted protectionist measures although he is indisputably the founder of the creed of free trade.

Santa Cruz and Belzu, on the other hand, were protectionists of very different sorts. While Santa Cruz's protectionism was geared towards to the owners of the workshops, and combined with a reactionary agrarian policy, Belzu's was something else: 'Through the mouths of superiors [. . .] the savage sensations, passions and fears of the mestizo masses of that society emerged from below.'[23]

Belzu represented, then, as Moreno notes, protectionism for artisanal production, slanted towards an appeal to the artisans themselves, and beyond this, nothing less than an alliance between the populist military faction, the artisans and the Indian peasant mobilization. In any case, it is entirely obvious that Belzu's protectionism included the masses and trade liberalism did not. That Belzu represented and desired the mobilization of the masses completely changes the nature of his protectionism. It was not, then, simply a hostile defence of regressive productive techniques. In essence, *Belcismo* expressed the domestic market to which the interpellative process centred in Potosí gave rise and perhaps in its rough outlines it was a programme with an economic content similar to that of Amaru's movement. In any case, to deny the 'mestizo masses' of the artisans the defence of their production would in effect be equivalent to a denial of the communities' right to fight for their survival. These

---

23 Gabriel René Moreno, *Bolivia y Argentina: Notas biográficas y bibliográficas* (Santiago: Imprenta Cervantes, 1901), p. 320.

were conservative acts of desperate masses and it's true that their victory would have led to a wretched fate, but this does not make their enemies right.

We have, on the other hand, what we might call the unconscious tasks of history. As we shall see when we review the conditions of the formation of the modern multitude in the twentieth century, this, the multitude, does not exist in itself but in the form of its determination. In general, it is said that the crisis of the state and, above all, its hegemonic fraying is the aperture through which the constitution of the multitude emerges. Belzu, like Katari, interpellated the masses. It's true that the Bolivian masses have a tumultuous and violent character, like Katari; they would thereafter be *belcistas* in a paradigmatic way, with their cult of spontaneity and the notion that the movement creates itself. In any case, for whatever reason, the introduction of the masses into history precipitated by Belzu (although not only by him) is what gives the period its true dimensions because it is part of the acquisition of a temperament.

Belzu, therefore, like Amaru and Katari, was the bearer of a progressive rallying flag in an objective sense. This does not require even that the objective tasks coincide with a consciousness of them. The artisans, for example, were an objectively more advanced force than other sectors of Bolivian society at the time. Like the *forasteros* of the countryside, they exhibited different levels of a *state of separation*. There is an important distinction to be made here. The *forastero* is literally detached from his traditional connection to the land; his condition in agriculture itself is already the condition of a man who has broken his ancestral ties because he is either in a land that is not his or that is his without imposing upon it the general paraphernalia of ideologemes that come with ancestral belonging. The artisan, meanwhile, is an individual and, if he has not been separated from his means of production, he benefits from the relative concentration of the city; he is an urban, or concentrated, individual. *Forasteros*, *ccajchas*, *belcista* artisans are part of the social legacy out of which the proletariat would later emerge.

We must keep in mind this question of the internal market as school. That is, the internal market is internal because it refers to itself or at least tends towards self-referentiality. It is a web of interests that want to be consolidated. We are of course speaking here of a market that was in the process of being dissolved, of what was left of this market after the conquest of the ports by British trade. However, two aspects of Belzu's actions warrant our attention. In the first place, the precocious recognition of the agitative, sometimes overwhelming role that the masses would assume in the history of the country, that is, the early detection of a factor that could never be ignored thereafter. This categorically contradicts the fantasy of the suppression or mediation of the multitude, which is proper to the political thought of the social Darwinists. The second is related to self-determinative tendencies. Perhaps because of the exogenous extraction of those who came from Europe to occupy a privileged position, perhaps because they were always few in number and with the threat from within they had to appeal continually for help from outside, whatever the reason, it is a fact that the oligarchy had no impetus towards self-determination. On the contrary, perhaps with the exception of Santa Cruz, when it comes to matters of sovereignty, it has always acted with absolute cowardice, as though surrendering from the outset—and this is true even today. In any event, in his relationship with Bustillo, in regard to the Chilean question, in his difficult relations with Lloyd, the British minister, and even with Brazil, although his general project lacked a vision of its subsequent development, it is unquestionable that Belzu had clear ideas about the conflicts that awaited Bolivia in the future.

We might say that the history of the country, those tensions that had sedimented within a sociability so little given to eclecticism, had sketched out the context of two parties, at once fundamental and fundamentalist, so that whatever occurred beyond their limits, whether it assumed the form of caudillism or of juridico-formal (constitutionalist, etc.) disputes, was but the superstructure or phenomenon of a deeper struggle. From even a minimally impartial perspective, we must recognize that each of these parties or class factions retained its position within the social order and that they were situated at entirely different ranks, just as they differed in their objectives in terms of their followings and even styles of action and, ultimately, in their whole conception of things. Still, both organized their inimical, contradictory existence within the same civil society. There was, of course, in the popular party a natural tendency to see everything from an inland perspective and there is no doubt that the seigneurial bloc, as we have seen, by blood, by virtue of its spiritual inheritance and by the most implacable necessities of group instinct, tended to see the world outside its borders as a source of civilization and of certainty. Still unstructured and with an overwhelming burden of collective unconscious contents, the two projects, nonetheless, had been born here and of the contradictions of this place, and they were therefore the legitimate offspring of the history of this society. From this point of view, it surely makes no sense to label the plebeian project as national and the elite, seigneurial project as inherently antinational, and such a claim merely demonstrates an affiliation or prejudice. Xenophilia was certainly the characteristic feature of *melgarejismo* before and after Melgarejo and for all practical purposes Arce's appeasement so closely approximated total desertion that he could scarcely be differentiated from that ferocious soldier. For this caste, however, the Indians were not only not the soul of the nation but also the fundamental obstacle to its existence.

We might attempt a rough summary of this antagonism as follows: A protectionist seigneurial current, that of Santa Cruz or that which he embodied at least in his early period, was added over the long term to a bloc made up of the artisanal sectors, bound by a solid legacy whether or not it was viable as the embryo of a capitalist project, and by the interests of the traditional peasantry that then and for a long time after would revolve around the defence of the communities, which is what they had fought tooth and nail to preserve of the past. This bloc, complex in its totality, is bonded by the *cement* that was the *weak currency*, a false solution which was nonetheless the only one possible, and had no chance of coming to power until it intersected with the division, through Belzu, of the repressive apparatus that was then the whole state or almost the whole state. Immediate violence was in reality the only manifestation of the force of that state that had not managed to solve its most basic problems.

We have, on the other hand, the seigneurial party organized around the general principle of free trade. It consists of landowners who in their origins belong to either the core of the seigneurial or to its fringe, who accumulate wealth by way of commercial capital, through which they are linked to the *dynamic zones* of British influence, Chile in particular, that had developed within the logic of the replacement of an economy of state monopolies and interior centres by one of ports, which signals the passage from colony to independence, especially following the Peace of Utrecht. It would perhaps be useful to add some remarks here on the seigneurial as nucleus, and its fringe or periphery. No ruling class or caste exists in isolation; it must have a kind of 'reserve army' or area of irradiation surrounding it. If it has been said that the ideas of the ruling class are 'in every age the ruling ideas', it is because, whatever their degree of latent legitimacy, their hegemonic reach or seductive capacity as a discourse must at least reach the area called the 'effective majority' within the sphere of the state, that is, the decisive areas in terms of social control. It is the sector of oligarchic reinforcement. This is what explains the easy relations between Melgarejo and Adolfo Ballivián or between poor hidalgos like Arce and Pacheco and the Aramayos—that is, from a long-term perspective, the oligarchy is the nucleus that emits the seigneurial interpellative call along with all those who believe in it and, above all, its margin of recruitment or reserve. It is important to take into account here the draw of upward mobility via politics or economic accumulation. Neither Montes nor Barrientos belonged to the seigneurial elite but only to its area of credibility or co-optation, which cannot include truly popular men. It is a sector equivalent to what Genovese calls that of the 'poor whites'.

If projects arise out of the nature of things, if reality itself organizes them, this is nonetheless something that requires organic
thinkers. Here it was certainly a task that demanded a concerted effort
because it unified a sector that was deeply submerged in *gamonalismo*
—in an absolute particularism—around an objective, which required
that it generate desire and the universality of consensus within the
class. That indeed such a project was organized in this way three
times—first with Melgarejo and the conservatives, then with the
Federal Revolution and, finally, with the democratic Revolution of
1952—speaks to the vitality of the seigneurial caste. In the process
of this programme of reconstruction, we see the element of decision,
the presence of the factual and the contingent in the central ideological construct of a political project. It would seem here that the oligarchy for an instant abandons the erratic style that had defined it
until then. Melgarejo, for example, was a caudillo and so was Belzu,
which means that the concept of the caudillo as such has no specificity in itself, because Melgarejo was savagely reactionary and Belzu
was a caudillo of the masses. In any case, the 'reds', although they
resorted to the most degenerate forms of corruption, and although
they gladly took refuge in systemic impunity and generalized violence
with Melgarejo, had previously resorted to a cathartic and ethicist
programme with Linares, which proclaimed a silent dictatorship as
a path of purification. Ultimately, they would inherit [Tómas] Frías
[Amettler]'s constitutionalist project, which was the first minimally
viable proposition of rationally verifiable forms of power.

In the middle of this clamour of ambitions, desertions and
atrocities, what was clear is that a programme was growing in the
belly of this class. This teaches us that a party's programme can only
be seen ex post, when it has been realized. What one says of oneself
is indeed not so important as what one carries within oneself, the
force of one's determinants, which are almost never consciously
known. Arce's or Pacheco's official and general practice of bribery
was the execution of Frías' programme. This was inevitable because
one who does not have consent must buy it. This stage, that of the

pseudoverifiable formation of power, would last a long time—with some variations, until 1978. This continual practice of electoral fraud and bribery, which was like a fools' game in which one is convinced of having won after having given himself the marked card, would last as long as it did because of a strange circumstance. Frías' proposal meant only that the success of the purely factual mode of enunciation of power was over. The stubborn application of these principles demonstrated, however, that even corrupt elections could have a certain effect of legitimation in a way that pure factual power does not.

All this, however, was nothing more than the theatrics of charlatans and casuits. With Melgarejo, who was implacable and corrupt, or with Linares, who was pure and implacable, with Ballivian, who had been legitimately elected but by no more than four families, or with Pacheco and Arce, electoral fraudsters in the truest sense, the ascendent programme was the reconstruction of the oligarchic caste and the terms of its material existence in the world; this, with regard to its two central ventures that were mining—with all that this implied in addition to itself—and that kind of conquest of the land that was the double expansion of the latifundia, along with everything it entailed.

*

To sum up: to say that the people contains the nation or is the nation itself is true only in the sense that if the nation does not include the whole people it is not truly national. To be a nation is to recognize all as the same, in some measure and in a particular habitat. This, however, would be a romantic version of nationalization, which is often a far more imperative and authoritarian event. It would seem logical to posit a process in which men act together to produce something common to all but not specifically corresponding to any of them. This is what best approximates the democratic revolution understood as a national revolution. It is a somewhat chimerical idea. In reality, nationalization has occurred through passive revolution, by the *junker* path, and of course there have been reactionary or forced nationalizations, just as there have been processes of nation-alization through a negative hegemony, and peoples tend to be the belated protagonists of processes to which they have been summoned under strictly enforced predefined terms. The statist constitution of the nation no doubt has to do with this kind of process.

We can say then that in principle there was no reason to deny the Arce–Baptista (Montes, etc.) project a certain national significance, although placing at its apex or point of convocation the seigneurial caste in the flesh. In their conception, of course, few programmes are intrinsically perverse. The past weighs heavily on men, however, and we can see how much good it did the generation of 1880 in Argentina, for example, to have almost no past. The depravity of its dissolute and treasonous history marked this project in a way that we could call *melgarejista*, in its inward vision—the land problem—as well as in the way in which it saw the 'other', that is, the foreigner. We might say that the former consisted from start to finish in taking all they could and the second in turning over to foreign hands whatever was asked.

The first legal measures of this virtual expropriation of the indigenous communities in favour of white and mestizo landowners, which translated into a feudalization of the countryside at least in the most populated areas of the country, were enacted by Melgarejo in 1866 but continued uninterrupted well into the twentieth century.

Consequences were quick to follow. Just a few years later, Santiváñez could write this:

These great accumulations (of landed property, acquired through the plunder of the *comunarios*) are precisely a con-sequence of the law of the 20th of September. Six or seven hundred landowners had replaced 75,000 *comunario* fami-lies; and if, as the defenders of this law affirm, the value of community lands rose to 40 or 50 million, it is clear that, having sold more than three-quarters of it, 700 landowners were worth 30 or 40 million previously held by 75,000.[24]

---

24 Cited in Luis Antezana Ergueta, 'La reforma agraria campesina en Bolivia (1956–1960)', *Revista Mexicana de Sociología* 31(2) (1969): 261.

We might say that it was a general seizure of the territory of one class by another and, indeed, in large measure, of one race by another.

Silvia Rivera [Cusicanqui] notes, in accordance with available data on the expansion of the feudal agrarian regime in the provinces of Pacajes of the department of La Paz between 1881 and 1920, which is the period that interests us:

> 8.4 per cent of the buyers acquired 66.8 per cent of the land, while what we might call the 'middle' stratum, which constituted 20.6 per cent of the total buyers, acquired 26.1 per cent of the land and the remaining 71 per cent of the buyers acquired only an area equivalent to 7.1 per cent of the land.[25]

To give a sense the proportions of this general dispossession: until 1860 only 10 per cent of the land was in the hands of 'feudal *hacendados*' while the remaining 90 per cent belonged to the peasants. Antezana calculated that 'the number of communities exceeded 10,000 and there were not a thousand haciendas in all the altiplano and the central valleys'.[26]

Dispossession not only modernized social stratification but also translated it into a kind of *second serfdom*: 'If previously the greater part of the land belonged to the peasants (and these were free men), beginning with Melgarejo's programme, most of the land was converted into feudal haciendas and free men became *colonos* and serfs bound to the land.'[27]

This was the process of transformation of the *comunario* into the *pongo* [servile worker on an estate]. What is at issue here, then, is the question of the fate of reforms, or of their reception.

The justification for the juridico-military assault on the lands of the Indians and on the communities was that they would be turned

---

25 Rivera Cusicanqui, 'La expansión del latifundio en el Altiplano boliviano', p. 204.

26 Luis Antezana Ergueta, *Bolivia: ¿Reforma o revolución agraria?* (Caracas: Poleo, 1976).

27 Ibid., p. 24.

into productive lands from a capitalist perspective. The proof that appearances deceive is that, formally, 'disentailment' was no different from the *clearing of the land* and the task of the English bourgeoisie in their assault on the enclosures. As for the other part of the programme, the insistence on a *conceptual non-separation* from foreign capital and the laissez-faire policy with respect to the national territory, an obsessive xenophilia comparable only to the obsession of El Dorado, we could also argue that it was a certain mode of 'being in the world' for a country that felt, with good reason, outside the world. Ultimately, even the Meiji 'opened' Japan.

Why, indeed, did the Black Plague produce bourgeois depeasantization in England and a second feudalism in Germany? The same social fact was received by different minds; each country lived it in its own way. How did they rationalize these reforms that were, ultimately, the most radical attempt to initiate a reactionary programme of economic development? For the seigneurial man, his *dominium*, his *ius abutendi* or sovereignty, refers to his own land, to which his lineage is connected, and not to the nation. Personal honour, an arrogance and supreme authority derived from a lineage take the place of national sentiment. While the silver surplus of Potosí flowed copiously over the caste, the Indians were successful in the preservation of traditional forms of organization, which does not mean that they were completely traditional.

Whether through outright theft of the land by military force, as with Melgarejo and Montes, or through purchase under invariably iniquitous conditions, there is no doubt that the object was the expansion, consolidation and supremacy of the seigneurial caste at the Indians' expense. The Indian is in effect the only recognized enemy of the state at the level of its substantive desires. The naturalness with which from Linares to Melgarejo the introduction, establishment and development of Chilean capital (and Chilean settlement in the area) was permitted, that sort of fascination with which the miners became attached to it and then set out to install themselves at the head of their conquests, according to Arce's formula, all this is not easy to explain. It is indeed astonishing. Objectively, it indicates the general feeling of a certain alienation of an entire social sector. In reality we should understand this in terms of the decadence or sickness of a hereditary caste. Servitude degraded the daily life of these men who later (and to this day) would become accustomed to seeing as mere facts of their routine existence what in reality were acts of a strange spiritual perversity. This is what brings them to a sustained practice in the manner of Melgarejo of what in principle might have had some hint of rationality (reactionary but rational). The problem, then, has to do with their fundamental conception of the world. Baptista, for example, who is an exemplary figure here, certainly loved Bolivia but was not prepared to abandon his prejudices for this reason. And so they behaved in an antinational way, although they perhaps believed themselves to be following projects that would benefit the nation. Under the banner of capitalist development, that is, of progress, they brought together all the conditions of its impossibility.

Free trade did not bring about the bourgeois revolution, or a non-revolutionary bourgeois accumulation, or even, ultimately, the introduction of the anticipated capital. In short, their worldview, which is what matters here and not the proclamation of free trade, was incompatible with all forms of 'progress' and not just with one of them. It would certainly have been madness to entrust the task of intellectual reform to a man like Baptista, who was the personification of counter-reformism; it might as well have been entrusted to Torquemada. On the other hand, if we consider the faction of his rivals, those who are accused and guilty of being utterly prebourgeois, we would have to see if they did not carry in embryonic form certain secular and egalitarian elements without which no democratic revolution would have been possible, including that of 1952.

The combination of the real or supposed xenophobia of Belzu and his protectionism is of course all too reminiscent of Dr Francia [José Gaspar Rodríguez de Francia y Velasco]. One certainly could argue that, whatever the circumstances, Belzu's expulsion of Lloyd was preferable to Megarejo's ceding Ladario in exchange for a horse. This xenophobia, at least as practised in a country that is in fact beleaguered on all sides as Bolivia was then, engenders incipient feelings of sovereignty. Certainly Belzu made too much of a distinction between the British and the Bolivian but Arce made no distinction at all between what was Chilean or British and what was Bolivian.

And Belzu's pact was with the artisans and the peasants, essentially *comunarios*, that is, noncapitalist and perhaps not even precapitalist classes. We are more interested in the way in which the bourgeois revolution transforms principles and elements that are not at all capitalist at their inception into capitalist ones, what we might call the *embourgeoisement of ideas*: we might cite here the French Revolution as the transformation of Frenchmen from Catholics to deists. It is a true feat of the art of politics to make god and the goddess of reason coexist in the same space, and the French did just this. The English artisans became inventors, and for this to occur the atmosphere could no longer be artisanal and hence the story that each woman felt herself to be the darling of the king, etc. One might also ask how 'capitalist' the peasants that rose up in the name of the myth of the 'freeborn Englishman' and in response to the suppression of their rights to the commons were. These are elements of what Thompson has called 'the moral economy of the crowd' and are not merely the *riotous diversions* of backward populations. In reality, there is not a single capitalist revolution in which the demands of these kinds of not-yet-capitalist masses are not present; this very action of the masses is a necessary condition of both the bourgeois and the proletarian revolutions, of capitalism and of socialism.

It remained to be seen, on the other hand, what was to replace the internal market of Potosí, defended ex post by Belzu's skilled workers, which was after all the only one, good or bad, that had ever existed. The indigenous community, meanwhile, was the traditional form of the only originary agricultural model of the country; it still remained to be proven whether the new haciendas in the hands of the 'enterprising, active, intelligent white race' of which [José Vicente]

Dorado spoke[28] would in fact be more productive. Indeed, very shortly afterwards, Santiváñez would practically prove the opposite and even the supposed reconstruction of the communities before 1952[29] in no way demonstrates the superiority of the hacienda in this form at least over the communities.

Things did not turn out as projected. What we might call the artisanal-commercial form of the internal market was destroyed, or its destruction was completed, but this only unleashed and renewed in a centrifugal manner what was unresolved, deteriorated and latent in the national question. Meanwhile, disentailment meant only a shift in terms of the application or collection of the surplus, because, strictly speaking, production itself, as a primary act, remained more or less untouched in its original form, whether in the communities or these so-called haciendas and even in a large portion of small-holdings. In short, at least in these areas (the altiplano and the valleys), other ways of working the land are practically unknown.

In our view, all this must be understood in other terms. It is indisputable that the two projects had as their object the capitalist development of Bolivia, and here we must consider the very different fate that a country can have depending on whether one form of capitalism or another develops. In both cases, there was a conceptual failure because they were non-contemporary visions of the contemporary. Protectionism, of course, never produces anything as such, that is, closing things off in no way guarantees their transformation and, moreover, the civilized form of existence in the world of our time is to exist at a certain distance from it but at the same time within it. To suppose, on the other hand, that the metropoles, through free trade, would come to develop Bolivia as a nation and even to preserve it is like a tale full of sound and fury told by an idiot.

28 José Vicente Dorado, 'Proyecto de repartición de tierras y venta de ellas entre los indígenas' (Sucre: Tipografía de Pedro España, 1864). Cited in Almaraz, *El poder y la caída*, p. 73.

29 Grieshaber, 'Survival of Indian Communities in Nineteenth-Century Bolivia'.

Every national project, capitalist or socialist, must develop the legacy of its collective history (from its productive foundation to its mode of being) until it achieves a modern form and so, for example, there can be no advanced agriculture in Bolivia if it does not take into account the foundation of the local traditional agricultural regime and a true industrialization would have sought to base itself in the distribution of what is called real subsumption in the previous flesh-and-blood agents of transformation, that is, in the artisans. In any case, the Darwinist elimination of all prior productive forms is in no way a necessary condition for industrialization or capitalism and much less for socialism. Utopian or not, Belzu's project was much closer to this kind of formulation. No country, and least of all Bolivia, has ever been successful in importing a model of accumulation. This is always local.

*

Bloch was ill-bred, neurotic and snobbish, and since he belonged to a family of little repute, he had to support, as on the floor of the ocean, the incalculable pressure of what was imposed on him not only by the Christians upon the surface but by all the intervening layers of Jewish castes superior to his own, each of them crushing with its contempt the one that was immediately beneath it.[30]

Marcel Proust

Such are the outlines of what can properly be called the battle of the two bloodlines or lineages in Bolivia. It is a theme that pervades not only this study but, of course, also the history itself that is its object. Every society, in fact—we saw this in the case of Chile—has a collection of 'invisible beliefs' or, as it were, a religion that binds it (*religatio*) in Durkheim's sense of this concept. The production of the *social substance* or general equivalence conceived as something that

---

30 Marcel Proust, *In Search of Lost Time, Volume 2: Within a Budding Grove* (C. K. Scott Moncrieff trans.) (London: Vintage, 2005), p. 374.

is not merely economic, in other words, the universal social cement, all this refers to the same thing.

On the other hand, a society can have several articulations or planes of articulation, something like different levels of life and of consciousness, or a single central articulation can be the immediate result of a pact among disparate elements, etc. The question of ideological unity or unconscious identity is one that remains unresolved in Bolivia because the two lineages or identities exhibit an unusual persistence over time. In a way, they don't want to be anything but what they are and they understand this as a will not to belong to one another, not to become integrated. It is an insistence on unfinished forms, of a distinct provisionality, or that are lived as provisional norms. This is significant and can even be advantageous in that in the cases we have mentioned (in one more than the other) this kind of dilemma, if it ever existed, was defined at least initially in a reactionary way. Here, as we have said, we have a duel in which nobody won. Bolivia did not become as viceroyalist as Peru and the besieging obstinacy of the popular prevented the implantation of an anti-indigenous authoritarianism like that of Chile. The ideas of the ruling class have succeeded here in becoming the ideas of the whole society only in a distorted, though persistent, way. However, before going into a matter that is extremely dense in itself, we must make some preliminary clarifications. To speak of two lineages is of course a simplification but not if we understand by this two historical projects that come into conflict with one another. It is a deeply rooted pact and one that is unresolved. The terms themselves rather than defining things can cause confusion because it is in reality a conflict between mestizos—such is the extent to which our bloods have mixed. We must therefore speak in terms of connotation or degree, and here the racial basis of social rank is merely the support for a doctrine or vision of the order of things. Nor should it be concluded from the name of this dispute that there was a separation of bloodlines; one could say, on the contrary, that it is the form of interference of one in the other and ultimately the impossibility of seeing one's own face without immediately seeing that of one's historical interlocutor that characterizes this problematic of Bolivian intersubjectivity.

The origin of seigneurial mediation in this society or in any of its American equivalents is unclear. Of course, we are familiar with the prevailing ideas among the conquistadores themselves: *iglesia o mar o casa real*.[31] In any case, it entailed a certain degree of prestige and of ease:

> The pride of ennoblement was far greater in Castilla, where the exemption from taxation, the ability to participate in the leadership of the town and perhaps other factors of a psychological nature made nobility more desirable. It was enough to have the means to maintain a horse and arms and then to be awarded military privileges.[32]

This, a consequence perhaps of great military need, could not but result in that

> in the beginning of the sixteenth century, the nobility represented more than one-tenth of the population; in the Basque Country this proportion approached 100 per cent and in León 50 per cent, 25 per cent in Burgos and 14 per cent in Galicia and Zamora.[33]

Romano and Tenenti credit the 'second sons' with giving a certain coloring to seigneurialism in America:

> The second wave of conquistadores includes an extraordinary number of 'second sons', younger sons of families of the

---

31 [Literally, 'church or sea or royal court', a proverb that is sometimes completed *quien quiera medrar* ('he who would prosper'), or *hacen y deshacen a los hombres* ('make and unmake men').]

32 [Jaime Vicens Vives, Santiago Sobrequés i Vidal and Guillermo Céspedes del Castillo, *Historia social y económica de España y América: Baja Edad Media, Reyes Católicos, Descubrimientos*, VOL. 2 (Barcelona: Ed. Vicens-Vives, 1972), pp. 115–16.]

33 Chaunu, *La España de Carlos V*, pp. 225–7.

high, middle and lower ranks of the aristocracy, also poor
devils, in a way, but who had known in the houses in which
they were born the feudal way of life, with its myths, its ideals, and its customs. [For them] the problem consisted in
reconstructing a life that only the right of primogeniture had
denied them. Thus in America—on virgin soil—that feudal
world, which in Europe had taken its first blows, would be
revived. [To which they add]: They had the advantage that
the subjugated upon whom they exercised their rights were
racially different, [which] allowed them to establish especially durable and inflexible relations of oppression.[34]

The vast supply of Indians and the decomposition of the
metropolitan seigneurial system (the seventeenth century was one
of acute crisis in Europe) surely only reinforced these tendencies.

From the above descriptions alone we can infer that we are not
speaking of the seigneurial in the feudal European sense, which generally has other characteristics. Here it is something that is constructed in the encounter with the Indian and therefore it is prevalent
in the areas where the Indians were least vulnerable, where there was
some form of state. In fact, it is interesting to note that, although in
an immediate sense to have a state and a relation of consent to the
state confers a margin of power to a society, pre-state societies are
nonetheless more socially resilient. The basic point here, however, is
that where there is no Indian there is no lord. The master recognizes
himself in the slave; the Indian becomes the foundation of the identity of the lord: 'The truth of independent consciousness is [. . .] the
servile consciousness of the bondsman.'[35]

The Indian, therefore, is the proof that the lord exists. This is
expressed, moreover, in the trauma of victory or the deformation
of the victor, which is a *mode of being* that always deceives itself:

34 Romano and Tenenti, *Los fundamentos del mundo moderno*, pp. 185–6.

35 G. W. F. Hegel, *Phenomenology of Spirit* (A. V. Miller trans.) (Oxford:
Oxford University Press, 1977), p. 117 (§193).

'[T]he lord [. . .] is the power over this thing, for he proved in the struggle that it is something merely negative.'[36]

The slave is also the foundation of the 'idealism' of the master because he, the master, is in a paradigmatic way the non-witness of material transformation; on the contrary, he is the man who does not touch the earth. So: 'The lord relates himself mediately to the thing through the bondsman.'[37]

This is, therefore, exactly the opposite of the *command of capital* and the decline of the bourgeoisie begins when it abandons this function of productive leadership and is depersonalized in relation to capital. This aspect is perhaps the most revealing of the conduct of the seigneurial caste in relation to the fundamental productive act of this society, which has always been agriculture. It is a sector that does not participate except in the appropriation of the surplus, that is, in the beginning of circulation, and, as a class that is in essence circulationist, its power derives from the repressive and monopolistic control of the market.

On the other hand, the slave or serf in a state of territorial fragmentation (although the very idea of the community raises doubts about this) is no more apt as a witness to the transformation of nature because he has access only to a magical or at least intuitive and pre-rational experience; but at least in him the possibility of acquiring that rationality exists since he is in close contact with the process of transformation. The master, meanwhile, is external to it in practice, is materially alien to the transformation of nature and, in his view, the slave becomes the part of his being (of his body) that is in contact with the thing. He sees, therefore, through the mediation of another.

In a somewhat crude understanding of the problem, the seigneurial is identified (with the certainty common to all popular conceptions) with the traditional ruling class, even over the course of its mutations and successions, and in this sense the total lord, that

---

36 Ibid., p. 115 (§190).
37 Ibid., pp. 115–16 (§190).

is, lordship across time, resembles the total capitalist. This identification is beyond doubt in that, in the conjunction of representation
and the repressive act, 'fear of the lord is [. . .] the beginning of wis-
dom'[38] and, ultimately, the conception of the world is universalized
until the slave effectively sees himself with the eyes of the master. If
hegemony arises with 'a class that considers itself capable of assimi-
lating the whole of society',[39] then this is a kind of hegemony.

In other words, the seigneurial articulation is that which is based
on an originary hierarchical pact, which can be factual or contractual, that is, it is not founded on equality but on an essential inequality among men. This is at once a mechanism for the construction of
consent because it constitutes a graduated hierarchical structure.
This means that there is always someone lower in rank (which can
be based on economic or racial criteria, or on lineage or even region).
The fact that no one is ever last and all are *hijos de algo*[40] legitimates
the entire conceptual scale.

That the logic of the master becomes that of the slave is aptly
demonstrated in *Memorial de los Charcas*: 'Now in this general visi-
tation that has been made by order of Don Franscisco of Toledo,
viceroy of these lands, we have been stripped of the authority and
lordship that we had over our subjects and vassals as though we were
not natural lords just as the dukes and counts and marquis are in
Spain, which we consider a great affront and injury.'[41]

Their desire, then, was to be assimilated into the Spanish power
structure and not for an instant the abolition of servitude, but the
return of their own Indian vassals [*yanaconas*]: 'They have stolen all
the *yanaconas* we had by making them tributary Indians.'[42]

---

38 Ibid., pp. 117–18 (§195).

39 Gramsci, *Selections from the Prison Notebooks*, p. 260.

40 The phrase (literally 'son of something') is the basis for the term *hidalgo*,
which is a nobleman.

41 Waldemar Espinoza Soriano, *El memorial de Charcas: crónica inédita de
1582* (Lima: Ed. Univ. Nacional de Educación, 1969), n.p.

42 Ibid., n.p.

On the other hand, the four years that Condorcanqui spent demanding recognition of his seigneurial status in no way represent a merely political act. It proves that there is a dissolution of popular identity based on this loyalty or spiritual submission to the seigneurial, a loyalty that clearly permeates all levels of society. Here, therefore, one who cannot claim the title of Spanish lord at least claims that of pre-Spanish lord, but the seigneurial reasoning remains intact. This valorization of the plethora of familial, racial, ethnic and regional hierarchical fetishes is infinite in practice. It is perhaps the most consistent conservative element of all those that exist in Bolivian society, the most general reactionary feeling.

To be a lord here (not in the sense of being master of oneself but in reference to those of inferior rank) is the ultimate object of life. And there is no lord without land. The relation to the land easily becomes feudal in the sense that it has no function except its symbolic value and the surplus it produces (which means the remainder after the reproduction of the productive act). We can speak then of the disintegrative function or the triumph of the seigneurial within the popular as the belief of the oppressed in the logic of the oppressor; but we may also speak of the oligarchic consequences of the seigneurial, that is, of the seigneurial in relation to itself.

What is at issue here is, first, the validity of the seigneurial as mediation or more or less universal articulation instituted by the crossing of the constitutive acts of this society; but also, in another sense, we must ask whether there are forms of the popular that irradiate towards the seigneurial sphere itself.

As for the first aspect, we need not assume that because it tends towards the *gamonalization* of the country, because it does not see the territory as nation-state or in terms of sovereignty but as inheritance or property, because it is not founded on a centralized power or it is founded on a power whose centralization is purely accidental, because of the dispersion of the vassals. For all this, we need not assume that the link between master and slave is interrupted. The truth is that to oppress is to belong to the oppressed, and the more personal the relation the more the slave contaminates the master with his servitude. The slave is the sickness of the master and not his freedom—he is his drug. It is, then, a destructive relation. It is something very different from the interaction between free men, where one is created in the image of the other; they penetrate one another but the freedom of one advances the freedom of the other and is in some measure its precondition. We must differentiate therefore between an oppressive solidarity and an organic and civil solidarity. The quality of the interaction naturally has much to do with the social optimum.

As for the second: All this is what impoverishes this society because the slave is oppressed not by an individual master but by the whole society, and this necessarily produces feelings of collective guilt. The Germans, for example, only exhibit solidarity among themselves against another or for irrational though profound reasons; in their daily life they have no solidarity but, rather, something like a resentment born of a sense of stagnation. Surely at the basis of this neurosis is the seigneurial articulation, unification from above or passive nationalization. *Mutatis mutandis*, we have seen that the seigneurial also exists as a certain popular feeling in Bolivia, in that a single drop of white blood will always allow one to feel more respectable and worthy than the Indian, that is, it will ensure, in the everyday self-conception of the people, that no one feels oppressed or that everyone feels only relatively oppressed. The Indian, in turn, and we are still referring the level of the quotidian, will wish not to be Indian but to be Spanish or will think that he can be Spanish, that is, he will dream as the oppressed dream rather than identify as oppressed. This is the conservative ground or spirit of the of the history of the country, its most precapitalist and most general essence. The persecuted here ensure the permanence of their persecution. We shall see, however, that this is not incompatible with a certain popular history.

Disorder, for example, is one of the characteristic forms of spontaneous discontent. The duty of a man who suffers is to break the order that causes his suffering. This inevitably leaves traces. Katari, his tactics not always structured, is the founder of maximalism for the Bolivian masses, while Amaru, the depeasantization of Potosí, and the internal market that it generated, represent the structural-democratic formulation of the nation, the legitimate ordering of the democratic, and Belzu represents certain nascent forms of the masses conceived as a sector captured by the state. This necessarily gives rise to the construction of memory. We shall see even more clearly the form that this acquisition of memory takes when we go into the analysis of the question of the proletariat. For now it is enough to assume that memory exists as an organizing principle.

It is also clear that a kind of internal history of the seigneurial caste exists, that is, not of the seigneurial as universal articulation but of a caste that occupies a specific position within this specific social formation. With this we return in a way to our point of departure in this chapter, to the relation between categorical forms and their historical subsumption. Arce, for example, or Pacheco would have been bourgeois in the same sense that Edison, Ford or Nobel were, or as Dreyfus was in Peru and as North was in Chile. In effect, if we adhere to the established and accepted definition, the bourgeois is but the owner of the means of production who buys labour power and transforms them both into productive capital. Of course each of these men contained a historical world and what is concrete in them within the general capitalist or bourgeois condition is the history of the individual or national context of each. Dreyfus and North, for example, are living representatives of the form that capitalism assumed in those countries and we could even say that the extent to which North became invested in Chile's military ventures while Dreyfus did not in Peru reflects the form of insertion of each formation in the world system. What is said of one level—*the capitalist qua individual*—is certainly valid to a far greater extent for other equally general categories like the proletariat or mode of production or accumulation. In short, these are categories that have no analytical utility if they are not subsumed in historical analysis.

We can now return to the nature of the seigneurial bloc of the second silver boom that, in its general outlines, founded the present bourgeois mentality in Bolivia. The most eloquent, as we have seen, is no doubt the mystery of its at once mythical and parasitic relation to the land, conceived as an ideal patrimony or material foundation of lordship, that is, as a kind of return to the origins of the bloodline. In the civil war that this fervour would precipitate we shall see the full extent of this insistence upon a retrogressive self-reconstruction. This, added to the zeal to assimilate to foreign capital and for the foreign in general, clearly indicates the presence of what Tamayo called a state of racial doubt. It is a general sense of loss or of uncertainty. It has been said that this came from the contingency of an accumulation based on the world market. A capitalism that does not understand contingency does not understand capitalism. The whole logic of the mode of production is based on the impersonality of collective classes and on expanded reproduction, which is the negation of simple reproduction, something that should be anticipated from its very nature.

On the other hand, it's clear that the uncertainty of the Bolivian oligarchic caste is existential in nature and is in effect a state of racial uncertainty. They are, as Medinaceli said, Spaniards exiled in the high plains but, at the same time, they have ceased to be Spaniards.[43] It is a class that, moreover, has taken significant blows. It did not live the Amaru rebellion as a political threat but in its immediate violence; but it is also extremely significant that the horizon of its wealth collapsed with the colonial world because, in effect, the mercury crisis only completed the work of independence. It is undeniable, on the other hand, that none of those who noted the persistence of the

---

43 [On Gabriel René Moreno, see, for example, Carlos Medinaceli, *Estudios críticos* (Sucre: Editorial Charcas, 1938), pp. 16–18.]

communities realized that it was an inevitable result of the form represented by Katari as well as of the struggle between the factions of the Fifteen Years' War, in which the very logistics of the war were based on the practical erasure of the landowning class. The threat of the mestizo and Indian masses is the *ultima ratio* of the racial uncertainty of the oligarchic caste. It is a permanent siege that has made the latter a defeatist and disloyal class. If we add to this events like those of Belzu, Zárate and 1952, we have a necessarily demoralized and profoundly perplexed class.

Under these conditions, it is indeed surprising that it would regain its strength and develop a true project, that of its reconstruction, on the basis of its racial uncertainty. It was destined, however, in putting this project into practice, to reproduce the ruined traces of its life. Xenophilia and social Darwinism were in fact but the consequences of an endogamic vision of the internal reproduction of the caste that led to an incapacity for hegemonic interpellation, to the reestablishment of the ideology of magical solutions or a mystical idea of history and the unmediated exercise of conquered power. We shall try to explain this even if only in summary terms.

Like many popular terms, that of the *rosca*[44] has a meaning worth taking into account. It underscores the endogamic mode of reproduction of this caste and its conduct would be the same with the conservatives as with the liberals and the neo-bourgeoisie of 1952. From the outset, for example, these are men of modest origins in terms of their economic background, like Arce and Pacheco, or even illegitimate sons of poor whites like Baptista. It is to this that we refer when we speak of the oligarchic caste and its fringe or area of recruitment or reserve. This has its own complex genealogical organization because it is fundamentally a country of illegitimate and poor relations, sometimes inferred on the basis of racial or regional origins; in any case, there is a certain necessary permissiveness that

---

44 [Literally, a screw thread. A local term for the political and economic elite during the period of the tin barons.]

can be called a tolerance of the 'one-eighth-blood' among a few hundred families, which excludes only the mestizo masses and the strictly indigenous, the excluded within the excluded.

The reductiveness of the ideologemes that sum up this conception of the world is also instructive. Not to see the world as something essentially contradictory already reveals the existence of an obscurantist worldview. Anthropocentrism, as such, means the substitution of revelation by doubt. That the Spaniards who came were pre-Renaissance men is evident in the simplicity of their accounts of conquests, discoveries and events in general, which are invariably narratives of grandeur. No Spaniard then would have been able to do anything like what Michelangelo did with *I Prigioni*, that is, the transformation of inorganic matter into human action within a single living being; anthropocentrism and its correlate, that is, a sense of internal contradiction within all things was replaced here by a psychology of *Santiago y cierra España*[45] or by the myth of El Dorado. The inevitable miracle of British capital or of the expropriation of the land by the whites, that is, the propensity for simple solutions to complex problems, reveals, beyond mere ignorance, a certain lack of a sense of reality proper to periods of decadence. Arce thought that surrendering to Chile would make Bolivia like Chile, and this is not just a manner of speaking. The same goes for the dogma of free trade that was, as always, destined to solve everything, or for the myth of the railroad. How could one explain to such people that gunpowder destroyed castles, but also ensured the survival of absolutism for a long time?

From the distance of time, one might marvel at the frankness with which the programme of oligarchic reconstruction is advanced, whether we listen to Arce or Dorado or Muñoz or, above all, Baptista, who was like the bearer of a revelation, as Salamanca would later be, always on the hunt for a 'symbolic man'[46] or charismatic solution that

45 ['Santiago and close ranks, Spain', a famous battle cry of the Reconquista.]
46 [An epithet for Salamanca (*El Hombre Símbolo*).]

never arrived. This, however, has a broader significance. The oligarchic caste, in its extreme backwardness, was incapable of marking out an ideological emission or hegemonic ideology, because it did not propose to seduce the Indians but to exterminate them. Hence the transparency of the Darwinist dogma. Nor did it consider for an instant accepting any form of mediation and whenever it could it exercised power itself, at least with Pacheco and Arce. The fate of this state system, as we shall see shortly, was that of all who fail to grasp the function of the relative autonomy of the state, certainly a bourgeois idea, so little understood by this bourgeoisie of Upper Peru. But why should we be surprised, knowing that these were men who had no notion that after all the principle of self-determination or sovereignty or being for itself is something as central to the 'rational state' or capitalist state as real subsumption itself? They served their ghosts and thus they killed their sons.

*

As much as we hold all this to be valid, the truth is that social Darwinism does not become a general ideology of all sectors of the Bolivian elite until after the Federal Revolution. What the Peruvian viceroyalists lived with Amaru the Bolivian oligarchs lived with Willka. It was like a spectral enactment of their real position within the unfolding of history. Indeed, it is worth noting how Willka would become a kind of Amaru, although with local overtones, and how the effects of the Chaco War would resemble those that the War of the Pacific had had in Peru as an efficient cause of a certain consciousness of things, more or less diffuse, and even of a certain intelligentsia. In any case, the physiognomy of the present oligarchy is that which emerges from this rupture or turn.

We can sum up what we have said up until now as follows: The oligarchy itself broke out of a kind of historical hiatus that had been prolonged, at least to some extent, by a certain lack of realism that also meant, as we have seen, a deviation from reality. It bore the weight of a tradition of language games as a substitute for thought and a patent intellectual decadence that ultimately became a kind of self-authorization (language games here almost paved the passage from one social class to another). It also bore the burden of another terrible, brutal truth—and that was the absence of exemplarity. It was a class without heroes and therefore without anything on which to found its cult of heroes, which is always a key element in aristocratic legitimation. Those whom they called their heroes were like the frontmen for something that never existed.

So, after the confusion of the mercury crisis and the devastation of the civil war, after Bolivia's erasure from the map or radical absence in the world, something extraordinary emerges here: a project. This cannot be attributed solely to the price of silver or to the new cheap mercury from California. Silver is sought out of a will to exist and, as Huallpa proved, existence is not derived from a fortuitous silver find.

As we have said, the act of oligarchic reconstruction is distributed among various figures and we might say that it occurs with a certain quiet grandeur with Linares (who, if not for his great intellectual poverty, would have been the father of the oligarchy along with José Ballivián) and in an eccentric fashion with Montes; atrociously with Megarejo, who gives the reconstruction its facticity together with Arce, both founders of a kind of social method; with a constitutional-legalist aspect with Adolfo Ballivián and Frías. Baptista, Arce and Pacheco would distort and execute the project (by bending it towards fraudulence, they made it possible).

In any case, it is clear that something like an oligarchic state existed in the sense of the weak nomenclature of Latin American sociology and we might even say that this is the state that existed between 1880 and 1952. In this phase, as we have suggested, at least for a long time a fraudulent method of legitimation was practised, which means that fraud also produces a kind of political credibility or legitimacy for the conservatives and then for the so-called *pax liberalis*. A contempt for the local is, moreover, something shared by contemporary figures of other countries, like Argentina. Free trade would be converted before long into a love of all things foreign and the oligarchic substrata would begin to be differentiated as pro-US, pro-British or pro-German, or as pro-Chilean, pro-Argentine or pro-Peruvian. There is no doubt that the founder of this manner of thinking, which is like a desire to disappear, is Aniceto Arce.

In all this we see how a class ideology is instituted. It is constructed by otherwise cultured and sensible men like Moreno and even Baptista, and by utterly practical men like Melgarejo and Arce. In any case, it is in the figure of Pando, in his transfiguration from the federal leader of the masses and defender of the territory into the architect of a strategic covenant and concrete author of Willka's assassination, where the final fate of the Federal Revolution is revealed, as we shall see below.

*

It is somewhat arbitrary, but also useful, to locate the beginning of the quinquennium of the great general crisis that would put into question the political, regional, ethnic and economic contents that had defined the Bolivian formation for at least the previous 40 years on 6 May 1896.

Groups of Aymara Indians began on that day to gather in La Ceja and El Alto and other towns surrounding the city of La Paz.

The urban population, restless and disconcerted, trembled with fright. The authorities enquired into the purpose of the masses. The peasants wanted only to congratulate Pando. The army reacted and dispersed the rioters. Prisoners were taken. The liberal candidate was held responsible for instigating disorder and unrest.[47]

In a typical conservative election, fraudulent and fixed, Pando lost to Fernández Alonso. 'For the first time in Bolivia, the electoral

---

47 Condarco Morales, *Zárate, el temible Willka*, p. 58.

question is tied up with the social question',[48] Baptista said then, although he could not have fully understood then the truth of what he said because things had only begun to unfold. Nor could Pando or Fernández Alonso, of course, who would be the visible actors of a tragedy of great masses. And so, just as an almost absolute reorganization of civil society was attempted (for this meant an inversion of the terms of the agrarian regime and the consolidation of the new supremacy of big mining firms over traditional manufacturers), that is, when it needed most to prove its unassailability and preponderance over it (over civil society), the political state, called to execute tasks that were entirely beyond its means, revealed its vulnerability, the form of its non-contemporaneity. To this we could add the decline of the new surplus, but only as an ancillary factor. It is in moments of crisis that a state reveals what it has accumulated as state capital, and the terms of its relation to civil society, that is, to its own cause or origin.

Heated from the beginning, the controversy revolved around the constitutional legitimacy of the government and the location of the capital, that is, the legitimacy and unity of the hegemonic axis, because at least in theory, the one—the capital—had to coincide with the other, the hegemonic axis. On this point we could say that a state relies more on symbols (and the capital is a symbol) when its unity is guaranteed largely by a decision or an explicit pact and less if its unity is the result of a slow, consensual and democratic process. In other words, if unity really exists, it matters little if parliament meets here one day and there another or where the emblem or insignia of that unity is located.

In claiming Sucre as the capital, Chuquisaca invoked the claim of having been the seat of the colonial government. In other words, to resolve something extremely urgent, it cited two events that

---

48 Cited in Leopoldo Zea, *Dos etapas del pensamiento en Hispanoamérica: Del romanticismo al positivismo* (Mexico City: El Colegio de México, 1949), p. 257.

belonged irremediably to the past: the bureaucratic unification whose support or definition came from its colonial ties and, on the other hand, the second silver boom located in the south that had already begun its decline. It invoked, in other words, the *last days of the colony*,[49] when the brutal realities of the present spoke of another time. Chuquisaca, therefore, was not Piamonte.

To compensate for the hegemonic deficiency that ensued at least in some measure from the custom of electoral fraud, practised consistently since Pacheco and Arce, that is, in the middle of the transition from a non-verifiable formation to rational-verifiable formation of power, when its prestige was in question because even the surplus was dwindling and when nobody had agreed to give Chuquisaca something that it had assumed as a given (its status as capital), Fernández Alonso pitched himself against his adversaries with sheer military force in the name of Chuquisaca, for arms to resolve what politics could not. But Chuquisaca was not Prussia.

Ultimately, the general uprising of the Indians in the midst of the Civil War was about to throw everyone and everything overboard: Chuquisaca and La Paz, whites and those who could count as white [*blancoides*], victors and vanquished, all spheres of the official country. The fact is that precariousness and confusion cannot build up from above without society itself taking on the task of filling in the holes and here everything was suspended in a state of uncertainty. And uncertainty is intolerable in politics. Uncertainty as to the territorial axis; uncertainty as to the composition of power or legitimacy; finally, uncertainty as to the effective social and military supremacy of the old ruling caste itself.

The tipping point was reached with the *Ley de Radicatoria* that declared that Sucre or Chuquisaca would be the permanent seat of the executive. The previous practice, which speaks to the volatility of the situation, was that the government would convene in any

---

49 The reference is to Gabriel René Moreno, *Últimos días coloniales en el Alto Perú* (La Paz: Juventud, 1970).

major city of the republic; it was a system of a *migrating capital*. The representatives of the north, that is, La Paz, opposed the law. Drawing on the demographic and economic strength of the region, which was nothing new in itself but now expressed a new balance of forces, La Paz swiftly organized a military force equal in size and might to the 'national' army itself. La Paz alone, solely on the strength of this militia, might have defeated Chuquisaca. La Paz's victory, however, would have to come from its alliance with the indigenous insurrection, essentially Aymara. This is in every respect one of the richest and most symbolic insurrectionary movements of Latin America.

No one knows how Pando obtained a certain measure of support, popularity and respect among the Indians. Before the events themselves, he was already called *tata Pando*, which proves a certain initial charismatic relation; but it also means that nothing happens in Bolivia without the participation of the Indians. The electoral system was designed to exclude the Indians and indeed to prevent society from appearing except in a particular predetermined context. The singular resonance of Pando's name indicates, however, that the disenfranchised regarded the elections with a certain interest and exerted some influence in them, if only by giving them a certain inflection. Pando's tone was effectively popular and Fernández Alonso's was seigneurial. We could speak here of an *external participation* in the electoral sphere and, conversely, it is quite clear that the previous elections had had effects that were registered within the collective life of the Indians despite their disenfranchisement. In any case, the horrified reaction of the city and of the troops before a merely symbolic demonstration like that of El Alto in May 1896, which, moreover, consisted of no more than 2,000 people, as later became known, is telling. It was not just the memory of Katari or of independence, which the descendants of Segurola surely kept, but perhaps even more than this—perhaps a memory of the conquest itself. In any case, there was an internalized fear. The stunned terror of any Indian multitude is perhaps the most ancestral impulse of the sectors that identify as non-indigenous in Bolivia. We could take this a step further to say that just as there is a collective obscuration of the independence of the state or the impersonality of the law, for example, to impede the constitution of the multitude by the Indians is a resolute and non-negotiable objective of a whole society built on their backs. Pando, in his deep cunning, used this feeling against Chuquisaca, perhaps because the cultural formation of La Paz as a city is less remote from the Indians than the culture of the Chuquisacan elite; but it was also mobilized by the Indians themselves, this time against Pando and La Paz.

The general revolt of the Indians is the direct result of the seigneurial reconstruction of the land tenure regime initiated by Melgarejo. The military uprising is not surprising if we consider the experiences of the preceding period. Indeed, a sombre, simmering agitation could be detected in the countryside. A La Paz newspaper described the situation in 1896 thus:

> In a relatively short space of time, indigenous groups have committed an interminable series of abuses and transgressions: the *comunarios* of Calamarca have set fire to Vilaque; those of Pucarani have repeatedly raided the property of Mr Tamayo, despite having been cleared out twice by the Murillo Battalion; those of Yaco have refused to pay the indigenous tribute, the *colonos* of Mr Goytia rise up interminably; those of Aigachi and Chililaya persist in continual skirmishes; those of Collana and Colquencha are exterminating one another; those of Desaguadero engaged in repugnant acts of cannibalism and, finally, most of them have perpetrated in recent years a hundred attacks on the property and lives of persons.[50]

The description gives us a fairly exhaustive picture of the times. Such 'abuses' on the part of men as oppressed as these, that they 'rise up interminably', could only be the prelude to rebellion, to the

---

50 Cited in Condarco Morales, *Zárate, el temible Willka*, p. 58.

jacquerie. That the *comunarios* of Calamarca set fire to Vilaque reveals the growing antagonism between peasants and townspeople, because the residents of the town were like the agents of the *small hacienda.* That those of Pucarani stormed Tamayo's lands was logical because Tamayo, who had collaborated with Melgarejo, surely acquired them through the dispossessions enacted by the latter. To refuse to pay the indigenous tribute, as those of Yaco did, is natural because, as we have explained, it was a tax on individuals qua Indians, a racial tribute. The constant sabotage of the telegraph lines committed by those of Tambillo was an act of sabotage against the state, but it was also a kind of training in guerrilla tactics that, as we shall see, would turn out to be useful. Such was the situation.

The active discontent of the Indians was a direct response to the appropriation of communal lands that took place between 1868 and 1871, in its first phase, and then between 1874 and 1899. For these reasons and various others, among them the conceptualization of the territory, Melgarejo would be one of the founders of this process with the *decree of consolidation* (which is a joke) of the property of the *comunarios* in 60 days, a policy resumed with the Law of Disentailment of 1874. The reaction was formidable from the beginning. That of 1868, according to a credible account, 'assumed the proportions of a general uprising':

> The narration of these battles offers scenes worthy of the conquest according to a source from the period. It is said, for example, that General Leonardo Antezana, 'Melgarejo's ferocious assassin [. . .] killed approximately 600 Indians in San Pedro' on the 28 June 1869. On the other hand, 'between the 2nd and the 5th of January 1870, the same Antezana once again took the lives of hundreds of people [400] in Huaicho.' According to Sanjinés Uriarte, the incursions of the army in Huaicho, Ancoraime, and Taraco left a total of 2,000 Indians dead.[51]

---

51 Ibid., p. 44.

This is the story of agrarian property in Bolivia. It would continue unchanged with Montes and would last until 1952.

*

It is no exaggeration to say that the features of this social-military movement are extraordinary.

Zárate himself, the Fearsome Willka, is from Sicasica. Specifically, from Imila Imilla, a village immediately bordering Sicasica, the land of Tupac Katari, a fact of which Zárate could not have been unaware. The birthplace of the originary impulse of the movement is located in Omasuyos, Pacajes, Sicasica and Inquisivi, that is, in what Condarco called the frontier of the expanding seigneurial agrarian regime in the reconstruction of the oligarchy.

The epithet 'Fearsome' comes from his white enemies, the Chiquisacans, who perceived him as such. 'Willka', meanwhile, a traditional title, designates the hereditary nature of his rank, a legacy with a long history just like the war in question. It is a millenarian movement operating within the specific conditions of the regional and class war of the Bolivian formation of the late nineteenth-century. It is an intervention in 'national' events that could not have been expected to be thus received. Zárate, then, is the unexpected. It is already significant that it was a Zárate (which does not mean that he was mestizo by blood) who called for 'the extermination of this race [the white race] and the constitution of an indigenous government'.[52]

We will return to this, which is surely a reverberation of Apaza's implacable maximalism. It is a collective validation of a hereditary symbolic charisma, of liturgico-military leadership. This is radically different from the Upper Peruvian conception of power in which the highly personalized individual struggle for power is one of the primary objectives of life. In that case, it is not a question of ruling in general but of ruling in one's own name; every hidalgo in Bolivia, rich or poor, strives for this. We might say that the infallible convictions of the seigneurial Bolivian are his unquestioned superiority

---

52 Ibid., p. 276.

over the Indian and his traditional and personal right to power. The *Willka* idea of power, in contrast, refers to a transpersonal assumption of command; the impersonality of power is what guarantees its perpetuity. The caudillos assume the position of Willka, that is, of leadership, and incorporate the title into their being; the family is the ayllu and the country is the final expansion of the ayllu.

There is, in fact, a first Willka, one who resisted Melgarejo's barbaric decree against the communities in 1866. This Willka's mother, a 'revered and stately' nonagenarian, was savagely murdered by Leonardo Antezana, Melgarejo's cousin. It was also a Willka who led that infernal pursuit of the Melgarejists, charging across the wilderness towards Peru. In the Federal Revolution itself, finally, there are at least three successive Willkas, although there is no doubt that Zárate is the Fearsome. The function of the title is similar to that of Caesar and there is certainly very little of a 'Western' flavour to it. In any case, if ever it has been possible to speak of historical memory, here, where Zárate is born in the same town as Apaza and a third or fourth Willka avenges the death of the first Willka's mother, where the same area that is pillaged under the leadership of a Willka is capable of responding with another Willka more than thirty years later, there is no doubt that this constitutes a perfect example.

Willka is, moreover, the 'representative of the ayllus subject to his authority',[53] like Zapata of Anenecuilco. How official this was, among Indians no doubt little inclined to legalistic disputes with written documents, is something that must be confirmed by further research. In any case, it is significant that they went to war 'with their own system of authorities',[54] which tells us that just as we maintain that the productive patterns of Andean agriculture were unchanged by the juridical form of appropriation of the surplus, we could go a step further to say that the apparent state system (chief magistrate, etc.) coexists, as it were, with the real state system or the furtive,

---

53 Ibid., p. 95.
54 Ibid., p. 348.

subterranean state form. What is certain is that Willka is the caudillo because he is the representative of the ayllus under his rule and because he follows the Aymara structure of authority below, above, and alongside the Bolivian state. This means that in its very existence it is essentially separatist or separate at least in relation to the state.

His contribution to the war was great, but it was also the fulfilment of a hereditary role. It is the technical, organizational, and affective continuation of ancestral practices. The problem of historical burden or legacy is decisive here. Willka would not have been possible without Katari or the Indian combatants of the Fifteen Years War. Nor would 1952, as we shall see, have happened without Willka. Social classes and men believe that they make history, when in reality they repeat it unconsciously, but transforming it. Just as the miners were the heirs of the *forastero*, the *ccajcha*, and the *mita*, the peasant struggle is no doubt interpellated by the old mobilizations of the communities and the ayllus. The same can be said, of course, of the oligarchic legacy.

*

It is worth pausing to consider the operative description of the war, which has a clear overtone of originality and creativity of a popular sort. We might say that the Aymara expropriate the war, that they occupy not only their own space, claiming hegemonic command of the scene, but also condition the non-indigenous space by immobilizing it, and even occupy the military actions themselves by imposing a *tempo*. The initiative in the end is almost entirely theirs. The horizon becomes *kolla*. We speak of the Aymara columns, the Aymara army, Aymara logistics, Aymara intelligence, the Aymara multitude, even the characteristic noise of the Aymara, and there is, in short, an Aymara conversion of historical memory and of geographical and territorial features into military assets. This is consistent with the account found in the diary of the drum major Vargas.[55]

---

55 Santos Vargas, *Diario de un comandante de la independencia americana.*

For example, at Crucero: 'From the moment Colonel Pando arrived at the head of the Murillo squad, he had time enough to reflect, prepare, and execute actions, conveniently protected by the thick indigenous "wall", to then command his frontline.'[56]

Not just to defeat Pando but to reach him, this wall had to be crossed. Or, rather, there is a wall between Paceños and Chuquisacans but it is a wall that protects the former; it is not neutral.

On the other hand, the logistical monopoly: 'His first and most important contribution to the victory [of La Paz] was the war of resources against the general headquarters of Viacha [those of the Chuquisacans].'[57]

Of course it was idiocy to base the encampment in the social heart of the enemy without any prior logistical connection. Meanwhile, a conscious use of psychological resources emerges, namely, the insinuation that something terrible that had happened in the past could suddenly happen again, here and now. The deer-like fear of the Indian siege emerges as a military weapon: 'The Indians completely surrounded the regular forces of both sides',[58] which proves that the regularity of these armies was tenuous and, moreover, that each side was disloyal in its own way.

Meanwhile, Pando's decision to admit an important 'sociological' fact—that the Indians would not fight except under the command of Indians—was extremely significant. Condarco writes that the Indians 'did not recognize any authority but that of their traditional military leadership'.[59]

A pragmatic act if ever there was one because in the negative correlation of the terms of the social equation in Bolivia, and this is evident in the Chaco War, the troops only prevailed when they assumed

---

56 Condarco Morales, *Zárate, el temible Willka*, p. 335.

57 Ibid., p. 208.

58 Ibid., p. 209.

59 Ibid., p. 208.

or were granted some level of autonomy in their operations. The problem of military legitimacy at the moment of battle is something that never even crossed the minds the Bolivian officers. When Pando decided not to recognize the 'traditional military authorities', he was almost defeated himself and in any case he had to fight ruthlessly, in hand-to-hand combat, against those who had secured his victory.

The methods of combat betrayed a complete tactical and technical inferiority, and a no less marked strategic and social superiority, namely:

First principle: 'Attacks targeting the scattered and isolated supply companies detached and at some distance from the area of operations.'

Second principle: Manoeuvres surrounding all enemy forces.

Third principle: Approach and attack, forcing the enemy to 'engage in hand-to-hand combat, with machetes rather than firearms'.

Fourth principle: 'Decisive and overwhelming offensives against the weakest enemy units.'

Fifth principle: Continuous struggle and tenacious pursuit.[60]

The Indians also took advantage of the old obsession with their numbers, with a clear understanding of the myth that the vanquished had instilled within the victor, that is, given that the factions had no knowledge of the dimensions of their enemy, the latter could exploit the baseless assumption of the numerical superiority of the Indians in every situation. According to Jáuregui Rosquellas, who offers what is perhaps the best chronicle of the events of his own faction, towards 8 January, 'the number of insurgents reached 40,000 just in the vicinity of La Paz'.[61] In reality, there were no more than 4,000 or 5,000.

---

60 Ibid., p. 208–9.

61 Alfredo Jáuregui Rosquellas, *La ciudad de los cuatro nombres, cronicario histórico* (Sucre: Imprenta La Glorieta, 1924), p. 302. Cited in Condarco Morales, *Zárate, el temible Willka*, p. 208–9.

The foundation of all this was a mastery of the terrain that translated into a military advantage. Thus, to say that 'a great number of Indians stretched out in a chain along the Andean routes and guarded the main roads'[62] reveals the strategic use of a *constant presence* or continuous struggle because there could be Paceño or Chuquisacan whites in one place or another, but there could never not be Aymara Indians. This produced a sense of insecurity and uncertainty in the former and a sense of perseverance in the Indian combatants. The peasant transformed his weakness—his dispersion—into a perpetual erosion of all others forces.

The endless siege of contiguity in space and time, identification through noise, that is, the calls of the blowing horn and *japapeos* (*oqueos*), and a symbolic presence in the elements: 'The dense clouds of dust kicked up by the Indian hordes.'[63] Thus it was not entirely true that 'the only arms used by the Indians were slings [*huarakas*], clubs [*macanas*], pikes and no more than one gun for every 20 men.'[64]

The application of these tactics produced a situation of general war that involved the entire population and all the resources offered by the environment. Such a total mobilization (which nonetheless would have its own internal contradictions) has three necessary conditions: first, the existence of an identity that is not just communal [*comunaria*] but ethnic in its millenarian expression; second, there must be a plan, and this means also recognized leadership and organized masses; third, the war must continuously expand because its prolongation in the previous terms would make it into regular war, which is the terrain of the *k'aras*.[65]

The basis of this insurrection, like that of any other, because this is something like a law of the revolutionary event, is the effective and

62 Blas Lanza, cited in Condarco Morales, *Zárate, el temible Willka*, p. 255.

63 Condarco Morales, *Zárate, el temible Willka*, p. 215.

64 Ibid., p. 217.

65 [Whites.]

not just formal division of the ruling class. In the subformation of La Paz, as we shall see, in part as the mode of being of Bolivian society and in part as a result of the outward flight from the nuclei of the old Potosí market, it was more or less to be expected that a staunch alliance would be forged between the two anti-Chuquisacan parties as in fact occurred here, and indeed, 'particularism [. . .] went hand in hand with a sense of community since both reflected the conditions of locally rooted lordship', which means that, in a fit of localist passion, the initial impromptu thought of the gentlemen of La Paz was *better the Aymara than the southerners*: 'The names of Pando and Willka went hand in hand.'[66]

This clearly attests to a great resolve on the part of the emergent oligarchy of La Paz. The Chuquisacans did not respond by mobilizing the Indians of the south because, among other reasons, they would not have been able to do so nor would it have been in their interest. It is remarkable how they perceived this gesture of the Paceños, which seemed artful to the point of disgust, as an act of treason against Bolivia. 'They resorted to the terrible and abhorrent extreme of rousing the indigenous race.'[67] This explains how Zárate could have reached the rank of Major General of the Federal Army. On the other hand, that the Aymara presence was readily accepted by the Paceños, naturally and even with a certain enthusiasm, is evident, for example, in the reference to 'Major Sargent Manuel Arancibia' as 'leader of the aboriginal vanguard'. It was, therefore, something official.

Pando, however, spoilt the audaciousness of the gesture—of the Aymara mobilization—with the absurd idea that they would act as *his* Indians or that a man like Zárate could be definitively bought with trifles like a generalship.

---

66 Ibid., p. 325.

67 Napoleón Fernández Antezana, *La hecatombe de Mohoza* (La Paz: Tipografía de La Unión, 1905), p. 26. Also cited in Condarco Morales, *Zárate, el temible Willka*, p. 172.

The Paceños not only benefitted from the 'aboriginal vanguard' but also, as Soria Galvarro said with a measure of bitterness, Pando 'found himself conveniently supplied by the Indians with accurate intelligence'.[68] This means only that while the state project of La Paz, in its most embryonic form, had some remote hegemonic resonance among the Indians (a substantial part of the nation as a whole), the Chuquisacans still had no such recognition at all and their situation was no different from what it would have been in a Chilean territory occupied by Chileans. This is the height of the alliance between the regionalist uprising of the Paceña oligarchy and the millenarian movement of the Fearsome Willka.

From then on the situation began to reveal its own contradictions, its necessary enigma. In short, no one knew to what point the intrepid and sinister general multitude of the Aymara race effectively played that ancillary role of threat and omen, of informant, or of exhausting the enemy, and to what point it had its own designs. In other words, no one knew to what extent they were defending the Paceños and La Paz itself and to what extent they were laying siege to the city. 'It was impossible to know "what was happening in La Paz" as a result of the Indian wall that encircled it.'[69]

The city was therefore held hostage by the very forces that represented its only true line of defence. '[T]he Indians having become the primary political factor',[70] then, the utter confusion of not knowing whether it represented a threat or offered protection escalated to a critical level as the Paceños were alarmed by the very manner in which they were defeating the enemy. Suddenly, the danger was the imminent extermination of the Chuquisacans.

68 Rodolfo Soria Galvarro, *Los últimos días del gobierno Alonso: Reportage para la historia* (Valparaíso: Universo de Gmo. Helfmann, 1899), p. 72.

69 Jáuregui Rosquellas, *La ciudad de los cuatro nombres*, p. 302. Cited in Condarco Morales, *Zárate, el temble Willka*, p. 196.

70 Cited in Condarco Morales, *Zárate, el temble Willka*, p. 258.

Colonel Pando, as Ismael Montes recounted, 'ordered the immediate advance on the cavalry with the end of pursuing the fleeing [Chuquisacans], mostly to protect them from the Indians'.[71]

This image of Montes, that of the 'fleeing cavalry', is one of a class on its way out, a metaphor he composed unwittingly. Pando himself, by then a man who knew the remote regions and the soul of the peoples of the interior, could no longer discern whether he was fighting with the Indians against the Chuquisacans or to save the Chuquisacans for the inevitable struggle against the Indians. A question, surely, that warrants some thought. The relations between Pando, Willka and the Chuquisacans is worth recapitulating. In any case, the masses can never be roused without consequences. Pando drowned in his own overwhelming success.

In the first place, Pando accepted the conjunction of his name and Willka's. What's more: he decided upon this conjunction. It is a fact that, at this point, Pando had counted Willka as an accomplice, as a military comrade and political ally. Willka's very presence at his side at the prefecture of Oruro, in an act that was significant given the circumstances, was no accident but 'a result of his unscrupulous cunning'.[72]

But suddenly things came to have two meanings and just as they didn't know whether to kill or rescue the Chuquisacans, if La Paz was protected by the Indians or besieged, they sensed what was happening beneath these unresolved tensions. In other words, indeed in those of Pando himself: 'The Indian mob began, of its own initiative, a war of extermination against the white race.'[73]

Montes, who would later prove so knowledgeable about their 'particular motives', depicted the situation in a distorted but revealing way: the 'Indian hordes', for 'particular motives' and in the interest

---

71 Ibid, p. 226.

72 Ibid., p. 138.

73 Cited in Sergio Almaraz, *El poder y la caída*, p. 79.

of 'self-preservation', 'took an interest in the conflict and then proceeded to make war of their own accord'.[74]

In any case, the horrific nature that the conflict assumed, especially after the massacres of Ayoayo, Umala and Mohoza, produced a kind of understandable solidarity between the warring armies of whites and mestizos, that is, a kind of solidarity against what they perceived to be a common enemy. It is instructive that Pando, Montes and Saavedra, the three major Paceña figures of the liberal-republican era, coincided in their line of reasoning on this. Saavedra, for example, thought that it was a long-hatched plan: 'Willka meditated the insurrection of the Aymara race of the Republic.'[75]

Pando, meanwhile, suggested that a race war had been latent in the country and that the obstinacy of the Chuquisacans had unleashed it: 'To these [the evils of the war] we can add an inevitable war of the races, which is already upon us by the initiative of the indigenous race itself.'[76]

Fernández Alonso's comment was already a lament: 'Bolivia will be engulfed', 'our united forces' will be hard-pressed 'to subdue it [the Indian horde]'.[77]

We have come to the critical moment of the event. It could hardly have been expressed more clearly: here not only the facts but even the explicit terms of their discourse indicate the existence of two countries and not one. There is the Bolivia of Fernández Alonso and Pando, and the *Indian patria*, that of Willka. There is no doubt, therefore, that what was at stake was the inauguration of 'Willka as the president of the Indian nation'.

Let us now turn to the programmatic points of Willka's party, in their strictest enunciation. Considered from a distance, they were in reality quite simple:

---

74 Cited in Condarco Morales, *Zárate, el temible Willka*, p. 173.

75 Cited in ibid., p. 275.

76 Cited in ibid., p. 295.

77 Cited in ibid., p. 295.

1. The restitution of aboriginal lands or 'conversion' of the estates into communities.

2. The subordination of the ruling castes to the aboriginal nationalities (the terms are Condarco's).

3. The constitution of an indigenous government.

4. The non-recognition of Pando's authority and of that of the other revolutionary leaders.

5. 'Obedience and fealty to Willka Zárate.'

6. The prohibition of garments not made from of traditional homespun cloth (the *bayeta*).[78]

It is quite clear, then, that all power was to be in the hands of Zárate and the Indians. The real problem was not, however, that Willka himself would advance this programme or even a more radical one, but that it was what was already in the souls of the people, what many thought even before Zárate put it into words. Such was the nature of this peace.

On the 'sorrowful night' of Mohoza (the brutal massacre of 120 whites), when the leaders of Pando's squadron, the elite troops of the Federalists, decided to return to the town, the news was conveyed (by [Commanding Officer Arturo] Eguino to [Father Jacinto] Escóbar, surnames that would later be tragically repeated): 'Father, we are lost; the Indian multitude has been roused; the war is no longer between parties, but between races: we cheered Pando and the Federation, and they answered, Long live Villca!'[79]

And, likewise, when they were approached by some 300 men in Coato, near Mohaza: 'Here there is no Pando but only Villca.'[80] What would Pando have thought then! He had unleashed something that he could never have imagined. In a Bonapartist gesture, because such was his inclination, he voted in favour of the law that made Sucre the

78 Ibid., p. 296.

79 Fernández Antezana, *La hecatombe de Mohoza*, p. 61.

80 Saavedra, 'Proceso Mohoza', p. 129.

de jure and de facto capital, with the argument that although he was a native of La Paz, he was a senator for Sucre. All of La Paz rose up in support of Pando, even as they voted against his proposal. In sum: he could not win the war without the Indians; he had to fight for the lives of the Chuquisacans against the Indians themselves; he ordered the death of the very man who was the symbol and instrument of his victory; and, in the end, he died in Kenko at the hands of Paceño whites perhaps because they suspected, even after Willka's death, that he was an accomplice of the Indians. A strange fate for a man forever adrift amid of the forces of history.

Let us see, then, what was contained within the millenarian ideologeme of the *patria india*.

*

The history of Zárate and its premises bring us back to the beginning of this excursus. The logic of reduction or sacrifice appears as a path that must be followed before a central thought-concrete that is also, within the logic of Marxism, a concrete appropriation or subordination of the captured object, can be obtained. It seems that history, which is something like the *longue durée* of politics, is the proof that the object of appropriation exists as such. And yet it also seems that this does not confer knowledge as the conscious organization of what has been appropriated if that particular class of subjects or determinants of the era that are the concrete forms of totalization is not produced. It's true that the 'original picture of the system of production and consumption as a circular process'[81] or the formation of a 'common foundation' or even of the 'historical foundation' pose the question of what constitutes the effective nucleus of the interpellative call. That is to say, of interpellation and totalization *when these exist*. It is clear, therefore, that there can be no totalization without reduction

---

81 Piero Sraffa, in reference to Quesnay's *Tableau économique*. See Sraffa, *Production of Commodities by Means of Commodities: Prelude to a Critique of Economic Theory* (Cambridge: Cambridge University Press, 1960), p. 93.

or sacrifice; that totalities are merely nominal before the acquisition of their historical personality but also that this, the real sequence, is not intelligible if there is no passage from apparent subjects to the universal subjects that are totalities. We maintain that we can speak of this only when it has occurred, although of course it is not impossible to detect other perhaps equally rich moments—for example, the phase of flux or incomplete definition of the conditions that precede totalization, that is, the forms of general equivalence not in a merely economic sense and even instances of capitulation or fragmentation of a process of incomplete totalization.

If we speak of the Bolivian *in situ* we must say that interaction or recognition as reciprocity, considered both in terms of the markets and further back, from its agrarian foundation, has given rise to a kind of Geist or aura. Nonetheless, the politico-spatial dissolution that followed Amaru's campaign continued with the decline of the general equivalent itself that had been produced by Potosí and that ultimately was Potosí (since Potosí is all there was of identification between Tucumán and Puno, or between Arequipa, Santa Cruz, and Córdoba) as a result of the collapse of the first silver boom, and then, at the superstructural level, with the de jure and de facto disappearance of the Audiencia of Charcas, a court 'much given to political intrusions in the business of government'[82] that had played the part of the patron, guard and architect of a routine-bureaucratic unification like that imparted by Lima to Peru. Ultimately, the substitution of the monopolistic system of the interior centres and of mining by the more contemporary idea of ports, modern textiles and free trade was no more than the inevitable result of the failure of a precarious, contingent unification.

The loss of the authoritarian effectivity of the Audiencia, whose legitimacy was indisputable even if only as a result of the reproduction of its juridical apparatus over three centuries of power, inevitably made itself felt among these men—so accustomed to power coming

---

82 Moreno, *Últimos días coloniales en el Alto Perú*, p. 207.

from above and from without to the intermittent and aleatory forms
of rule—by way of the pronouncements of the caudillos, barbaric or
not, who responded to fortuitous forms of determination that came
from a base that now had no surviving articulation between its parts
except the aura that remained from the habit of coexistence.

The caudillos are, however, only an expression of the gamonalization of power, that is, the latifundium as the horizon of visibility
once the traditional spatial links of the Potosí market and even of the
crushing juridical authority of Charcas had been destroyed or weakened. A book like *Últimos días coloniales en el Alto Perú* [The Last
Days of the Colonial Era in Upper Peru] reveals the point to which
this, the colonial subcentres and subcultures, certainly not without
their own charms and provincial patriotism, contained second-hand
cultural and political frameworks of a closed, localist kind, like
Chuquisaca: 'a ceremonious, contentious, and false court',[83] which
included the doctors, a class 'of that instinct no less rationalist than
idle, which always trained its members in colonial society to understand and consult and lead, and whose members on more than one
occasion had shown a proud esprit de corps'.[84]

The motley composition of the colonial, interrupted only by the
continual crises that surfaced with such terrifying force with Katari,
the Fifteen Days' War, Belzu, and Willka, was therefore like an omen
of the inevitable splintering of a certain mutilated unification that
had lost its fetishistic and seductive power.

In politics in general, and even more so in what we might call
structural politics (as opposed to what is known as superstructural
politics), unresolved questions weigh so heavily that they impede the
functioning of the whole relation. The moveable capital was like a
symbol of this dissociation because it was obvious that it represented
a decision continually deferred. Later came what we might call the
second spatial question, with the lack of effective legitimacy in a

---

83 Ibid., p. 140.
84 Ibid., p. 297.

legitimate territory such as Cobija. Finally, the challenge posed to Chuquisaca by La Paz. The process reached its culmination only with the Willka insurrection. It would last another several decades but really it is then that it became clear that there was little left for the oligarchy as a bloc to do.

There is no doubt that events were putting the national question on the table as a problem that knit together all other problems. And so we must consider this issue in its general context, in an analysis focused on Bolivia.

*

Marx wrote that 'The community itself appears as the first great force of production.'[85] The form of socialization or of the collective is something that has always been of great importance and we have always known that some forms are more effective than others, at least in relation to certain ends. The problem of the optimum itself, which we addressed in the previous chapter, in fact has to do with this. The nation, for example, is a specific form of civil existence and association, but not every civil society is a nation. In principle, therefore, this tells us only that there are homogeneous men who share a single identity. In other words, it would seem to be a problem belonging to the *value sphere*, as Weber would have it: the nation exists where men feel themselves to be a nation. It is understandable, of course, that it is thought logical that homogeneous men produce a unified political will more readily or that the will of the state is expanded and fulfilled more efficiently, more directly, in a civil society that receives it with homogeneous forms, forms that respond in a similar way to the same incitement. But things are surely more contradictory and complicated than this because what we might call the depth or density of the constitution of a nation is of no small importance, nor is the certainty or penetration of the state, because a state can have at its disposal forms that are very advanced but alien to its society, etc.

---

85 Marx, *Grundrisse*, p. 495.

In essence, the question can be summed up as follows: We can hardly speak of capitalism in the strict sense except with the general dissemination of the market or what has been called the generalization of market relations. We might say that the general market is a feature of the capitalist mode of production along with, for example, expanded reproduction and free men. It is truly a crucial attribute and before this we can speak only in terms of a higher or lower phase of originary accumulation, that is, of the prehistory of capital. This means that one always produces for another and never for himself. This implies, first of all, the suppression of the logic of the village and domestic production.

> Things are in themselves external to man, and therefore alienable. In order that this alienation may be reciprocal, it is only necessary for men to agree tacitly to treat each other as private owners of those alienable things, and, precisely for that reason, *as persons who are independent of each other.* But this relationship of *reciprocal isolation and foreignness* does not exist for the members of a primitive community of natural origin, whether it takes the form of a patriarchal family, an ancient Indian commune or an Inca state. The exchange of commodities begins where communities have their boundaries [. . .][86]

There are a number of crucial points here: In the first place, it is not a matter of free men in general or in isolation but of men who recognize one another as such (they 'must therefore, recognize each other as owners'[87]). Second, and most importantly, where the *state of separation* or independence has not been produced, the community or collective ground is also false, that is, mechanical and not organic as it must be in the national reconstruction of capitalism.

It is, therefore, not interaction in general but the interaction of free men who recognize one another as such. This is something that

---

86 Marx, *Capital,* VOL. 1, p. 182. [Zavaleta's emphasis.]
87 Ibid., p. 178.

cannot occur without consequences. It gives rise, therefore, to a type of *subjectification* (to be distinguished from *subjectivity* because here subjects are constituted) at once determined and determinant in relation to the immediate *other*. It is to this generalized interaction or intersubjectivity, which is the effect of total circulation upon subjects, to which we must attribute the construction of the great modern forms of totalization, from the social class (which does not resemble any social class from any prior era) to the multitude or the masses themselves, from the nation to the state. In their interpenetration, individuals produce social substance: 'the independence of the individuals from each other has as its counterpart and supplement a system of all-round material dependence'.[88] And also:

> The social character of activity, as well as the social form of the product, and the share of individuals in production here appear as something alien and objective, confronting the individuals, not as their relation to one another, but as their subordination to relations which subsist independently of them and which arise out of collisions between mutually indifferent individuals.[89]

The 'practically indestructible' nature that Weber ascribes to the *rational state*[90] derives from this no doubt unprecedented form of intersubjectification. It is based on the destruction or abolition of the old individual—because one who has not been *separated* cannot be united in the modern sense—and also of its environment, which is the family and the village. The consequences of such environments are, for example, the despotic state or non-equivalent exchange, etc. The consciousness of the individual cannot be recovered then in what he no longer is but only in what he is and this is not possible without a thinking of totality. Such is the importance of this problem in relation to our whole era.

---

88 Ibid., pp. 202–3.

89 Marx, *Grundrisse*, p. 157.

90 Weber, *Economy and Society*, p. 987.

By nation, therefore, in principle and in general, we mean the collective self or socialized substance that is the result of the most basic premises of capitalism. It is, therefore, a self made up of the imaginary confluence of men in a state of detachment—alienated men. The relation between one and the other, the national self and the revocation of the prior communal identity or of a mechanical and inorganic solidarity, is not merely circumstantial, but entails a necessary causality; if the latter does not occur, the former cannot exist: 'The dissolution of all products and activities into exchange values presupposes the dissolution of all fixed personal (historic) relations of dependence in production, as well as the all-sided dependence of the producers on one another.'[91]

Therefore: 'Personal independence founded on *objective* [*sachlicher*] dependence is the second great form, in which a system of general social metabolism, of universal relations, of all-round needs and universal capacities is formed for the first time.'[92]

The nation and its complex derivative, the nation state, would then be something like the expression of this 'universal metabolism'. In other words, for the nation to exist, an event that involves the dissolution of the 'fixed personal relations of dependence' and the emergence of a transpersonal link, or at least an event that amounts to this in its pretensions of validity, must take place. We will consider the hypothesis of precapitalist nationalization below.

In this sense, it is composed of men who are free of themselves for an instant (because the self contains here the prior ideological mode of insertion) and, consequently, now indeed free men plain and simple, facing a kind of interpellation or call, men who are subsumed (*real subsumption*). This runs exactly parallel to the moment of formal subsumption because subsumption indeed refers to the subjection of labour to capital, but it designates, beyond this, the act of internalization of a new conception of time. Men accept the

---

91 Marx, *Grundrisse*, p. 156.
92 Ibid., p. 158.

authority that regulates their discipline and, consequently, they experience a multiplication of time. Meanwhile, just as a man who frees himself through a confrontation with industrial capital differs from one who frees himself from commercial capital and all this is also contingent upon on the extent to which capital thinks of itself as industrial, that is, with a mentality as capitalist as its own productive acts, so also the nature of the interpellation will depend on the degree of its externality. It is one thing for the nucleus of interpellation to be constructed by a collective-democratic action or process, and another for it to be received from an external constitutive moment, to which it has contributed nothing.

Indeed, when Lenin wrote that the nation-state is the ideal context for the development of capitalism, he was certainly adhering to a principle that is implicit in all of Marx's works, although his scientific contempt, like that of Marx himself, for the heterogeneous [lo abigarrado] would later have important political consequences. In other words: Nobody doubts that capitalist development can take place before the nation exists in the form of its theoretical paradigm. England itself, with its yeoman-citizen-depeasantization-Baconism-industrialization model, is an example of how this process is not incompatible with certain residues, sometimes of considerable proportions, of noncapitalist forms. We must acknowledge, at the same time, that a cushion of this kind is not indispensable for real subsumption, that is, the application en masse of science as a general rationality, of technology and the machine to the productive act. There are authoritarian forms of real subsumption, like the Japanese, which cannot be said to have coincided with intellectual reform except within the Meiji elite, or postcapitalist forms as occurred in the Soviet Union. All this is true. However, whether the implantation of capitalism or of postcapitalist industrialization takes place on a national stage (of prior intersubjectivity) or the degree to which a national logic is constructed or not, the measure in which the subsumption of science itself under production and daily life is incorporated into the spirit of the masses, that is, the internal contours of society, all this surely indicates one level or another of development of the 'productive force' that is totalization. The sometimes tragic force of classes and of the multitude but also of states and of nations in our time is the manifestation of these profound social events.

The problem, as is well known, is larger than all this. Nations, of course, are the basis or the units of the world market, that is, the mediations between globality and concrete labour. In a kind of double life, however, the world system is a rival to the constitution of nation-states and at the same time the measure of its success depends largely on the extent to which it is capable of being internalized within nation-states, which means obstructing their identity or sovereignty, and this is the catch. Every nation-state, on the other hand, is the enemy of another nation-state; no rhetoric can change this and in this regard no one looks out for anything but one's own interests understood as something utterly non-negotiable. This occurs to an extreme degree in the relations between the original nation-states and the latecomers.

The ideal internalization of the core nation-state in the periphery is clearly demonstrable: not for nothing do we speak of the national-popular and, on the other hand, all the peripheral ruling classes are unconditional partisans of the logic of the world market.

We can derive from the foregoing propositions certain limitations of the nation-state in the world today. It is certainly true that, on the one hand, the privileged locus for the realization or honing of certain productive forces like the free man and his correlate that is impersonal power, formal subsumption as a precondition for the primacy of the ideological as the memory of punishment above actual punishment or force or the repressive apparatus, is the nation-state. On the other hand, real subsumption itself holds little interest for us as something devised in Galileo's tower but only insofar as it is converted, like equality, which is its premise, into a general intuition, and it is clear that this, real subsumption, is more effective, so to speak, in a nation or nation-state. All this is obvious. But it is no less obvious that the nation-state, as pre-defined will and tied to a single continuous body, does not exist in such purity. After the core nations, there can only be pathetic forms of modernization of nation-states outside of them.

The nation-state is what occurs when society has become a nation, when the state desires in the name of the nation what the nation wants it to desire for it. The state, certainly, can be the condition of the nation, preceding it, and this is what has almost always occurred; but the inverse is also possible, where the nation pre-exists the state.

*

The present discussion interests us here only insofar as it relates to the situation in Bolivia during the general national crisis of the Federal War. In the war itself, a set of interconnected prior events surfaced. One such event, for example, was the inevitable rupture of the false nationalization derived from administrative centralization and its contingent equivalence. The silver of Potosí, in any case, was not the same thing as the wheat of Italy because as long as Italy exists its wheat will exist; silver, on the other hand, is something that will run out. To continue with the comparison, Chuquisaca, which wanted to rule but not to lead—not to contain the interests of the led in a hegemonic fashion—did not fulfil then what has been called the 'function of Piedmont'.[93] La Paz, in turn, seemed to be a kind of miniature Prussia in its victory over Chuquisaca but it did not assume this role in relation to Chile (nor could it have) and so, since its consciousness of the loss of the coast was so vague and tenuous, there was no France to play the role of unifying incentive for Germany. But we must ask why here all paths become tortuous along

---

93 Gramsci, *Selections from the Prison Notebooks*, pp. 104–6.

the way and end in frustration and which elements of the nation have indeed been effectively achieved in Bolivia.

It is not unprofitable to refer to Stalin's definition since, although nobody speaks in these terms today, it is still the most succinct.[94] For example, with regard to the 'stable community, historically constituted', what is meant here surely is that it is not simply a matter of a racial community or of a tribal contract but refers instead to a 'series of significant chronological groupings', as Pierre Vilar puts it. This is true, but nobody can deny that the racial community (and even more so the ethnic community) is a contributing element, favourable and sometimes decisive in processes of nationalization. If it is an imprecise and evaluative category, it nonetheless belongs to the order of powerful and primary facts. It is not necessary to claim that this category lacks effective significance in order to fight racism. Man's physical externalization surely constitutes a sign that cannot be dismissed, although of course, perhaps as a result of its very irrefutability, it produces only an apparent identity. The force of its manifestation stands in stark contrast to the relativity of its content. It's true that a deep intersubjectivity is often founded on the supremacy of identity over heterogeneity and this is a manner of approach like any other. It is good, moreover, that men insist on what they are.

It is a fact, however, that is always preliminary and rudimentary and peoples that locate the key to their community in this are necessarily primitive peoples or nonprimitive peoples that have reverted to the primitive. Still, it is undeniable that in many cases (and this proves that it is senseless to theorize the national independently of historical context or particular cases) racial sympathy has constituted a causal link in the process of national recognition. Moreover, there is no doubt that the nature of the events incorporated determines the national selection, and this is what we might call a constitutive

94 Stalin, *Marxism and the National Question*.

moment or significant chronological grouping. Men always return to certain profound events that serve as points of departure.

Things are more complicated when it comes to the territory, although its function and task is no less fluid. The event of revelation or nationalization (interpellation) is of course experienced by a living body and a face but as important or more than this is the fact that it occurs within a landscape or environment. The hermeneutic function of space is, however, a dependent factor because it is qualified by what occurs within it. Some peoples (and this is the case in Bolivia) are not intelligible outside of their space. The *appropriated* existence of the space is subject to its own organizational models, although certainly they have been determined by it originally. It is something largely determined by agriculture and even by the type of livestock (since neither can be practised in a spontaneous fashion) because the harvest was of course very scant. The persistence of men is in reality a response to the rejection of the land, which creates an intense symbiosis.

There is nonetheless no reason why this should be any less instrumental. In the end, our discussion of this question, in such limited terms, might seem to suggest a state of subordination to the natural and the cosmic, which would of course be an overstatement. The optimism in the face of the cosmos shown by men like Marx is a consequence the fact that they were the sons of an age in which real subsumption had just occurred.

Nor is it necessary to expand on the posteriority that the territory can sometimes have vis-à-vis the nation. There is no doubt that the Anglo-Americans, who still have no toponym of their own to refer to themselves but who do indeed have a coherent identity, existed first and then gave themselves their space, although it is also true to some extent that neither Texas nor Atacama will ever be truly American or Chilean. In any case, it's clear that the *raison d'être* of the territory is subordinated in general to the act of articulation, which is the essence of the national.

It's true, on the other hand, as Gramsci (who was Sardinian) said, that a language is a conception of the world. Language is also, however, a dynamic process. What we call a national language is ultimately nothing but the *modus vivendi* between the languages or elements that take part in the process of nationalization or, as it were, the linguistic terms in which the pact has been instituted and, in this case (not for nothing does Gramsci himself say that 'the new culture [. . .] was born in dialect'[95]), they qualify the centralizing language or the latter is imposed through a Darwinian process of selection, that is, through the destruction of other languages. As conceptions of the world, languages traverse and exceed their formalization. Thus conceived, a language should contain the subjection, oppression and expression of the thing and its opposites, that is to say, it is a discourse on the world. In any case, it is not a neutral social fact. If discourse is nothing but representation, it is nothing at all: it is assumed to morphologically absorb the social fact and it is at the same time the programme that a society lays out for itself. The indigenous or African inflection of the different varieties of Spanish spoken in Bolivia and in the rest of the Americas does not constitute a mere deficit in relation to Golden Age Spanish. It is the form of appropriation of the language or the linguistic consequences of its insertion in a new world.

The linguistic and interlinguistic elements in Bolivia serve as a point of entry into this problematic. Not just because of the patently Darwinian suppression of Puquina but also as a result of the tenacity or persistence of Aymara, which is the linguistic equivalent in its power of resistance of the communal form as conceived by Grieshaber and others. In any case, Quechua, which is now seen by many as an originary language, was in reality adopted as a result of the introduction of *mitima*[96] colonies, that is, it was a cultural impo-

---

95 Gramsci, *Prison Notebooks*, VOL. 3, p. 97 (Q6 §116).

96 An Inca system of population resettlement to facilitate state military and political control as well as economic production.

sition or a typical case of negative hegemony. Forced Quechuization was a prelude to the forced de-Quechuization attempted by [José Antonio de] Areche. It then became one of the general languages of Peru and finally the lingua franca of Potosí, that is, of the alienation determined by the market system of Potosí. This role played by the Quechua language, which is now the most widely used in the country with the exception of Spanish, as a conquering language, the language imposed universally in all regions except the Cuzco Valley, with the Incas, with colonial mining, or with the *forasteros*, expresses a particular social matrix. Whether the form of nationalization would amount here to forced Hispanicization or to the various bilingual forms also depends, therefore, on the resolution of the cultural contents of the class struggle. It would not be incorrect to maintain that there is a 'moral economy' of linguistic distribution.

Nor is it necessary to dwell too much on the *reductio ad absurdum* of Stalin's proposition: that without a prior common language, the French or the Italians would not have succeeded in becoming a nation. The decisive barrier would here seem to be the lack of a distinct, previously unified language. We can challenge this by saying, and this is undeniable, that the formation of the language is often a concurrent part of the formation of the nation and here the role of Dante or Luther is one thing and the popular formation of the Spanish language is another. This has been called the 'historical knot':

> The original defect of the new bourgeois state, which had
> not known to found its constitution on the broad economic
> and social base of an agrarian and peasant revolution that
> would destroy, along with the landholding monopoly, a
> semifeudal backwardness and not only of the Mezzogiorno.[97]

In other words, the logic of the *junker* path was inherent in the birth of Hochdeutsch and the unification of the language was a herald of events to come. A different story no doubt from that of the successful Basque, Catalan or Galician resistance to Spanish or the

---

97 [From Gramsci, although the exact source cannot be traced.]

incorporation of French by the Italians of Nice or by the Basques or the Bretons, and, in short, by all the peoples, Alsace included, in the *interlocution* of the French Revolution. Under these conditions, would not the gamonalization of the Bolivian social formation have something to do with the fragmentation, if not of Quechua or Aymara, of Spanish itself as it is spoken in these regions? Is it not even to this day significant that Paraguay, a country with a considerable indigenous population or where the indigenous maintains a strong presence and without a seigneurial property regime (without a traditional landed aristocracy de facto), developed a fluid, effortless bilingualism while this occurred only sporadically in Mexico, Peru and Bolivia and in Guatemala and El Salvador there was a true linguistic persecution? All these, the non-bilingual countries, are countries with a predominantly servile productive model. In Bolivia, Cochabamba, whose fundamental characteristics we will consider below, stands out as an important exception. Here we have the beginnings of a project that does not come out of nowhere. It is what proves that monolinguist or bilinguist dogmatism necessarily refers to what is called a *mass project*, a democratic pact. What matters, therefore, are the consensus of the masses, that is, the modality adopted, spontaneously or not, by the men who take part in the act of nationalization. In other words, what matters is the scope of intersubjectivity and not its linguistic form. The language is only a sign of nationalization and not its condition. In the moment of its communicative intensity, a people can abandon its language since it has been proven that peoples are capable of retreating from their vision of the world and language is, indeed, nothing but a conception of the world. To hold bilingualism to be a limitation or obstacle to Paraguayan or Cochabamban identity is nonsense. Bilingualism, on the contrary, is their identity. Where it effectively reflects a universal sensibility of the people, it is a typical popular solution. But here we are referring only to a certain bilingualism, that of a self-determined, democratic identity. In other circumstances, of course, bilingualism can be a form of oppression. It seems that this is how the Basques and Catalans experience it.

With all the importance that his racial, spatial, and especially linguistic arguments might have had, what Stalin called problems of 'economic life' and 'psychology' or the community of culture are undoubtedly those which have the most decisive value, although they can have only a relative meaning if we do not look back to their originary phase, that is, to the problematic of the constitutive moment.

In principle at least, both economic and psychological life would have to do with the concept, which is more conspicuous in certain advanced capitalist countries, of depeasantization or the Western form of originary accumulation (the way in which originary accumulation affects the agrarian culture). This, however, is rudimentary *ab origine*. In the end, to speak simply of a 'common economic life' is idiocy. In the first place, because it's obvious that there are non-market forms of economic life in common. If we take a step back to recapitulate, we could say that if the market form is decisive it is not because things are bought and sold but because of the strength or perfect hegemony that it acquires.

'Money does not arise by convention, any more than the state does. It arises out of exchange, and arises naturally out of exchange; it is a product of the same.'[98]

Given that the mercantile *alter* or referent is such a decisive condition of the self, it should give rise to a kind of compulsive reciprocity or interpenetration. This necessarily requires the factual validity of the state of alienation, the advent of the juridically free individual, which is a kind of economic citizenship; but also the immediate subsumption under the market, that is, formal subsumption, which is a contract between capital and labour. This same form of 'economic life in common' can occur, therefore, with a greater level of participation on the part of the alienated individual or as a fact imposed

---

98 Marx, *Grundrisse*, p. 165.

upon the individual. The level of consensus with which formal sub-sumption takes place of course gives a distinct connotation to each constitutive pact. It is this generalized interaction that produces the social or national substance that can also be called value and herein lies the material base of the national in the capitalist mode of production.

If we agree, then, that there are different economic lives in common, we could say that on the contrary the existence of pre-market forms of economic life in common is sometimes the most formidable obstacle to a nationalization of the capitalist sort because it crystalizes and preserves the precapitalist or noncapitalist 'nation'.

In this regard, if horizontal integration is extremely important (from the suppression of tariffs to the erection of a national market infrastructure to the abolition of non-rational units of exchange, such as women's currency, etc.), the aspect of vertical integration is even more important because it relates to the democratic conceptualization of society. Equality is unity, or at least there is no true unity except among equals. Hence the mass base of self-determination: a people made up of equal men tends naturally towards self-determination; non-democratic self-determination, therefore, is founded in a mere messianic impulse or depends on the whim of those who rule; it is not a structural fact.

On the other hand, the composition of the total worker and of the general capitalist cannot be external to elements like those we have just described and are therefore results of the collective habits originating in the market understood as universal interaction. This is especially true with regard to the latter, the collective capitalist, because the less private the retention of surplus value the more national it is. In other words, it's not enough for things to be national in appearance or on the surface; the circulation of surplus value and even the rate of the rotation of capital (because certainly the more it circulates the more unified it is) speak to the qualitative implications of unification. The state, ultimately, is nothing but the production of political will (because it 'desires' in the name of the nation) in relation to the social body. In any case, it's clear that not all 'economic lives in common' are equal nor do they all have the same effects. The deep market develops gradually. It is what indicates beyond all doubt the level of organization of the collectivity as productive force. A society can persist in the same common pastoral practices and even in a centralized system of taxation with no nationalizing effects in the capitalist sense. On the other hand, with a sophisticated process of rotation, it is possible for this to be achieved without a common language or even a common psychology.

On the subject of the mercantile production of the nation, we must make two more remarks. Fragmentary or scattered forms of the market require that the support of the social substance—as noted with regard to Potosí—be something durable or constant. The disappearance of this support with the mercury crisis led to the disarticulation of that nascent domestic market. The situation in Potosí was volatile not only because it was a contingent and ephemeral market but because it was founded, in terms of its base, on forced commercialization and controlled trade. This aggravated the gamonalization of the economy and differentiated the regional patterns of social development to a considerable extent, besides giving rise to a centrifugal model of development. We might say that the social formation experienced a regression because never before had such dispersive tendencies been so powerfully expressed as in the interregional and class struggle that arose under the common banner of the Federal Revolution, which compares unfavourably with the Potosí market and even with its pre-Hispanic precursor. As to the former, it was certainly a case of what Sereni calls 'a national market of adjacent regional markets'.[99] In reality, the ideological matrix of this age or its interpenetration is the only thing that allowed the nation to survive the clearly centrifugal and sometimes liquidationist programme of the ruling classes of the republic. As to the

---

99 Emilio Sereni, *Capitalismo y mercado nacional* (Barcelona: Crítica, 1980).

pre-Hispanic element, there had been a certain passive homogeneity, proper to this type of accumulation, that was utterly dependent on the cement of the state; these were statolatrous societies, so that when the Spaniards took the apex of the system, it immediately lost its organicity and fell back to its elemental bastions of resistance, to agriculture and quiet discontent.

*

The economic moment of national formation, which can also be conceived as that of the passage from contingent exchange to general exchange, and its ideological or cultural correlate, the formation of the collective unconscious, are both founded in the vicissitudes of the constitutive moment. A materialist conception of history must struggle consciously against a misappropriation of this concept, that is, against the cult of the primal, which would explain all of life on the basis of protomemories or protophantasies of collective archetypes. This, as is well known, has an ultra-reactionary derivation in Jung; but that does not discredit the truth that 'As the individual is not just a single, separate being, but by his very existence presupposes a collective relationship, it follows that the process of individuation must lead to more intense and broader collective relationships and not to isolation.'[100] The very assumption of predestination in history leads irremediably to an irrationalist and ultimately Darwinian conception of the social. The myth of the finality of destiny has had no course but this. On the other hand, it is well known that every society lives constitutive moments of different intensities and positions in the course of its development and that there can be moreover what we might call a hegemonic shift or successive constitution, although this occurs only within the logic of an advanced social optimum. This is how democratic selection operates, with all the limitations that come with the framework set by its class character and by the simultaneous

---

100 Carl Jung, *Collected Works of C. G. Jung* (Gerhard Adler ed., R. F. C. Hull trans.) (Princeton, NJ: Princeton University, 1966), p. 2508.

production of state receptivity and a rational political will. The revolutionary event itself is a cathartic and catastrophic form of amendment of history and implies a process of selection by the masses in that they constitute the social man (of our time) in practice.

If it is clear that such an originary act cannot be explained independently of the conjuncture proper to man in a state of alienation, it does not follow that forced depeasantization, following the English or Stanilist model, is the only path. The 'dissolution of all fixed personal (historic) relations of dependence',[101] as the French example proves, does not necessarily require a social Darwinist solution. It must be said that in this matter monist interpretations have had disastrous results. There is a kind of positivist nihilism that arises from this and it has come to constitute a school of thought among scholars of the problems of development. Nonetheless, it is impossible to proceed with our discussion without a certain description of this paradigm.

That of the English is indeed a quintessential constitutive moment. At least it is the most familiar. There was an almost miraculous convergence of conditions that all seem post hoc to tend towards the construction of the same thing—the English process: not only the relative brevity of English feudalism, which certainly should have left fewer *feudal memories* than the French millennium, but also a sequence beginning with the self-destruction of its aristocratic source in the War of the Roses, which suppresses it in practice in the name of an appeal to aristocratic purity, that is, that it is a young country, having shed the burden of the old nobility; that the tradition was pastoral, and wool tends towards industry just as winemaking tends towards smallholding; and finally, the drastic depopulation of the countryside with the Black Plague. But this, as we know, is important only from the perspective of the effects of the demographic catastrophe: the abrupt death of half the population in two years cannot but leave lasting ideological traces. A world of representations

---

101 Marx, *Grundrisse*, p. 156.

dies with the victims and this is why unprecedented (unforeseeable) loss of life always has such a great ideological impact. The Black Death itself was common to the Europeans; its reception here, on the other hand, was English because its consequences were very different in Germany or Poland. That a man famous for elevating his sexuality to the level of state doctrine like Henry VIII had to do with this proves how little heroes matter in such processes. In fact, the (belated) substitution of personal services by tribute in kind and of the latter by centralized rent, and the shift, through the price revolution, towards the constitution of free men produces at once a modernization of the myth of the ('freeborn') Englishman, that is, the yeoman origin of individualism, but also a multitude of 'separated' but famished men, the unequivocal root of 'possessive individualism'. All this no doubt configures a distinct constitutive moment. Here, however, we see the inadequacy of the designation of this cycle as a moment, although it is true that the idea of the act is not absent in some of its features, such as the enclosures and the expulsion of the farmers. The English structural and superstructural forms, even the eclecticism of a primitive bourgeois revolution crowned by the political failure of the bourgeoisie and the contractual rebirth of its enemy, constituted the phases of development of this narrative whose secret perhaps lies in the construction of the agrarian foundation of industrialization. For Englishmen from that point on this tabula rasa, the land before its commodification, that is, the pre-mercantile moment of the conception of the land, is but the prehistory of agriculture.

In England, in short, the substitution of the traditional temporality of man, which was that of agriculture, occurred in this way. Depeasantization, therefore, was the English mode of destruction of the point of reference or scene of peasant culture, which was the cellular base of all previous modes of production. Thus the first rupture takes place between man and his traditional means of production, which is the land, and his solitude or independence in relation to the soil begins; this had to be accompanied by what we call juridical equality, that 'one pre-historical condition [that] comprises a world's history'.[102] This is what has been called the advent of the self.

It is so brutal an event that it is almost indescribable. The *state of separation* presupposes a collective state of ideological void or the emptying of a conception of the world. The loss of the erratic logic of the peasant or pre-national forms of reasoning (or of a rationality internal to the peasantry) that followed could be successfully supplemented by an anthropocentric worldview. In other words, where there is no alienation, it is doubtful that intellectual reform, which is the medium of real subsumption, will occur; without this, without a reform of the intellect, the logic of the factory itself is but a superimposition. The combination of these factors constitutes an example of the optimum or equation: 'Whatever the British advance was due to, it was not scientific and technological superiority. In the natural sciences the French were almost certainly ahead of the of the British.'[103]

This means that while it is certainly false that Arkwright invented the factory, it is true, on the other hand, that the idea of the factory was brewing in the English social process and therefore Bacon could be to philosophy what Stephenson was to the extraction of coal—men with the same social reasoning.

The sociologists know the importance of a moment of receptivity or permeability. It is not something that happens every day and in essence all social science is the study of significant exceptionality. It is then that the essential call that is only part of the interpellative process can be produced, the precise convocation or implantation of the distribution or character of the social formation. This of course will follow a particular course depending on whether the interpellation is imposed by a more properly bourgeois bourgeoisie, by a

---

102 Marx, *Capital*, VOL. 1, p. 274.

103 Eric Hobsbawm, *The Age of Revolution, 1789–1848* (New York: Vintage, 1962), p. 29.

democratic revolutionary class (perhaps secretly harbouring bourgeois desires), or by a class of despotic reformers. Any one of these is possible.

Returning to the English example, that kind of political poverty or infirmity of the aristocracy after the War of the Roses would cause the aristocratic programme to remain in the hands of a false aristocracy, a social placebo: the essential feudal convictions would be irreparably dampened. This is compounded by the parallel hegemonic incapacity of the bourgeoisie, which 'had lost even its personality' and was resigned to paying a very significant lip service to the aristocracy. In an infinite syncretism, ennoblement itself would serve the function of bureaucratic recruitment and the selection of state personnel. The hubris of the formation is aptly exemplified by Arkwright, who, after inventing the factory system, bought himself a landed estate. On the other hand, the hypothesis that if the favourable circumstances of the environment for the passage from real subsumption to a mode of reasoning of the masses were duly appreciated it was because of what has been called 'the existence of a vast proletariat', that is, the great number of men in a state of perplexity and displacement, is not implausible. This of course favours democratization rather than rigid stratification. There is, in short, a base with a powerful capitalist force and a superstructure with undeniable feudal parameters. In the end, neither those at the top nor those at the bottom were disinclined to do business. The religious schism of Henry VIII itself seems to be nothing but a secularization of religion, that is to say, Anglicanism was the deism of the English and they would rather have their king be also their pope than make the pope king of England. An entirely different thing no doubt from Spain's nationalization (so to speak) sealed by the Reconquista, military supremacy and Catholicism understood precisely as counterreformation, with the visible predominance of commercial capital.

Of course, fascinating as it is, in recalling this process we must not fall into a fetishization of what has been called depeasantization.

This is in fact only one of the catastrophic forms of social parricide or succession, supposing that there are non-catastrophic or non-pathetic modes of reform of collective ideas. What is important about the *state of separation* is the openness to a substitution of beliefs and the revocation of essential loyalties, that is, the substitution of one conception of the world for another. Here receptivity itself is what matters and not depeasantization, which is its English version. The French Revolution produced a similar state of receptivity without voluntary long-term depeasantization. Moreover, it would be wrong to believe that in Russia receptivity arose from forced collectivization. Such a barbaric act was indeed possible because there was a pre-existing social receptivity. This demonstrates that revolutionary pathos is a natural vehicle for the production of general receptivity within the parameters of our era. If this is true, it is no less true, however, that war, natural catastrophes and great plagues or epidemics can produce similar states of consent or dramatic dislocation, all this apart from the democratic logic of transformism.

*

We can now sum up the situation of the national problem in Bolivia at the moment of the general national crisis of 1899 as follows: Potosí had constituted a kind of commercial unit or contingent market in an area that spanned (at least) the present Bolivian territory plus the south of Peru and the north of Argentina. On this base a powerful administrative superstructure—the Audiencia of Charcas—was erected. To the above factors we must add the nature of the composition of this market that was based on depeasantization by the *mita* and the so-called *forasteros*, on the one hand, and on the other, by the repressive formation of the market or controlled trade (forced commercialization). The aleatory elements of this, which can be considered the first market, are clear, and not only because the inevitable 'non-equivalent exchange', which is one of the sources of regionalism, that is, of the political regime of the gamonal, could only give rise to what is called an 'irrational capitalism', which is at the very core of the formation. Hence the question arises as to whether this capitalism is reformable or if, as in Russia, it is a matter of tasks that can only be fulfilled by socialism. At the same time, given that the logic of this market was determined by the silver mining industry, it was a contingent and impermanent system of exchange and it effectively perished even before the mercury crisis as a result of the decline of Potosí, with the mercury market itself and the debt of the mercury miners and, subsequently, with the devastation and forcible return to a natural economy that came with the War of Independence. Finally, given that the support or protection of the 'sovereignty' of the Audiencia was exogenous, there could not but be an administrative debacle with the factual disappearance of Spain form the panorama, first with Napoleon and then with independence.

The colonial regime created a deeply ingrained seigneurial-servile culture. In successfully resisting the social formations of the colony, with the artisans and the communities, a kind of centrifugal solution arose: territorial losses, the fragmentation of the land and the gamonalization of what was left are all one and the same. With ideas steeped in a racist and anti-popular discourse, and with great resentment in its soul, this caste unaccustomed to thinking of anything beyond the legitimacy or illegitimacy of its pedigree constructed a kind of provincial seigneurial subsystem, with epicentres now utterly scattered, with a distinct culture, decadent but not without a certain malevolent grace that nonetheless had a local stamp, which was popular, with its pleasures, its hypocrisy and its idleness. The very circumstances of the world market fostered a kind of modernization of this caste that threw itself into the venture of self-reconstruction with the second silver boom and the assault on the communal lands. It followed the logic of all doomed classes. It aspired to become a powerful axis, but neither La Paz nor Chuquisaca, its capitals, were in any condition for such a thing. They did not consider for an instant undergoing a serious embourgeoisement and perhaps they did not even know what that meant; rather, they wasted whatever they could snatch up of the accidental surplus in the augmentation of their seigneurial symbols, land in particular. After Melgarejo and the farce of free trade with the conservatives, they could not aspire, moreover, to any kind of moral-political prestige, rural or urban.

CHAPTER THREE

The Torpor of Centuries

Does what has been called 'Darwin's immanence' mean that natural selection was an inevitable myth or ideologeme of the circumstances of originary accumulation? We could say, indeed, that this and its extension to the social sciences that is social Darwinism, the claim that 'the supremacy of one people over another was the inevitable outcome of the biological laws of the universe',[1] were ideas too contemporary with a certain specific process, which is nothing less than the rise of the West. Darwin himself, to be sure, seems to have had little to do with these particular opinions. They constitute, rather, a certain reading of the so-called *dismal science* (that of Malthus) by way of Spencer. An exegetic and facile reading, moreover, like everything that man wrote or thought. He founded a school of abhorrent but powerful ideas.

But what doubt is there that the first element in man's self-recognition (and recognition should mean to re-encounter oneself) is his appearance, his material face, his mode of appearing before the world, his existence as phenomenon? To be, certainly, is also to appear. We must, however, distinguish between this 'folk racism, a popular system of prejudice'[2] (because prejudices constitute the history of the world) through which every group harbours an essential mistrust and abhorrence of its neighbour (at least provisionally), what can be called a universal and ancestral contempt among men, who despise all that they do not know, that is, 'folk racism', and the rather doctrinarian intent to systematize this as an interpretation of

---

1 Marvin Harris, *The Rise of Anthropological Theory: A History of Theories of Culture* (Walnut Creek, CA: AltaMira Press, 2001), p. 81.
2 Ibid.

the world. That such thinking is dangerous, like almost any other used in this way, is abundantly clear. But it is equally clear that it is a danger to which man's basic nature tends. The natural sciences themselves are today imbued with and enveloped in these prejudices, whence we can see that it is an ideologeme that runs right through to the final flourishes in the construction of the scientific paradigms themselves. It has always been a matter of proving pre-existing prejudices.

In any case, it was Wallace, who had been the co-author of some work by Darwin, who wrote: 'In every generation the inferior would inevitably be killed off and the superior would remain—that is, the fittest would survive,'[3] whence Spencer deduced the expression 'survival of the fittest'. It was a creed destined for formidable success. Its emergence, if we wish to contextualize it, must be located in the process of universal subjectification (the constitution of subjects) that derives from the 'entitlement' or birth of the *state of separation* that is from the beginning simultaneous with or attended by what has been called possessive individualism.

We maintain, therefore, first, that racial difference as appearance or phenomenon is an originary fact. It is not something that can be ignored in the process of *anagnorisis*. Second, that we are speaking here of an ancient feeling among men, that of group empathy, whose ancestral tendency towards a mistrust of the other is but the form of aversion or resistance to the unknown whose object is human. Finally, that the intense subjectification proper to the new forms of totalization was not possible without a negation of its constitutive or original points of reference, which were precisely the germs of other totalities or nations.

It seems to us that with race the same thing happens as with many other ideologemes: they need not be rational in themselves in order to serve rational ends. Anti-Semitism is barbaric but it has produced certain instances of 'national recognition' which is not

---

3 Cited in ibid., p. 123.

barbaric. A common belief in an absurdity can bind men together, although this ends up poisoning the resultant collectivity. To grant another recognition of identity with oneself or not to do so is an act of valorization and not a rational act per se. The result of these groundless acts of acceptance is the collectivity or nation, which is, however, a rationally valid totality because, at least in the world we live in, it is better to be a nation than not to be one and the form of *being in the age* is the national form.

In any case, nationalization through depeasantization or the 'Darwinian' destruction of the peasantry, which is in effect the traditional form, is inferior in our view to a political process of nationalization, like that of the French, in which the dissemination of a discourse of equality overdetermines the forms of economic unification. Similarly, an interpellative process, national or not, centred on essentially irrational or valorative premises like that of race is not the same thing as one founded on rational models such as that of democratic articulation. And there is no doubt that equality derives from a rational process while race is a mythic construct, founded on the conviction of an originary inequality. Things are of course more complicated than this, because even an externally antidemocratic interpellation can have internally democratic consequences, etc. Nonetheless, history itself would later prove that whenever a people opts for primitive or magical (though precocious) forms of unification, these will be reborn in time as despotic. The pragmatic idea of neutrality with regard to the contents of the interpellative call (in general, the vindication of fallacious but successful forms of interpellation) is no doubt a voluntarist idea, despite all appearances. It is always of crucial importance to determine the ideas around which a people has been unified.

*

In any event, since ours is an age that has chosen to recognize itself through its great men, in a kind of heroic conception of a history that has had no true heroes, social Darwinism became a pervasive creed in Bolivia, one that cut across the entire social fabric. Indeed, perhaps nowhere else is the condemnation of the national man so habitual. The catalogue of such denunciations is formidable.

According to José Domingo Cortés, perhaps our first historian, who claimed to have been well acquainted with the Indians:

> The Indian is vigilant in his own business and lazy in all else; he know no virtue and praises what is evil; he seeks always to deceive, and believes himself to be cheated; he is sired by self-interest and the father of envy; when he appears to give he sells; he is so opposed to truth that he lies with his very countenance; he holds himself to be innocent when he is malice itself; he treats his mistress as his wife and his wife as a slave; he appears chaste and sleeps in lechery; when you beg him he grows haughty; when given orders, he feigns exhaustion; he loves no one and mistreats himself; he is all mistrust and suspects even himself; he speaks well of no one, much less of God and this because he does not know Him; he perseveres in idolatry and affects religiosity; devotion in him is mere ceremony; he uses worship as a means to inebriation and this he uses to commit atrocities; he murmurs when he seems to pray; he eats just enough to live, and sleeps without a care; he knows no sacrament and makes a sacrament of everything; he believes all that is false and repudiates all that is true; he falls ill like a beast and dies without fear of God.[4]

This represents a widely held view. [Mariano] Baptista said that the 'lettered and Christian class, that which lives in an atmosphere of civilization, has a great horror of the Aymara.'[5] Here is his portrait of the Aymara man:

---

4 José Domingo Cortés, *La República de Bolivia* (Santiago: Imp. de El Independiente, 1872), pp. 119–20.

5 Cited in Condarco Morales, *Zárate, el temible Willka*, p. 38

This Indian's face, his gaze, his features, are of stone like the granite of his mountains. There is no expression in that face: there are no contractions; it chews and swallows inertly. I have studied it many times, since my childhood, filled with fear for humanity. The Aymara walks past the white man without looking at him, or glancing at him out of the corner or his eye. In the high peaks, in the immense steppes, only the traveller, cholo or viracocha, crosses his path. It seems that on such occasions, a spontaneous sympathy should instinctively draw man to man, but the Aymara never greets you. Not a syllable of his barbarous dialect issues from his throat: and we hardly hear its timbre when, crouching in the door of his hovel, he answers gruffly: *janihua*, which is a refusal of all service.

And then: 'What kind of sensations stir in him? . . . And how can we discover them with our fear of the unthinkable? They don't speak in their stuttering, they only gesticulate like imbeciles.'

These are the words of Baptista who, according to Prudencio Bustillo, was 'the greatest political mind ever produced by the Bolivian race.'[6]

On the other hand, Gabriel René Moreno, the most renowned of Bolivian writers, took for granted that mestizos and Indians were subalterns 'as a consequence of the very cells that make up their wicked nature and deficient minds';[7] and he spoke of the Inca Indian as 'sombre, foul, elusive, meek, stupid and sordid';[8] therefore:

The men of Chuquisaca wanted to subject [it] to the Indian laws and decrees of Toledo; laws and decrees made to crush and wring the Inca Indian, shrewd, devious, filthy, taciturn,

---

6 Cited in ibid., p. 39.

7 Cited in ibid., p. 40.

8 Cited in Augusto Guzmán, *Baptista: Biografía de un orador político* (La Paz: Juventud, 1957), p. 121.

abject, a stranger to truth, never surrendering body and soul to the Spaniard like the neophyte of Moxos.[9]

Even *mestizaje* itself through illegitimate unions 'meant the institutional degeneration of the country'.[10]

Let us consider now the thoughts of Pando himself, called Tata in memory of Belzu: 'What would it cost to implement a policy of universal education? How long would it take? [. . .] The task would be impractical. It would be far more practical, then, to eliminate them.'

And: 'The Indians are inferior beings and their elimination is not a crime but a "natural selection", a difficult and repugnant task but one that is imposed by the necessities of industry'.[11]

Or also: 'The problem of this race of savages seems to be unsolvable: the Indian's tiny brain cannot, even through intellectual cultivation, develop like a muscle'.[12]

And he decreed their 'necessary slavery' and inevitable extinction. Zárate would seem an unlikely ally.

Saavedra's words are even more telling because in the Mohoza trial he acted as a spokesperson for the whole Hispanic bloc in the judgement of the events of the Federal Revolution. The Mohoza massacre was

> The manifestation of a ferocious and savage outbreak of a morally atrophied race, or one degenerate to the point of dehumanization. [The Indians] feign an 'abject submission' when they find themselves in an inferior position, but in groups they are haughty, stubborn, audacious, and can become fearsome beasts.[13]

---

9 Gabriel René Moreno, *Nicomedes Antelo* (Santa Cruz: UGRM, 1960), p. 53.

10 Ibid., p. 32.

11 Cited in Juan Albarracín Millán, *Orígenes del pensamiento social contemporáneo de Bolivia* (La Paz: Juventud, 1976), p. 193.

12 Cited in ibid., p. 194.

13 Saavedra, 'Proceso Mohoza', n.p.

As to Willka's ideals, Saavedra does not deny them but for him they are the 'obsessions' of 'bloodthirsty orangutans'. It is, in short, 'a degenerate race in the process of its final dissolution'. Saavedra who is, moreover, as leader of the artisans, a kind of predecessor of populism, is then the author of this 'tragic racist pamphlet' that according to Albarracín is 'perhaps the most anti-Indian piece of literature in all of Bolivian sociology as a document of white racism'.[14] The Indian is 'no more than a beast of burden, miserable and abject, who warrants no compassion and must be exploited to the point of inhumanity and indignity'[15] and, in short, 'if we must eliminate them, because they constitute an obstacle to our programme, let us do it frankly and energetically';[16] 'If he [the Indian], consumed by suffering, rebels against his oppressors [. . .] then he must be crushed like a dangerous animal.'[17]

States, like individuals—like men—cannot live things without representing them, that is, without conceptualizing them. These are the founders of the ideology of the oligarchic state. They were based, as we will see in the following chapters (which look at the state that was constructed against this one), on something that long preceded the oligarchic state and that would survive long after its destruction. It is one of the elements of the deep ideology of this society, at least that of the elite, seigneurial and Hispanic stratum. As we have seen in the particular articulation of the seigneurial (the structure of complicity), this itself necessarily includes important sectors of the oppressed because there is always one beneath the last of the inferior ranks and the consecration of hierarchies does not recognize an intelligible logic. What is interesting in this case is that the ideology of the historical foundation, in a kind of suicidal outburst, expresses itself also

14 Juan Albarracín Millán, *El gran debate: Positivismo e irracionalismo en el estudio de la sociedad boliviana* (La Paz: Universo, 1978), p. 243.

15 Saavedra, 'Proceso Mohoza', p. 145.

16 Ibid., p. 146.

17 Ibid., p. 145.

as appearance or phenomenon. In its explicit ideology, for example, the US state is Jeffersonian but it knows what its inner ideology is. There is always in every state a set of ideological premises that are the secret of the state and that are transmitted and reproduced but that cannot be made explicit within the logic of the apparent formation, which is proper to the institutions of capitalism. The whole of the history condensed in Willka turned out to be so maddening that it forced these men to unwittingly commit the mortal sin of betraying the secret of the state. The necessary split between the eternal and esoteric ends of the state and its apparent ends would only be recovered with revolutionary nationalism, which would find in this inflection one of its indisputable advantages over the oligarchic state.

Whether he was 'the greatest political mind ever produced by Bolivia'[18] or not, that this was said of him proves the importance of the figure of Baptista. One can forgive certain conspiratorial desertions and even a certain servility towards the mining families of the time; we can also understand that he was deeply affected by the death of his son. For this very reason, a man like him should have grasped that with those facile remarks, still common today among whites, he was poisoning a long legacy. He was, nonetheless, our Martí.

With Pando or Saavedra, as with Moreno, who reached his rank as a result of his great talent (although it was less significant in politics itself), the contradictions become insuperable. But contradictions, as we will see in the three cases, can take on a life of their own.

The best of Pando undoubtedly lies in a certain practical obsession with the territory. If the men of his time had had the same geographic conception as he did, perhaps things would have been different, or at least so some have thought. Pando was able to recognize that that 'passion for the territory' was irreconcilable with the elimination of the men who belonged to that space. Furthermore, when he was the idol of the Aymara and was waging a winning fight

---

18 Ignacio Prudencio Bustillo. See note 8.

thanks to their support, it was incongruous for him to share the theses of the very men he had defeated, those of Baptista or Saavedra, who called for the unsparing and immediate extermination of the Aymara. That all this would end in the consolidation of so anodyne and so 'Montista' a government proves that a kind of impersonal reason was being fulfilled. Within this logic it was acceptable to exterminate the 'cambas', to solicit Willka's support, to betray and murder Willka, and then later or simultaneously to express the opinion that the 'cambas' should be exterminated and the Aymara leader eliminated. Pando's conscience was clear after all this because this is how an entire community thought (within the scope of the caste).

Moreno, in turn, a thoroughly modern man, had thoroughly understood the logic of Argentine Europeanization. Indeed, he had denounced

> the plan to isolate and Europeanize Argentina in America [and the] so-called *porteñismo* of the isolation of Río de la Plata to achieve this Europeanization of workers, capital, and commerce most expediently. [. . .] So Buenos Aires, which had invited her sisters, the most properly Argentinian provinces, to reap the fruits of Europeanization, will break its American ties decisively for itself and in their name, to enjoy this Europeanization together.[19]

If this same man could so lucidly grasp the interpellation of Charcas, that is, the subsequent Potosí market, as well as the role played by Belcismo, for which he was himself labelled a red like his countryman the illustrious but confused [Andrés] Ibáñez, even if only out of envy or intrigue, why did he have to succumb to such a humiliating role as that of a regional intellectual, as had occurred already in a more ambiguous way in *Archivo de Moxos y Chiquitos* and in a unequivocal, that is, a purely provincialist way in *Nicomedes Antelo*?

---

19 Gabriel René Moreno, *Ayacucho en Buenos Aires, y Prevaricación de Rivadavia* (Madrid: Editorial América, 1917), pp. 65–7.

Moreno had already said things as significant as this with regard to the undignified conduct of the Bolivians in the government of the time: 'A generation like the present one in Upper Peru, let them say what they will with their acolytes and sycophants within, has not known how to preserve intact, above all human error or interest, the territorial inheritance of their forefathers, etc.'[20], evidently expressing a certain characteristic Eastern sentiment of the frontier, which is typical. However, the provincialism that followed selected the worst of Moreno, the most parochial. Why not also vindicate his anti-Europeanism, which is a form of nationalism even if of the right, and his own Belcismo *in partibus*? Because they were factors inimical to the construction of the new oligarchic thought that was not so complex as Moreno's, which was at once anti-European and anti-indigenous, nationalist and regionalist, pro-Belcista and Charqueño? There is no worse enemy of a contradictory thinking than its minor contradictors.

As for Saavedra, whose thought was perhaps the most organized and the most modern among the men of his time (which is not saying much), however, there is no doubt that he is considered the man of the greatest popular sensibility of those who belonged to the conservative-liberal-republican period. For this very reason, because he was an energetic man little accustomed to making concessions, his is no doubt the prevailing vision in this society, which had become so reactionary with its renewed terror of the Indian threat. By no means should one believe that his were unpopular ideas within those ranks. It would be ingenuous to suppose that a state was constructed with no social base: in reality, a broad sector of those not excluded through an ancestral marginality must have shared this thinking and, like the *sheep of Achacachi*, they accepted it as perfectly

20 Gabriel René Moreno, *Biblioteca boliviana: Catálogo del archivo de Mojos y Chiquitos* (Bolivian Library: Catalogue of the Archive of Mojos and Chiquitos) (Santiago: Impr. Gutenberg, 1888) [La Paz: Juventud, 1974], p. 110.

natural. This is an early expression of the distinction between towns-people [*vecinos*] and Indians, which would be of vital importance.

Voltaire's racism and Goethe's anti-Semitism were troubling because these were diseased elements in great spirits who are like the stewards of the soul of the age. Spencer's racism is not, because it is to be expected that small-minded men cultivate prejudices. Ulti-mately, the survival of the fittest would be demonstrated in the inevitable disappearance of his eminently forgettable *oeuvre*. The same can be said of Alcides Arguedas, whom we have deliberately not cited because he was clearly an insignificant writer of bad prose, of great pretensions and inferior ideas poorly expressed. The irony consists in that the illustrious learned from the mediocre. They, the illustrious, embodied the essence of the age and in a way they founded it, if only in following it to its root. We must ask ourselves what happened to them.

*

Every age has an ideology. There are certainly ages that have only a vague notion of their own ideological contents but this, ideology, will take its final shape sooner or later; this is what Marx meant when he said that the ideas of the age are those of the ruling class, although we could also say this the other way around: the ruling class becomes the ruling class by reading, from its position of lucidity, the ideas that will be dominant or that are dominant only in a potential and obscure way. In other words, ideology results from the social sub-stance and not the social substance from ideology; even negative or critical ideology expresses elements that will develop inexorably. Therefore, the struggle has predefined the context in which the ideas that will make it explicit will emerge.

This clearly applies to the case that constitutes the object of our study. Social Darwinism, the idolization of the surplus, even xenophilia, were the results of class struggle in the specific context of the defeat of the diffuse and vast party that was called Belcismo.

The state, then, shifted, according to a logic that permitted a resolution, at least in theory, of the seemingly eternal stalemate between the plebeian party and the evolution of Ballivianismo. With the exclusion of the Indians and the artisans, the effective civil society, that which was capable of producing political effects (which of course did not coincide with the real civil society), now thought in social Darwinist terms and in all else they restored the thinking of the oligarchic state. With minor variations, Moreno expressed the same thing as Baptista and Pando. It was therefore an epochal ideology. They merely formalized as thought what had been assumed in society following the political expulsion of the Indians and cholos. Willka, in contrast, provided the affective conditions for this to be expressed decisively. Not to vanquish at the right time always creates a supervictory for the enemy; it exaggerates the enemy's triumph.

But to this argument we must add another: the relative ease with which the oligarchic party imposed itself weakened it, as often happens, because victory is not always to one's benefit. If there is an overarching ideology of the age, it can also be said that the state has its own *tempo*, which is only relatively dependent upon this ideology. In its very nature, the capitalist state must at once serve a logic of the market (which is egalitarian, the 'paradise of the rights of man') and a logic of surplus-value, which is not. So, surplus-value must be hidden so that it does not disappear, and hence the substantive schizophrenia of the formulation of the social facts of capitalism: surplus-value must appear as profit, value as price, inequality as equality. This is commodity fetishism, or the problem of what in Marx are called *apparent formations*.[21] The same occurs with the state: a state must always have a legitimating or explicit ideology; but it would be incomplete if it did not have an ideology or representation of the world as identity, that is, of self-reference, which is what

21 See René Zavaleta Mercado, 'Las formaciones aparentes en Marx' in *Historia y Sociedad: Revista Latinoamericana de Pensamiento Marxista* (Mexico) 18 (1978): 3–27.

Hegel called *self-certainty* and what we can call the *form* of its class character. On both ends, if this, which is a law of the modern state, is not fulfilled, we have a kind of failure. An identity between legitimation or the explicit ideological emission and self-consciousness exists, for example, in backward states. The result is that this reactionary synthesis produces a transience or instability of the state. On the other extreme, a true identity between what the state is and how it appears would make the state useless. It would have to disappear ipso facto. And yet, the state can only develop self-certainty in accordance with the requirements of civil society, which it serves through its legitimating or explicit ideology. Here Bacon's dictum holds true: nature—like society—to be commanded must be obeyed.

How did the oligarchic state behave in relation to this law? With a heedlessness that cost it dearly. It exaggerated the significance of its victory and identified its internal ideology with its explicit ideology. It's easy to have a certain unanimity if you exclude all your enemies and this is what the oligarchic state did with its victory over Belcismo and Willka; but very soon a 'subterranean revenge' would come, as we shall see. That the warring parties—conservatives, liberals, republicans—were so much in agreement as to the spirit of the state shows that it was a question of dissension within the *state party*. It also indicates that, after the exclusion of the Indians and the plebeian masses from the politico-legal country, the system enjoyed a kind of deformed hegemony: it was the country that had been besieged by Willka and the proclamation of its ideological programme was an excess of the hour of victory. Meanwhile, that the supposed discourse of legitimation, the outward ideology, and the discourse of the state's identity coincided is what explains the brevity of its life and the suddenness of its downfall.

The revolutionary-nationalist school labelled this line of thought anti-patriotic. This led to an ethico-Manichean discourse on the national-popular. What is certain is that all of them, with the exception again of Arguedas, who was nothing but a bureaucratic hack in search of sinecures, were men profoundly committed to their country. Pando, for example, is more than his cruelty towards Willka; he is also the source of the state's feeling of connection to the territory or at least one of its sources. Moreno, in turn, if he is the founder of a school of prejudices in the society of the East, also showed the greatest national pride, with Bolívar and the Colombians or with Melgarejo's disregard for the integrity of the national territory, in short, at all times. Baptista himself, if we dismiss his understandable though illegitimate resentment towards the Aymara and his desertion or liquidationist position in his relations with Argentina, was no doubt a scrupulous negotiator with Chile in unenviable circumstances.

Nor can a position like that of *Sartor Resartor*[22] on the Chaco question be understood only on the basis of that supreme enmity between Saavedra and Salamanca. Still, a total inattention to appearances, especially when founded on a contingent triumphalism, is never without consequences.

But the real problem lies elsewhere. These men unconsciously laboured against their country, against the only one that existed and against themselves. They inflicted concrete injury on what they loved in the abstract. This indeed reveals a psychology of *the last of a line.*[23] We must, of course, distinguish the qualitative aspects of racism according to its different subjects. For example, Spencer's racism or the Anglocentrism expressed by Disraeli, who once said that he preferred the rights of Englishmen to the rights of man, constituted attitudes of integrated men, belonging, beyond all doubt, for better or worse, to a collectivity. They might be poor arguments, but these were men who cultivated arguments in their own interest. In other words, Disraeli's theses were in the interest of the English as a whole. *Mutatis mutandis*, the same could be said of Alberdi and Sarmiento, who made a number of idiotic remarks (not to mention Mitre, who in his language and attitude is a precursor to Arguedas), but there

---

22 Pamphlet by Bautista Saavedra published in La Paz in 1933.

23 The expression is Carlos Medinaceli's.

was no doubt that their anti-Americanism was not anti-Argentinian. The repudiation of America was their way of constructing the Argentinian. De-Americanization and de-indigenization were understood in the same way as de-peasantization in the English process. This was the Argentinian form of nationalization, one of a social Darwinist mould, and Roca ultimately did no more in his military campaign than what Alberdi proposed, a purge of the indigenous population.

Still, we must consider here the alterity of the Indian. For an Argentinian or a Chilean, the Indian's presence indeed represented a negation. Neither *La Araucana* nor *Martín Fierro* came out of nowhere. This is largely because they were pre-state Indians, as we saw in the first chapter, fierce Indians who could be subjugated only at the cost of great difficulties. Cultures are defined by their modalities of resistance. The Eastern Indian, for example, either did not submit or submitted only to disappear immediately. Hence Moreno's preference for the Inca, because he 'never surrendered body and soul like the neophyte of the Moxo missions'.[24] A culture of resistance is a habit of organized men, as is the case with the Andeans, whose originary principle is organization, because otherwise life would have been impossible. Moreno was surely more repulsed by the grime of the Andeans than by that of the Spaniards, but between one and the other there was little difference.

In any case, we are talking about countries and societies constructed *against* the Indians. *Martín Fierro*, however anti-indigenous, is unquestionably a national epic. It is natural that, overtly or not, a war that has been waged and won would be glorified, although this would certainly instill racist and Europeanist elements that are unmistakable in the specific form of alienation of those societies. This is not the Bolivian model. We cannot say categorically that Bolivia will be Indian or it will not exist, but, at least, among all its programmes with any degree of viability, there is not one that posits

24 Moreno, *Biblioteca boliviana*, p. 51.

a country without Indians. The least that could be done would be to grant them an indisputable status within the nation. That, however, is not what one might deduce from the reasoning of those founders of the state: it is an entirely anti-hegemonic idea. The material reconstruction of the flesh-and-blood society was attempted on the basis of a fifth of its population. Men will form opinions that suit their needs and it is obvious that the most candid subjectivity is subjectivity for itself. The problem lies, rather, in discerning the social conditions in which one reasons against oneself. The starting point is the following: Saavedra or Moreno, one as much as the other, thought that Bolivia as such was lost but not Moreno or Saavedra himself; this indicates a split between the conception of the individual being and its environment. They simply did not feel themselves to be a part of it and, like the Argentinians and the Chileans, could not conceive of their countrymen, the Indians, as such.

Let us leave aside the limited information that these men had at their disposal, ultimately a result of living in what can be called the most provincial of the provinces. But it is not simply a question of a lack of information. That the idea of a European Argentina was viable was proven by its de facto Europeanization, a clear case of correspondence between reality and a prior utopia. The idea of a European Chile, being false, at least proved to be a useful argument for the construction of a nation in a certain sense: it was a lie that had become plausible and what mattered then was the unanimity of self-representation. A European Bolivia, on the other hand, was a radical falsehood, an implausible impossibility. In other words, the pan-Europeanism of the country's heroes could not even serve as a political lie or a productive fantasy. But they did not espouse it out of ignorance. The facts are more terrible, more cruel. They were the unconscious expression certain tragic social forces.

It was a kind of schizophrenia (understood as 'mental dissociation, that is, hallucinations, fantastical illusions, and a disorganized emotional life, together with a relative intellectual consistency'[25]) because in this muddled apology for the white race and in locating the viability of Bolivia in the whites, they were in fact defending the viability of the *vecinos* who had proven to be anti-Bolivian almost without exception, and this surely provided their enemies with the arguments they needed. Why did they do it? This is the terrible thing: because they believed in it. They believed in it to the peril of their lives, unless we are to accept that this 10 or 15 per cent of Bolivia stood any chance, as opposed to 90 per cent in Argentina or 30 per cent in Chile. It was, then, a doctrine based on the expectation of imminent defeat, accepted and inevitable even if disguised as a certain final honour as with Moreno, Saavedra or even Salamanca himself.

This pessimism, the depressed spirit of an irremediably fallen caste, a profound internalization of defeat—these are the conditions that make it possible to reason against one's own country as those Bolivians did then. They preferred to be lost along with the 10 per cent whose chimeras had led the entire country to ruin rather than to accept the principles, explicit or not, of the opposing majority. One can surely consent in a moment of greatness to sacrifice oneself for a misconceived truth, but here this truth turned out to be no more than a class prejudice, a truth of convenience. In general, truth in politics is too voluble a thing to sacrifice one's life for it. One must fight for one's own truth, which is the only one that can be known. General truth is an idea with which the powerful persecute the oppressed. The proof of this is that the descendants of these Europeanists today must encapsulate their arguments within an indigenism as contingent as that Europeanism. That is, it was a 'truth' destined to be short-lived.

The word *disease* has been thrown around. Here Arguedas indeed had his reasons. The pathological here lies in that the caudillos reviled the men who granted them that rank and therefore took

---

25 Beatriz Barba de Piña Chán, *La expansión de la magia* (Mexico City: Instituto Nacional de Antropología e Historia, 1980), p. 227.

for granted that it constituted a sort of recognition of a certain innate privilege. We are dealing with a kind of sickness or neurosis—that of men who reason against themselves. It's like a salesman arguing that he should be paid less. Why did they do this? Because of a seigneurial conception of life in which salvation and perdition are tied to the lineage. They felt that Bolivia's adversities concerned them only indirectly; they thought, in short, that some (the lords) would yet be saved, by virtue of their blood, when all was lost. This is the most extreme case of a rupture of solidarity, of even a pragmatic solidarity, with the country itself. Not all of them, however, lost their composure as easily as Montes or Arce. For this, to save himself, Moreno placed his hopes in his elegant prose, Baptista in who knows what, other than a discourse, and Saavedra, in power; but they all thought the same thing: there was no solidarity or identity at all among the lords and masters.

The underlying problem is that of self-interest or the instinct of self-preservation in the realm of thought. It must be said that to reason against one's life is a grave sin. All men are indebted first of all to themselves, to their identity. To fully possess oneself, that is, to determine oneself, enables one to think of other things. First one has to be oneself in order then to contribute something, if possible. A certain degree of healthy selfishness is the key to sovereignty, but also to class consciousness or to personality, to all forms of self-determination. Therefore, just as Moreno hated with all the purity of his legitimate rage those who had not known how to defend their inheritance, we too can vehemently condemn those who failed to give us reasons to defend it today. It is a charge no less terrible and no less obvious.

In the study of the state, space, for example, does not have the same content as in cartography; what exists on the map might not exist for the state—we are referring to a space in which the state has validity, to the habitat in which the authority of the state is enforceable, to the human terms of this enforceability. The same can be said of the population; in this sense the only population that exists is that which has been incorporated into the state or, as Kelsen said, into the 'human sphere of validity of the state', which certainly need not be equivalent to what exists in crude demographic terms. The Indians of the Amazon are self-determined in the middle of the rainforest and therefore do not exist for Brazil as a state except when they become an obstacle to it, because we are using a technical definition and not an ethical one. These are well-known principles. Now, the object of the state with regard to ideas is also the production of the substance of the state or of ideas valid for the state, not of *all* ideas. The same can be said of the state as producer: when the state produces steel, it does not produce steel but state substance and this would be equally true if it produced shoes. In the sphere of ideas, what should interest it are the ideas that can be validated within the state, that is, ideas that can become the spirit of the state, for the sate itself and also for civil society. When a ruling class produces ideas that cannot be metabolized as its own by civil society, the state necessarily exists in a relation of non-belonging to its very object or end which is, precisely, society. To be durable, of course, domination must be to some extent in the interest of the dominated; otherwise, solidarity is blocked from the outset.

It is said, to absolve Pando or Saavedra or Montes, that they merely shared the ideas of their time; we could just as well claim that they were, on the other hand, incapable of being contemporary with their own time. All this is debatable, but to forget oneself, which is something concrete, in the service of the general spirit of the times, is already the beginning of one's dependency or non-self-determination. If the 'ideas of the age' said all this, it would mean that the world's ideas favour the good fortune of some nations and the decline or elimination of others. The role of truth would be terrible indeed if its function were always to serve the victor. What is clear, in any case, is that there are no neutral ideas and that the ideas of the world serve those who produce them and who have succeeded in imposing them.

If this proposition is to be carried through to its logical conclusion, although it is true that we are now on shaky terrain, we must return to the question of the validity or efficacy of ideas in the sphere of the state. In short, an idea, false or not but adapted to its object, even to a mythical one, can be valid from the point of view of the state, as was Portales' anti-indigenous order, for example. In the case of these Bolivians, setting aside the inconsistency of their reasoning and even the ethical infirmity of not knowing how to use their own intellectual authority, the objective alienation of their spirits was expressed in the essential inviability of their ideas as state ideas. All this, moreover, with fallacious arguments. The solution for Moreno, for example, consisted in:

1. 'That [the Indian] be crushed under the foot of European immigration.' Why, then, protest against the Europeanization of Argentina?

2. That racial 'purification' be carried out to produce the 'unification' of the national race, assuming of course that the national race is one's own.

3. 'That miscegenation be encouraged with the Camba Indian, but never with the Aymara or Quechua.'[26]

Which means, in a word: no Indians; but if there must remain something of any of them, let it be of mine. Pando thought the same but the other way around: 'The Eastern Indians, that is, the Cambas, had to be exterminated.'[27] In an evidently arbitrary judgement, Saavedra, in turn, within his general anti-indigenism, considered the Aymara civilization to be 'vast, great and ancient like the Incan,'[28]

---

26 Albarracín Millán, *Orígenes del pensamiento social contemporáneo de Bolivia*, p. 156.

27 José Manuel Pando, 'Viaje a la región de la goma elástica (N.O. de Bolivia)', *Revista del Museo de La Plata*, VOL. 6 (La Plata: Talleres de publicaciones del Museo, 1895), pp. 141–220. Cited in Albarracín Millán, *Orígenes del pensamiento social contemporáneo de Bolivia*, p. 185.

28 Saavedra, *El ayllu: Estudios sociológicos* (La Paz: Juventud, 1971), p. 51.

presumably because he identified the Aymara with his own region. All this is patently absurd. In all three cases, under the pretext of imagining an illusory community (for Moreno, without Kollas but with Charcas; for Pando, without Cambas but defending the territory they inhabited; for Saavedra, without Indians but with labour legislation), they repudiated the real, living, flesh-and-blood collectivity that was Bolivia with its Indian—Camba and Kolla—majority. It was a true act of substitution of reality that could not be without consequence, because to supplant the real is necessarily to lose one's mind. It is a loss of or deviation from the real that derives from the seigneurialist roots of their thought, taken to the point of aberrance. To return to the examples cited above, which could of course be multiplied, Alberdi's plan or Portales' ideas were legitimate from the point of view of the state. It matters little, as we have said, that the Chileans were mestizos (as Lipschutz has shown)[29] so long as feeling European was an effective part of their identity, because the decisive thing ultimately is identity or the intersubjective discourse and not the fact of being European. In Argentina this became a concrete fact and not just an anti-Rosist utopia. It makes no sense to compare these ideas because a project of this kind was fundamentally incongruous in Bolivia. That men with the lucidity of those under discussion proposed such absurdities cannot simply be ascribed to their error: it tells us that the clan to which they belonged, which was the traditional caste, was, as such, as a human group, coming to the dead end of abject consciousness.

Whether or not they truly believed, as they surely did, in such appalling ideas is irrelevant except insofar as it proves that they were poor spiritual leaders and weak men of power, precarious masters of a dark hour. The primary task of the state is always legitimation or credibility. In other words, what cannot be legitimated does not exist. This shows that the constitution of the oligarchic state at that moment was flooded with an unprecedented fury, which defers all

---

29 Alejandro Lipschutz, *Perfil de Indoamérica de nuestro tiempo* (La Habana: Ed. Ciencias Sociales, 1972).

rational organization. Moreno was the founder of Bolivia's national history (as historiography); Saavedra for decades was a university professor of great prestige; Pando was the caudillo of the Indian masses, whose elimination he decreed—all this cannot be explained except as a profound sense of disorientation on the part of the collectivity to which they belonged.

If, in rather broad terms, we maintain that the first symptom lies in reasoning against one's own life, proposing what cannot occur by any means, the second consists in not finding the will to exist or to vanquish, in not taking account of the world such as it is. Their ideas, however, prevailed even if only in the narrow sphere that they had created for their poor victory. The ideas of those illustrious men founded a discourse and preserved the ancestral fury of Pizarro and Almagro in a way that lives on today in every seigneurial heart. They led to where they had to lead, to the permanent subordination of Bolivia and to their own subordination because it was the last country capable of accomplishing such horrific, abhorrent and impossible tasks. Only the action of the wretched of the earth would be able to save the scraps that could still be rescued from the legacy of that society in its absolute dislocation.

No racist thinks that in speaking of the subject he does not exaggerate. The radicality of the prejudices of our founders prevents us, however, from thinking of them as hyperbolic. The men of this country, especially those of its ruling class, had entered a state of chaos. Social Darwinism was exacerbated as a result of the double catastrophe of the Pacific, which subdued them to the point of admiration for their enemy, and Willka's war, which terrified them to the point of abhorrence of their brothers. The Indians—Baptista testifies to this— are the Jews of Bolivia (as [Antonio de la] Calancha had noted),[30] its scapegoats. This, then, is the basis of the discourse of the oligarchic state that in its four sub-phases (conservative, liberal, republican and military) always maintains the same ideal foundation.

---

30 See Saavedra, *El ayllu*, p. 36.

From these poisoned roots arose that tree that wanted only to fall. The problem is that all this could not remain shut up in the closet, but would necessarily break out. Things would come to light fully only when the state came to face the rest of the world, which it would do through war. This is perhaps the central problem with which any student of the events of Bolivian history since then and even since the War of the Pacific must contend: the sense of ground-lessness and bewilderment that all these events assume, as if life had lost its skeleton, a generalized absurdity. Incoherence, then, is not a mere metaphor but the defining attribute of the character of that state, as it would later be of its conduct in the Chaco War, of its behaviour in relation to the surplus, of the mad fanaticism with which the upper echelon of this society fought against all democratic forms, even the most basic.

What is strange in all this is the impotence of the intellect. Salamanca was not, by any means, a man of less talent than Batlle, as anyone who had known him would have attested. Baptista is said to have been a brilliant man; Moreno was unquestionably a better writer than Vicuña Mackena or Rodó; Saavedra was a man as impos-ing as Irigoyen and more cultured. Toro, as we shall see, was at least potentially a man of no less talent than Estigarribia. Here personalist interpretations of all kinds are clearly inadequate. We can presume, however, that Batlle believed in the equality of immigrants because he himself was an immigrant in a country of immigrants. Each in his own way felt himself to be part of what he did. In other words: knowledge cannot be constructed against reality with impunity, nor is knowledge ever independent from what one is.

*

An age of contempt, this period was described by Cuadros Quiroga as '40 years of recklessness'.[31] The era as a whole, if not for Willka's

---

31 Reference to an article titled 'Cuarenta años de vida perdularia' by José Cuadros Quiroga, published in 1940 in the newspaper *La Calle*.

war, which opens this phase of the state, the Chaco War, which reveals its aspiration , and the April insurrection, which neutralizes it, would have only a grotesque atmosphere, like a maelstrom of depravity and monstrosity in the midst of a burning house. The substance of the era is determined by the oligarchy in its pristine form, that is, by the seigneurial regrouping around the mining surplus and its major firms. We see here, uninterrupted by caudillos (in the manner of the nineteenth century) or popular uprisings, the oligarchy in its historical form, in the full deployment of its beliefs, rituals and principles. The people as such had been eclipsed with Melgarejo's victory and Zárate's disastrous campaign. We could say that this is the period of the *rosca* in its actuality or nakedness, certainly invaluable for the biography of a class but inexorable in demonstrating the inviability of capitalism in Bolivia.

The devastating failure of the oligarchic project stands in stark contrast to the cheerful certainty of its formulations. It is an era of bold assertions. Everyone seemed to know where things were going and it was an age in which Bolivia was unwavering. Amid the ruins of an exclusive sphere of public opinion, it was a society that believed too firmly. It was also, of course, the time when Bolivia was closest to political and national extinction. Montes and his foolish, triumphant pride turned Bolivia into a panglossian village, starving to death and capable of nothing but self-satisfied. Although based on a kind of apartheid, in this at least the liberals were unarguably successful: in selling consent almost by the pound. This shift towards groundless illusions was part of a certain enigmatic fantasy that enveloped the misfortune of the age.

It is, then, the age of abject consciousness or of false consciousness. The local political jargon speaks of the superstate or feudal-mining state, all terms that are modest approximations of varying efficacy to the scrutiny of an obvious fact that was the merely apparent or pseudological existence of the state, an existence tangled up in its real subordination to the dominant nucleus of 'big mining' and its periphery, the *rosca*, that is, the mining superstate. And so when the university reform movement launched the slogan 'mines to the state and land to the Indians' it became a pivotal rallying call, because in Bolivia the main oppressed groups were the Indians and the state. It was a slogan that perfectly fulfilled its function as such, incisively and with perfect concision.

It is here that we must begin a digression on sovereignty or self-certainty or authority, which is the ethos of the state and means being beholden only to itself. This is something that should not be reduced to the absurd. Obviously, no one has or can acquire infinite self-determination. What the concept implies is that a self-determinative ethos is always present in the spirit of one's acts. In any case, not to know what one is at least in the materiality of one's historicity is already a form of non-existence or subordination.

We should perhaps emphasize the solipsistic nature of the sterile digressions of recent attempts at a general theory of the state, based on the principle of alocalism in political analysis. Indeed, if we can speak of a mode of production in universal terms we must stop at the moment of the regulative model, which is the limit of its validity, that is, it can only comprehend the most strictly quantifiable aspects of abstract labour and no more than some general outlines of the superstructural phenomena, such as the freedom of modern men. It is in a way a discussion exhausted not through elucidation but through sheer accretion. In any case, it is clear that if there is a structural order through which there exists a certain univocality with regard to the capitalist mode of production or regulative model in such different formations as France, the US, Mexico and Argentina, this implies the principle of mundiality, that is, the logic of world history, which is a new dimension like the sense of temporality. Mundiality as generalization means, in a way that seems somewhat paradoxical, that nations or particularities are also deeper and more differentiated. In the past, the identity of a nation came from its isolation; here it is a choice because each nation must define itself in relation to mundiality. This is why the generalized framework of the regulative model tells us very little about the social equation or the specific difference of these countries, which is better expressed through the concept of the socioeconomic formation. Since the type of articulation between the relations of production and the super-structure is one of the meanings of this concept, in this sense the study of the superstructural sum has a local and historical connota-tion; it does not have a logical explanation, but a causal-factual one. This is why superstructures, even when the form of their autochthony is reduced to the particular mode of reception of the flow of mundiality, turn out to be a nucleus of irradiation because they are the modified synthesis of the set of determinants that derive from the subjects and conditions that, therefore, produce a kind of active predicate of society. Ideological, state or juridico-political pro-cesses always have as their structural explanation the accumulation of their internal history. In the case at hand, there was an excess of the world (or mundiality) in Bolivia but only because the Bolivian historical process was incapable, in the first place, of producing a viable articulation of the territory and, second, of building structures of self-determination.

This is where the problem of the general will (or *moi commun*) and that of equality intersect. At some point in time someone acquires the ability to 'desire' for society and in its name. This means to assume the general will or have the capacity to make one's own will the general will. The conditions for this are, of course, the objec-tive social possibility of the production of a general will and, sec-ondly, the power to read this faculty as political state. Where there is no general will there is only a sporadic, contingent and volatile will. The general will is something that must not only include everyone, horizontally but also all past generations and their legacy over the course of time: over the *longue durée* subjectivity can only exist in the form of a collectivity. In the very act of political excommunica-tion of the Indians and of the masses as a whole, the oligarchic state renounced from the outset the task of the production of a general will; but the generality of its will is the specific force of the state and this state was therefore the architect of its own impossibility.

It is important, however, given everything we have said, to try to situate the oligarchic state in Bolivia within a general theory of the moments of the state. We must of course consider that historical analysis always turns out to be better suited to its object than classifications according to generalities. What are construed as schools of thought or doctrines regarding the state turn out to be verifiable historical situations in different contexts and perhaps this indicates that state theory, sociology or historical materialism all in fact rely on the practical proof of historical subsumption.

In any case, with regard to the situation of the oligarchic state, we can distinguish at least four moments:

1. We have, in the first place, the situation in which formal or ornamental elements of the modern state exist but not the foundations of its substantive existence. This occurred with all the Latin American countries at the moment of independence. It is an apparent state because the cartographic dimensions do not correspond to the effective space of the state, nor does its demographic volume correspond to its enforceable legitimacy.

2. There is, on the other hand, a configuration opposite to the first. Through pathos or pure chance, men who differ from one another in their daily lives place themselves in a position of offering or receptivity. The political state is constituted as a more or less indefinite power over civil society and therefore an almost general capacity for the transformation of political habits is produced. The state is capable of governing routine existence and there is a contractual reform of daily life. This is what has been called, with a certain intellectual vulgarity, the Hegelian state.

3. Here we must consider the situation in which the dominant element in civil society becomes the political state itself, in the flesh, that is, in a special apparatus separated from society. The ruling class not only occupies the state, but one and the other become the same. The subordination of the state to the dominant group is so complete that there is no communication between civil society as a whole and the state, but the ruling class imposes itself upon both. In this sense, the Leninist or Engelsian sense of the state (if it can be simplified in this way), what is known as the instrumental concept, is not an archaic conception but a discrete historical moment. One has an instrumentalist conception of tsarism or of Somozism not because one is an instrumentalist but because Somozism and tsarism were.

4. Finally, we have organized capitalism. Here the state is clearly separated. It is the practice of what Marx called the relative autonomy of the state. It is a hegemonic exercise in which the dominant element 'learns' [aprende] (apprehends [aprehende]) the appropriate forms of domination from the dominated; the logic of the oppressor aspires in a sophisticated way to contain within itself the logic of the oppressed. This conception is present in Lenin's theory of dictatorship. Dictatorship then is democracy for us, the internal democracy of the proletarian dictatorship, in the same way that what is called democracy in general is democracy within bourgeois dictatorship. Thus the categories of dictatorship and democracy acquire a constant binary nature.

If we adhere to this schema—one that is surely incomplete and whose value is largely taxonomical—the oligarchic state in its physiognomy, and even in its character, oscillated between the apparent state and the instrumental state. Its most pronounced distortion is undoubtedly spatial. Space is a central fact of the past but it also contains what a country aspires to be—it contains the principle of hope. In its conception of the territory, which it did not aspire to integrate nationally but to organize around the requirements of the mining companies (an impermanent fetish) and of course in outright denial of the spatial foundations of social memory, it was clearly a state incapable of realizing its own objectives. In its conception of a sphere of legitimacy that was oligarchic in its origin, which means exclusive, based on the logic of the separation of citizens and *pongos* or *interdictos*, it was a state that condemned itself to an apparent or spectral existence. It ultimately accepted the demographic and spatial boundaries conceded by its neighbours. Given that during the entire period there was not a single president without some degree of connection to the mining companies, with the obvious exceptions of Busch and Villarroel, who already belong to the phase of its dissolution and decline, it is undeniable that to speak here of the relative autonomy of the state is ludicrous. The concept of the modern state did not exist in the proud and empty heads of the men of the oligarchic caste.

What characterized this power bloc that only for ease of exposition we call the oligarchy, in brief, was a certain lack of appetite for self-determination. This must be conceived in terms of a long process. It is not a question of the necessary mobilization of self-determinative action by a catastrophic event: it is, rather, the social production of a systematic desire or impetus. If self-determination had to be realized immediately, there would only be such an impulse when it—self-determination—existed fully, which is absurd. The peculiarity of this state is that in none of its acts was there a true desire for self-determination or when such a desire existed—we are thinking of Salamanca and his party—it was in relation to factors that were absolutely secondary like the Paraguayans and not in relation to the central problems of sovereignty. For Salamanca sovereignty was about the Gran Chaco and not about history. The miners' conception of space seemed entirely compatible to him with an utterly imperative attitude towards a peripheral territorial dispute.

*

Willka's masses emerged at the same time as the oligarchic programme of La Paz, that is, with Pandismo. Pando *in tuito persona* embodied the enviable possibility of a victory at once regional and popular, which would not only expel the conservatives and Chuquisacans but would also give rise to a certain potential hegemonic platform that would have been inconceivable from the Southern perspective. And yet, in reacting in accordance with its ancestral reflexes and not its sound judgement, the Pando liberals, which means all of them, sealed the antipopular character of the state they founded. The inclusion of the popular sectors would never go beyond the narrow front of the Saavedrist artisans and *Achacachi's sheep*; there was an explicit disjunction or externality vis-à-vis the popular. With this, the liberals washed their hands of what could have been a formidable burden but, at the same time, they completely deflated the margins of their project which would henceforth be slight. The existing power, exploiting what receptivity was left after having squandered the hegemonic capacity of Willka's masses, followed the path of the psychology of its class, a psychology with little sense of power or of its mediations and none whatsoever of sovereignty. In a way, the timidity or lack of desire for self-determinative habits in the oligarchy was a response to a certain tradition, one that stands in contrast to the sensibility of the masses. The ready acceptance of all things foreign is significant in contrast to the thoroughly local self-determinative style of the masses.

This has certain structural effects. We have come to an important problem—in the discourse of dependency, we know that we are dependent but not when our dependency ends. Countries are of course always dependent up until a certain point. Whether we look at Germany or Japan or Italy or Russia, there is a moment of popular acquisition of a sense of self-determination or at least such a sense is acquired in the discourse of the state.

It is a true break in the form of power. It is not an arbitrary will, but a structure of self-determination, that is, a kind of transpersonal conviction, which does not depend on the support of power but that instead provides a framework or norm whose transgression is illegitimate. Hence, when we speak of self-determination, we must distinguish between accidental or pathetic acts and what we are calling a *structure of self-determination*: this, the structure, is an objective fact, at least to the extent that collective and unrenounceable beliefs can be objective. The emergence of such structures remains enigmatic, at least in part, although it is clear that it must be attended by certain instances of surrender or opening to the general will. Self-determination itself is really an aspect of the general will and self-determinative acts are accidental or fortuitous to the extent that they fail to acquire a certain pattern of repetition in time—to the extent that they do not come to constitute a structure.

The case of the oligarchic state is a counterexample. First, because a generality of the will did not exist even as a utopian idea, while the constitutive pact was based on a regime of exclusion. Montes, Salamanca or Saavedra could perhaps believe to some extent in a certain dignity of the state but the idea of the self-determination of Bolivia as a society and as a state was unquestionably alien to them. The subordinate character of the country seemed to them to be determined by fate, a natural fact. This is the perspective from which it was said that 'we are a poor country and we must live like a poor country'.[32] It is an extreme case of docility in the face of a collective loss of freedom.

In certain circumstances, self-determination can be derived from a charismatic interpellation (as occurred in Belzu's era), but this lasts as long as the power that sustains it. The social base in which self-determination is rooted is therefore crucial to explain its

---

32 The phrase is attributed to president Carlos Blanco Galindo (1930).

emergence. In other words, the most consistent self-determination is that which derives from democratic exchange because in it the shared identity takes the form of equality. Self-determination is the collective or national extension of personal dignity, that is, of the extent to which the free individual exists, and if the collectivity has the strength that it has in capitalism it is because it is the result of interpenetration or interdiscursivity among free men. Surely it is a false personal dignity that is founded on the erosion of the dignity of another, because this exclusivizes or isolates instead of generalizing its meaning. This means that the free man tends naturally to extend his liberty towards the political and certain profound tendencies towards political democracy and self-determination are hence derived. It is this mass element that gives sovereignty its corporeality. Where men are not homogeneous or do not have active symbolic elements of homogeneity, they tend not to identify their Other as Other because their identity is obscured: the seigneurial caste thinks the Other is the Indian, not the foreigner. The opposition here is between a racial-culturalist project and a national project. The internal Other is a much more powerful negative point of reference than the true or external other. The extension of homogeneity, or of inter-subjective sympathy, so to speak, determines the emergence of feelings of self-determination.

Democracy is of course only the paradigmatic form of the emergence of this modern myth. We cannot say that it is the only one—it has certainly taken authoritarian forms. The Prussians acquired this impulse from the French invasions and a reasonable fear of the West triggered it in Meiji Japan, although there were conditions in both cases that preceded these. Why did the same thing not occur with a humiliation so terrible, so needlessly atrocious, as that inflicted by Chile in Peru or Bolivia? Men who come from elsewhere take much longer than one might think to become incorporated into their new space; it is a debt that must be paid over the long term or in dramatic events (because the drama consists in an act that is not gratuitous: one who witnesses it emerges a different man). The liturgical market,

that is, economic privilege based on race and religion, only accentuated this alienation and those who profited from it ended up constructing their own tiny country or subculture, which was the
oligarchy. An oligarchy that had barely begun to crack the protocul-
tural codes of the place could not counterpose a national idea to that
of their foreign assailants because they felt more alien to the Aymara
or Quechua multitude than to the Chilean army. Everything indicated
to them that ultimately their allies were latter—the foreigners—and
not the former. It's not that they had no patriotic feeling but that in
them the logic of the lineage, exaggerated to the point of absurdity,
had always been more decisive than the logic of the nation.

　　With power monopolized in so few hands, in which the suppression of the principles of equality and dignity was legally sanctioned
and was practically a tenet of the state, Montes and his cohort of sell-
outs acted, after Zárate's defeat, in accordance with all the deep convictions of a caste so mysteriously alien to its own home.

*

We can identify certain regularities here. In the formation of the axis
or equation, the state, furiously possessed by a kind of messianic rage,
relates to society on social Darwinist terms. The development or formulation of the social Darwinist discourse, however, is one thing,
and the ideological practice of social Darwinism, its brutal manifestation, is another. From Baptista to Saavedra, from Moreno to Pando,
the ideas formulated are in fact collective ideas; but they are those of
a collectivity that could not imagine itself beyond its existing boundaries. It was a caste that, within the gamonal conception of space,
was united only through the negation of its enemies. As [Alberto]
Gutiérrez would say, it's clear that Melgarejismo was not a spiritual
and material enterprise that began and ended with Melgarejo but the
horizon of the mode of being of this class.[33] Just as Montes would

---

33 Alberto Gutiérrez, *El melgarejismo antes y después de Melgarejo* (La Paz:
Velarde, 1916).

negotiate the territory in terms identical to Melgarejo's, now as minister of defence he directed the leader of the Abaroa regiment in Viacha against what he called the 'Insurrection of the Indian horde': 'In resorting to arms, we must shoot to kill; warning shots that serve no purpose but to diminish respect for the armed forces are prohibited.'[34]

There is nothing new here and, on the contrary, it is simply an extension of what some have called the expansion of the seigneurial landholding regime systematically instituted with Melgarejo.[35] Montes himself, creator of the brilliant tactic of *shooting to kill*, almost obscenely, would come into possession of the Taraco hacienda, expelling its peasant community. These are the origins not only of the oligarchy of the 50s but also of the present one; as we shall see later, the descendants of these men are present and active in today's society.

With this observation we mean only to say that it is the climate of the era, in this case its stale, foul air, which enabled the espousal of social Darwinism by some of its ideologues and not the ideologues themselves: they conformed to a general conception of things. This has a material origin—what the effective collectivity thinks is a synthesis of the results of the class struggle. The victors want to erect their flag in the name of all. This is the reactionary unconscious of Bolivian society. It is its secret ideology and its 'domination complex' that produce the instinctive acts of the state in a process whose rationalization is beside the point; in this case the genocidal instincts of the oligarchic spirit surfaced in a literal way. It is the ideology in which this state existed; social Darwinism as *Weltanschauung* and the dispossession of the Indians as a *bare right*, with the dogma of the surplus as the only (illusory) basis of legitimation.

---

34 Cited in Gregorio Iriarte, *Sindicalismo campesino: Ayer, hoy y mañana* (La Paz, CIPCA, 1980), p. 15.
35 Rivera Cusicanqui, 'La expansión del latifundio en el Altiplano boliviano', pp. 95–118.

In describing this landscape we are inclined towards the usual irony with which one views the past, because those who came before us always seem so ingenuous. But this should not be exaggerated. It was, in fact, a successful project. The response on the part of the sub-merged society was weak, dispossession was a reality, and the sur-plus, though it did not exist in the promised proportions, did indeed exist, at least as a general fantasy.

We must distinguish between the moment of the construction of this ideological foundation and what it becomes once it has been integrated. Practice qualifies collective hypotheses and terror can be Kant put into practice, as Merleau-Ponty said. These ideas contained some contradictions in Moreno or Baptista but we see them fully developed, with a certain terrible magnificence, in Montes' actions and Saavedra's or Arguedas' thought, which is their final form. In the histories of states, the moment of interpellation tends to have a cer-tain grandeur, because interpellation is impossible with weak incen-tives. Only the extreme degree of self-destruction of the peasantry, the structural impossibility of transforming its ethnic-corporative demands into a general democratic programme, in other words, the necessary failure of all backward ultimatumism, can explain the rudi-mentary character of the utopian moment of the oligarchic state: there was a sense that all things could be founded *ex nihilo*. Willka's project is, in any case, proof of the sterility of the oligarchy as state. Carranza could have defeated Zapata but he adopted his programme, although, naturally, in a modified form, because that is the right of the victor. The liberals wanted to destroy not only Willka but also his programme and yet this has long survived him. They had not the faintest notion of the process of assimilation by the state of the propositions of the social base.

In other words, this state, like all states at the moment of their constitution, had to make certain choices or undertake a process of selection. In doing so, it revealed the hollowness of its hegemonic ambitions. The great agrarian movement nonetheless gave rise to the elements of a certain hegemonic engagement. As in any such act of refoundation, Pando could not prevail without mobilizing the masses. It was the right moment to do it, since he somewhat inexplicably commanded the respect of the Indians. But ultimately he held his own prejudices dearer.

*

Not all of their thought was so utterly bankrupt. It was Tamayo, certainly an audacious man whose thought went beyond mere conformity to the era while still its prisoner, who knew that mulitvocality was a natural feature of all social propositions, that they should be— and are always—*biunivocal*, although he expressed this in a discourse mired in contradictions that end up destroying the logic of his exposition. It is nonetheless instructive to follow the thread of this discourse, even if only in the most summary way.

In the first place, a powerful but Manichean reaction against the social Darwinist dogma that was so prevalent at the time:

> If by the manifestation of a moral superiority we understand that air of gravity with which man faces all the events of his existence, and a profound sense of justice, and more than justice, of equality, and still more than equality, of love; if morality consists in being one's own master and only abandoning oneself and one's own interest for love and service towards one's fellow; if great morality is manifested in the accentuation of one's personality, without prejudice and rather to the benefit of others; if it is, somewhat more precisely, the expression of certain general virtues, such as working from the time one is able and until one can work no longer, moderation and observance of customs and the translation of this into an orderly bodily health; absence of all radical evil, truthfulness, gravity, absence of all spirit of mockery, gentleness as a general condition, humanity and harmlessness, and, along with this, as intellectual qualities, simplicity, rectitude, precision and moderation; if all this is a manifestation of moral superiority, no one possesses such

superiority to a greater degree than the Indian of whom we speak.[36]

The consequence of this was a *centrality* of the Indian, which was like an inverted social Darwinism: 'The foundation of all superior morality is in a real physical superiority; in this sense, what is most moral, what is strongest in Bolivia is the Indian; then the mestizo, because of his Indian blood, and lastly the white man.'[37]

It was the resurrection of pan-Aymarism, an indigenism that we insist is too reductive. Tamayo, however, in attempting to put his exultant messianism into positivist syllogisms, unwittingly founded a whole school of thought: the entire subsequent Aymarist discourse —Katarism—consists in believing in oneself and this is ethnocentric, although its justifications were not. To be Aymara, however, implies universality, that is, to embody symbolically the persecuted of the earth in a carnality of the here and now. But one cannot logically be simultaneously Aymara and gamonal. All of Tamayo, but especially his formidable sociological pamphlet on the society of La Paz, makes a double tribute to the seigneurial and the indigenous core of the national, which could only end in a kind of mystification or decomposition of his thought. It is not easy, however, to convey a conceptual contradiction of such magnitude with such eloquence, fervour and consistency. As a landowner himself and even as a direct heir of Melgarejismo, Tamayo of course could not see the Indians as anything but born labourers. Nor did such radical protests impede him from praising Montes himself, whereby he revealed himself, in a way, as no more than an *enfant terrible* of this, of Montismo. A great personality, however, transcends its own caprices, and this is clearly the case with Tamayo, in whose discourse on the country we find certain lines that are indispensable for our understanding of the subject.

---

36 Tamayo, *Creación de la pedagogía nacional*, CHAP. 34.
37 Ibid.

Tamayo proposes to imitate the spirit of the Japanese example when the Meiji Restoration was in process, that is, very early on. Japan, in his view, had obtained in the first place a stark and disenchanted objective vision of the world: 'It is evident that what lives most intensely in the world is Europe.'[38]

But Japan is not overwhelmed by this knowledge; on the contrary, it sets out to capture 'all the objective, external elements of European life.' 'Only fools speak of the Europeanization of Japan.'[39] Tamayo then invokes the distinction between culture and civilization, so in vogue especially among the Germans: 'In Japan there is a European civilization: but the whole culture, its soul and substance, is Japanese.'[40]

Translating this into other terms, we can affirm that there is here a clear idea that being is being in the world and that, conversely, only in the world (in one's mode of exchange with the world, which is civilization, the currency of this market) is one oneself (one's own culture). Against a class and an atmosphere that lack that kind of sentiment and presentiment, Tamayo's call for self-determination or for what he called a 'national pedagogy' remains the most categorical historical manifesto of these principles. Its limitations, however, were obvious. Tamayo resembled Fichte but Montes was no Bismarck.

One could ask, for example, why Patiño was able to succeed in the world despite the fact that his 'soul and substance' were not Bolivian. The ability to appropriate the technology of the world was comparable in the two cases but not the cultural—or spiritual—sensibility with which this was achieved or, rather, not their national accumulation. Tamayo, in the tremendous muddle of his thought, lacked the objective class position necessary to understand the decisive relation between self-determination and democracy.

---

38 Ibid., CHAP. 8.

39 Ibid.

40 Ibid.

There is certainly a demagogic Tamayo, in Unamuno's sense (a pedagogue of peoples). The fundamentalist or millenarian aspect of his discourse today serves interests that he surely would not have shared, because he was conceptually torn. Tamayo, contradicting himself, nonetheless proposes a principle that, in our view, is absolutely central to the analysis of the national question in Bolivia: that of human interaction in its development, certainly the most intelligent and profound thesis of this exceptional text:

> And at this point in our study of the national character we necessarily encounter another factor that is definitive for many sociologists, and we too, with certain reservations, are inclined to hold it as such. This factor is the environment, And the environment is the land, to use a less dryly scientific term. Man is made by the land.[41]

The environment or atmosphere of the social—this much is recuperable. The land itself, of which we have already spoken, is a very significant element here. But the land, as modified land, is the modification of the land and not the land itself, even if the land has determined its modification. In Tamayo, it is not a question of a mere reduction to geography but of the necessary interaction, which is already the condition of a local form of intersubjectivity:

> In speaking of the national character, American whites, mestizos, and Indians all have two powerful factors in common: our history and our environment. [. . .] Our common land and permanent coexistence are two forces that work ceaselessly in the same direction despite the resistance of the exotic races and the historical oppression of the autochthonous races. The human species can exhibit deviations, strange modifications, diverse tendencies, etc. It matters little; an anonymous and powerful will emerges from the land and in it there is a confluence of all human currents: volitional, intellectual and emotional. And this is

41 Ibid., CHAP. 43.

the true meaning of nations [. . .]. Men sometimes fail to grasp this, and worse, sometimes a delusion, a false inter- pretation of their own history, an inherited prejudice, blinds them to the true meaning of their life, and this is a hindrance to history and an obstacle to life. Thus, the white man among us, implicitly or explicitly, imagines himself to be at an immense distance from our Indian; and not only does he imagine this but, on this false premise, he indeed harbours no feeling but of contempt for the Indian or, in the best of cases, indifference. He does not see that between him and the Indian there is much less distance than between him and the white man of Europe [. . .]. In America, there are no whites, at least not in the strictly European sense.[42]

These arguments belong to the best strain of our essayistic dis- course, which is to a great extent (as the novel would later become) the chosen genre in America. Tamayo could not have read Murra or Choy (who certainly had read Tamayo), he despised Rousseau for no apparent reason and read Schopenhauer seriously and Nietzsche rather literarily. But the question of the land, whether as the originary scene of ideology, the agrarian question itself (for example, in the characteristic dichotomy of productive 'persistence' and the preda- tory but not incorporative style of the landholder or, more generally, of the extractor of the surplus and the society of the landholders), or the very logic of spatial belonging or the unrenouceability of space, are elements present in *Creación de la pedagogía nacional* of an indis- putable validity today. The recognition of the effects of premercantile or protomercantile intersubjectivity in the general development of a common identity is no doubt a very advanced intuition regarding the production of the self-consciousness of this society.

Tamayo intuited or remembered, in the Platonic sense, another aspect of the general state of fluidity that had occurred recently in Bolivia, with the emergence of the indigenous masses and the

---

42 Ibid., CHAP. 44.

conflict around what we have been calling the axis or equation. He found that in the very body of interdiscursivity or psychological activity of the environment (which here should not be understood as mere geography) it was necessary to determine what the axis of interpellation would be. In his view, this unquestionably had to be the indigenous: 'The two fundamental features of our national character are persistence and resistance. [. . .] The main root of our nationality is necessarily formed in every way by the indigenous blood which, as we have seen, is the true reservoir of national energy.'[43]

The conjunction of the principle of intersubjectivity and this, which is an interpellation from the indigenous pole, invites a new reading of this programme, although it is of course a deductive reading. We must differentiate between utopia and illusion. Men who do not organize utopias do not truly exist, while illusions are often merely an escape from existence. It is not easy, moreover, to turn a feeling of contempt into a programme. The officially or ideally Hispanic caste had always failed in Bolivia in the embittered illusion of a Europeanization of society, perhaps because it referred to a Europe that had ceased to exist. Even if we presume that such a programme might have admitted a syncretic existence, this would only have been possible with a significant degree of ethico-state absorption of the propositions of the Indian masses, that is, with a hegemonic and not cultural-genocidal or fetishistic project. The current millenarian movements certainly take up and develop the centrality of the indigenous that Tamayo proposed and in their good sense they proclaim the right of every recognizable body (and here we speak of a considerable portion of the social entity) to qualify the terms on which equality must occur, that is, the right to formulate interpellative propositions.

It is with Pando that the possibility of a modern state collapsed, because an opening or fluidity of the masses had come about and

---

43 Ibid., CHAP. 48.

was closed to him at the level of the quotidian. Pando chose to serve his savage dogmas and to pay slavish tribute to ill-conceived ideas rather than to take on the national programme that was latent in the form of the rebellion; he sanctioned the legal exile of the Indians, who, moreover, had risen up in his name. Such a mobilization of support for Pando had its own meanings. It is true that even in the decade of 1910–20 his name maintained a certain resonance among the Aymara. It was nonetheless tragic that the Indians themselves invoked a man with such nefarious racist ideas, which means, frankly, that in their perplexity, they themselves still harboured the seeds of their own servitude. That is, they lacked information. Without this, they could not win.

The cast of leading characters of that era was of course radically incapable of discerning such glimmers of analytic greatness in Tamayo. He himself, moreover, acted for that society, filled his poetry with marvellous elements and gushed the imperiousness of a facile erudition to the point of disgust, and ended up shut up in a room for decades. To a considerable extent, the comfortable superiority that he enjoyed over the men of his time led him to lose all self-perspective and distorted him. The ultranationalist military regime of the 40s republished his essays, but they reformed neither the society of the time nor their own institution in accordance with them and, in general, instead of discerning the transformative lines of this thought, they made Tamayo into one more household god.

*

We could say that originary accumulation, which leads to the construction of the generalized market, is also a constitutive moment of the nation in the capitalist sense. It is not, of course, the only possible constitutive moment, nor, as we have seen, is the capitalist form the only possible national form. It is also clearly possible to imagine a process of originary accumulation without a national orientation in its discourse, that is, not all originary accumulation produces a nation. The expansion of the seigneurial land regime and the triumph of free trade at the level of the state certainly amounted to such a moment of accumulation. In this process there was, then, a conflict between different axes of proposition and interpellation, and Willka's defeat surely expressed by contrast the fully developed form of the non-national character that defined the period. In the confrontation between the endogenous forces of the 'moral economy' of communitarian resistance and the primitive protectionism of the artisans and the exogenous forces of the silver boom and Chilean interests, the latter prevailed. The truth is that neither the popular demands, at once extremist and conservative (because they proposed nothing but the complete restoration of the indigenous community), nor the intellectual expression of the oligarchic victory fulfilled the basic conditions of a national-bourgeois solution to the contingencies of the class struggle, that they offered a simple, reactionary solution. There was, as we have seen, a vanguardist and exclusionary programme within a kind of eternal return of the masses that struggled ferociously for amorphous objectives and a seigneurial one that up to that point had always succeeded in reconstructing spaces for its own repetition or persistence. In the long run, as will also occur in this phase, both failed because an elite programme that does not ultimately succeed in seducing or including the masses is insubstantial. A mass programme that is not viable, that is, fully national or collective, in turn, inevitably provokes a reactionary response.

The consequence of this limited resolution of the problem was the mentality of the miners, that is, of the flesh-and-blood bourgeoisie, who put into practice these theories that were in turn the expression of a social process.

*

Let us see in a summary manner some of the elements of the fascinating history of the tin mines. Production went from 1000 tons per year in 1890 to 3,500 in 1899 and 15,000 in 1905.[44] In 1929 it reached

---

44 Herbert S. Klein, 'The Creation of the Patiño Tin Empire', *Inter-American Economic Affairs* 19(2) (1965): 7.

48,000 tons. Exports rose from 20,014,100 Bolivian pesos in 1895 to 93,721,800 in 1913.

Leaving aside the loss of the great surplus of the nitrate fields and copper mines of the coast, if we consider that during many decades Bolivia had effectively disappeared from the world market or barely participated in it, it's clear that, in relation to the life that had been organized in those conditions, here two new surpluses worth taking into account had been produced, that of the second silver boom and that of the tin mines. This is in addition to that produced by the rubber industry, which was not insignificant. So the problem to be addressed is not the absence of a surplus but the capacity for its local metabolization or assimilation. This was of course non-existent.

The Huanchaca mine set a precedent that would be repeated. In 1885, for example, while the state revenue was just over 4 million pesos, Huanchaca alone made 5 million for its shareholders.

Moreover, in the context of Bolivia's virtual non-existence in the world market, Huanchaca came to produce 850,000 marks of silver and paid 40 per cent per annum to its shareholders in dividends. Since the export rights were 0.08 Bolivian pesos per mark, of course nothing was left and it was as if it had never existed.

The same can be said after the rubber boom, which between 1906 and 1911 came to represent 20 per cent of Bolivian exports.

The history of the tin mines is no different. Between 1900 and 1920, exports totalled 1,023,329,090 Bolivian pesos, of which the state retained 48,026,040, or less than 5 per cent. The former liberal minister of finance Edmundo Vásquez calculated that in a single decade, from 1920 to 1930, exports totalled 2,660,000,000 Bolivian pesos but, as Vásquez said, 'this capital has not been reinvested in the country'.[45] Meanwhile, 'while the national revenue during the entire term of the liberal administration did not surpass 31,000,000

45 Albarracín Millán, *El poder minero en la administración liberal*, p. 164.

[Bolivian pesos], until 1920 La Salvadora [Patiño's main mine] alone was valued at 2,000,000,000 bolivianos.'[46]

Until 1952, the year they were nationalized, Bolivian mines produced 300,000 tons of tin.

In 1902, Pando introduced an extremely modest tax of 3 per cent on net profits. In 1904, according to the *Report of the Finance Committee of the Chamber of Deputies*, only two companies, Abelli and the Quechisla Mining Company, paid this tax. The former paid 583,077 Bolivian pesos and the latter 861,540. Disobedience on the part of the Indians was harshly punished; in this case, incompliance had no consequence but the expiration of the law because it had 'fallen into disuse': 'The law of 13 December 1902 fell into disuse' and 'as of 1905, none of the companies paid the tax.'[47]

The same thing happened with the other minerals. With a certain degree of naivety, Montes, who felt that he had nothing to do with it, wrote in his 1914 report to Congress: 'The antimony exported for a value of 17 million Bolivian pesos has not left a single cent in taxes [and Montes' minister of finance, Darío Gutiérrez, would say in 1918 that] the fiscal yield on antimony exports was zero, *because no export tax is levied.*'[48]

If we compare this figure with the national budget, which did not exceed 16 million pesos in the same year, it would be fair to protest that 'the direct export of 17 million pesos, with no duties of any kind, could not be conceived as anything but outright plunder.'[49]

General Montes' indifference did not stop there and the same report added: 'We must add that the same applies to lead and zinc, which are exported duty-free.'[50]

---

46 Ibid., p. 319.

47 Ibid., p.159.

48 Cited in ibid., pp. 161–2. [Zavaleta's emphasis.]

49 Ibid., p. 162.

50 Cited in ibid., p. 163.

As for wolfram, of which Bolivia was the world's primary producer, 97,000 Bolivian pesos were left in the country of 5,600,000 in exports. This, however, was considered 'a miracle'.

Vásquez had said that all profits from exports up until 1930 were 'distributed to foreign shareholders',[51] a claim that was corroborated by Montes himself, according to whom '98 per cent of the mining companies, whose shareholders pay tax on dividends, were foreigners and collected their dividends outside the country'.[52]

The last president of the liberal era, José Gutiérrez Guerra, attempted to tax mineral exports and it is entirely possible that this was the immediate cause that brought this era to a close:

> Between 1900 and 1920, during two decades of mineral exports, the percentage of customs duties was almost invariable, fluctuating between 3 per cent and 3.4 per cent [. . .] Taxes were not levied on tin profits, nor did any other kind of tax apply, because the only tax law, instituted in 1902, was not observed; on the rest of the mineral wealth, including antimony, no taxes were levied, not even customs. Copper, sliver and gold were constantly exempted of export duties through express ministerial orders.[53]

This means, quite simply, that there was no retention of the surplus. Let us leave aside the basic ineptitude in the defence of greatest surplus after Potosí, which was the surrender of the nitrate fields and the copper mines. The fetishization of the surplus was so extreme that the absurdity was committed of sacrificing a large existing surplus—that of the nitrate fields—for the prospect of a future surplus. The model, therefore, was Chile but only because of a pathological Chile-philia—Chile as appendix or partner of the British and not the Chile that had coveted and conquered a surplus. This is what Montismo did with this so central element of its conception of the

---

51 Cited in ibid., p. 164.

52 Cited in ibid.

53 Ibid., pp. 120–1.

world, with its philosopher's stone. If by surplus we mean access to resources that do not merely reproduce the previous levels but exceed them, that is, a favourable change in the means of social reproduction, it was unquestionable that Bolivia had embarked upon a new era in terms of its surplus. The men of the oligarchy squandered it with an unfathomable insouciance.

This refers not only to Bolivia's loss of a million square kilometers between 1889 and 1909, which was serious above all because of the acquiescent manner in which the loss was born. It was not just a case of simple defeatism in the sense of not believing in what was officially theirs. It was something more that this. We could say that every state programme has a territorial feeling as part of its conception of things. These are relations that are not always conscious. Moreno, for example, as a member of this state, at the hour of his death felt the grief of seeing Bolivia transformed into a mining factory; it was, however, too late even for regret because the gamonal conception of the territory of the state was only the extension of the destruction of its human wealth, whose origin was the racial chauvinism of which Moreno himself had been a prophet.

These feelings were applied outwardly as well as inwardly, and what happened with the railway network is of a terrible eloquence. The sale of territory (because the peace treaties with Chile and Brazil were nothing more or less than this) translated into an investment in a kind of infrastructure based on the Sisson Report. They gave rise to the network called Speyer-Montes, designed for no purpose at all but to serve the mining industry, as Sisson himself acknowledged.[54] On the remains of the derailed prior internal market, which was a residue of the nucleus of Potosí, which had collapsed for all practical purposes with Belzu's artisans and Willka's *comunarios*, since the participation of the regions was interrupted, a new, shrunken internal market, if it can be called this, was constructed, circumscribed to the

---

54 W. Lee Sisson, *Reconnoissance Report upon Proposed System of Bolivian Railways* (La Paz: Impr. Heitman y Cornejo, 1905).

mining districts and a few valleys, Cochabamba in particular. The foundations of the old protected market (sugarcane, wheat) destroyed, its breadth was reduced and this affected important regions like Santa Cruz:

> The Cochabamba flour industry slowly disappeared; the looms and garment industry only made strange things that not even the Indians wore; the sugar of Santa Cruz was made into alcohol and was eclipsed by imported liquor from Peru. If not Chilean, Brazilian, Argentinian and Peruvian, the products that flooded the consumer market were US imports.[55]

A phenomenon that will only be seen in its full expression when we discuss the problems of mentality in the conduct of the Chaco War, that is, the tenacious, inevitable and general slippage towards an active inconsistency of behaviour, understood as a collective tendency, appears here in its early stages. The lack of coherence, not to mention of national orientation or self-determination, was expressed here in the simplest negotiations. For example, despite the fact that the Speyer contract was like a derivation of the Chilean indemnification, that is, that the same thing occurred with the railway as with the coast, 'the bankers of the Speyer trust left business in the hands of The Bolivian Railway Co., which in turn transferred its rights to the Anglo-Chilean subsidiary, the Antofagasta & Bolivian Railway Co., moved by the same interests that produced the treaty of 1914'.[56]

The money, acquired at the immense price of territorial dispossession, was returned to US and Chilean hands, that is, directly to the plunderers.

These habits of the state in relation to the territory were also translated into their internal equivalent, which made up what can be called the enclave system. Here the tin miners simply inherited practices instituted by their immediate predecessors. A commission of the Chamber of Deputies reported in 1900: 'The Huanchaca com-

---

55 Albarracín Millán, *El poder minero en la administración liberal*, p. 329.
56 Ibid., p. 92.

pany, in a grave offense against the Constitution and the republic, dictates its will and governs a population of eight thousand souls.'[57]

The mines and the rubber plantations were preserves closed to any form of state action. The company was forbidden to pay in vouchers and to impede trade and freedom of movement among the population. To little avail: 'In this area it was impossible to enforce the law [. . .] [because] "the managers of Huanchaca and Pulacayo named authorities who should administer the towns so that all the authorities were subordinated to the company".'[58]

This situation persisted in practice until well into the 1940s. In any case, Tejada Sorzano, as the liberal minister, certified that in 1919 the system had not changed. He asked: 'What could the sub-prefects, intendants or magistrates do against the big companies? They unfortunately had no choice but to submit to the whims of the companies or leave their dominions.'[59]

In principle, the explanation for this would be the incapacity for a bourgeois use of wealth, and this would be the cause of the lack of will to self-determination exhibited by the state, that is, the social entity did not assume the desire for either. In those conditions, it is reasonable to suppose that the same thing that happened with the second silver boom and the tin mines would have happened with the nitrate fields and the copper mines, as indeed occurred with Chile. This will lead us at some point in this exposition to other levels of analysis. It is remarkable considering that we are speaking of a country with some measure of mercantile and even capitalist experience. It is no accident that Patiño almost unconsciously worked out the model that has been called that of 'cross-mutations',[60] that is, he tended towards the incorporation of technology as if he

---

57 Cited in ibid., p. 251.

58 Ibid., p. 251.

59 Cited in ibid., p. 272.

60 T. S. Ashton, *The Industrial Revolution, 1760–1830* (London: Oxford University Press, 1948).

had been born in it and, at the same time, towards the subsumption of the *manager* model under traditional forms of exploitation. Patiño was living proof that there were no true cultural obstructions to a rather comprehensive understanding of the world or of capitalism. It is evident, on the contrary, that he himself represented a case of possessive individualism without a nation, that is, it was the nation or those who assumed the monopoly of its name who lacked such notions of individuality and possession. The seigneurial elements in Aramayo or Arce were more important, even if only by osmosis, and cosmopolitan elements were dominant in Hochschild. The real leader or corporate caudillo, however, was Patiño. This is why we must ask under what conditions it was possible to perform all the tasks proper to a bourgeois logic and at the same time to directly renounce its extension as a national logic. The favourable combination of low consumption and a relatively high level of adaptation to advanced technology on the part of the workers, along with the pre-existence of a certain internal market, seemed to invite a kind of mimetic effect in the development of capitalism. However, Patiño constituted himself as an exemplar of spurious embourgeoisement because, bourgeois to the core of his being, he was formally capitalist but not national. It is in the study of the great figures of the bourgeois class that we find evidence of the insidious limits of embourgeoisement in a formation like the Bolivian. The fact is that it turned out to be an inhospitable land for it.

Patiño, a man from a modest background (although from within a very particular popular setting, that of Cochabamba, which despite being a non-industrial subformation was perhaps the oldest and most distinctly mercantile of Bolivia), acquired the notions that would take him so far first as an employee of a supply company (Fricke) and later of Huanchaca itself, then the biggest company in the country. We could say that here certain ideas take hold of him, such as the particular and subordinate position of Bolivia in the world market, but also the advantages of industrial concentration.

This is the origin of the deeply rooted fusion of formal subsumption and exploitation that defines his character as an entrepreneur.

We can perhaps accept [Herbert] Klein's claim that 'his first move was the creation of a modern technical administration under the management of competent European engineers'.[61] But there is no doubt that, in their long relationship, we certainly cannot speak of an attitude of deference towards the foreign technocrats on Patiño's part. In reality, he subordinated, even psychologically, a vast body of European and US administrators and engineers to achieve his ends, which were not those of Bolivia—but not those of the foreigners either. In this sense, he is an entrepreneur of the classic mould because he never abandons, from beginning to end, what Marx called the *command of capital*. This is significant because the manner in which real subsumption occurs determines the form of power in capitalism and we can perhaps even say that it is the earliest moment of the foundation of the state. If this did not extend towards society it was not because of any particular fault of Patiño's (although it was also this) but because of a certain incapacity for absorption on the part of the social body. The local pre-bourgeoisie, to the modest extent that it existed, was far from the spirit of command of capital in any form that would exceed the the purely despotic framework of originary accumulation.

Patiño had a profound instinct for technology and this would have extended, in other conditions, towards society. Almost from the outset he bought a refining mill worth a million dollars, which in his time was a truly considerable investment.

> The mill called Miraflores started working in 1905. With electric energy and other improvements, La Salvadora jumped from 10,797 tons in 1904 to a pre-refined production level of 42,409 tons in 1905. In 1910, La Salvadora was already producing 10 per cent of the world's tin.[62]

61 Klein, 'The Creation of the Patiño Tin Empire', p. 9.
62 Ibid.

This means that the two basic moments, formal subsumption or the formalization of command, which entails the assimilation of the new sense of time, and real subsumption, as freedom from the constraints of the traditional forces of production, were present in him. The latter, as we know, is the civilizing moment of the bourgeoisie, its hour of vitality and substance, and Patiño belonged to it. Carrasco speaks of his exercise of this aptitude until the end:

> When I went up to the Harrison gallery—Patiño writes—I saw that metal carts were leaving the mine only half full, a grave error because it wastes material. The *palliris*[63] send boxes to the foundry and the machinery gets ruined with no one to oversee it. There are too many workers in the mines, and there is no control. I am surprised that you have not noticed this or that, having noticed it, you have have not taken steps to remedy it . . . I must tell you that you are the only one answerable to me for the lack of order and the lack of compliance on the part of your subordinates in their duties.[64]

Almaraz narrates another no less eloquent anecdote:

> Just before he died, his technicians from Huanuni announced the that the mine was exhausted. Despite having been absent for twenty years, he ordered that work be continued in the site called Boca Grande. He died before the outcome of the this exploration was known: Huanuni became one of the richest mines of the group.[65]

The three big miners, Patiño, Hochschild and Aramayo, were known as the 'tin barons'. Patiño, however, had not a trace of aristocratic caprice; his temperament was entirely pragmatic. The variation between some 'barons' and others is telling. Hochschild, for example, is the embodiment of cosmopolitan capital. He himself came to

---

63 Women who sorted through the minerals retrieved from the mines.

64 Manuel Carrasco, *Simón I. Patiño: Un prócer industrial* (Cochabamba: Editorial Canelas, 1964), p. 81.

65 Almaraz, *El poder y la caída*, p. 31

Bolivia, it is said, with an inheritance of 200,000 pounds sterling and a doctorate in mining; therefore, his fortune was his doctorate in action. He was cosmopolitan and he conducted himself as such, although he was almost killed in the most local manner. His case could hardly have become paradigmatic. As for Pacheco, Aramayo, or Arce, if we have said that one can find in them a certain popular element, far from becoming bourgeois, they became lords and ended up, as Mitre says, buying manors in Sucre and ranches all over the country.[66] It's true that Arkwright also ended up buying rural land and properties but he clearly never abandoned a secular and worldly style. The same can be said of Patiño, who was like the personification of capital: Pairumani, the ranch he bought in the valley, always meant little to him and he regarded his non-mining investments, including an electric plant in Cochabamba, with a certain disinterest. He seems to have been a man endowed with a somewhat brutal good sense in which the impulse of accumulation predominated and not that of the protestant ethic; a good sense, moreover, that was purely capitalist, a conception of the world through profit. He believed in nothing else. His attitude towards the national ideology as well as the national reality, for example, is clear. While he was not known to have any religious ideas or convictions of any kind other than entrepreneurial, he nonetheless realized that it could be useful for others to believe in nonsense. This explains the fact that Alcides Arguedas dedicated his *Historia de Bolivia* to him. He would have laughed heartily if someone had told him that he was to industry what Montes was to politics or Arguedas to public opinion because he did not often notice the existence of his employees nor was he in interested in their opinions. Still, he did not spurn Arguedas' dedications and he even subscribed to his doctrines to some extent.

The truth is that he saw Bolivia as nothing more than an exploitable portion of the world, and one that surely he knew better than anybody else. But he was not only bourgeois in form: he was a

---

66 See Mitre, *Los patriarcas de la plata.*

bourgeois-in-the-world. In 1908, he opened his first office in Hamburg, perhaps influenced by Fricke or perhaps because the Germans had come to be important purchasers of Bolivian minerals before the First World War. He believed no more in Germany than in Bolivia, of course, because it was not his style to admire countries; that is, if he believed in it, he interrupted his belief when his interests moved him to do so just as one changes one's clothes. In defending his most concrete interests, he was capable of doing fierce battle with the Chilean capitalists, whose plans he frustrated to a large extent although it's clear that by then they and Chile as such were biting off more than they could chew.

Two moments stand out as proof that he was a man who moved with a comfortable certainty in the world. First, when he makes an ally of the US National Lead Company and takes over Williams Harvey, the British tin foundry that was the largest in the world. Second, in his role in the formation of the International Tin Committee in response to the bust of 1929. By then, of course, between La Salvadora, Uncía and Llallagua, he controlled 49 per cent of Bolivia's tin and 11 per cent of global production. The subsequent expansion of his business is just the extension of these unerring intuitions about the world.

That certainty is matched only by the utter lack of patriotism or the moral indifference with which he regarded his own country, which can be seen in his relation—common to the entire oligarchy—to the local labour force and also to the Bolivian state.

The conditions were always atrocious in the 'mining cemeteries'. Of Huanchaca, a foreign observer once said: 'Of the 400 born every year, about 360 die within three months.'[67] In 1909, Lima found that in Corocoro, '75 per cent had developed clearly detectable lesions in their lungs'.[68] Pasley, a British engineer, 'made it known that the

67 Almaraz, El poder y la caída, p. 21.
68 Cited in Albarracín Millán, El poder minero en la administración liberal, p. 263.

transport of minerals from the interior of the mine to the surface was performed by workers carrying sacks of metal on their backs. These sacks had a capacity of 75 kilograms and only two trips could be made.'[69]

Barbier affirmed that 'The pulverization, the sulphur emissions from the silver, the handling of minerals made into bars to be sent to Europe, killed them like flies.'[70]

It was a labour regime that seemed to indicate that for the companies everything was important except those men. It was, however, something socially accepted, as was made evident when in 1903 a law was passed making Sunday a mandatory day of rest for all, with the exception of the mine workers. The loss of human life through overexploitation of labour was seen to the end as part of the nature of things, to the point that Aramayo wrote in his famous *Memorandum*, which lays out his project for the country: 'The Bolivian worker, as a result of his primitive education, does not yet have the same needs that more advanced peoples have.'[71]

This has been illustrated, in a descriptive mode, in the observation that 'The company [. . .] did not hesitate, despite its heavy investment in machinery and advanced techniques, to employ women and children above ground in sorting metals and other tasks which required extensive labour [. . .].'[72]

All this is only to say that then and much earlier the exploitation of the labour force was an established custom. Indeed, the mining industry only continued the Spanish tradition of extermination through work, which is a systematic practice that persists to this day and is incorporated into the everyday life of this society.

*

69 Cited in ibid., p. 237.
70 Cited in ibid., p. 239.
71 Cited in Almaraz, *El poder y la caída*, p. 106.
72 Klein, 'The Creation of the Patiño Tin Empire', p. 18.

There is a problematic knot that we can call the aporia of Patiño. The sordid and dense enigma of his trajectory has generally been explained either as the product of a singular personality or as a result of the call of the world market. When the world needed tin, it produced Patiño, etc. These elements of course figure in the process of the enigma but they do not totally resolve it. Hochschild is an example of the world coming not to Bolivia but to its tin. And to inherit a fortune as Aramayo did is not the same thing as to make one. Patiño was at once local, because he was formed here, and contemporary, that is, originary.

We should perhaps take into account the problems of a mentality proper to an outwardly oriented economy. The very capacity for participation in the world market is conditioned by the level of consolidation of the nation-state, which means that it is dangerous to become essentially a part of the world before becoming a nation. This kind of extroversion not only deforms the internal congruence of the economy but also defines the ideological belonging or loyalty of the bourgeoisie, even if it has developed locally. It is a complex problem because exportation deforms, and at the same time the notion of existence outside of the world is chimeric. On the other hand, a class is always the class plus its culture or environment, which exceeds it. Patiño, as we have seen, as an individual was a man of a wholly bourgeois character. He introduced technical innovations at the global level, such as Patiño motors, and he succeeded in transnationalizing himself in an unorthodox manner, that is, from the periphery to the centre. He was undoubtedly the dominant figure of the era, entirely without peer; having assumed such perfect mastery over the country, it would have seemed logical that he would reconstruct it in his image. For some reason, such a dissemination of the capitalist spirit did not occur and Patiño himself seemed to share the logic of exclusion and non-incorporation that was proper to the ruling class. He achieved only a weak and instrumental unification of the dominant bloc, which would inevitably lead to its collapse. As for self-determination, not only was no such thing attempted but it was never given a thought either—on the contrary, it was strictly impeded, as the history of the foundry ovens shows.

The question of why Patiño's programme, which involved the entire economic cycle of the mining industry and its corporate integration but not an ideologico-institutional transformation, was interrupted at the very point at which it became strategic for the country and for his own class warrants a few more precise hypotheses. It is a problem that has to do with the democratic (or undemocratic) skeleton of the social. The assimilation of free labour in formal subsumption need not occur in a purely despotic manner and, in any case, that act of subjection is limited by the free man himself. The power of this moment lies in the democratic infusion of the productive moment as an objective factor, that is, democracy as a force of production, residing in the essence of the act of production and not merely a superstructural reflection of it. It is (in effect) a moral-historical element because the morality of history (which is the proposition of freedom) qualifies the mode of participation in the historical horizon. As to real subsumption or the technological principle, which is already the highest moment of the reform of production, it is largely an inextricable relation between freedom and the state. Of the state, insofar as it entails the principle of totalization, which is the ultimate result of concentration plus the advent of the new sense of temporality. Of freedom, because the total worker is its *mass force* and a necessary condition of real subsumption. To believe that the culminating moment of this process (the machine in production) can be achieved without producing its social base (totalization, determined by the degree of democratization), sooner or later, leads this base to cripple or paralyse its false expression. Patiño's motors in the end were useless because the workers rebelled against Patiño.

Patiño, therefore, aptly expressed the schizophrenia of this formation. There was an unresolved conflict between his tortured impatience to incorporate himself into the world, a result of the amputation of the Pacific coast and an obsession with the surplus, and a resolve not to alter the terms of the internal class relations and even to undertake their reactionary reform. Patiño, then, as the most advanced stage of this bloc, wanted to combine real subsumption with the massive exploitation of labour power.

This, as a discursive model, was tenacious and even successful in its final expression but it lacked long-term viability. Ultimately, there are only two ways to build structures of self-determination. The first, which we have already cited, is through the receptivity that ensues from democratic concentration. The second is the authoritarian form or the method of negative hegemony. For this to occur there must be a kind of absolute victory, implacable and prolonged, to create the foundation that receives the authoritarian command; but, also, a coherent continuity of authoritarian rule because at a certain moment this indefinite over-domination turns on the one charged with exercising it. This form, therefore, requires a state like the one imagined by Hegel, a state with an ultimate internal certainty. The project derived from Patiño's process suggests that an authoritarian route was sought that would submit labour to exploitation by both capital and the state. The core of its inviability was, however, in its conception of the state as an instrument of obstruction and subjugation.

To affirm that Bolivia lacked structures of embourgeoisement raises the question of latent ideas. In principle, a pioneer is a pioneer —but he should also be a model. Society should at once produce him and receive him, transformed, as proof of its potential. Patiño's ideas, applied to politics, did not make the Patiñist state more powerful. This was because he only gathered together latent ideas with his power. The structures of embourgeoisement or the socialization of bourgeois ideals, the ideologeme transformed into a popular myth, must be preceded by or simultaneous with intellectual reform. Instead, in that Bolivia what had taken place was a popular movement that clung, rightly or wrongly, to archaic forms of its constitution that were nonetheless capable of laying siege in a fierce (and we would add, counterproductive) way to the whole of the ruling class and its fringe. The latter, in turn, too attached to a simplified version of the Chilean model, could not help but embrace social Darwinism, which came to represent the ex-post rationalization of something that had already happened. The complicity of the great minds of the country, in proportion to their talent, is clear.

＊

In that kind of involuntary omnipresence, Patiño was also the cause of a grave deformation in the development of the state. In 1899, Patiño held a mysterious meeting with Pando. This was just shortly before the violent action with which Patiño, 'with Indians and armed men', took La Salvadora never to relinquish it. This episode represented the beginning of the end of Anglo-Chilean economic expansionism, which then had very concrete designs. It is also, however, a significant event for other reasons. The miners, we must say, did not govern directly and there was indeed a certain political class. Still the specificity of this state consisted in the subordination of the political class to what was therefore called the superstate. It is an anecdote that illustrates the original, essential and definitive subordination of the oligarchic state to 'big mining', a subordination that becomes a kind of second nature for the politicians, that is, there is an absorption of sovereignty by the irrefutable apex of that society. It would be helpful at this point to describe the form in which this was expressed. For this we turn to the personnel of the 'establishment' itself.

Tejada Sorzano, who was Gutiérrez Guerra's minister at the time, describes it best, in 1919:

> The power [of the Bolivian state] is increasingly inferior to that of a group of industrial firms which, as a result of important interests, have become a political force in the development of the Bolivian nation [...]. The phenomenon consists in that the development of great fortunes does not

run parallel to the development of public finances; that a single citizen or a small group of citizens alone has at its disposal greater resources than the entire nation and that the predominance of their interests increasingly determines an imbalance in the distribution of the country's energy, these interests weighing evermore heavily on the opposite side of the scale to that of the interests of the nation.[73]

This was entirely obvious. The modest 30,000 kilowatts generated in the mines was more energy than that consumed by the rest of the country together. The capital produced by a single mine (La Salvadora) in a single year (1920) was equal to 70 times the total revenue of the Bolivian state in 20 years. Under these conditions, things could not but be as they were.

It is not surprising then that Villazón, a former manager of the firm, would maintain upon completing his presidential term that 'We have concentrated our efforts in protecting the mining industry'. In his view: 'The government [. . .] should be exclusively devoted to administrative tasks [. . .] *our fellow citizens cannot and should not ask for more*' because 'we have work to do; our task comes down to that of exportation'.[74] The 'symbolic man' himself, Salamanca, whose significance we shall see below, had declared: 'The miners are not to be touched'.[75]

Such official and openly acknowledged supremacy could not but have immense consequences for the conception of the state, for example, with regard to its spatial self-conception and even the legitimacy or authority of the state in its new space. In Zalles' opinion, the mines 'constitute an independent community that is territorially coextensive with the Republic'.[76] Zalles had been a presidential

73 Cited in Albarracín Millán, *El poder minero en la administración liberal*, pp. 335–6.
74 Cited in ibid., pp. 123–4.
75 Cited in ibid., p. 112.
76 Cited in ibid., p. 252.

candidate—we do not know who successfully commanded him to step down; this he did but said what everyone thought and denounced 'an unchecked, omnifarious power' within the Liberal Party.[77]

This translated into specific modalities of the constitution of power, which abdicated all legitimation *eo ipso*. Electoral participation did not exceed 1 per cent of the population and, nonetheless, as the official organ of Patiñismo, *El Diario*, acknowledged: 'In the political sphere, Simón I. Patiño has control of the province of Bustillos in the department of Potosí and of Huanumi in the department of Oruro, a decisive control certain to tilt the balance towards the side to which he inclines', and therefore, 'Patiño [. . .] no longer holds only the economic centre of the country, but extensive control of the electoral activity of the nation.'[78]

Extraterritoriality of the enclaves, the literal exclusion of the population in the constitution of power, and direct control of the electorate that was left. On top of this, considering that the intellectual who had been proclaimed 'the teacher of youth', Daniel Sánchez Bustamante, had said, 'Attracting the interest of the Yankee is our primary task',[79] it seemed entirely natural that the xenophilia of that atmosphere would pride itself on its consummate appeasement. An American even occupied the post of minister of mines and petroleum for several years. A Frenchman, Jaques Sever, was chief of the general staff from 1905 to 1909 and the German Hans Kundt occupied the same post in 1910. He would go on to lead a crucial part of the Chaco campaign. Even education was organized under the leadership of a Belgian mission and the Kemmerer mission reshaped the country's fiscal policy with absolute authority. Not to mention the terrible affair of the loans that gave rise to Margaret

77 Cited in ibid., p. 221.
78 Cited in ibid., pp. 191–2.
79 See Conrado Ríos Gallardo, *Después de la paz . . .* : *Las relaciones chileno-bolivianas* (Santiago: Imp. Universitaria, 1926), p. 317.

Marsh's classic account, *The Bankers in Bolivia*.[80] Such acts of appeasement cost Bolivia dearly, as we shall see.

In discussing the crisis of the oligarchic structure, we must consider the conditions under which a society is capable of producing relative objectivity in the form of shared cognitive premises or criteria of valorization. In a way, we could say that those who need self-knowledge most, the countries that must face history in an already deteriorated state, are least able to acquire the necessary conditions to do so. If Zárate, Belzu or Patiño himself—who (in their way) advanced propositions that in principle contained realizable elements (that could be made real) of a social project—had constructed intermediate spaces, they would have thereby modified the oligarchic political society. This, in turn, would necessarily have existed with a less spurious independence than that which it assumed. It is a series of successive ruptures. Not even the most successful personal and entrepreneurial bourgeois experiments, like Patiño's, included a project of intellectual reform within their horizon, that is, their fortunes were capitalist but their invisible beliefs were not and they were in no way prepared to contribute anything to the formation of the state. In their very character, they were individual capitalists who rejected from the first the idea of the general capitalist. On the other hand, the intellectuals turned out to be all too organic in relation to the proclamation of an absolute victory over the Indians. Enamoured of their own prejudices, they did not for an instant abandon them; they made them into the units of a general structure of thought (which was a compendium of abject chimeras) and nothing of this had the slightest potential of becoming a national programme, which, moreover, would have supposed certain minimal democratic elements, that is, from the outset, the gradual substitution of a mode of life. But men do not replace their mode of life—they develop it or they die for it. They were operating under impossible premises. They

80 Margaret Alexander Marsh, *The Bankers in Bolivia: A Study in American Foreign Investment* (New York: Vanguard Press, 1928).

wanted something like a bourgeois state without capitalist ideas. In a Jeremian apotheosis, they lamented their national inferiority but no one ever proposed the elimination of the efficient cause, which was inequality.

The form of politics has real consequences. In other words, we tend to think that things can be expressed in different ways but, in reality, they have a single necessary expression and thus we come to the problem of the necessary forms of politics. Iconic power and a denial of reality are constitutive of the present form of this state system. It was a society that replaced every project of effective homogeneity with an illusory homogeneity, through the legal anathematization of the Indians. It was what is called an act of suppression: since history had unfolded unfavourably, history did not exist; it was replaced by an irrational optimism.

This is what occurred with the flesh-and-blood men of the foundation of the oligarchy, that is, with its intellectual sources and the founders of its lineage. Let us see now what happened with its *first actors*, who were already only the figureheads of that founding. The volatile logic of this state itself led to a non-rationality in the constitution of power and to its charismatic or ritual legitimation. It should not be assumed that this assertion necessarily rests on premises that favour a rational-bourgeois constitution or reiterable rationality and a bureaucratic-transpersonal nomination of its organs. Clearly, even a power that is non-rational in its routine operation and in quantitative terms can have an unquestioned validity. Belzu was not directly elected but no one was as popular as he. On the other hand, charismatic election is proper to prophetic forms and of course today no one would deny the validity of millenarian forms of legitimation. In this case, however, there was a restriction to the interregional logic of the lords, that is, the lords after Willka, intoxicated with the power of their monopoly.

In its very nature, this power bloc, the miners and landholders (not only the *latifundistas*, and this is important, because even a small plot of land signalled the assumption of lordship—hence the Melgarejist hunger for all land and not just productive land), could believe neither deeply nor superficially in what is called representative democracy, that is, in the logic that supposes that where there is one man there must be one vote. This itself is not the culmination of democracy but its formal principle; at best it is a poor expression of the democratic essentialism of Rousseau or Paine. Through a mental act that transformed Montesquieu's system into *Rojas' Candidacy* or *huayraleva*[81] *democracy*, this system expressed with great factual eloquence what was inherent in the structure of the Bolivia that emerged from the Federal Revolution. For all political purposes, it was a country that had resolved to exist without the vanquished and that further declared the political monopoly of the victors through restricted suffrage in a way that is only comparable to the American South or to South Africa today. In certain sociological conceptions of politics as a white-collar privilege, it is an idea that is still alive today. If it's true that one does not think beyond what the available concepts of one's society allow one to think, this society could not imagine democracy except in Rojas' terms. This proves its incongruence because the fraudulent constitution of power cannot but lead to power's not knowing what it's made of; it is not something that only has consequences for the oppressed and it is, therefore, above all a form of self-deception. What is absurd about this caucus is that it was accountable only to itself, but its true excess lay in that it still aspired to a charismatic appeal. It was, therefore, a state that could not exist without its own weakness. The forms of its debility guaranteed its own precarious existence and it was, in short, a *rosca*, that is, a vicious circle.

In accordance with its own tradition, its particular style, this society tended towards grace and not virtue, towards bouts of excess

---

81 [Local pejorative term for a member of the elite; Augusto Céspedes uses the phrase *huayraleva democracy* to refer to electoral democracy restricted to a very narrow political class.]

and not historical process. Its life is like a never-ending party where bad news is not admitted. Perhaps for this reason, the political phase now before us, on the contrary, is characterized by the stubborn attempt to establish the criterion of exemplarity over processual logic in the explanation of events. The project was crude in its essence because it was based on the political annihilation of the masses, but it aspired to construct a closed political society that believed in a kind of reinvention of history, a heroic history constructed almost without heroes because what heroes there were were elsewhere, their names unknown.

Salamanca inherited the paradigm of the 'symbolic man' from Linares. It is a process full of feelings of inexplicability or disorientation. The oligarchic society had squandered one opportunity for charismatic leadership after another, although certainly, instinctively, it sought them without end; the pursuit of a charismatic solution to the unresolved problem of the legitimacy of power is only natural where the principle of the rational legitimation of power has been abdicated.

If we adhere to the descriptions offered by Saavedra's few biographers, we must believe that his intellectual horizon was more contemporary than Tamayo's. Siles himself, although he was on the fringes of the *rosca* gentry, with a conventional training as a Charcas attorney, was a man with a certain intellectual dignity. Both, however, stand out as peaks on an otherwise flat landscape. It was a society obsessed with mere appearances, a collective case of submerged consciousness. It was Montes who, through sheer noise, showered this political society with his paralogy because, with his formidable euphoria directed primarily towards itself, with his innate sense of boundless self-satisfaction, he belonged to an environment enamoured of this, of an optimism that issued from the fervour for the surplus.

The surplus, however, came, existed in some small measure and vanished immediately. Then the 'symbolic man' emerged, 'the most meditative and coldest of the Bolivian politicians and also the most distinguished', with an 'intelligence [that] was self-sufficient without any kind of intercourse with new ideas', according to Céspedes' magnificent observation.[82]

It seemed that this society had finally reached its objective. With 'the simplicity of his oratory, precise and eloquent, rare in those times in its lack of rhetorical excess',[83] Salamanca's sobriety, which was like a kind of inertia, however, came too late because it was impossible for the system and it was, in any case, accompanied by an illusory vision of the world that was of the greatest significance. And so, when the 'symbolic man' appeared, it was said that the misfortunes of the nation had come to an end.

In the following pages, we will see to what point Salamanca's ideas about Bolivia corresponded to the radical falsity proper to his class position: he himself, as a landholder, entirely seigneurial yet a mestizo, had Indians but could not see them. Even in his disheartened vision of a man given over to death from the beginning, he was confined by a social blindness in the style of Candide, a general optimism that explains how Bolivia could follow him into a hopeless venture like that of the Gran Chaco. Here indeed an entire state organized its own defeat. In this more general sense, if in the microhistory of the oligarchic state Montes means something different from Saavedra or Salamanca from Siles, they all nonetheless merely constitute different moments in the process of a state that would run its course. We are not particularly interested in this discussion or in the banal internal history of oligarchic democracy between republicans and liberals but, rather, in its role in determining subsequent events and above all in the apocalyptic ordeal that was the Chaco War. None of them, in the end, figures as more than a straggling

---

82 Augusto Céspedes, *Salamanca o El metafísico del fracaso* (La Paz: Juventud, 1973), pp. 15, 19.

83 Ibid., p. 18.

piper in a parade of disaster and disgrace. In this catastrophe, the essence of its epitasis can be read.

*

War, according to Clausewitz, 'is [. . .] closer to politics which, in turn, may be considered as a kind of commerce on a larger scale'.[84] It seems to us that here Clausewitz establishes an apt comparison between the essence or spirit behind each of these three forms of interaction. A war is, in effect, a crisis and, as such, has an unusual and extraordinary effect of trans-subjectivity. Politics and commerce, in turn, have the same content but in a perennial way. This proposition serves as the basis on which we can advance a hypothesis. Indeed, we know the limitations of a theoretical reduction of the national question to its mercantile desideratum. Reality itself suggests that there have been nonmercantile or premercantile forms of nationalization. In fact, politics is the commerce of power, war is the crisis of politics and politics is the distribution of crisis while war is the violence of commerce. All of these are forms of communication between men. In the Bolivian case, this great mobilization, which moreover entailed a significant death toll that is socially productive, if we can say this in these terms, was one of the elements, and perhaps the most important, in the constitution of the multitude, which is to say, we are speaking of an important indirect form of institution of the national. The Chaco mobilization was the pathetic revival of the elements of unification that had existed with the Potosí market and its consequences for the masses, such as the Amaru uprising.[85]

---

84 Karl von Clausewitz, *On War* (Michael Eliot Howard and Peter Paret trans) (Princeton, NJ: Princeton University Press, 1989), p. 75.

85 The following paragraphs are from Zavaleta's *Consideraciones generales sobre la historia de Bolivia, 1932–71* (1977), available in Zavaleta Mercado, *Obra Completa*, VOL. 2, pp. 35–96.

Love, power, war—these are the true elements of life. It was in the Gran Chaco that Bolivia came to ask itself what its life meant. Here, where the wilderness itself writhes in dry pain, is the starting point for all of modern Bolivia. Boquerón, Nanawa, Kilometre 7, Picuiba, Cañada Strongest are no longer inert toponyms; they now contain their own dead. These are names that are alive for all Bolivians. It is as if only there history (at least for Bolivia) shed its routine existence and it is undoubtedly then, only then, that Bolivia realized that power is destiny, that is, something sacred, something for which ultimately one must kill or die.

The war, of course, was avoidable. Notwithstanding the motley array of claims laid by the two parties, whatever the gravity of the incidents that preceded the war itself, it is evident that it was possible to agree upon a solution. It is bad state policy to think that the only solution to everything is the imposition of one's own position and this was of course the approach taken by the negotiators, the 'Chacologists'. Why, indeed, did the two poorest, most backward and emptiest countries of the region feel compelled to throw themselves into a venture that proved so uncertain and so lethal? It was as if they acted out of a sense of duty to themselves, perhaps because they felt that all they had left was their honour. A negotiated solution was what reason demanded and what followed from the outcome of the war; but those who had to conduct the negotiations were not reasonable men. Arbitrage would have been possible but only between countries not subjected to such accumulated emotional pressure that had never been rationally examined. This, which seems to be almost a will to submit to a trial by fire, something nihilistic, mysterious and primitive, is perhaps where we must attempt an explanation not based on a reasoning coetaneous with the events, but on the charge that conditioned that reasoning, that is, in the *historical foundation* of these countries. All rational arguments demanded that they unite, and yet they mustered, from the recesses of their impotence, arguments to attack one another. Charcas, of course, was Charcas, like the pearl of inland America. Asunción, meanwhile, had its own prestige. Was it not, after all, the epicentre of colonial expansion in the whole of Río de la Plata and then a modest country but also progressive and harmonious, comparable in this to the Chile of the time, but perhaps in a healthier way? There was undoubtedly a kind of weak arrogance on the part of Charcas and there was no reason why Asunción should not have harboured a certain vindicationism that was not related to the Gran Chaco. There is a misunderstanding here. People tend to see countries from the perspective of the present and they are not necessarily wrong to do so because things are known in their conclusion; each country, on the other hand, sees itself with the eyes of its memory. That a country's memory stagnates at a moment in its past or that it becomes mythicized is not really important because here what matters is what a country believes itself to be. The component of collective memory in the ideological register is no doubt greater than is commonly assumed. The Paraguayans, then, carried their own historical burden.

This is also the case with Charcas. It is generally taken for granted that the viceroyalty of Río de la Plata is the relevant frame of reference for Bolivia in terms of its juridical origins. It is often assumed that the centre of the viceroyalty was always Buenos Aires. But the truth is that it was not Charcas that existed in its relation to the viceroyalty but the viceroyalty that was constituted with its foundation in Charcas. In principle, the territory of the viceroyalty was Charcas. The viceroyalty of Peru was made up of the two *audiencias* and that of Charcas comprised what is today Argentina, Bolivia, Paraguay and Uruguay. Even when another *audiencia* was created, that of Buenos Aires, now within the viceroyalty, half of the provinces and most of the population remained in Charcas. The entire region, moreover, lived off of Potosí and was constituted by its relation to it.

In both cases, we are dealing with countries whose relative importance in the region had done none nothing but decline continuously. This, as we shall see, radicalizes the mood of intensity, of national uncertainty. Both countries were hurt by the new economic order of South America, by the substitution of a state-monopoly economy based in the interior centres and fuelled by a lust for precious metals by an economy centred on the commercial periphery of the ports, largely induced by the expansive phase of the English textile industry.

Paraguay, as far as we know (although with a knowledge coloured by the exultation of our sources) was certainly one of the most interesting centres of those that revolved around Potosí. Following the separation of the United Provinces (or of the Confederation, as Dr Francia would have preferred to say), it was certainly a more populated province than the others, considered individually. It was a country constructed by the despotic-theological discourse of the Jesuits (and this perhaps explains its politics which consists almost exclusively of long cycles). The seigneurial landholding sector was therefore insignificant and control of the land quickly passed to the state, although under negotiated terms that produced a virtual small-holding peasantry. The dictators—Francia and the López family— ratified the Jesuit laws and developed them in their own way and thus fashioned a despotic, paternalistic and dogmatic republic—but also a more egalitarian one, in its most basic principles: legitimate power, men who are free in practice. Our records of the country before the war of the Triple Alliance show evidence of a certain sober wellbeing in the life of the people, of a higher literacy rate than anywhere else on the continent in any case and, in short, of a kind of poor but utopian polis. Paraguay was among the first Latin American countries to build a railway—although its effective utility is unclear— and also, more importantly, its own shipyards and a military industry. All this, naturally, with the proportions of a small and isolated country. It was, at the same time, a country that had been shut off not only to foreigners in general but also specifically to British trade, which was seen, as it is now, as civilization itself. The vicissitudes of the opening of trade, and, above all, the political reaction to the

Paraguayan schism, allowed the new capitals of British commerce in the region—Buenos Aires, Rio de Janeiro and Montevideo—to organize the war of the Triple Alliance, to plunder the country and to produce a kind of demographic catastrophe from which Paraguay never recovered.

The history of Bolivia in the nineteenth century is different but its point of arrival is similar. The country itself, in its nineteenth-century form, is the result of two events: the mercury crisis, which was a consequence of Napoleon's embargo against British trade and the ruin of the Huancavelica mines, and the brutal agrarian war, the Fifteen Years' War or the war of the little republics [*republiquetas*] or factions (the irregular endemic war that involved the whole country) between 1809 and 1824. Only in New Granada was there such a levelling of the forces of production as a consequence of war. With the mercury crisis, the Potosí economy, which was already in steep decline, finally collapsed. Potosí, meanwhile, was the key to unification with the upper provinces and the concrete link was therefore lost. Upper Peru was now nothing but violence in the manner of Facundo, so that the leaders of Buenos Aires, starting with Rivadavia (bearing in mind that all of Argentina in the nineteenth century and perhaps longer is nothing but the development of Rivadavia's Europeanist and racist ideas), saw the retention of the Upper Provinces as utterly undesirable, while these provinces indeed wanted this, as part of the confederation. With a greater population than all the other territories together, they could only reinforce the provinces of the north that, on the other hand, would not be reduced to the emerging power of Buenos Aires until the second half of the century.

Bolívar, as is evident in his correspondence with Sucre, could not understand that the same capital—Buenos Aires—that had displayed an extraordinary lack of interest in these provinces, despite the fact that these were the territories that kept the border region independent from the rest of the viceroyalty, at once showed an almost passionate interest in their separation. In short, Alvear, a man from Buenos Aires, negotiated a deal with Bolívar in which what was called Upper Peru (or Charcas, more precisely) at the end of the colonial period would not be part of the United Provinces whose constitution they had nonetheless endorsed. The will of the country that had received Sucre with the blue and white flag of Belgrano opposed this; but Bolívar, dictator of Peru, that is, of a place that had never lost its Hispanophilic flavour, felt then perhaps for the first time his Gran Colombianism and decreed that the formation of an enormous country bordering Gran Colombia to the south that would be the product of the almost natural union of Upper and Lower Peru was undesirable. It was, therefore, something that nobody wanted and if Buenos Aires, which after all had been a powerful revolutionary centre, was mistrustful of the defiant spirit of the Upper Peruvian provinces, Lima had been—financially, militarily and spiritually— the place from which these were pursued in their solitary struggle. Lima, moreover, was a land whose independence had been won against its will and Upper Peru, or Charcas, with the bankrupt oligarchy of the mercury miners and with a hundred little republics founded upon the violence of an invincible geography, constituted by a kind of direct democracy of war and, with an autonomous organizational capacity, a territorial-political aggregate with no hegemonic nucleus, was incapable of resolving by itself and for itself the grave question of its political power. The Upper Peruvians themselves, who with a clear conscience had raised the flag of Belgrano upon the arrival of Bolívar's army, had to accept, and not without a certain perplexity, their status as an independent country.

Even so, the events themselves could have warned them (if they had been prudent men, but the ruling class only has prudent men at its height, that is, in the early stages of its rule) that something was changing in what they thought of as the nature of things. With this we perhaps mean to justify, but by *argumentum a contrario*, the certain arrogance or unjustified sureness of itself with which this republic, destined to suffer all the perils of the world, was born. It was, however, a sureness that did not come from itself and we can discern in it a paranoia that would later be repeated, if it's true that paranoia consists in a split between intellect and sensibility. The factions or little republics themselves demonstrated not only an inexplicable and sometimes atrocious capacity for resistance (given that they were never vanquished by anyone) but also the centrifugal nature of power for which they laid the foundations (which explains their inelegant designation as *republiquetas*). Much later, this would take the form of a permeation of the national by the indigenous. In other words, since leaders were nominated by the combatants and the logistics were determined by the Indians, given that the very existence of a faction means, in concrete terms (although not in a legal sense), that the landowners do not hold possession of their properties so long as the military democracy lasts, it is a mass war with all the features of the classic peasant wars: strong resistance and little chance of victory. For those fond of transhistorical comparisons, for Toynbee, for example, Amaru's war or even the war of independence and Münzer's would bear an uncanny resemblance. This is passed down to the republic and would become a feature of the national character. It would be a country of great military capacity in its masses, always unyielding in their home territory, reproducing certain Incan limitations because it would be a state with little ability to wage wars outside its own habitat, as if as a result of an excessive adaptation to its environment. The faction, with the habits of democracy in arms, would leave as its legacy a country of what Alcides Arguedas would call, with all the bitterness of his soul, the 'barbarous caudillos' and the 'plebs in action'. This explains the great distance between two countries that are otherwise as similar as Peru and Bolivia. It is here, in part, where the distinctive features of its social character are forged.

The catastrophic silver bust would put an end to the mercury mining oligarchy and this meant that it was a country born isolated from the world, just as others—for example, Argentina—are born through their interaction with the world. Isolated, moreover, from a world that it itself had produced. It would therefore be a kind of contingent state that would have to live till the last third of the nineteenth century on indigenous tribute, a racial tax on the Indians as such, which means that it would be a state in perpetual war with its own population.

The learned men of Charcas,[86] who were the recipients of independence, gave no thought to any of this. They thought of the sumptuous glories of the Potosí of Arzáns de Orsúa y Vela, of its splendour; they felt like the indisputable centre of things and could not be convinced that they had been left behind even when the Argentinians told them as much as emphatically as possible through Alvear, Anchorena or any number of others who had spoken on the issue. The vanity with which Charcas thought of independence, its affectation and self-satisfaction, can only be explained as the style of a class that had never worked, that had grown accustomed to being the unquestioned axis of things. Potosí's silver and the servitude of the Indians poisoned the country, and what might be understood as its human counterpart everywhere lacked the ability to concretize into a power structure.[87]

*

War teaches us a great deal about things. The two least powerful countries of South America waged the greatest military conflict the region has ever seen. The Chaco War has been called 'the vicious war'[88] and perhaps for this reason it is so instructive to consider the technical military analysis of its events together with the sociological

---

86 *Los doctores de Charcas*, a term for the intellectual and political elite at independence, often mocking its distance from the populace.

87 End of passage from *Consideraciones generales sobre la historia de Bolivia*.

88 Charles Arnade, *La dramática insurgencia de Bolivia* (La Paz: Juventud, 1964), p. 11.

premises that surrounded them. We will try to do this primarily from the perspective of the existing Bolivian state, because this is the general object of our analysis. Meanwhile, we think that David Zook's study[89] is the most objective and also the most useful for this manner of stocktaking, although it is clear that in availing ourselves of this work we must ignore its eminently contemporary orientation, that is, the poverty of its historical horizon.

In the first place, with regard to the very conception of the war: the Paraguayans were convinced 'that Bolivia was contemplating a full-scale conflict', and consequently '[o]n 30 June [1932] [General Estigarribia] called for commitment in the Isla Poí sector within twenty days of "all the available population of the country" to vanquish the enemy and save the Paraguayan Republic.'[90]

It must be said that such a mobilization never occurred in Bolivia, perhaps because in essence this formation, because of its heterogeneity [*abigarramiento*], was incapable of conceiving the idea of a 'general mobilization'. Perhaps the closest precedents were the non-indigenous mobilization in the siege of La Paz by Katari and that of Cochabamba against Goyeneche's advance. In any case, it is clear that, for one reason or another, the attribute 'national' was automatically ascribed to the war in Paraguay and not at all in Bolivia. Here a more or less complex problem arises, which is the construction of the image of the war that must be waged, that is, the ideologeme under which men will fight. To launch a national war without a certain radical concept of it, that is, without considering the possibility of generalizing it, is in itself a great risk; in insurrections, as in wars, one must always be willing to carry them through to the end or not wage them at all. On the other hand, it is difficult to engage the degree of mobilization necessary for a war in the twentieth century without giving it the necessary elements of a national war

---

89 Zook, *The Conduct of the Chaco War.*

90 Ibid., p. 84.

because, indeed, it is here, in the national war, that war 'recovers its true nature'.

What remains to be determined then is whether Salamanca, as the 'symbolic man', expressed only himself or if he was the cathartic fulfilment of a compulsion, that is, if he expressed the necessity of a real form of something that had already appeared (the oligarchic state) or if the entire country simply followed him in a fit of temper. In any case, in contrast to the Paraguayans of Isla Poí, Paraguay was for Salamanca 'the little devil'[91] and the war not only presented no danger but it also became an 'opportunity that had bestowed great fortune [upon Bolivia]'.[92] An opportunity that, moreover, could not be squandered in the service of pettifogging schemes: 'Possesssion of the Gran Chaco cannot be the subject of protocols, of arbitrage or negotiations.'[93]

In short, the figure that constituted the symbolic condensation of the oligarchic political civilization and of course acted as moral leader of the war from the outset proposed that peace be made in Asunción because he was obsessed with what we might aptly call the cartographic objectives of the conflict. At this point, Salamanca's charismatic style was obviously largely founded on the non-negotiable attitude of a Belcista programme that stirred up internal public opinion. This, however, consisted in dangerous boasts in which not even they themselves believed except when they were turned against them. Neither society as such nor its heteronational apex seriously believed that the Gran Chaco was a vital part of the country, and if it was, as the 'symbol' claimed, an existential matter, this was true for Paraguay but not for Bolivia. Some have attributed this hyperbolization to a Petrópolis complex. Salamanca, however, identified the country with the oligarchic political system (to which he had only to supplement

---

91 Querejazu Calvo, *Masamaclay*, p. 162.

92 Céspedes, *Salamanca o El metafísico del fracaso*, p. 28.

93 David Alvéstegui, *Salamanca: Su gravitación sobre el destino de Bolivia*, VOL. 3 (La Paz: Talleres Gráficos, 1957), p. 185.

with Salamanquismo what was subtracted of Montismo) to such an extent that he thought that with the catharsis of the Gran Chaco the nation's faith in itself, lost in the War of the Pacific, could be restored. He thought, in short, that Bolivia was guaranteed an easy and cheap military victory, an assumption based in an alienation proper to the Panglossian vision of the oligarchic state.

Bolivia's underestimation of her opponent was astonishing. [...] In December 1931 a twenty-six-page Operations Plan #1, prepared by G-3, argued that since war of maneuver would be impossible in the Chaco, five reinforced battalions of 812 men each, with integral batteries of mountain guns, would be adequate for a war with Paraguay.[94]

Already in 1924, Kundt, the eternal optimist, had maintained that 'since the Paraguayans are poor soldiers, Asunción could be taken with 3,000 men'.[95] Not only this, but 'he believed that twenty thousand men would be sufficient to achieve their objectives in the Pacific'.[96]

All this, of course, only illustrates certain general sentiments of that period overrun by more of the same. Patiño would certainly have done a better job of managing the war.

'The Austrians,' it has been said, 'proceeded with such indolence, calculation, reticence, that they completely forgot their objective.' Kundt, in short, was a theorist of the 'cheap war' that fit so well with Salamanca's soma because the former believed in what the latter wanted: a sweeping victory at a low cost. True superiority, political or military, is not an abstract or general fact but the sum of the factors at play. In this case, it is not only, as is conventionally said, that Bolivia once again paid dearly for having unpopulated territory. We could say that this is a crude assertion because then a country would always have to wait until it had a literal demographic presence before

---

94 Zook, *The Conduct of the Chaco War*, p. 90.

95 Ibid.

96 Ibid., p. 126.

it could defend a territory while in reality there are many other forms of belonging to a space, but here there was none at all. Bolivia lacked any kind of territorial sovereignty in the Gran Chaco and there was not even a ritual relation of legitimacy of the state with the Toba people; this distinguishes it thoroughly from Atacama. In any case, Bolivia wasted its unprecedented relative demographic superiority (unprecedented because this was the only possible case) and surrendered to Paraguay's geographic superiority:

> Had Bolivia conducted general mobilization during August and struck promptly, she would likely have attained the river and won the war. Instead she remained passive, mobilizing in dribbles; this enabled Paraguay to bring to bear her decisive advantage in space, and to achieve earlier concentration of numerically superior forces.[97]

We cannot say that Paraguay then had an advanced social equation as we can, even if only in comparative terms, of Chile in 1879. Between a civil society levelled by the Triple Alliance and an exogenous state, which succeeded only in being pro-Argentine or pro-Brazilian, one could not have expected much. Despite these difficulties, the relation between the state and society was more favourable than in Bolivia and this in itself tells us that the idea of the state optimum does not necessarily refer to fully developed positions. It was the right state for the corresponding social situation under the circumstance of an intense mobilizing force. Meanwhile, in Bolivia, the period was marked by the decline of a state constituted against its society, out of options and rallied around a kind of jingoist, arrogant patriotism.

All the Bolivian authors subscribe to Querejazu's claim that Bolivia threw itself into the war 'when there was a total of 1,251 men spread out over that vast territory'[98] (some 200,000 square kilometres), which would prove only that it was a nation of fools. If this was

---

97 Ibid., p. 91.

98 Querejazu Calvo, *Masamaclay*, p. 63.

the case, it was necessary to make peace at any price, even if only to gain time to recruit. On the other hand, there would have had to be a revolution if they had come to such an extreme situation with such weak preparation, which is to say in which the state didn't see it coming at all.

Zook's account is more realistic: 'At the beginning of October of 1932, each country had total forces of around 20,000, the vital difference being in their deployment. In the main theatre, Bolivia had about 5,500 with 2,000 more en route, while Paraguay fielded 12,000.'[99]

The operative idea here is that of deployment. The sterile relation between the population and the territory is not so important. The circulation of men in the territory lends the population itself a greater productivity of state or national substance. A territory, ultimately, belongs to us insofar as we can deploy ourselves towards it more swiftly and with a greater sense of identity than anyone else. In other words, where we can say: 'We exist there.' On the other hand, to go to an unincorporated space is perhaps the most difficult military task for any state.

This is a result of the process of decomposition of war, which the Bolivian armed forces should have learned better from Bolivian history than the Paraguayans from theirs. Not only the war of communications but also an ecological war had begun, and it became clear that the poverty of the post-Potosí system of circulation produced men who belonged to their own immediate terrain and not to their historical landscape. Hence the invariable consequence of the constant numerical superiority of the Paraguayans over the course of the entire campaign. In fact, it must be acknowledged that a greater human presence in a given place is proof of possession. Indeed:

The Andean Indian [. . .] was transported from the Altiplano to the Chaco like a beast, unaware of his purpose, and

---

99 Zook, *The Conduct of the Chaco War*, p. 102.

then thrust untrained into combat. He was seldom employed in sufficient numbers at a given tactical moment. Although in the course of the war Bolivia mobilized nearly 250,000 as against 140,000 Paraguayans, her forces rarely possessed numerical superiority.[100]

This is one of Zook's few expressions of sympathy for the Bolivian soldier, and it is therefore quite objective. The Indian was not only transported like a beast, but was treated like a beast in all aspects of life. It was a society founded on treating Indians like beasts. 'Combat training' is really a relation to the state and no such thing had existed in a normal way except with Belzu, that is, if by training we understand a relation of reciprocity with the state, this had been nearly impossible for a long time. What is inexplicable here, on the contrary, is the profound, unconditional loyalty towards an antagonistic state objective, which expressed the deep horizon of identity: the struggle for a future identity. Finally, the senseless decimation of these men reveals a secret desire to exterminate them, which was in the logic of social Darwinism.

It bears repeating that a country's inability to mobilize its own potential when it must is already eloquent. This, contrary to what might be assumed, does not attest to Bolivia's inferiority, unless we believe, as in what Gramsci called the fetishism of unification, that the entire country is better off when it is more standardized. It is obvious that the secret of countries like Bolivia or Italy resides in the multiplicity of their micro-universes, unless, of course, these paralyse the formation of a modern unity. Let us leave aside the fact that Paraguay was like an overgrown and homogeneous province, and that therefore its internal relation to its population was more efficient than that of Bolivia. The Gran Chaco, moreover, was certainly better linked to its central territorial character than to Bolivia's. On the other hand, the simple administrative explanation of under-mobilization is insufficient, although it merits discussion in its own

---

100 Ibid., p. 149.

right, because it would have been reasonable to expect of the oligarchic elite at least the bureaucratic control of its own society. The fact is that the Bolivian state did not correspond to its own theoretical demographic proportions and, in any case, it acted with the concrete capacity that it possessed in its internal integration: it could not reach its own men or rally them to its objectives when the time came.

Two logics, then, were brought into opposition. One, that of Estigarribia, who knew that Paraguay could not defeat Bolivia, but also that it could realistically defend itself against Bolivia. The other, that of Salamanca, who clung to the fantasy of an easy symbolic victory, a cartographic victory that would entail nothing less than the conquest of Paraguay, that is, a possible objective and an impossible one, because as with Bolivia in the Pacific, and the Chileans knew this, it was conceivable to conquer Paraguay but not incorporate it. To set impossible objectives in military matters is, of course, to invite disaster.

Estigarribia, a modest but more powerful man, was aware of three fundamental facts:

1. Paraguay's essential superiority with regard to the terrain: 'Logistically Paraguay, with her shorter lines of supply and communication, was superior to Bolivia, an advantage which largely negated the greater size and wealth of the Altiplano-centred republic [. . .]. Here river vessels complemented this facility [that of the railway] at Puerto Casado, thus forming a cohesive transportation system of relative quality.'[101]

   Indeed, from the end of the railway line to the theatre of operations there was a distance of only 200 kilometres and Paraguay was able to deploy 16,000 men in 36 days.

2. What is summed up in Estigarribia's assertion: 'We are entering a war of communications', a lucid response to the problem of expanse. Communication is more important

---

101 Ibid., p. 92.

where it is more difficult. With the robust and simple linearity of his thought he arrived at 'the revolution in logistics occasioned by the motor truck'.[102] This is brilliant. Not an admiration of technology in general but of the truck, which was the means by which technology could come to the Gran Chaco. At the same time, Salamanca, within the logic of the economical war (which is to say, a cheap or free war, a precapitalist concept), refuses to buy 600 trucks in April 1932 while in July '[h]e compounded his error by launching [. . .] reprisals without resolving the fundamental problem of transport',[103] in a typical seigneurial fashion: they must be punished; how the punishment is to be carried out is not the lord's the concern.

3. Estigarribia's (and also Zook's) reflection on the problem of water. It was an essential resource of the area and also the scarcest. The water supply determined the forms of combat. 'The lessons of the day [Boquerón] were explicit and foretold the character of the entire war. *Water* was a vital factor. [. . .] It was obvious that a lack of water could of itself destroy an army in the Chaco. As in the World War, *defence*, when field fortifications the fire power of numerous automatic weapons, was vastly superior to frontal assault.'[104]

Water, Bolivia's old obsession. It suppressed, moreover, another profoundly national faculty, which was the inclination towards frontal attack. (On this subject, Kundt simply offers a reading of the national temperament.) It is enough to resist the savage fury of the Bolivians for the key to their undoing to appear. Here we have come to the heart of the matter.

---

102 Ibid., p. 84.

103 Ibid., p. 92.

104 Ibid., p. 94.

Clausewitz says: 'Nothing is more important in life than finding the right standpoint for seeing and judging events, and then adhering to it. One point, and one only, yields an integrated view of all phenomena; and only by holding to that point of view can one avoid inconsistency.'[105] This means that no matter how many ideas one might have, one must, in one's conduct at least, follow a certain, central, master idea, that is, one must manoeuvre according to what is most thoroughly verified. Estigarribia clearly incorporated into his reasoning these early lessons of the war—the strategic rather than tactical importance of water, the new role of defensive warfare—in a kind of conceptual construction proper to the war. It has indeed been said that insurrection is an art; but *combat is an art* in a very particular sense: it is a situation that only allows for a synthetic or artistic characterization of things; it does not readily lend itself to a scholastic and calculable knowledge; therefore, the necessity arises of adhering to what little knowledge is essentially verifiable, such as the importance of water and the defense of Boquerón. Salamanca could not grasp either of these among other things because he had not been there and the government, in short, lacked structures of mediation linking it to the rest of society, that which fought and that which waited. Therefore, since he could not know, he believed in effect in an inspired knowledge. Zook says this well: Estigarriba

> 'demonstrated from the beginning of the war that he possessed the primordial qualities of a genuine *caudillo* of military command: *Tener una idea.*' That idea was to seek annihilation of the Bolivian army as far as possible from nuclear Paraguay.[106]

This was the antithesis of the Bolivian command. Since Salamanca was the intellectual leader, it could not be expected of

---

105 Clausewitz, *On War*, p. 532.

106 Zook, *The Conduct of the Chaco War*, p. 127. The quoted text in the passage is from José Carlos Fernández, *La Guerra del Chaco*, VOL. 2 (Buenos Aires: n.p., 1962), p. 325.

such an abstract thinking (or, rather, one so poisoned by poor but successful abstractions) that it address certain decisive minutiae such as water or even logistics. The senile optimism of the oligarchy tragically coincided, moreover, with the character of the modern Bolivian masses, which tended incessantly towards the logic of frontal attack. From this perspective, that of the masses, the inclination towards the offensive no doubt has to do with a pathetic unification; it is the performance of *unity through passion* of men who are not united in their daily lives. On the other hand, if Kundt confused stubbornness with efficiency (as a certain prototype of German men tends to do), we cannot attribute to him what constituted a whole idea of war, surely an idea that was readily apparent: that which is based on the underestimation of the enemy and disregard for loss of life, ultimately because it was a loss Indian lives, that is, an entirely palatable loss. This—the conscious desire to trade Indian lives for a particular fetish that was the a grandeur conceived in territorial terms—is evident throughout the war.

The desertion of men of the upper ranks, moreover, remarkably coincided with the invitation extended to Kundt and other foreigners to direct the war. As one well versed in the subject has aptly said: 'Experience has shown that only princes and armed republics achieve solid success and that mercenaries bring nothing but loss.'[107]

The truth is that Bolivia was a society in a state of error and this was the root of the mistakes made by its political and military leaders. If Estigarribia and Toro had suddenly appeared at the same time, for example (not to mention Peñaranda, who was a stupid man), the latter—Toro—would not have seemed so bad. He seems to have represented, as few men have, a culture of sophistry and a frivolousness extolled by certain Chuquisacan conventions, since language games are a tradition there. Meanwhile, Salamanca would certainly have compared favourably to Alaya. At another level and on both sides,

107 Niccolo Machiavelli, *The Prince* (George Bull trans.) (Harmondsworth: Penguin, 1975), p. 49.

the officials and soldiers displayed tremendous bravery and it is there whence names like Busch, Bilbao or Ustárez emerged, all of plebeian origin. In spite of this, at least assuming that they were of similar stock or were 'equivalent men', as they surely were, here we come to what is inexplicable: some acted in an absurd manner, which seemed demented and self-destructive, while others adhered to the rule of sound logic, which turned out to be more than enough. We need, of course, a material explanation of all this because it has to do with the social foundation of Bolivia. For some reason, there was something that tended to go wrong invariably or almost invariably, however great the sacrifices made.

Let us turn now to the consequences of this in the construction of politics. When all opinions are always final and irreconcilable, it means that the political has not been constituted, that it has not been autonomized. There is a point to which a syncretic attitude is what defines civilized man. We know, on the other hand, that debate in times of great peril is a serious matter. Disobedience in war is equivalent to a failure of the only possible pilots to agree in the operation of a plane. Defiance and dissent have a long history in Bolivia; in reality, they come from a long tradition of treason, anarchy and insurrection because all experience produces habits.

The relationship between Estigarribia and Alaya, meanwhile, was one of two men in a state of normality. The latter wrote in an eloquent letter to the former:

> This nervous population, which is already sensitive to panic [. . .] The people pass from enthusiasm and depression according to the information from the front [. . .] In any case, [he stressed] you can be assured that my personal and official authority will be on your side in good and, above all, in bad conditions.[108]

---

108 Cited in Zook, *The Conduct of the Chaco War*, p. 137.

Relying on this support, at one point Estigarribia dismissed a high-ranking officer on the spot on his own account and was duly backed up.

Things were different within the Bolivian leadership. In principle, it is not that the military leaders were injudicious.

> The army would require definite objectives, not mere historical aspirations [. . .]. The historical hypothesis of Salamanca, which aimed at total reintegration, would require a nation in arms to sustain military occupation of the entire Chaco and dictate peace at Asunción. [. . .] The military objective of the command, however, remained Olimpo and the river above.[109]

Zook continues: 'Obviously, such a settlement would have given Daniel Salamanca apoplexy, although it was more realistic than his own proposals. In reality, however, Bolivia laced the transport to implement either plan.'[110]

At least there was an awareness of the difficulty of radicalizing the ambition of a 'nation in arms' and a certain resistance to the Salamancan assumption that titles proffer victories. This moral discontent or technical reserve had to undergo an anomic development. Indeed, evident in the observation that 'Peñaranda's inability to command Colonel Toro . . . was tragic for Bolivia', there was something more than breaches of discipline that, moreover, should have been foreseen and prevented. Toro became 'the sinister power behind the command' but this itself was a consequence of 'the weakness of Peñaranda and his utter misunderstanding of his own proper role [which was] so patent as to require no comment', ultimately a consequence of his 'impotent pusillanimity'.[111]

---

109 Ibid., pp. 88–9.
110 Ibid., p. 89.
111 Ibid., pp. 198–9.

If the nature of modern power lies in rationality and trans-personalism and verifiability, we have here just the opposite. There is unquestionably a personalized conception of the exercise of power, as if it were an inherent or inalienable attribute of the its subject. The paucity of real legitimacy of power, on the other hand, in a country that was moreover accustomed to not recognizing anyone in power, was ultimately based only on the exaggerated authority of Salamanca or his symbolic construction, which, precisely because it was exaggerated, necessarily produced persistent forms of insubordination, furtive dissent and, finally, outright rebellion.

> The command, he wrote, acted as if 'military assignments are intangible personal rights, even when necessities of discipline and of defence demand convenient changes'. The exchange of recriminations, misunderstandings, lack of discipline and hatred between President and General, Díaz observes, led Bolivia down the road to defeat, culminating first in the overthrow of Salamanca and finally in loss of the Chaco.[112]

The attribution of authority not to a rationally and normatively revocable appointment but to 'intangible personal right' belongs to the purest seigneurial reason. The impassioned excess of power, moreover, was a pure fantasy and, in any case, it would have to be successful to become valid. Rodríguez and Toro, Salamanca and Kundt represented two mutually impossible styles, which were nonetheless durable in a perverse way. In descriptive terms, insubordination was a paradoxical result of what came from above, from Salamanca's deification, which need not have occurred in an almost elegiac fashion in him (because he was like a dead man attending his own glorious funeral), since it had occurred before in the limited society that had elected him (that which was left after the exclusion of the popular sectors). Salamanca, in short, had an attitude of intel-

---

112 Ibid., p. 210.

lectual arrogance that was characteristic of that social sector and of that time. He was no doubt an intelligent man and lucid in his conceptual articulation. This does not mean that he was intelligent in his grasp of reality. In any case, everything seems to indicate that his knowledge of the world was very limited because he was not prepared to believe that the world could be something other than what he thought it was. Upon becoming the formal, affective, embodied culmination of a system that had been looking for just that, for a symbolic man, he indeed behaved like a symbolic man, like someone bearing prescient truths. His contempt for a public opinion as equable as that of the oligarchy (a bunch of quasi-intellectuals and their cronies) nonetheless did not stop him from almost perfectly expressing the prejudices of his age. He was anticommunist, as had been his countryman Baptista, even before there were any communists. His stubborn optimism with regard to Paraguay was that of Montes, who surely assumed that with the Chilean indemnification he could buy the whole world, which (from his point of view) was not very big. We will have to return to this problem of the visibility (or invisibility) of the world.

With this curriculum vitae it is understandable that Salamanca not only presumed to understand the problem, like anyone else, but also to personally orchestrate its solution: 'Salamanca, since the beginning of the penetration plan, had exercised an increasingly personal influence on military decisions. [...] Although abjectly ignorant of tactical considerations, he sought to direct operations.'[113]

The incident of Pitiantuta is exemplary here: Major Moscoso saw a great lagoon from the air. The general staff 'with the knowledge of His Excellency the President of the Republic', then ordered the Fourth Division to 'occupy the Great Lagoon immediately', because 'the latest accords in neutral Washington negotiations would pressure litigating countries urgently to precisely identify their most

---

113 Ibid., p. 103.

advanced positions'.[114] In June 1932, Moscoso carried out the order and the Paraguayans fled. Salamanca then felt betrayed:

'The news came like a lightning bolt out of nowhere', for he had ordered the occupation to be implemented 'abstaining from all contact with the enemy', proceeding 'with the utmost circumspection' and 'if a Paraguayan approach is detected [...] the unit will proceed cautiously to establish Bolivian forts or posts at a distance of 20 or 30 kilometres from the Paraguayan posts.'[115]

As Céspedes says, '20 or 30 kilometres without water in the Chaco wilderness is an unthinkable distance',[116] which means that to 'abstain from contact' would have been absurd. Still, Salamanca ordered 'the immediate abandonment of the Paraguayan fort'.[117] Moscoso later commented:

For a unit that for 20 days had suffered water shortages and covered an extensive area tellingly called Campo de Deso-lación [Desolation Fields, thus christened by Ustárez], the presence of an inexhaustible water source stimulated their patriotism and the desire to conquer it. Any official instructed to avoid clashes with the enemy, after the distance I had crossed with my soldiers [...] would have attacked the fort.[118]

The dismissal of Osorio, one of the leaders of the first phase of the war, is a similar story. Salamanca answered the objections to this saying that 'Osorio had been removed with popular approval'.[119]

It was a stupid thing to say in any case because this is not an argument. If war were waged through popular consensus on every

114 Céspedes, *Salamanca o El metafísico del fracaso*, p. 64.
115 Ibid., p. 65.
116 Ibid.
117 Ibid.
118 Ibid., p. 66.
119 Zook, *The Conduct of the Chaco War*, p. 104.

decision there would be no battles but only plebiscites. The affair, as was inevitable, ended while the fighting went on, with Salamanca saying that 'the command had lost the "sympathy of the people"' while, just as inevitably, the command (Peñaranda) said that 'the government had "lost the confidence of the Army"',[120] which was, in any case, more serious.

This is more important than it seems. The measure of hegemony, that is, of the optimum, consists in the extent to which contradictions can be absorbed in it, that is, in something beyond its subjects or within a subject capable of containing all subjects. That in its ideologico-political formalization the liberal state had to resort to a pontifical mode of power, in a strange combination of personalization and lack of effective personal power, the very fact that it had to appeal, to survive, to its most stringent *internal critic*, all this proved, of course, the system's loss of coherence. But the situation continued to deteriorate. It was a state that had to appeal to its last resort, Salamanca, a cross between Linares and Baptista. This is not something that would have occurred in a state of normality. Moreover, that in his impenitent antipathy towards the military Salamanca turned to extreme acts of humiliation such as the appointment of a German as national commander, or attempting to designate Joaquín Espada as civil inspector of an army in the midst of a war, or, finally, inviting Ismael Montes to serve as commander when he had become no more than a vestige of his former self, all of this indicates a lack of national coherence.

The rift between the military and Salamanca (the political class incarnate) already reveals the division of the state. This would be forcefully expressed later on and it is in fact one of the sources of the revolutionary crisis of 1952. Indeed, where there is no division of the ruling class, there is no revolutionary crisis. In essence, however, even more fundamentally, this shows that the political suppression of the majority of the population produced a situation of intellectual, psy-

---

120 Ibid., p. 198.

chological and behavioural anomaly that explains the fact that these men, surely intelligent enough in principle, acted in an erratic and divisive way. The horizon of visibility of the world was determined by the social base; this is proof of the effectivity of the social base upon cognitive activity. It is what explains the persistent degenerative tendencies of the Bolivian state even after 1952 in its constant inclination towards the oligarchization of power.

Zook then falls into the error of insufficient generality in believing that 'the close cooperation of President Alaya and Estigarribia lent added strength to the country and was in no small measure responsible for the outcome of the war'.[121] This is almost like the attribution of success to the protestant ethic. On the contrary, this cooperation was possible because behind it was Paraguay such as it was. This was essentially founded on the ideological conception of the war as an absolute danger, a conception that was correct but that also served an organizing function. On the other hand, it was made possible by the survival of certain hereditary forms of 'health' that came, in their positive aspect, from the non-aristocratizing and non-seigneurial formation of that society (largely by the Jesuits) and also from the internalized habit of compliance with authority, whatever this might be, a not especially positive inheritance from the great dictators.

At Christmas 1934, a melancholy Salamanca, now deposed, would say that 'militarism, which had not been capable of repelling the foreign enemy, has already imposed its domination in Bolivia.'[122] Since a military approach to things was adopted, there was nothing unusual in the fact that that things would become militaristic. But the collapse of the oligarchic state continued implacably and not only because of the inauguration of a period of military rule.

It translated, for example, into an absolute lack of faith in the men of the country and of the system. Salamanca's xenophobia was applied contemptuously to the Paraguayans and timorously to the

---

121 Ibid., p. 199.
122 Cited in ibid., p. 214.

Chileans, but within a context of confidence in the foreign that, as we have seen, characterizes the entire oligarchic state and perhaps an entire caste. When Kundt left, hated by all, Salamanca brought in a Czech military mission and even his own interior police chief was a Mexican *cristero*.

The deterioration of the Bolivian troops continued in the way imagined by Kundt and applied by Salamanca and his men. In Nanawa, for example, '[t]he Bolivians repeated their common errors of inadequate coordination, lack of intelligence, violation of the principle of economy of force and underestimation of the enemy.'[123] The result: 'In 10 days' fighting, the defenders suffered only 248 casualties against 2,000 Bolivian losses. Nanawa could not be subdued and insufficient were available to lay siege.'[124] It was the greatest frontal assault of the 'aggressive Andeans' (Zook): 'at 0905, nearly 7,000 charged across no-man's-land. [. . .] The German [Kundt] sacrificed the best of his army. Over 2,000 Altiplano soldiers died futilely in front of the III Corps defences.'[125] This is the story of more or less the entire war. In Toledo:

> By 5 March, the Bolivians had lost nearly 2,000. They were short of food and water; some men even lacked clothes, fighting in their shorts; the stench of 700 unburied dead in no-man's-land was unbearable. [. . .] Insubordination was rife and on the night of 16 March the 30th Infantry fled, shooting at the officers.[126]

> Insubordination, which Toro and Quintanilla had set in motion among officers, spread rapidly to the fatigued Andean troops, deteriorating their faith in the *jefes*. Defeated,

---

123 Ibid., p. 129.
124 Ibid., p. 130.
125 Ibid., p. 146.
126 Ibid., p. 132.

poorly supplied and even lacking a mail service, the Bolivian soldiers were easily demoralized.[127]

This closely resembles Russia leading up to the Treaty of Brest Litovsk. The country, however, seemed indefatigable and what is striking is the constant capacity for construction of the army: three armies are organized over the course of the war. All this is very strange because the normal thing would be for people to refuse to fight, especially after adversities and disasters that revealed such a patent ineffectiveness of the state and of the command. To accept such losses was to truly accept the absurd. *To go on fighting still when all is lost*, to fight, as they said, 'for the honour of the regiment', is perhaps what best expresses the heroism of the people at that moment. The sense of reconstruction and of resistance of the Bolivian troops ultimately frustrated the Paraguayan offensive, in keeping with the most basic prognoses with regard to this absurd war. A single battle like Campo Vía, although notable for the military success of Estigarribia, would cost Paraguay 15,000 casualties between the dead and the wounded.

The consequences of the Chaco War were enormous for Bolivia. We cannot say that there was a political class in the liberal-oligarchic state, but there was a kind of elite based on charismatic-seigneurial election that is more or less arbitrary [*ocasional*] or pertains only to a limited social base. With Salamanca came the disbandment of this sector. The praetorianization of power, power as the monopoly of bad military men, is its result. The state finally resorts, inevitably, to a state of emergency, that is, to the army. Thus begins the first military period of Bolivian history in the twentieth century, a period that would last until 1952. To this we must add the decline of the tin mining industry. It was, then, truly a state living on its reserves.

The situation, as the stubborn capacity for *struggle in defeat* proves, is different with regard to civil society. The Chaco War was

---

127 Ibid., p. 106.

a true constitutive moment. Some 50,000 men died of 240,000 who were deployed—at least one in five. The country lost 2 per cent of its population. This death toll is less significant than Cuba's at the end of the nineteenth century or that of the Mexican Revolution, but we must consider that the figure includes only young men. A kind of identification is forged through the war, that form of historical commerce of which Clausewitz spoke. It is certainly a nationalizing event that would have formidable consequences. The Paraguayan death toll was also high (3.5 per cent of the population). Victory, however, even a Pyrrhic victory, has its satisfactions, which here were badly needed, and the result was a certain weak local form of ratification of the model of domination. In Bolivia, on the other hand, the result was a generalized hegemonic contestation of the state, unanimous at least among veterans. We have come, then, to the deep causes of the multitude of 1952 and the order of things that attended the constitution of the next phase of the Bolivian state, which is the state of 1952.

Afterword

ANNE FREELAND

A Note on the Translation

René Zavaleta Mercado's prose is famously idiosyncratic, and it will be helpful to discuss some of the problems of translation of terms that refer to central concepts in his work.

Abigarramiento. The most salient of these terms is *sociedad abigarrada*, translated here as 'motley' or sometimes simply 'heterogeneous' society (also discussed in my Note on the Text). Zavaleta uses *heterogéneo* to refer to the same quality but the specific connotations of the more distinctive *abigarrado* should be borne in mind. The term does not refer to difference in the sense of pluralism or multiculturalism but, at least in its initial formulation, to the overlapping of multiple modes of production, and, therefore, of multiple historical moments, within a territory claimed by a single nation-state. Unlike the more neutral *heterogéneo*, *abigarrado* connotes disjointedness, incongruousness, beyond mere difference.

Disponibilidad. This term refers to a society's readiness (a cognate would be 'disposition') to receive or respond to the interpellation of a new hegemonic project, to fundamentally alter its conception of the world and of itself. The standard English equivalent of *disponibilidad* is 'availability', but I have translated it here as 'receptivity', which I think is a more precise rendering in this case. My translation, however, is perhaps too passive, and there are places where I even leant towards using 'will'. It is a willingness to enter into a new set of social relations and an openness to the epistemic transformation that such a repositioning of the subject entails.

Patético. 'Pathetic' should always be read here as the adjectival form of *pathos* and not in the colloquial sense. It does not, however, refer to rhetoric but to the affective element of social identification and collective subject formation.

Óptimo/ecuación social. Translated literally here as 'social optimum' or 'social equation', these terms are used interchangeably to refer to the level of articulation or communication between society and the state. A high 'social optimum' is characteristic of what Gramsci called the integral state in which the institutions of civil society are thoroughly integrated into the ethico-political programme of political society, or the state in the narrow sense.

Irresistibilidad. Always an attribute of the state, this term generally refers to the effective capacity to rule in a given territory. I have used a number of different words in different contexts: usually 'authority', but sometimes 'enforceability', 'power', 'coercion'; on one occasion 'solidity'; and, in the context of 'a superstition of the *irresistibilidad* of the state', meaning an inability to envision the transformation or replacement of the state in the broad sense, 'indestructibility'. While each of these conveys the sense of the respective passages better than a single word applicable to all could, the specific import of the concept developed through the repetition of the term, and the unity of these different senses, is lost.

Verificable. As a modifier of the form of power, this refers to the principle of rational-legal authority. It is generally translated as 'verifiable' but I have also used 'rational' where this helps to clarify the sense. Zavaleta regularly draws explicitly upon Weber, and also uses *rational* in this sense, and so I think the citation is justified. I have also translated the noun *constatabilidad*, in one instance, as 'rationality'.

A Note on the Text

Zavaleta came of age with Bolivia's National Revolution of 1952, an event that marked the emergence of organized labour as a major political force in the country and a shift in the national discourse comparable to that which took place in 2005 with the election of Evo Morales as the continent's first indigenous president. Zavaleta was active in the political life of the MNR, serving briefly as minister of mines and petroleum in addition to holding diplomatic posts in Uruguay and Chile and contributing regularly to national and regional newspapers. In these early years, prior to his official break with the MNR in 1969, Zavaleta had positioned himself within a critical left wing of the diverse coalition that formed the base of a regime that he would later acknowledge had effectively been co-opted by local elites and US interests within its first four years and which finally collapsed in 1964, followed by two decades of military rule. During this period, Zavaleta moved towards a more rigorously Marxist intellectual framework and he was a founding member of the Movimiento de la Izquierda Revolucionaria [Revolutionary Left Movement or MIR], which he left shortly after to join the Partido Comunista de Bolivia [Communist Party of Bolivia or PCB]. In 1971, he was arrested by the military regime and went into exile in Chile; following the Pinochet coup of 1973, he fled to Mexico where he was the first director of the Facultad Latinoamericano de Ciencias Sociales (FLACSO) and where he lived until his early death in 1984, leaving behind an unfinished manuscript of the present book.

Zavaleta is often described as a forgotten or understudied figure of the Latin American left, and yet when he is cited it is to assign to him a position at once singular and emblematic within a certain canon. He has been read as a 'local' and localist theorist of the Bolivian social text, and the work published as *Lo nacional-popular en Bolivia* is held to represent this quality most consummately, as the most mature expression of his thought. This reading is supported by two overlapping narratives: one at the level of a certain tradition of the Latin American left as a whole, the other at the level of Zavaleta's individual work. Within the macronarrative of Latin Americanist social thought, he is placed at the intersection of a discourse governed by the categories of class, people and nation, and one centred on indigeneity, heterogeneity and subalternity. In the current scholarship on Zavaleta, his intellectual trajectory is conventionally periodized into (1) a youthful, nationalist period, (2) an orthodox Marxist period, and (3) a final, critical Marxist period in which universal (metropolitan) categories are rejected as inoperable for the theoretical production of non-metropolitan societies.

The concept-metaphor most commonly associated with Zavaleta and cited to situate him at the threshold of a passage from a traditional Marxist left to a discourse aligned with the struggles of indigenous movements is that of *abigarramiento*, translated here sometimes simply as 'heterogeneity' or, in its adjectival form, following existing English citations of the term, as 'motley'. *Abigarramiento* refers to the coexistence of multiple modes of production and multiple conceptions of the world within a single national territory and, therefore, complicates the sequential and deterministic modes-of-production narrative and constitutes an obstacle to the methods of both modern social-scientific analysis and liberal democratic politics premised on the existence of a more or less unified national citizenry. The Bolivian social formation, for Zavaleta, is *abigarrada* because precapitalist (feudal) or noncapitalist (Andean 'communitarian') social relations persist within the space claimed by a formally capitalist nation-state.

As a concept that supplements those received from European social theory to designate the specificity of a peripheral society, *abigarramiento* (too readily taken to stand for Zavaleta's theoretical apparatus as a whole) tends to be read in a vindicatory key, as multicultural diversity or least as a force of anticolonial resistance. Even Luis Tapia, the most prominent scholar of Zavaleta's work, who correctly identifies and refutes the multiculturalist interpretation, nonetheless remains within a localist framework, placing Zavaleta in a pivotal but intermediary position in a progression from metropolitan to thoroughly local thought (see *The Production of Local Knowledge*, translated for Elsewhere Texts by Alison Spedding, forthcoming from Seagull Books). Walter Mignolo, writing from the US academy, situates Zavaleta in an early stage in a process of epitemic decolonization—he marks a break from metropolitan orthodoxy but falls short of a fully local expression.[1] The bio-bibliographical narrative of a passage from nationalism to orthodoxy to a more critical, original, and therefore *authentic* perspective likewise represents a dialectical development that ends in a vindication of a regionalist disciplinary demarcation.

This double schematic frame is not unfounded and it is not without value, but it is necessarily reductive and has served certain forms of appropriation and instrumentalization of Zavaleta's thought. Every translation implies a challenge to this kind of fetishization of the local, even as it recognizes its own inevitable insufficiency. Zavaleta indeed insists upon the necessity of a methodological modification—beginning with a historicist grounding and qualification of abstract categories—in social inquiry in 'peripheral' or 'motley' societies. He does so almost apologetically at first (in the prologue to this book, he writes: 'In defence of this method it must be said that no social science is possible otherwise in a country like Bolivia'),[2] but his text comes to suggest that this method is itself generalizable—that attention to history, to the singular, to contingency, to the epistemic ruptures that occur in moments of crisis, to what escapes every model, should inform the study of any society. The epigraph to the first chapter of the book, like the title itself, after all, is a citation of Gramsci; Zavaleta

---

1 'The colonial matrix of power was introduced after Zavaleta Mercado died (and of course, Zavaleta's contribution fueled that conceptualization) [. . .] the tensions juggled in a conceptual apparatus inherited from Karl Marx and Antonio Gramsci, but growing out of Bolivian society' (Walter Mignolo, 'On Subalterns and Other Agencies', *Postcolonial Studies: Culture, Politics, Economy* 8[4] [2005]: 381–407; here p. 397).

2 See p. 1 of this volume.

situates himself within a Marxist tradition that is already at once critical—in the deep sense of the term and not in the sense of factiousness, apostasy, or even transcendence that is sometimes implied by the localist scholarship—and committed to the (always imperfect) translatability of theoretical categories. This translation is offered to the reader, then, in the hope that it will be received as an invitation to learn *from* a particular historical process with Zavaleta, rather than *about* an insular local history and its specific intellectual expression.

Context and Afterlife

Between the 1960s and 80s, an academic Latin Americanism of the left was constructed largely by a community of exiles—intellectuals displaced and brought together by the US-backed military dictatorships that had seized power in much of the region. One of the central discourses that pervaded the field was that of dependency theory, in its varying kinds and degrees of articulation with Marxist thought.[3] It is largely against dependency theory—and therefore against a certain structuralism[4]—that Zavaleta's 'localism' is directed; he maintains that a history of a country like Bolivia—even if one predominantly marked by defeat, oppression and stagnation—can be written

---

3 The foundational text of dependency theory is Argentine economist Raúl Prebisch's 'The Economic Development of Latin America and its Principal Problems' (United Nations Economic Commission for Latin America, 1950); among the most influential scholars of the Marxist strain is the German-American economist and sociologist Andre Gunder Frank (see *Capitalism and Underdevelopment in Latin America* [New York: Monthly Review Press, 1967]).

4 World-systems theory (see, in particular, the work of Immanuel Wallerstein and Giovanni Arrighi) builds upon dependency theory in a away that illuminates the affinity with structuralist thought; the periphery is conceived only in relation to the centre, and vice versa. But the claim of the effectivity of local history (undetermined by the colonial power or neocolonial metropole) also challenges the structuralist Marxism of Louis Althusser or Nicos Poulantzas, which seeks to formulate a theory of social reproduction devoid of all historicism.

Zavaleta
vs
dependency
theory

from within, without giving priority to the coercion of external conditions, which is not to say without acknowledging their force. At a time when Marxism in Latin America was to a great extent synonymous with the thought of the French philosopher Louis Althusser, Zavaleta speaks of *interpellation*—an Althusserian concept of ideological 'hailing'—with an emphasis on subjectivity rather than subjection; on the indigenous as subject or nucleus of a 'national-popular' interpellation with the 1780 uprising led by Tupac Amaru II, for example, but also on the active intersubjectivity of the interpellated masses. The epistemic constraints of structural position within a global order are taken for granted, and it is the possibility of rupture and of a reorganization of these conditions, which are necessarily both limiting and enabling, that Zavaleta is interested in examining.

We read his text now from the perspective of a different theoretical and political conjuncture. Zavaleta wrote within a discourse marked by a negation of the social productivity of local histories; he is now also used as a prefiguration of a nationalist identitarian teleology.

Bolivia, 1879–1934: The War of the Pacific, the Federal Revolution and the Chaco War

In the prologue of the manuscript bearing the title *Elementos para una historia de lo nacional-popular en Bolivia: 1879–1980* (my translation, *Towards a History of the National-Popular in Bolivia, 1879–1980*, is a rough pragmatic equivalent),[5] Zavaleta writes that he

---

5 The manuscript was first published in book form in Mexico (by Siglo XXI) under the title *Lo nacional-popular en Bolivia* (*The National-Popular in Bolivia*) in 1986, and has been republished under the same title in 2013 by Plural in Bolivia, in Volume 2 of Zavaleta's complete works, scrupulously edited and annotated by Mauricio Souza. I have chosen not to abbreviate the original title of the manuscript as the Spanish editors do, since neither the rudimentariness conveyed by the term *elementos* nor the reference to the historical are without significance. I also think it is worth keeping the dates that

intends to conduct a theoretical inquiry into 'the national-popular in Bolivia, that is, the connection between what Weber called social democratization and state form', grounded in a study of Bolivian history during the period between 1952 (the so-called National Revolution) and 1980 (just four years prior to Zavaleta's death, and a moment that he identifies elsewhere as one of general crisis[6]), adding that 'its causal explanation will bring us back to the War of the Pacific (1879–83)'.[7] The three chapters he wrote address the War of the Pacific, the Federal War (1898–99; also known as the Federal Revolution) and the Chaco War (1932–35), the last identified in the final sentence of the manuscript as a condition of possibility of the 'multitude of 1952', and, therefore, of the 'state of 1952'. The book we have ends at its intended point of departure.

Since Zavaleta assumes a reader familiar with Bolivian history, and only selectively provides narrative accounts of the events that form the basis of his analysis, I hope it will be helpful to attempt at least a rudimentary outline of the historical background here.

In 1878, Bolivia imposed a small export tax on the Chilean nitrate operations that dominated the economy of its coastal region and threatened to expropriate the Antofagasta Nitrate & Railway Company when it would not comply. The Chilean army occupied the territory, launching the War of the Pacific that ended in the annexation of the Atacama Desert by Chile, leaving Bolivia landlocked. This territorial amputation still weighs heavily in the national imaginary today, and Zavaleta uses the event to illustrate a radical absence of the the relation that he proposes to examine between the social corpus and the state. A state that had achieved the autonomous subjectivity necessary to act in its own national interest and that had

Zavaleta chose to frame his study, which betray its unfinished condition as well as a gap between the book imagined in the prologue and one that clearly had taken a different course.

6 'Las masas en noviembre', discussed at the end of this Afterword.

7 See p. 1 of this volume.

built structures of social mediation through which to mobilize its population, he argues, could never have suffered such a defeat.

Zavaleta's account of this failure of the Bolivian oligarchic (and 'xenophilic') state—against which the discourse of the state of 1952 would be constructed—while sometimes resonant with a whole genre of nationalist Latin American historiography on the period, is not organized by the same Manichean principles. He writes with a sometimes passionate contempt for his subjects—the leading players of what he calls the oligarchic caste—and yet without for an instant falling into reductive moralization. His analysis of the conflict serves, in the first place, to elucidate the concept of the 'social optimum' (óptimo social, also called ecuación), Zavaleta's term for the state–society relation proper to what Gramsci calls the integral state, through its conspicuous absence. While Zavaleta acknowledges his debt to Gramsci, he warns against the assumption of a Eurocentric world-historical teleology that, he claims, underlies Gramsci's concept of the 'Western' state, in which there is a 'proper relation' to civil society, an organized system of mediations. This should alert us to the difference between Zavaleta's critique of the oligarchic state as non-national and that of a 'stagist' Marxism (which of course is not Gramsci's either) that sees the bourgeois nationalist revolution as the immediate task of 'backward' (precapitalist) societies. It is equally important to keep in mind that a high social optimum, although it implies a military advantage, carries no inherent virtue.

In Zavaleta's concrete historical analysis, a high optimum is shown to enable an authoritarian state (that of late-nineteenth-century Chile) to bolster its economy in a moment of economic crisis (a result of Canadian and Argentine competition in the world wheat market and Spanish and US copper) through the outright conquest and annexation of its neighbours' resource-rich territories, while in his theoretical exposition of the concept by way of Gramsci in the same chapter, it refers to an epistemic apparatus through which the liberal state reads and adapts to its shifting social base in order to

maintain the existing structure of domination; Zavaleta's examina-
tion of the failure of the Bolivian state, which is contrasted alternately
with both, does not readily suggest a desirable alternative and
attempts to read something like a prescriptive programme here are
ill-founded.

If the War of the Pacific was what Zavaleta calls an interstate war,
that is, one confined to the level of the state (at least for its vanquished, Bolivia and Peru), the Federal War of 1889–99 began as an
intrastate war between opposing factions within the Bolivian oligarchic caste but ultimately came to reveal 'the vital core of the
paradigmatic conflicts of civil society'.[8] Against the ruling Conservative Party dominated by silver-mining interests and centred in Sucre
and Potosí, the Liberal Party based in La Paz was gaining strength
with the support of the rising tin magnates that had begun to outpace
the old silver elite. The Liberal regionalist revolt that sought to establish the thriving city of La Paz as the capital, however, would not have
been able to defeat the national army without resorting to an unprecedented political and military strategy: an alliance with indigenous
forces. The Liberal, Federalist leader General José Manuel Pando had
gained the confidence of the indigenous communities that had been
under assault for decades,[9] and the La Paz faction was able to secure
the upper hand with the help of an indigenous army commanded by
the the Aymara leader Pablo Zárate 'Willka'. But rather than waiting
for a Liberal victory for Pando to make good on his promise to
restore communal land rights, Zárate's forces incorporated their own
political programme into their military campaign, reclaiming lands
and assailing creole towns not fighting with the Conservative troops
(most famously in the village of Mohoza) and finally occupying the
city of Oruro. After the Conservative leader Severo Fernández
Alonso fled to Antofagasta (now in Chile) and a Liberal victory was

8 See p. 19 of this volume.

9 Most recently, since the large-scale expropriation of communal lands initiated by president Mariano Melgarejo in 1864.

secure, Pando sought a swift peace with his Southern counterparts and turned to the suppression of what creole society as a whole now perceived as an infinitely more terrible threat: the *indiada* (a derogatory term evoking an undifferentiated and hostile mass, which I have sometimes rendered as the *Indian hordes* or *Indian mob*). Zárate and other indigenous leaders were executed, privatization and expropriation of communal lands continued, and the political class regrouped, now with La Paz as the de facto seat of the federal government while Sucre retained its status as the official capital, an arrangement symbolic of the truce or stalemate between the factions of the white and mestizo elite still in force today. If the initial lesson of the Federal War was the internal weakness and disunity of the dominant bloc, its true eloquence for Zavaleta lies in the revelation that what cohesion it could muster derived from the construction and exclusion of the *indiada* as its constitutive enemy.

Bolivia entered another border dispute in 1927, this time with Paraguay, the only other landlocked country in the Americas and, like Bolivia, one of the poorest. Zavaleta maintains that the territory in question here—the region of the Río de la Plata basin called the Gran Chaco—was not 'socially incorporated', that is, unlike the Atacama Desert that separated the rest of the country from the sea, it was not an integral part of the Bolivian social formation and should never have been the object of a war; moreover, a diplomatic solution was entirely feasible. Instead, a bloody military campaign was launched in 1932 and when a ceasefire was finally negotiated in 1935, most of the disputed region went to Paraguay. Here the incompetence of the government of the Liberal president Daniel Salamanca in managing the war—in Zavaleta's account a result of his disconnection from the reality on the ground and disregard for the lives of the almost exclusively indigenous and poor mestizo troops—created a rift between the state and the army; this implied at once a more explicit division between the state and its social base and a division internal to the ruling class. This dissension, Zavaleta argues, was a necessary condition for the revolution of 1952. But the lack of an

organic relation between society and the state was already evident,
in this analysis, at least since the War of the Pacific; the difference
here is that a large portion of the population *was* effectively mobilized, and it is this mobilization that gave rise to a collective subject
(Zavaleta would say an intersubjectivity) capable of apprehending its
exclusion and thus of producing an organic crisis and ultimately an
alternative hegemonic project—that of the 'state of 1952'.

*Constitution and Crisis of the 'Revolutionary Nationalist' State,
1952–79*

It seems clear that had Zavaleta lived to finish the book, it would not
have coincided with the one imagined in the prologue, since after
almost 300 pages of groundwork on the 'causal explanations' of his
subject and possibly only one chapter remaining (more on which
below), he had not yet arrived at its beginning. Yet the events of the
chapters or chapter that remain(s) unwritten—which would have covered the period of Bolivian history that Zavaleta lived through and in
which he was an active participant—are nonetheless central to the substance and texture of the book even in the form in which it exists and
must therefore be included in a discussion of its historical framing.

Mauricio Souza proposes that all of Zavaleta's books can be read
as chapters in a biography of the state of 1952,[10] and this process can
indeed be conceived as a complex and polyvalent figure for the formation of an intersubjectivity or the (frustrated) emergence of a self-
determined popular collectivity in relation to which prior and
subsequent events can be read. The absent centre of *The National-
Popular in Bolivia* is an event that came to represent a prefiguration
of something that would remain in the mode of the to come. The
'state of 1952' names at once the nationalization and democratization

10 'Apuntes sobre la obra de René Zavaleta Mercado' (Notes on the Work of
René Zavaleta Mercado) in René Zavaleta Mercado, *Obra completa*, VOL. 1 (La
Paz: Plural, 2011). In a 1983 interview, Zavaleta says that he has 'suffered no
disillusionment at all' with regard to what he believed in 1952, when he was
14 years old; that his position has not changed but has only developed.

of the state and the reconstruction of its oligarchic core. These moments can be understood sequentially—but also as simultaneous. There was unquestionably a real moment of democratization and an emergence of new political subjects; the same event, however, was also from the beginning a process of adaptation on the part of the political class.

Tapia cites an outline in one of Zavaleta's notebooks that includes a fourth and final chapter, 'The Song of María Barzola', after the martyred leader of the march that ended in the Catavi Massacre of 21 December 1942.[11] We have no further clue as to its intended contents. Tapia proposes, however, that we might read one of Zavaleta's last essays, 'The Masses in November' ('Las masas en noviembre'), as a stand-in for this final chapter.[12] Taking up this astute suggestion, I conclude this Afterword with a brief reflection on the present book in light of this almost contemporary text that takes us, at least chronologically, (almost) to its projected point of completion, to the general strike of November 1979.

Zavaleta's analysis here indeed supplements and recasts that of *The National-Popular in Bolivia* in its existing form, which is structured as a reading of the crisis of the Liberal oligarchic state that led to the constitution of the state of 1952; 'The Masses in November' focuses on the crisis of the state of 1952 (which is at once a 'recomposition of the alliance of 1952' between the workers and the peasantry) as the opening that will lead to a hegemonic configuration still to come. The conceptual guiding thread designated in the //

---

11 Luis Tapia, *La producción del conocimiento local* (The Production of Local Knowledge) (La Paz: Muela del Diablo Editores, 2002), p. 335. Tapia told me in a email that he recalls seeing the outline in a notebook in a drawer in the Zavaleta family's home but does not have a copy of it; Zavaleta's son Diego tells me he has no knowledge of the notebook. There is a reference in the third chapter of *The National-Popular in Bolivia* to the 'following chapters', in the plural (specifically to say that these will address the state constructed against the oligarchic one, which is the subject of the first three chapters).

12 Tapia, *La producción del conocimiento local*, p. 336.

prologue to this book is the 'optimum', which is understood as the constitutive relation of the integral state in the Gramscian sense, and in the final pages is equated with hegemony, insofar as its deficiency in Bolivia supplied the conditions of possibility of crisis; at the centre of 'The Masses in November' is an exposition of the moment of crisis itself as productive epistemological opening. Each of these concepts contains the other, and each is prominent in both texts. But the shift in focus from constitution to crisis, and the pattern of repetition (with a difference) configured by their conjunction, suggests some useful points of entry into this book and Zavaleta's work as a whole.

In the first place, it takes us back to the question of theory in and of 'motley' societies. In 'Las masas', Zavaleta presents the specificity of local theory not as a negation of the universalizing drive of metropolitan theory, but as antidote to the dismissal of the rest of the world as untheorizable, which can only serve a reactionary politics: 'All this [the theory of crisis as epistemological method] is necessary to controvert the reactionary theory that seeks to segregate intelligible countries from unintelligible ones'. The decolonialist appropriation of Zavaleta as a figure of vindication of the local can be seen as the mirror image of this kind of 'segregation'. The second and final point from 'The Masses in November' that I will mention here is that the production of (self-)knowledge through crisis does not amount to a passage from unconsciousness to a final, transparent self-consciousness; rather, it is a moment of substitution of one representation of the self in relation to the world by another. In the best of cases, this new relation is more democratic than the one it replaces. Critical knowledge, that is, knowledge in and through crisis, is a process and not something that is acquired once and for all. This should not be forgotten in reading Zavaleta now, as the increasingly obvious failures of the electoral left of the so-called Pink Tide in Bolivia and Latin America enters a new hegemonic crisis.

Primarily in terms of racialized 'caste' rather than class, the question of gender is completely absent here. A similar process of critique for the present must take gendered power relations into account in supplementing the current discourse of indigeneity. For an anti-colonial feminist perspective, the reader might turn to the work of Silvia Rivera Cusicanqui, the most robust scholar of contemporary indigenous movements in Bolivia and of their cooptation from both the neoliberal and left-populist positions.

Bibliography

ALBARRACÍN MILLÁN, Juan. *El poder minero en la administración liberal* [The Power of the Miners in the Liberal Administration], VOL. 1. La Paz: Urquizo, 1972.

——. *Orígenes del pensamiento social contemporáneo de Bolivia* [Origins of Contemporary Social Thought in Bolivia]. La Paz: Juventud, 1976.

——. *El gran debate: Positivismo e irracionalismo en el estudio de la sociedad boliviana* [The Great Debate: Positivism and Irrationalism in the Study of Bolivian Society]. La Paz: Universo, 1978.

ALMARAZ, Sergio. *El poder y la caída: El estaño en la historia de Bolivia* [Power and Decline: Tin in the History of Bolivia]. La Paz: Los Amigos del Libro, 1967.

ALTHUSSER, Louis. 'Ideology and Ideological State Apparatuses' in '*Lenin and Philosophy' and Other Essays* (Ben Brewster trans.). London: New Left Books, 1971, pp. 127–88.

ALVÉSTEGUI, David. *Salamanca: Su gravitación sobre el destino de Bolivia* [Salamanca: His Role in the Fate of Bolivia], 4 VOLS. La Paz: Talleres Gráficos Bolivianos, 1957–70.

ANDRADE, Víctor. *My Missions for Revolutionary Bolivia, 1944–1962*. Pittsburgh, PA: University of Pittsburgh Press, 1976.

ANTEZANA ERGUETA, Luis. 'La reforma agraria campesina en Bolivia (1956–1960)' [Peasant Agrarian Reform in Bolivia, 1956–60]. *Revista Mexicana de Sociología* 31(2) (1969): 245–321

——. *Bolivia: ¿Reforma o revolución agraria?* [Bolivia: Agrarian Reform or Revolution?]. Caracas: Poleo, 1976.

ANTEZANA JUÁREZ, Luis H. 'Sistema y proceso ideológicos en Bolivia (1935–1979)' [The Ideological System and Process in Bolivia, 1935–1979] in René Zavaleta Mercado (ed.), *Bolivia hoy* [Bolivia Today]. Mexico City: Siglo XXI, 1983, pp. 60–84.

ARGUEDAS, Alcides. *Historia general de Bolivia* [General History of Bolivia] in *Obras completas*, VOL. 2. Mexico City: Aguilar, 1960.

———. *Raza de bronce* [Race of Bronze]. Buenos Aires: Losada, 1972.

ARNADE, Charles W. *La dramática insurgencia de Bolivia* [Bolivia's Dramatic Insurgency]. La Paz: Juventud, 1964.

ASHTON, T. S. *The Industrial Revolution, 1760–1830*. London: Oxford University Press, 1948.

AYALA MERCADO, Ernesto. *¿Qué es la Revolución Boliviana?* [What Is the Bolivian Revolution?]. La Paz: Talleres Burillo, 1956.

BACIA, Hubert. 'La predisposición autoritaria' [The Authoritarian Personality] in Wolfgang Abendroth et al., *Capital monopolista y sociedad autoritaria: La involución autoritaria en la R.F.A.* [Monopolistic Capital and Authoritarian Society: The Authoritarian Involution in the RFA]. Barcelona: Fontanella, 1973, pp. 209–17.

BADÍA MALAGRIDA, Carlos. *El factor geográfico en la política sudamericana* [The Geographic Factor in South American Politics]. Madrid: Reus, 1946.

BAPTISTA GUMUCIO, Mariano. *Yo fui el orgullo. Vida y pensamiento de Franz Tamayo* [I Was the Pride: Life and Thought of Franz Tamayo]. La Paz: Los Amigos del Libro, 1978.

BARAN, Paul Alexander. *La economía política del crecimiento* [The Political Economy of Growth]. Mexico City: FCE, 1959.

———. *Excedente económico e irracionalidad capitalista* [Economic Surplus and Capitalist Irrationality]. Mexico City: Cuadernos de Pasado y Presente, 1980.

BARBA DE PIÑA CHÁN, Beatriz. *La expansión de la magia* [The Spread of Magic]. Mexico City: Instituto Nacional de Antropología e Historia, 1980.

BARNADAS, Josep M. *Charcas: Orígenes históricos de una sociedad colonial (1535–1565)* [Charcas: Historical Origins of a Colonial Society, 1535–1565]. La Paz: CIPCA, 1973.

BARRAGÁN, Rossana. *Indios, mujeres y ciudadanos. Legislación y ejercicio de la ciudadanía en Bolivia (siglo XIX)* [Indians, Women and Citizens: Legislation and Exercise of Citizenship in Bolivia (Nineteenth Century)]. La Paz: Fundación Diálogo / Embajada del Reino de Dinamarca en Bolivia, 1999.

BARRIOS DE CHUNGARA, Domitila, and Moema Viezzer (ed.). '*Si me permiten hablar*': *Testimonio de Domitila, una mujer de las minas de Bolivia*. Mexico City: Siglo XXI, 1977. Available in English as: *Let Me Speak! Testimony of Domitila, a Woman of the Bolivian Mines*. New York: Monthly Review Press, 1978.

BASADRE, Jorge. *Historia de la república del Perú, 1822–1933* [History of the Republic of Peru], 17 VOLS. Lima: Editorial Universitaria, 1968–70.

BELL, Diane. *Daughters of the Dreaming*. Minneapolis: University of Minnesota Press, 1993.

BLOCH, Ernst. *Sujeto-Objeto: El pensamiento de Hegel* [Subject-Object: Hegel's Thought]. Mexico City: FCE, 1949.

———. *The Principle of Hope*, 3 VOLS (Neville Plaice, Stephen Plaice and Paul Knight trans). Cambridge: MIT Press, 1986.

BOLÍVAR, Simon. *El Libertador: Writings of Simon Bolivar* (Frederick H. Fornoff trans.). Oxford: Oxford University Press, 2003.

BONILLA, Heraclio. *Guano y burguesía en el Perú* [Guano and the Bourgeoisie in Peru]. Lima: IEP, 1974.

———. *Un siglo a la deriva: Ensayos sobre el Perú, Bolivia y la Guerra* [A Century Adrift: Essays on Peru, Bolivia and the War of the Pacific]. Lima: IEP, 1980.

BULNES, Gonzalo. *Resumen de la Guerra del Pacífico* [Overview of the War of the Pacific]. Santiago: Ediciones del Pacífico, 1976.

CARRASCO, Manuel. *Simón I. Patiño: Un prócer industrial* [Simón I. Patiño: A Giant of Industry]. Cochabamba: Editorial Canelas, 1964.

CÉSPEDES, Augusto. *Salamanca o El metafísico del fracas* [Salamanca or the Metaphysician of Failure]. La Paz: Juventud, 1973.

CHAUNU, Pierre. *La España de Carlos V* [The Spain of Charles V]. Barcelona: Península, 1976.

CHOY MA, Emilio. *Antropología e historia* [Anthropology and History]. Lima: UNMSM, 1979.

CHURATA, Gamaliel. *El pez de oro: Retablos del Laykhakuy* [The Golden Fish: Retablos del Laykhakuy]. La Paz: Canata, 1957.

CLAUSEWITZ, Karl von. *On War* (Michael Eliot Howard and Peter Paret trans). Princeton, NJ: Princeton University Press, 1989.

CONDARCO MORALES, Ramiro. *Zárate, el temible Willka: Historia de la rebelión indígena de 1899* [Zárate, the Fearsome Willka: History of the Indigenous Rebellion of 1899]. La Paz: Talleres Gráficos Bolivianos, 1965.

———. *El escenario andino y el hombre: Ecología y antropogeografía de los Andes Centrales* [The Andean Environment: Ecology and Antrhopogeography in the Central Andes]. La Paz: Librería Renovación, 1971.

COOK, Sherburne Friend, and Woodrow Wilson Borah. *Ensayos sobre historia de la población: México y el Caribe*. Mexico: Siglo XXI, 1977. Available in English as: *Essays in Population History: Mexico and the Caribbean*. Berkeley: University of California Press, 1971.

CORNBLIT, Oscar. 'Levantamientos de masas en Perú y Bolivia durante el siglo dieciocho' [Mass Uprisings in Peru and Bolivia during the Eighteenth Century] in Tulio Halperín Donghi (ed.), *El ocaso del orden colonial en Hispanoamérica* [The Decline of the Colonial Order in Latin America]. Buenos Aires: Sudamericana, 1978, pp. 57–117.

CORTÉS, José Domingo. *La República de Bolivia* [The Republic of Bolivia]. Santiago: Imp. de El Independiente, 1872.

CORTÉS CONDE, Roberto. 'El "boom" argentino: ¿una oportunidad desperdiciada?' [The Argentine 'Boom': A Missed Opportunity?] in Tulio Halperín Donghi and Torcuato S. Di Tella, *Los fragmentos del poder: De la oligarquía a la poliarquía argentina* [The Fragments of Power: From Oligarchy to Argentine Polyarchy]. Buenos Aires: J. Álvarez, 1969, pp. 217–41.

COTLER, Julio. *Clases, Estado y nación en el Perú* [Classes, State and Nation in Peru]. Lima: IEP, 1978.

CUSSET, François. *French Theory: Foucault, Derrida, Deleuze et Cie et les mutations de la vie intellectuelle aux États-Unis*. Paris: Éditions la Découverte, 2003. Available in English as: *French Theory: How Foucault, Derrida, Deleuze, & Co. Transformed the Intellectual Life of the United States* (Jeff Fort trans., with Josephine Berganza and Marlon Jones). Minneapolis: University of Minnesota Press, 2008.

DALENCE, José María. *Bosquejo estadístico de Bolivia* [A Statistical Sketch of Bolivia]. Chuquisaca: Ymprenta de Sucre, 1851.

DANDLER, Jorge. *El sindicalismo campesino en Bolivia: Los cambios estructurales en Ucureña* [Peasant Syndicalism in Bolivia: Structural Changes in Ucureña]. Mexico: Instituto Indigenista Interamericano, 1969.

DE GIOVANNI, Biagio. 'Crisis orgánica y Estado en Gramsci' [Organic Crisis and the State in Gramsci] in Giacomo Marramao et al., *Teoría marxista de la política* [The Marxist Theory of Politics]. Mexico City: Cuadernos de Pasado y Presente, no. 89, 1981.

DEMÉLAS, Marie Danielle. *Nationalisme sans nation? La Bolivie aux XIXe–XXe siècles* [Nationalism without the Nation? Bolivia of the Nineteenth and Twentieth Centuries]. Paris: Éditions du C.N.R.S, 1980.

DERRIDA, Jacques. *The Other Heading: Reflections on Today's Europe* (Pascale-Anne Brault and Michael B. Naas trans). Bloomington: Indiana University Press, 1992.

DORADO, José Vicente. *Proyecto de repartición de tierras y venta de ellas entre los indígenas* [The Land Redistribution Programme among the Indians]. Sucre: Tipografía de Pedro España, 1864.

ENCINA, Francisco Antonio. *Resumen de la historia de Chile* [A Survey of Chilean History], 3 VOLS. Santiago de Chile: Zig-Zag, 1954.

ERCILLA, Alonso de. *La araucana.* Madrid: Aguilar, 1963.

ESCÓBAR, Alberto (ed.). *El reto del multilingüismo en el Perú* [The Challenge of Multilingualism in Peru]. Lima: IEP, 1972.

ESCOBARI CUSICANQUI, Jorge. *Historia diplomática de Bolivia: Política internacional* [Diplomatic History of Bolivia: Foreign Policy]. La Paz: Casa Municipal de la Cultura Franz Tamayo, 1975.

ESPINOZA SORIANO, Waldemar. *El memorial de Charcas: Crónica inédita de 1582* [Memorial of Charcas: Unpublished Chronicle of 1582]. Lima: Ed. Univ. Nacional de Educación, 1969.

ESTEVES, Luis Raúl. *Apuntes para la historia económica del Perú* [Notes for an Economic History of Peru]. Lima: Imprenta Calle de Huallaga, 1882.

FELLMAN VELARDE, Jose. *Réquiem para una rebeldía* [Requiem for a Rebellion]. La Paz: Los Amigos del Libro, 1967.

———. *Historia de Bolivia, tomo II: La bolivianidad semifeudal* [History of Bolivia, Volume 2: Bolivian Semifeudality]. La Paz: Los Amigos del Libro, 1970.

FERNÁNDEZ, Carlos José. *La Guerra del Chaco* [The Chaco War], 4 VOLS. Buenos Aires: n.p., 1962.

FERNÁNDEZ ANTEZANA, Napoleón. *La hecatombe de Mohoza* [The Mohoza Massacre]. La Paz: Tipografía de La Unión, 1905.

FIFER, J. Valerie. *Bolivia: Land, Location and Politics since 1825*. Cambridge: Cambridge University Press, 1972.

FLORES GALINDO, Alberto. *Arequipa y el sur andino: Ensayo, de historia regional (siglos XVII–XX)* [Arequipa and the Southern Andes: Essays on the History of the Region, Seventeenth to Twentieth Centuries]. Lima: Horizonte, 1977.

FRANCOVICH, Guillermo. *La filosofía en Bolivia* [Philosophy in Bolivia]. La Paz: Juventud, 1966.

FRANK, A. G. *Capitalism and Underdevelopment in Latin America*. New York: Monthly Review Press, 1967.

———. *Mexican Agriculture, 1521–1630: Transformation of the Mode of Production*. Cambridge: Cambridge University Press, 1981.

FREELAND, Anne. 'Gramsci in Latin America: Reconstitutions of the State'. PhD dissertation, Department of Latin American and Iberian Cultures, Columbia University, New York, 2017.

GARAVAGLIA, Juan Carlos. 'Un modo de producción subsidiario: la organización económica de las comunidades guaranizadas durante los siglos XVII-XVIII en la formación regional altoperuana-rioplatense' [A Subsidiary Mode of Production: The Economic Organization of the Guaranized Communities during the Seventeenth and Eighteenth Centuries in the Regional Formation of Upper Peru and the River Plate] in Carlos Sempat Assadourian, Ciro Flamarión S. Cardoso, Horacio Ciafardini, Juan Carlos Garavaglia and Ernesto Laclau, *Modos de producción en América Latina* [Modes of Production in Latin America]. Buenos Aires: Siglo XXI, 1973, pp. 161–92.

GARCÍA LINERA, Alvaro. *El retorno de la Bolivia plebeya* [The Return of Plebeian Bolivia]. La Paz: Muela del Diablo, 2000.

GATES JR., Henry Louis. 'The Black Letters on the Sign: W. E. B. Du Bois and the Canon' in *The Oxford W. E. B. Du Bois, Volume 8: Black Folk Then and Now: An Essay in the History and Sociology of the Negro Race*. New York: Oxford University Press, 2007, pp. *xi–xxiv*.

GENOVESE, Eugene D. *The Political Economy of Slavery: Studies in the Economy and Society of the Slave South*. New York: Pantheon Books, 1965.

GOLD, David A., Clarence Y. H. Lo and Erik Olin Wright. 'Recientes desarrollos en la teoría marxista del Estado capitalista' [Recent Developments in the Marxist Theory of the Capitalist State] in Heinz Rudolf Sonntag and Héctor Vallecilos (eds), *El Estado en el capitalismo contemporáneo* [The State in Contemporary Capitalism]. Mexico City: Siglo XXI, 1977, pp. 23–61.

GRAMSCI, Antonio. *Selections from the Prison Notebooks* (Quintin Hoare and Geoffrey Nowell Smith eds and trans). New York: International Publishers, 1971.

———. *Prison Notebooks*, 3 VOLS (Joseph A. Buttigieg and Antonio Callari eds and trans). New York: Columbia University Press, 2007.

GRIESHABER, Erwin. 'Survival of Indian Communities in Nineteenth-Century Bolivia'. PhD Dissertation, University of North Carolina, Chapel Hill, 1977.

GUEVARA ARZE, Walter. *Plan inmediato de política económica del gobierno de la Revolución Nacional* [Political-Economic Policy of the National Revolutionary Government]. La Paz: Ed. Letras, 1955.

———. *Radiografía de la negociación con Chile* [Analysis of the Negotiations with Chile]. La Paz: Universo, 1978.

———. 'Los militares en Bolivia' [The Military in Bolivia]. Unpublished manuscript, 1980.

GUTIÉRREZ, Alberto. *El melgarejismo antes y después de Melgarejo* [The *Melgarejismo* before and after Melgarejo]. La Paz: Velarde, 1916.

GUTIÉRREZ AGUILAR, Raquel. *Desandar el laberinto. Introspección en la feminidad contemporánea* [Return the Labyrinth: Introspection in Contemporary Femininity]. La Paz: Comuna, 1999.

———. 'Políticas en feminino: Transformaciones y subversiones no centradas en el estado' [Politics in a Feminine Key: Non-State-Centred Transformations and Subversions] in *Horizontes comunitario-populares. Producción de lo común más allá de las políticas estado-céntricas* [Popular-Communitarian Horizons: The Production of the Common behind State-Centred Politics]. Madrid: Traficantes de Sueños, 2017.

GUZMÁN, Augusto. *Baptista: Biografía de un orador politico* [Baptista: Biography of a Political Orator]. La Paz: Juventud, 1957.

HALPERÍN DONGHI, Tulio. *Revolución y guerra: Formación de una élite dirigente en la Argentina criolla* [Revolution and War: Formation of a Ruling Elite in Creole Argentina]. Mexico City: Siglo XXI, 1972.

—— and Torcuato S. Di Tella. *Los fragmentos del poder: De la oligarquía a la poliarquía argentina* [The Fragments of Power: From Oligarchy to Argentine Polyarchy]. Buenos Aires: Álvarez, 1972.

HARRIS, Marvin. *The Rise of Anthropological Theory: A History of Theories of Culture.* Walnut Creek, CA: AltaMira Press, 2001.

HEGEL, G. W. F. *Phenomenology of Spirit* (A. V. Miller trans.). Oxford: Oxford University Press, 1977.

——. *Philosophy of Right* (T. M. Knox trans.). London: Oxford University Press, 1979[1952].

HEIDEGGER, Martin. *What Is Called Thinking?* (J. Glenn Gray trans. and introd.). New York: Harper and Row, 1968.

HOBSBAWM, Eric. *The Age of Revolution, 1789–1848.* New York: Vintage, 1962.

IRIARTE, Gregorio. *Sindicalismo campesino: Ayer, hoy y mañana* [Peasant Unionism: Yesterday, Today and Tomorrow]. La Paz: CIPCA, 1980.

JARA, Álvaro. *Guerra y sociedad en Chile: La transformación de la guerra de Arauco y la esclavitud de los indios* [War and Society in Chile: The Transformation of the Arauco War and the Enslavement of the Indians]. Santiago: Ed. Universitaria, 1971.

JÁUREGUI ROSQUELLAS, Alfredo. *La ciudad de los cuatro nombres, cronicario histórico* [The City of Four Names: Historical Chronicles]. Sucre: Imprenta La Glorieta, 1924.

JOBET, Julio César. *Ensayo crítico del desarrollo económico-social de Chile* [Critical Essay on the Socioeconomic Development of Chile]. Mexico: Centro de Estudios del Movimiento Obrero Salvador Allende, 1982.

JUNG, C. G. *Collected Works of C. G. Jung* (Gerhard Adler ed., R. F. C. Hull trans.). Princeton, NJ: Princeton University Press, 1966.

JUSTO, Liborio. *Bolivia: La revolución derrotada* [Bolivia: The Defeated Revolution]. Buenos Aires: Juárez Editor, 1971.

KLEIN, Herbert S. 'The Creation of the Patiño Tin Empire'. *Inter-American Economic Affairs* 19(2) (1965): 3–24.

——. *Orígenes de la revolución nacional boliviana: La crisis de la generación del Chaco* [The Origins of the Bolivian National Revolution: The Crisis of the Chaco Generation]. La Paz: Juventud, 1968.

KÑAKAL, Jan. *Vinculaciones de las empresas transnacionales con la industria del estaño en Bolivia* [Transnational Companies and the Bolivian Tin Industry]. Santiago: CEPAL, 1981.

KOSIK, Karel. *Dialectics of the Concrete: A Study on Problems of Man and World* (Karel Kovanda, with James Schmidt trans). Boston: D. Riedel, 1976.

KULA, Witold. *Teoría económica del sistema feudal.* Mexico City: Siglo XXI, 1979. Available in English as: *An Economic Theory of the Feudal System: Towards a Model of the Polish Economy, 1500–1800.* New York: Verso, 1987.

LACLAU, Ernest. *Política e ideología en la teoría marxista.* Mexico City: Siglo XXI, 1978. Available in English as: *Politics and Ideology in Marxist Theory: Capitalism, Fascism, Populism.* London: Verso, 1977.

LEITCH, Vincent B. (ed.). *The Norton Anthology of Theory and Criticism.* New York: W. W. Norton, 2010.

LEMOINE, Jaquín de. *Biografía del general Eliodoro Camacho* [Biography of General Eliodoro Camacho]. Buenos Aires: Peuser, 1885.

LENIN, V. I. 'The Agrarian Question in Russia towards the Close of the Nineteenth Century' in *Collected Works,* VOL. 15. Moscow: Foreign Languages Publishing, 1963.

———. *Imperialism, the Highest Stage of Capitalism* (1917) in *Selected Works,* VOL. 1. Moscow: Progress Publishers, 1963, pp. 667–776.

LEWIN, Boleslao. *La rebelión de Tupac Amaru* (The Tupac Amaru Rebellion). Buenos Aires: Hachette, 1943.

LIPSCHUTZ, Alejandro. *Perfil de Indoamérica de nuestro tiempo* [Profile of Indigenous America of Our Time]. La Habana: Ed. Ciencias Sociales, 1972.

LORA, Guillermo. *La revolución boliviana: Análisis critic* [The Bolivian Revolution: A Critical Analysis]. La Paz: Difusión, 1964.

———. *Historia del movimiento obrero boliviano* [History of the Bolivian Labour Movement]. 5 VOLS. La Paz: Los Amigos del Libro, 1967–70.

LYOTARD, Jean-François. *The Differend: Phrases in Dispute* (Georges Van Den Abbeele trans.). Minneapolis: University of Minnesota Press, 1988.

MACHIAVELLI, Niccolo, *The Prince.* (George Bull trans.). Harmondsworth: Penguin, 1975.

Malavé Mata, Héctor. *Formación histórica del antidesarrollo de Venezuela* [Historical Formation of Venezuela's Anti-development]. Havana: Casa de las Américas, 1974.

Manrique, Nelson. *Las guerrillas indígenas en la guerra con Chile* [Indigenous Guerrillas in the Chilean War]. Lima: Centro de Investigación y Capacitación, 1981.

Mariátegui, José Carlos. *Siete ensayos de interpretación de la realidad peruana*. Lima: Amauta, 1975[1928]. Available in English as: *Seven Interpretative Essays On Peruvian Reality* (Marjory Urquidi trans.). Austin: University of Texas Press, 1971.

Marsh, Margaret Alexander. *The Bankers in Bolivia: A Study in American Foreign Investment*. New York: Vanguard Press, 1928.

Marx, Karl. *Capital: A Critique of Political Economy*, VOL. 1 (Ben Fowkes trans.). London: Penguin, 1990.

———. *Capital: A Critique of Political Economy*, VOL. 2 (David Fernbach trans.). London: Penguin, 1992.

———. *Grundrisse: Foundations of the Critique of Political Economy* (Martin Nicolaus trans.). London: Penguin, 1993.

——— and Friedrich Engels. *The German Ideology*, PART 1. New York: International Publishers, 1970.

Matthew, W. M. 'The Imperialism of Free Trade: Peru, 1820–70', *Economic History Review* 21(3) (December 1968): 562–79.

Medinaceli, Carlos. *Estudios críticos* (Critical Studies). La Paz: Los Amigos del Libro, 1969.

Mendoza, Jaime. *En las tierras de Potosí* [In the Lands of Potosí]. Barcelona: Viuda de Luis Tasso, 1911

———. *El macizo boliviano* [The Bolivian Massif]. La Paz: Imp. Arnó hnos, 1935.

Mignolo, Walter. 'On Subalterns and Other Agencies'. *Postcolonial Studies: Culture, Politics, Economy* 8(4) (2005): 381–407.

Ministerio de Planificación y Coordinación. *Estrategia socioeconómica del desarrollo nacional, 1971–1991* [Socioeconomic Strategies of National Development, 1971–91], 2 VOLS. La Paz: Ministerio de Planificación y Coordinación, 1970.

MITRE, Antonio. *Los patriarcas de la plata: Estructura socioeconómica de la minería boliviana en el siglo XIX* [The Silver Patriarchs: Socioeconomic Structure of Bolivian Mining in the Nineteenth Century]. Lima: IEP, 1981.

MONTENEGRO, Carlos. *Documentos*. La Paz: Editorial Imprenta Nacional, 1954.

———. *Nacionalismo y coloniaje* [Nationalism and Colonialism]. Buenos Aires: Pleamar, 1967.

MORENO, Gabriel René. *Biblioteca boliviana: Catálogo del archivo de Mojos y Chiquitos* [Bolivian Library: Catalogue of the Archive of Mojos and Chiquitos]. Santiago: Impr. Gutenberg, 1888. [La Paz: Juventud, 1974.]

———. *Bolivia y Argentina: Notas biográficas y bibliográficas* [Bolivia and Argentina: Biographical and Bibliographic Notes]. Santiago: Imprenta Cervantes, 1901.

———. *Ayacucho en Buenos Aires, y Prevaricación de Rivadavia* [Ayacucho in Buenos Aires, and the Corruption of Rivadavia]. Madrid: Editorial América, 1917.

———. *La Audiencia de Charcas* [The Audience of Charcas]. La Paz: Ministerio de Educación y Cultura, 1970.

———. *Últimos días coloniales en el Alto Perú* [Last Days of the Colonial Era in Upper Peru]. La Paz: Juventud, 1970.

———. *Nicomedes Antelo*. Santa Cruz: UGRM, 1960.

MOUSSA, Pierre. *Les nations Prolétaires* [The Proletarian Nations]. Paris: Presses Universitaires de France, 1959.

MURRA, John V. *Formaciones económicas y políticas del mundo andino* [Economic and Political Formations of the Andean World]. Lima: IEP, 1975.

———. *La organización económica del Estado inca*. Mexico City: Siglo XXI, 1978. Available in English as: *The Economic Organization of the Inca State*. New Haven, CT: JAI Press, 1980.

NEGT, Oskar. 'Hacia una sociedad autoritaria' [Towards an Authoritarian Society] in Wolfgang Abendroth et al., *Capital monopolista y sociedad autoritaria: La involución autoritaria en la R.F.A.* [Monopolistic Capital and Authoritarian Society: The Authoritarian Involution in the RFA]. Barcelona, Fontanella, 1973, pp. 236–50.

OBLITAS, Edgar. *Historia secreta de la Guerra del Pacífico* [Secret History of the War of the Pacific]. Buenos Aires: Peña Lillo, 1978.

OFFE, Claus. 'The Abolition of Market Control and the Problem of Legitimacy'. *Kapitalistate* 1–2 (1973–74): 109–16.

PANDO, José Manuel 'Viaje a la región de la goma elástica (N.O. de Bolivia)' [Journey to the Rubber Region, Northwestern Bolivia] in *Revista del Museo de La Plata*, VOL. 6. La Plata: Talleres de publicaciones del Museo, 1895, pp. 141–220.

PARKER, Gary. 'Falacias y verdades acerca del quechua' [Some Fallacies and Truths about the Quechua Language] in Alberto Escóbar (ed.), *El reto del multilingüismo en el Perú* [The Challenge of Multilingualism in Peru]. Lima: IEP, 1972, 111–21.

PEÑALOZA, Luis. *Historia del Movimiento Nacionalista Revolucionario, 1941–1952* [History of the Revolutionary Nationalist Movement, 1941–1952]. La Paz: Dirección Nacional de Informaciones, 1963.

——. *Historia económica de Bolivia* [Economic History of Bolivia]. La Paz: El Progreso, 1953.

PORRAS BARRENECHEA, Raúl. *Pizarro*. Lima: Ed. Pizarro, 1978.

PROUST, Marcle. *In Search of Lost Time, Volume 2: Within a Budding Grove* (C. K. Scott Moncrieff trans.). London: Vintage, 2005.

PRUDENCIO BUSTILLO, Ignacio. *La misión Bustillo: Más antecedentes de la Guerra del Pacífico* [The Bustillo Mission: Background of the War of the Pacific]. Sucre: Imprenta Bolívar, 1919.

QUEREJAZU CALVO, Roberto. *Masamaclay: Historia política, diplomática y militar de la Guerra del Chaco* [Masamaclay: Politial, Diplomatic and Military History of the Chaco War]. La Paz: Los Amigos del Libro, 1975.

——. *Guano, salitre, sangre: Historia de la Guerra del Pacífico* [Guano, Nitrate, Blood: A History of the War of the Pacific]. La Paz: Los Amigos del Libro, 1979.

QUIJANO, Aníbal. *Dependencia, urbanización y cambio social en Latinoamérica* [Dependency, Urbanization and Social Change in Latin America]. Lima: Mosca Azul Editores, 1977.

QUIROGA SANTA CRUZ, Marcelo. *La victoria de abril sobre la nación.* [The April Victory over the Nation]. La Paz: Burillo, 1964.

RAMÍREZ NECOCHEA, Hernán. *Balmaceda y la contrarrevolución de 1891* [Balmaceda and the Counterrevolution of 1891]. Santiago: Ed. Universitaria, 1969.

———. *Historia del imperialismo en Chile* [History of Imperialism in Chile]. Santiago: Austral, 1970.

REINAGA, Fausto. *La revolución india* [The Indian Revolution]. La Paz: Partido Indio de Bolivia, 1969.

RÍOS GALLARDO, Conrado. *Después de la paz . . . : Las relaciones chileno-bolivianas* [After the Peace . . . : Chile–Bolivia Relations]. Santiago: Imp. Universitaria, 1926.

RIBEIRO, Darcy. *Configuraciones histórico-culturales americanas* [American Historical-Cultural Configurations]. Montevideo: Centro de Estudios Latinoamericanos, 1972.

RIGOBERTO PAREDES, Manuel. *Melgarejo y su tiempo* [Melgarejo and His Time]. La Paz: Isla, 1962.

RIVERA CUSICANQUI, Silvia. 'La expansión del latifundio en el Altiplano boliviano: Elementos para la caracterización de una oligarquía regional' [The Expansion of the Latifundium in the Bolivian Highlands: Towards a Characterization of the Regional Oligarchy]. *Allpanchis. Revista de Pastoral Andina* 13 (1979): 189–218. Also published in: *Avances* 2 (1978): 95–118.

———. 'Apuntes para la historia de las luchas campesinas en Bolivia (1900–1978)' [Notes for a History of the Peasant Struggles in Bolivia, 1900–1978] in Pablo González Casanova (ed.), *Historia política de los campesinos latinoamericanos* [A Political History of Latin American Peasants], VOL. 3. Mexico City: Siglo XXI, 1985.

——— and Rossana Barragán (eds). *Debates post coloniales: Una introducción a los estudios de la subalternidad* [Postcolonial Debates: An Introduction to Subaltern Studies]. La Paz: SEPHIS/Aruwyiri, 1997.

RIVKIN, Julie, and Michael Ryan (eds). *Literary Theory: An Anthology*. Malden, MA: Wiley Blackwell, 2004.

ROJAS, Juan, and June C. Nash. *He agotado mi vida en la mina: Una historia de vida* [A Life Spent in the Mines]. Buenos Aires: Nueva Visión, 1976.

ROMANO, Ruggiero, and Alberto Tenenti. *Los fundamentos del mundo moderno: Edad Media tardía, Renacimiento, Reforma* [Foundations of the

Modern World: Late Middle Ages, Renaissance, Reform]. Mexico City: Siglo XXI, 1979.

ROMERO, Gonzalo. *Reflexiones para una interpretación de la historia de Bolivia* [Notes for an Interpretation of Bolivian History]. Buenos Aires: Imprenta López, 1960.

ROWE, John H. 'El movimiento nacional inca del siglo XVIII' [The Inca National Movement of the Eighteenth Century] in Alberto Flores Galindo (ed.), *Sociedad colonial y sublevaciones populares: Tupac Amaru II, 1780* [Colonial Society and Popular Uprisings: Tupac Amaru II, 1780]. Lima: Retablo de Papel, 1976, pp. 11–66.

SAAVEDRA, Bautista. *El ayllu: Estudios sociológicos* [The Ayllu: Sociological Studies]. La Paz: Juventud, 1971.

———. 'Proceso Mohoza. Defensa del abogado pronunciada en la audiencia del 12 de octubre de 1901' [The Mohoza Trial: Defence Pronounced in the Hearing of 12 October 1901] in *El ayllu: Estudios sociológicos* [The Ayllu: Sociological Studies]. La Paz: Juventud, 1971, pp. 133–56.

SADER, Emir. *The New Mole: Paths of the Latin American Left*. New York: Verso, 2011.

SANABRIA FERNÁNDEZ, Hernando. 'Preámbulo' [Foreword] in Gabriel René Moreno, *La Audiencia de Charcas* [The Audiencia of Charcas]. La Paz: Ministerio de Educación y Cultura, 1970.

———. *Breve historia de Santa Cruz* [Brief History of Santa Cruz]. La Paz: Juventud, 1973.

———. *En busca de El Dorado: La colonización del oriente boliviano por los cruceños* [In Search of El Dorado: The Colonization of Eastern Bolivia from Santa Cruz]. La Paz: Juventud, 1973.

SÁNCHEZ-ALBORNOZ, Nicolás. *La población de América Latina: Desde los tiempos precolombinos al año 2000* [The Population of Latin America: From Pre-Columbian Times to the Year 2000]. Madrid: Alianza, 1973.

———. 'Tributo abolido, tributo repuesto. Invariantes socioeconómicas en la Bolivia republicana' [Tribute Abolished and Reinstated: Socioeconomic Constants in Republican Bolivia] in Tulio Halperín Donghi et al., *El ocaso del orden colonial en Hispanoamérica* [The Decline of the Colonial Order in Spanish America]. Buenos Aires: Sudamericana, 1978, pp. 159–200.

SÁNCHEZ BUSTAMANTE, Daniel. *Bolivia: Su estructura y sus derechos en el Pacífico* [Bolivia: Its Structure and Rights in the Pacific]. La Paz: Banc Central-Academia Boliviana de la Historia, 1979.

SANTIVÁÑEZ, José María. 'Reivindicación de los terrenos de comunidad o sea refutación del folleto titulado "Lejitimidad de las compras de tierras realengas"' [Cochabamba, 1871] [Claiming Community Land or Refutation of the Brochure Entitled 'Lejitimidad de las compras de tierras realengas']. *Illimani* (La Paz) 8–9 (1976): 151–82.

SANTOS MARTÍNEZ, Pedro. *Las industrias durante el Virreinato (1776–1810)* [Industry During the Viceroyalty, 1776–1810]. Buenos Aires: Eudeba, 1969.

SEMPAT ASSADOURIAN, Carlos, Ciro Flamarión S. Cardoso, Horacio Ciafardani, Juan Carlos Garavaglia and Ernesto Laclau. *Modos de producción en América Latina* [Modes of Production in Latin America]. Buenos Aires: Siglo XXI, 1973.

SERENI, Emilio. *La categoría de 'formación económica y social'* [The Category of 'Economic and Social Formation']. Mexico City: Roca, 1973.

———. *Capitalismo y mercado nacional* [Capitalism and the National Market]. Barcelona: Crítica, 1980.

SILES SALINAS, Jorge. *La aventura y el orden. Reflexiones sobre la revolución boliviana* [Spontaneity and Order: Reflections on the Bolivian Revolution]. Santiago: Bustos y Letelier, 1956.

———. 'Reflexiones sobre la ejemplaridad' [Reflections on Exemplarity] in *Lecciones de una revolución: Bolivia, 1952–1959* [Lessons of a Revolution: Bolivia, 1952–1959]. Santiago: Editorial Universidad Católica, 1959, pp. 27–36.

SISSON, W. Lee. *Reconnoissance Report upon Proposed System of Bolivian Railways*. La Paz: Impr. Heitman y Cornejo, 1905.

SORIA GALVARRO, Carlos. *Con la revolución en las venas: Los mineros de Siglo XX en la resistencia antifascista* [Revolution in the Veins: Twentieth-Century Miners in Anti-fascist Resistance]. La Paz: Editorial Roalva, 1980.

SORIA GALVARRO, Rodolfo. *Los últimos días del Gobierno-Alonso: Reportage para la historia* [The Last Days of the Alonso Government: A Historical Report]. Valparaíso: Universo de Gmo. Helfmann, 1899.

SOZINA, Svetlana Alekseevna. *En el horizonte está El Dorado* [El Dorado Is on the Horizon]. La Habana: Casa de las Américas, 1982.

SPIVAK, Gayatri Chakravorty. 'Inscription: Of Truth to Size' in *Outside in the Teaching Machine*. New York: Routledge, 2009, pp. 201–16.

SRAFFA, Piero. *Production of Commodities by Means of Commodities: Prelude to a Critique of Economic Theory*. Cambridge: Cambridge University Press, 1960.

STALIN, Joseph. *Marxism and the National Question: Selected Writings and Speeches*. New York: International Publishers, 1942.

STERN, Steve J. 'Feudalism, Capitalism, and the World-System in the Perspective of Latin America and the Caribbean'. *The American Historical Review* 93(4) (October 1988): 829–72.

SUVIN, Darko. 'Tko se ne bori zajedno, izgubi pojedinačno . . .' [Whoever Doesn't Fight Collectively Loses Singly], interview with Saša Hrnjez, July–August 2015. Available at: https://goo.gl/X7Kkto (last accessed on 7 January 2018).

SZEMINSKI, Jan. 'La insurrección de Tupac Amaru II: ¿Guerra de independencia o revolución?' [The Insurrection of Tupac Amaru II: War of Independence or Revolution?]. *Estudios Latinoamericanos* 2 (1974): 9–40.

TAMAYO, Franz. *Creación de la pedagogía nacional* [Creation of the National Pedagogy]. La Paz: Biblioteca del Sesquicentenario de Bolivia, 1975[1910].

TAPIA, Luis. *La producción del conocimiento local. Historia y política en René Zavaleta Mercado*. La Paz: Muela del Diablo, 2002. Forthcoming from Seagull Books as: *The Production of Local Knowledge: History and Politics in the Work of René Zavaleta Mercado* (Alison Spedding trans.).

THOMPSON, E. P. 'The Moral Economy of the English Crowd in the Eighteenth Century'. *Past and Present* 50 (1971): 76–136.

TOCQUEVILLE, Alexis de. *Democracy in America* (Arthur Goldhammer trans.). New York: Library of America, 2004[1835].

TORERO, Alfredo. *El quechua y la historia social andina* [The Quechua and Andean Social History]. Lima: Studium, 1975.

VACA GUZMÁN, Santiago. *El doctor Arce y su rol en la política boliviana; examen de sus opiniones concernientes a la celebración de la paz entre Bolivia y Chile* [Doctor Arce and His Role in Bolivian Politics: Analysis of His

Opinions Concerning the Peace between Bolivia and Chile]. Buenos Aires: Coni, 1881.

VACCA, Giuseppe. 'Forma-stato y forma-valore' [State-Form and Value-Form] in Louis Althusser et al., *Discutere lo Stato: Posizioni a confronto su una tesi di Louis Althusser* [Discussing the Status: Comparing Positions on a Thesis by Louis Althusser]. Bari: De Donato, 1978.

VALDÉS, Julio César. *Bolivia y Chile*. Santiago: La Prensa, 1900.

VARGAS, José Santos. *Diario de un comandante de la independencia americana (1814–1825)* [Diary of a General of the American Wars of Independence, 1814–1825]. Mexico City: Siglo XXI, 1982.

VERGARA VICUÑA, Aquiles. *Historia de la Guerra del Chaco* [History of the Chaco War]. La Paz: Litografía e Imprenta Unidas, 1940–44.

VICENS VIVES, Jaime, Santiago Sobrequés i Vidal and Guillermo Céspedes del Castillo. *Historia social y económica de España y América: Baja Edad Media, Reyes Católicos, Descubrimientos* [Social and Economic History of Spain and America: Late Middle Ages, Catholic Kings, Discoveries], VOL. 2. Barcelona: Vicens-Vives, 1972.

VILAR, Pierre. *A History of Gold and Money, 1450–1920* (Judith White trans.). New York: Verso, 1991.

WEBER, Max. *Economy and Society: An Outline of Interpretive Sociology* (Guenther Roth and Clauss Wittich eds; Ephraim Fischoff, Hans Gerth and A. M. Henderson trans). Berkley: University of California Press, 1978.

WENNERGREN, E. Boyd, and Morris D. Whitaker. *The Status of Bolivian Agriculture*. New York: Praeger, 1975.

WHITEHEAD, Laurence. *The United States and Bolivia: A Case of Neocolonialism*. Oxford: Haslemere, 1969.

YEPES DEL CASTILLO, Ernesto. *Perú 1820-1920: Un siglo de desarrollo capitalista* [Peru, 1820–1920: A Century of Capitalist Development]. Lima: IEP, 1972.

——. 'Burguesía y gamonalismo en el Perú' [The Bourgeoisie and Gamonalism in Peru]. *Análisis. Cuadernos de Investigación* (Lima) 7 (1979): 31–66.

ZANETTI, Oscar. 'El comercio exterior de la República Neocolonial' [Foreign Trade in the Neocolonial Republic] in Juan Pérez de la Riva, Oscar Zanetti, Francisco Lopez Segrera and Federic Perez De La Riva Chang,

La República Neocolonial. Anuario de estudios cubanos [The Neocolonial Republic: Yearbook of Cuban Studies], VOL. 1. Havana: Ed. de Ciencias Sociales, 1975, pp. 45–126.

ZAVALA, Silvio. *New Viewpoints on the Spanish Colonization of America.* Philadelphia: University of Pennsylvania Press, 1943.

ZAVALETA MERCADO, René. *Bolivia: el desarrollo de la conciencia nacional.* Montevideo: Marcha, 1967.

——. 'El Che en el Churo' [Che in El Churo]. *Semanario Marcha* (Mexico), 10 October 1969, pp. 16–18.

——. *El poder dual en América Latina: Estudios de los casos de Bolivia y Chile* [Dual Power in Latin America: Case Studies from Bolivia and Chile]. Mexico: Siglo XXI, 1974.

——. 'Movimiento obrero y ciencia social. La revolución democrática de 1952 en Bolivia y las tendencias sociológicas emergentes' [The Labour Movement and Social Science: The Democratic Revolution of 1952 in Bolivia and Emerging Trends in Sociology]. *Historia y Sociedad. Revista Latinoamericana de Pensamiento Marxista*, (Mexico) 2(3) (1974): 3–35.

——. 'Clase y conocimiento' [Class and Knowledge]. *Historia y Sociedad. Revista Latinoamericana de Pensamiento Marxista* (Mexico) 2(7) (1975): 3–8.

——. 'Las formaciones aparentes en Marx' [Apparent Formations in Marx]. *Historia y Sociedad. Revista Latinoamericana de Pensamiento Marxista* (Mexico) 18 (1978): 3–27.

——. 'De Banzer a Guevara Arze: La fuerza de la masa' [From Banzer to Guevara Arze: The Force of the Masses]. *Cuadernos de Marcha* (Mexico) 2(3) (September–October 1979): 29–41.

——. 'Bolivia: Algunos problemas acerca de la democracia, el movimiento popular y la crisis revolucionaria' [Bolivia: Questions of Democracy, the Popular Movement and the Revolutionary Crisis] in René Zavaleta Mercado (ed.), *América Latina 80: Democracia y movimiento popular* [Latin America 80: Democracy and Popular Movement]. Lima: DESCO, 1981, pp. 39–61.

——. 'Cuatro conceptos de la democracia' [Four Concepts of Democracy]. *Bases: Expresiones del pensamiento marxista boliviano* 1 (1981): 101–24.

——. *Las masas en noviembre* [The Masses in November]. La Paz: Juventud, 1983.

——. *Obra Completa de René Zavaleta Mercado* [Complete Works of René Zavaleta Mercado], 3 VOLS. La Paz: Plural, 2011–15.

——. 'Forma primordial y determinacion dependiente' [Primordial Form and Dependent Determination] in *Obra completa*, VOL. 2. La Paz: Plural, 2013.

——. 'Las masas en noviembre' [The Masses in November] in *Obra completa*, VOL. 2. La Paz: Plural, 2013.

ZEA, Leopoldo. *Dos etapas del pensamiento en Hispanoamérica*: *Del romanticismo al positivismo* [Two Periods in Spanish American Thought: From Romanticism to Positivism]. Mexico: El Colegio de México, 1949.

ZIADE, Khaled. *Neighborhood and Boulevard*: *Reading through the Modern Arab City* (Samah Selim trans., Hosam Aboul-Ela introd.). New York: Palgrave MacMillan, 2011.

ZOOK, David H. *The Conduct of the Chaco War*. New York: Bookman Associated, 1961.